5/15 4x

8/14

TOMLINSON HILL

TOMLINSON HILL

The Remarkable Story of Two Families Who Share the Tomlinson Name—One White, One Black

CHRIS TOMLINSON

Foreword by
LaDainian Tomlinson

THOMAS DUNNE BOOKS

ST. MARTIN'S PRESS ⚏ NEW YORK

THOMAS DUNNE BOOKS.
An imprint of St. Martin's Press.

TOMLINSON HILL. Copyright © 2014 by Chris Tomlinson. Foreword copyright © 2014 by LaDainian Tomlinson. All rights reserved. Printed in the United States of America. For information, address St. Martin's Press, 175 Fifth Avenue, New York, N.Y. 10010.

www.thomasdunnebooks.com
www.stmartins.com

Designed by Kelly S. Too

Library of Congress Cataloging-in-Publication Data

Tomlinson, Chris.
    Tomlinson Hill: the remarkable story of two families who share the Tomlinson name—one white, one black / by Chris Tomlinson; foreword by LaDanian Tomlinson. — 1st ed.
        p. cm.
    ISBN 978-1-250-00547-2 (hardcover)
    ISBN 978-1-4668-5050-7 (e-book)
    1. Tomlinson, Chris—Family.   2. Tomlinson, LaDainian—Family.   3. Tomlinson Hill (Tex.)—Biography.   4. African Americans—Texas—Tomlinson Hill—Biography. 5. Whites—Texas—Tomlinson Hill—Biography.   6. Slaves—Texas—Tomlinson Hill— Biography.   7. Slaveholders—Texas—Tomlinson Hill—Biography.   8. Plantations— Texas—Tomlinson Hill—History.   9. Slavery—Texas—Tomlinson Hill—History. 10. Tomlinson Hill (Tex.)—Race relations.   I. Title.
    F394.T65T66 2014
    305.896'073076428600922—dc23
    [B]   2014008825

St. Martin's Press books may be purchased for educational, business, or promotional use. For information on bulk purchases, please contact Macmillan Corporate and Premium Sales Department at 1-800-221-7945, extension 5442, or write specialmarkets@macmillan.com.

First Edition: July 2014

10   9   8   7   6   5   4   3   2   1

To Shalini

CONTENTS

Foreword   ix

Introduction   1

Chapter One   5

Chapter Two   19

Chapter Three   31

Chapter Four   47

Chapter Five   57

Chapter Six   69

Chapter Seven   81

Chapter Eight   101

Chapter Nine   115

Chapter Ten   123

Chapter Eleven   141

Chapter Twelve 161

Chapter Thirteen 177

Chapter Fourteen 195

Chapter Fifteen 221

Chapter Sixteen 243

Chapter Seventeen 263

Chapter Eighteen 287

Chapter Nineteen 301

Chapter Twenty 317

Chapter Twenty-one 331

Chapter Twenty-two 341

Chapter Twenty-three 353

Epilogue 371

Endnotes 381

Acknowledgments 415

Index 417

FOREWORD

My earliest memories are of Tomlinson Hill, where my parents spent their early years. Living in my father's house and spending days at my grandma Julie's house filled me with joy. We ran up and down the dirt roads to visit cousins or to the store to buy candy. There was no area off-limits for us and we could do whatever, whenever we wanted. No cares in the world. But what I remember most is having a lot of brothers, sisters, and cousins and enjoying great picnics and family reunions on the Hill.

We would often go to Grandma Julie's house, and she would always love to have us sit on her lap. I could sit there for hours and watch TV with her. She was a great cook, and the breakfasts that she used to make were unbelievable. Bacon, scrambled eggs, and homemade sausage— everything came from the Hill. She was so gentle and always enjoyed having us around. She just had that kind of soul and personality that you gravitate to and, as a kid, I always felt like her favorite. She liked to keep everyone around the Hill. Three generations after the end of slavery, she felt like they could be safe there.

We didn't have much, but we didn't know that. The family did their best to shelter us from the outside world. We were very self-sufficient. I used to help my dad tend to the pigs, and there was one particular pig I felt a bond with. It became my pig, the pig that I took care of the most. As a kid, it doesn't hit home that pigs are your food. One day, my father took my brother and me to the house of one of his friends, and the men had hung a goat in the tree. That was our first lesson about butchering an animal and making it your dinner. I must have been six or seven years old and I was the type of kid who was very sensitive about killing animals. I didn't take to it very well. I cried, and my father sat me down and said, "Son, this is what life is about." Even after I left the Hill, the lessons I learned there remained a big part of me. I am still a country boy.

My father, Oliver Terry "O.T." Tomlinson, used to tell me that Tomlinson Hill got its name from our family, because that's where our family originated from and it was where we had always been. That made me proud, because the Hill had my name on it. It was our place.

My father, though, was just being protective of us, trying to shelter us from a tough world with a brutal history. My paternal grandfather, Vincent, died before I was born, and my father rarely talked about the family's history. We learned about slavery in school, but the teachers didn't talk about the slaveholding in Falls County. The only thing my father ever told me about Grandpa Vincent was that he worked long hours tending a farm and picking cotton for a white man, and that my dad wasn't allowed to visit. My father never talked to me about his years picking cotton. I think he didn't tell me because he was ashamed, for whatever reason. Or maybe he felt like I wasn't ready to know the family history. O.T. was also born after his grandfather Peter had died, so I'm not sure how much he knew himself. Now that he's gone, I'll never know.

Growing up, I had white friends, and to me this was totally normal. There was nothing odd or weird about it. I can't recall a single time where there was a white person who tried to oppress me. I think sports makes a difference in how you see race, because you see people for who they are, and at times when they're tired and they're hurt. And so you get to see them for who they are, rather than thinking about their skin color, especially when you're all trying to win a game, and after that game, when you celebrate winning. It's a happy time when you've all worked together to accomplish one thing. To fight, and try to break that apart, just because of a difference in skin color—I always felt that was silly.

When I got older, after my parents divorced, I began to experience what my dad and Grandma Julie had wanted to protect me from. During one high school football game, people in the crowd started calling me "nigger" after I scored a touchdown. I couldn't believe this was happening in the 1990s. But then I realized that they were just trying to make me angry. They were trying to belittle me, put me back in the cotton fields, where my ancestors had suffered. They wanted to make me angry so they could have power over me, just as their ancestors had power over mine. More than anything, it made me run harder. I never let them have the power to make me angry. The best way to make someone like that mad is to ignore them, so that's always been my approach.

The one time that felt a little awkward was at the NFL Combine, where all of the teams send their staff to inspect potential draft picks. You stand in the middle of the room, wearing only your drawers, and you have all these personnel decision makers measuring you, looking at your body structure and all types of things. Many people say it looks a lot like an old slave auction block. But the difference is that you're getting paid a king's ransom to play a game. And so I know if I am a decision maker, I want to see the body structure of a man who has to play a physical, rough game to judge whether he can hold up. But it does kind of make you feel strange when you stand up there.

I have retired from playing football now and am beginning the second act of my life. In all of my years as a running back, I have never run from my past. I look back at those early years on the Hill and realize that my family gave me a great perspective on life. Growing up in the country taught me self-reliance and an understanding of the circle of life. I know how important it is to understand your past in order to discover your future.

The two Tomlinson families, white and black, have lived and worked together for almost two hundred years. I am happy that Chris and I can work together today, as sons of slaves and sons of slaveholders, to share our common history and what it says about our nation. Our families are far from unique, and by telling the story of our shared heritage, this book also tells a larger story about race in Texas and in America as a whole. I have learned through this book new details about six generations of my family, and it gives me pride and an understanding of what my father, grandfather, and great-grandfather went through to give me the opportunity to have the life I lead today.

I have never been more proud to be a Tomlinson, or to come from Tomlinson Hill. I understand that while the Hill's name may have come from a white man, it belongs as much to my family as to Chris's. I hope to one day buy a ranch nearby and continue what my family has built, because it remains a part of me. I will also make sure the next generation of Tomlinsons knows our history. My son Daylen Oliver Tomlinson was born July 7, 2010, and, like me and my father, he will never know his grandfather. But I will make sure he knows the story of Tomlinson Hill and carries its lessons wherever he may go.

—LaDainian Tomlinson

TOMLINSON HILL

INTRODUCTION

On a hot September afternoon, I stood in a cotton field in Falls County, Texas, with Charles Tomlinson, and he taught me a skill he had learned seventy-five years earlier, almost as soon as he could walk. To pick cotton, you have to stick your fingers into the boll, trying not to scrape your cuticles on the sharp, dried-out shell around the linty white ball. He told me this was the hard method but that the cotton would be cleaner for the gin. The quicker, easier method was to pull cotton. He grabbed the entire boll, shell and all, and pulled it off the shrub. I asked Charles, a former sharecropper, to teach me these skills so I could understand exactly what my ancestors had demanded from his ancestors, the slaves of Tomlinson Hill.

Charles was immensely patient as we walked the Hill together, allowing me to pepper him and his wife, Zelma, with questions about the legacy of slavery and the Civil War and how it affected their family. Here I was, a blue-eyed middle-aged white man, asking him to drive from his home in Kansas to meet me on the Hill he had escaped, all so I could learn about his life as a sharecropper renting land from my relatives. He agreed to fulfill my childhood fantasy of living out

Dr. Martin Luther King, Jr.'s dream: to have the sons of slaves and the sons of slaveholders meet in brotherhood. I needed Charles's help to tell the story of our two families, a small part of the story of America.

Two families who share one name: One is white, the other black. Both trace their heritage to a Texas slave plantation that bore that name. The story begins with the first Tomlinson to arrive on the Hill and ends with the last Tomlinson to leave. For five years, I researched these two families and the larger events that shaped their lives.

From this mosaic of accounts, I found some heroes and villains, but mostly I learned about people who wanted to give their children a life better than theirs. In reading letters and articles and listening to people tell their stories, I found a full chorus to tell the story of the Tomlinsons of Falls County. I have let people speak for themselves whenever possible, because they tell their stories better than I can. I don't intend to provide a comprehensive history; I only want to examine America's history of race and bigotry through the paternal lines of these two families.

I come to this story after spending eleven years covering wars for The Associated Press, most of it in Africa, but with time also spent in Iraq and Afghanistan. I risked my life in nine war zones throughout those years because I believe in the journalistic mission to bear witness. Many times, I was the only foreign correspondent for hundreds of miles, either visiting child soldiers in Congo or interviewing al-Qaeda members in Somalia. I believe in revealing the facts, no matter how dangerous, to "write the first draft of history," as Mark Twain said. In the same spirit of exposing injustices and atrocities where I find them, I don't turn away from those I found within my own family history.

Every conflict I covered included an element of bigotry. In South Africa, I covered the end of apartheid, a political system based on the supposed inferiority of blacks. In Rwanda, I reported on the country's recovery from genocide. In Somalia, the most homogenous nation in the world, bigotry was based not on clan, but on sub-sub-clan. I found that in every instance, the bigotry was based on a human drive to divide ourselves up in order to hoard power and privilege. Science tells us that race, tribe, and clan have nothing do with biology—they are inventions of society.

On my last trip to Rwanda, I tried to understand how a country could recover from the mass slaughter of one million members of a minority by several million members of the majority. I went to the village of Mayange, where I met Cecile Mukagasana, a Tutsi, and Xavier Nemeye, a member of the Hutu majority. They lived as neighbors, and their children played together in front of their huts. The two had undergone a reconciliation program, where, among other things, they learned about the myth of ethnic difference in their culture. They were learning to not be Hutu or Tutsi, but simply to be Rwandans.

Xavier explained to me how he'd killed six of Cecile's friends with a machete. He described the years he spent in an overcrowded prison, hoping for the chance to kill again. Eventually, though, he came to accept responsibility for his crimes with the help of a preacher. During the day we spent together, Xavier taught me something I'd never thought about. "When you confess and ask for forgiveness, you are asking that person for something," he told me. "To forgive is to give something, and that is much more difficult than confessing."

Instead of asking Cecile and the rest of the victims in the village to forgive him, Xavier went to work constructing new homes for Cecile and the other genocide survivors. Cecile told me that watching and working with Xavier, listening to him take responsibility for what he'd done and witnessing his contrition was what finally made it possible for her to reconcile with him.

In the eleven years I spent in Africa, I learned about many different forms of justice, from sharia law to blood price. The one thing all forms of justice share is the need to establish the truth about what happened, and why. South African Archbishop Desmond Tutu chaired the Truth and Reconciliation Commission because he understood the futility of jailing people for decades for crimes against humanity, but he also recognized the societal value of an honest accounting of the past. Only once the truth is known can there be true reconciliation.

My heritage as a white Texan and my identity as a Tomlinson determined who I could become and what opportunities I could enjoy. I have borne witness to enough injustice, hatred, violence, and bigotry to know that the accident of one's gender, race, nationality, and wealth determines one's future more than one's personal intelligence or moti-vation. I left Africa feeling a responsibility to discover what happened on my family's land, to confront the possible crimes of my ancestors, and to examine if I had benefited from them. In beginning this book, I did not intend to ask for forgiveness, but to make an honest account-ing. My great-great-grandfather owned slaves, and I know there is no such thing as a good slaveholder. But what crimes had my ancestors committed to maintain their power and privilege? Did they know what they did was wrong? As an American and Texan, I wanted to under-stand the sins of our fathers.

ONE

They loved us so much, they took Tomlinson as their last name.

—Tommy Tomlinson

When I was a child, my father told me about Tomlinson Hill. He said it was not much of a hill; just a plot of flat land along the Brazos River. But it was the place our family came from, the origin of our Texaness. My great-grandfather bought the Hill in 1856, grew cotton, and owned slaves. Yet my father never took me there. I was told it was just a boring open field, with a picnic pavilion for Memorial Day barbecues and family reunions. My parents never went to those reunions, but other Tomlinsons did.

When I spent the night at my grandparents' house on Twin Tree Lane in Dallas, I slept in my father's childhood bed. Stacked on a bookshelf in his room sat some old leather-bound scrapbooks. The articles, on amber-colored newsprint, were written in English and German. Most of them were about my grandmother's family, the Fretzes, but I wanted to know what it meant to be a Tomlinson. I already knew my middle name, Lee, was my father's middle name, my grandfather's middle name, and my great-grandfather's middle name. I found a folded-up obituary for a Robert Edward Lee Tomlinson in the back of one scrapbook. He was born on Tomlinson Hill in 1861.

The old family photos and newspaper articles talked about Texas Rangers, cowboys, and proud southerners. My father had told me I was a fifth-generation Texan, something few white people could claim. There was also talk about a Tomlinson who died defending the Alamo. The clippings suggested an epic family history, and I created elaborate fantasies about my ancestors and their exploits.

The reality of my home life prompted much of this. My father, Bob Tomlinson, co-owned a bowling-supply shop with his father. We didn't have much money, and Dad spent his evenings and weekends in bowling alleys. When he was home, my parents fought, usually about money and often about my father's lack of ambition. He was overweight, wore his hair long, and had a 1970s mustache. He wore garish shirts and high-heeled boots and listened to jazz on Sunday mornings in his bathrobe. He believed in corporal punishment, usually administered with a belt.

My paternal grandfather, Albert "Tommy" Tomlinson, was a taciturn man, and he and my father fought a lot, too. My memories of him are few, but I know he wore a small gray Stetson, which made him look like President Lyndon B. Johnson. My grandmother Mary cautioned me not to make a lot of noise or bother him while I was at their house, as he was easily angered. I spent most of my time in the kitchen with her and their African-American housekeeper, Faye.

So I was excited to find the scrapbooks. The obituaries and anniversary notices mentioned Tomlinson Hill but provided no details. When I asked about it, relatives provided me with only one fact about the old slave plantation: When emancipation came, the former slaves had taken our name as their own. There were black Tomlinsons, too.

To a white boy growing up in the midst of civil rights turmoil in Dallas, this was a staggering revelation. In the early 1970s, it was perhaps the most important topic in Dallas, where the school board was dragging its feet on desegregation and everyone worried about the consequences. Parents and activists, teachers and politicians, liberals and conservatives were all fighting over how to deal with generations of bigotry and discrimination. We watched race riots sparked by busing in Boston on the nightly news, and I wondered if that would happen at my school.

Before he died, on New Year's Eve in 1973, my grandfather tried to make me proud of being a Texan. My father tried to keep me from becoming a racist. And bringing both points home in my young imagination was the knowledge that somewhere in rural Texas there were black Tomlinsons who shared our heritage.

My ancestors had owned their ancestors.

I tried to imagine the black Tomlinsons. Could their family have moved to Dallas, too? Were they still in the country? What an irony that would be. I had always imagined blacks to be urban and the countryside to be white. To me, rural Texas was the backwoods, a place where the sun didn't reach the forest floor, where rednecks still grew cotton, hunted deer, gigged frogs, and fried catfish. It was the place where the Ku Klux Klan roamed the red clay roads and burned crosses at night. The country was where the bogeyman lived.

TWO TOMLINSONS

Thirty years later, I was standing on a mountain ridge near Tora Bora, covering Osama bin Laden's last stand in Afghanistan. Fighter jets screamed through the bitterly cold winter sky, dropping laser-guided bombs on the caves where al-Qaeda had fled following the September eleventh terrorist attacks. At night, I slept in a mud hut a farmer had been using to dry peanuts. His compound was the closest shelter to the front line. The Associated Press team and a handful of other writers and photographers huddled around propane heaters to escape the mountain cold. We could hear the relentless explosions of two-thousand-pound bombs in the next valley over, but occasionally one would go astray and fall close enough to shake the walls of our shack.

We spent our days with the mujahideen at the front lines as they fought their way to reach Osama's redoubt. At night, we sipped tea with Pashtu warlords, transmitted our stories and photographs by satellite phone, and planned for the next day.

At the same time, on the other side of the planet, a young African-American athlete worked hard to prove himself in his rookie year in the National Football League. LaDainian Tomlinson had led the NCAA in rushing his senior year at Texas Christian University, carrying the ball for 2,158 yards and scoring twenty-two touchdowns. The San Diego Chargers recognized his talent and picked him in the first round of the 2001 draft. LaDainian was one of the best running backs in the NFL, but the Chargers were one of the worst teams. He planned to change that.

On December 15, 2001, I was sitting in the sun with Afghan warlords while they used a walkie-talkie to negotiate the surrender of al-Qaeda fighters, who were decimated and demoralized by American air power. LaDainian was in Qualcomm Stadium in San Diego, being pummeled by the Oakland Raiders in a game that would end with a 6-13 loss for the Chargers.

We had never met, but we shared a common legacy. We both traced our heritage to Tomlinson Hill. And we both had traveled far from Texas to create better lives for ourselves. I was the city boy who became a foreign correspondent; he was the country boy who became a millionaire football player.

My father first told me about LaDainian in 1999 and guessed he must be a descendant of Tomlinson Hill slaves. He was right. LaDainian had spent summers with his grandparents playing in the fields where his great-grandfather had been a slave and picked cotton.

RETURNING FROM AFRICA

By 2007, I was growing weary after eleven years covering war and destruction in Africa and the Middle East. I had spent most of 2006 traveling to Somalia, getting to know the clan leaders and covering the war there, and I had lost my stomach for it. I wasn't frightened for my life, nor was I feeling any foreboding. I had just stopped enjoying my work. I didn't want to be surrounded by teenagers with assault rifles anymore; I didn't want to see any more starving babies. Somalia had already been destroyed by civil war and fourteen years of anarchy. I had just witnessed another wave of violence, and I knew there was another one coming. For the first time, I felt despair.

And then Anthony died.

When I became the East Africa bureau chief, I knew one of my staff would likely die on assignment. The two bureau chiefs before me had both lost someone. But I had worked hard to train everyone to stay alive in the four war zones we covered from Nairobi. I lectured endlessly on tactics and procedures. I had felt especially responsible for Anthony Mitchell. He had been expelled from Ethiopia because of his reporting, and as a result, his wife had lost her job, their main source of income. I couldn't do much to help him in terms of money, but I tried to give him special assignments that he enjoyed, hoping to make up for his low pay and long hours. Coming home from one of those assignments, his plane crashed nose-first into a jungle in Cameroon, leaving his two small children without a father. Telling Catherine that her husband's plane was lost and that Anthony was likely dead tripped a circuit breaker in my heart. I'd had enough death. So a few months later, when my wife, Shalini, told me she had an interview scheduled for an exciting job in Texas, I knew fate was telling me it was time to go home.

The return to Texas was fraught with emotional land mines. Since I had left home at seventeen, I'd rarely spoken to any of my relatives. When I left for South Africa in 1993, my maternal grandmother was sure that even if I managed to escape the tribal violence, a wild animal would maul me. To people without passports and little knowledge of the world, my decision to go to Africa was unfathomable. No one ever directly asked me why I wanted to go, but neither did I offer any explanation except to say I wanted adventure. Meeting Nelson Mandela or marching through eastern Congo with Laurent Kabila's rebel army did not impress them. They would occasionally ask me if I was making enough money, but that was about all.

After years of avoiding what Shalini called my "southern gothic" family, we moved to Austin, just a few hours' drive away from my father. I was at a stage where I was ready to tackle whatever skeletons would leap out of the Tomlinson closet. I had made friends with Somali warlords, negotiated with drunken child soldiers, and faced down a mob of angry Rwandan refugees. How bad could my family really be? Besides, I was also going to live in my favorite city with my closest friends, whom I loved deeply.

Once we settled in Austin, I kept working for the AP on a part-time basis, making trips from Austin to Iraq and Africa on special assignments. But in between my overseas trips, I was remembering what it means to be a Texan. I saw my best friend from high school several times a week. Shalini and I would take walks on the University of Texas campus, where we had met. But I was also excited to learn the truth about my family and its legacy. I planned to go to Tomlinson Hill for the first time, and I wanted to find the black Tomlinsons.

FATHER AND SON REUNION

I decided the first step was to find those old scrapbooks. I hoped my father, Bob, would still have them and tell me more about our family. The only problem was our strained relationship. We rarely called each other on the phone. I thought maybe this would be a chance to bridge the gap.

Bob had the scrapbooks tucked away in a rented storage locker, along with his favorite bowling balls. Most of his life had been spent in bowling alleys, in one capacity or another. In the early 1980s, he started collecting cameras, and that became a part-time business. Now retired, he supplemented his Social Security check by trolling garage sales, buying old cameras for pennies and then selling them for dollars on eBay.

I drove to his home in McKinney, north of Dallas, and parked in front of the small brick house he shared with his third wife. I knocked on the hollow steel door, causing a startling amount of noise. I heard a muffled voice inside shout "Come in." When I walked inside, Dad was at a table, which was covered with haphazardly stacked cardboard boxes, bubble wrap, plastic bags, a few screwdrivers, and four old cameras. Despite a recent bout of colon cancer that took forty pounds off his frame, he was obese again and his breathing was labored. He complained about allergies, and I could see why. The house had not been properly cleaned in years. The royal blue carpet was blotted with large stains that turned it black in places. Pet food was strewn around the house and a cat was perched on a side table next to a water bowl. A deaf and blind seventeen-year-old dog of indeterminable breed sniffed around the clutter. Allergic to animal hair since childhood, I had taken two antihistamine tablets in the car, but the smell of animals and mildew made me wonder if the pills would do any good.

On the right-hand corner of the dining table, Dad had cleared a spot, and a scrapbook was open before him. He had pulled out some loose newspaper clippings and set them aside. "I've been going through this stuff to see what you might need," he said, with no acknowledgment that we hadn't seen each other in four years. He was being the smooth bowling ball salesman of my youth, living up to my friends' nickname for him: "Smilin' Bob."

The scrapbook had a red leather cover, but the binding had disintegrated long ago. Someone had glued the closely trimmed newspaper articles to the pages in a way that made use of every square inch. Most of the stories were from the early 1900s. The majority of the clips were in English, but there were also a good number of German clippings. I had learned German in school and in the army, but when my father asked me to read some of the articles, I discovered they were from a local Dallas newspaper that published its articles in an archaic form of Swiss German. I could understand some of what was written, but most parts left me flummoxed.

"This scrapbook was kept by my grandmother on the Fretz side," Dad explained. "I'm not sure who began it, but maybe my great-grandmother, judging by the age of the clippings."

The vast majority of the stories were about the Fretz family and the Swiss German community in Dallas. Emil A. Fretz, my great-grandfather, had founded the Dallas Parks Board. On the day the Marsalis Dallas Zoo opened, a photo of Emil's daughter Mary—my grandmother—was on the front page of the *Dallas Morning News*. She was cuddling a baby cheetah.

"The smartest thing your grandfather ever did was marry your grandmother, because the Fretzes were a wealthy family," Dad said. "She is largely the reason he was able to retire at fifty."

After my grandparents married in 1926, the scrapbook's breadth expanded to include the Tomlinsons. The entries were mostly obituaries or family announcements clipped from the *Dallas Morning News* and other newspapers. Unlike most of the Fretz articles, the Tomlinson clippings were not glued in; someone had dropped them inside the back cover.

These carefully folded pieces of newsprint, some held together with straight pins, had once provided the earliest knowledge of my family history. They had launched my curiosity and imagination. But now that I saw these clippings, they were far fewer and shorter than I remembered. There were just eleven articles, eight of them obituaries. One was my grandparent's wedding announcement, another a story about a fiftieth wedding anniversary, and the last was a story about a bridge collapse that had killed a cousin of my great-grandfather Robert Edward Lee Tomlinson.

I also discovered the fallibility of an eight-year-old's memory. I had conflated my great-grandfather's life with that of his brother Eldridge Alexander Tomlinson. Eldridge had been the Texas Ranger and cowboy, while R.E.L. had been a farmer, a real estate agent, and a schoolteacher.

> Trained in the art of teaching, R. E. L. Tomlinson took his place as chief pedagogue at Busby School where the Blue Back Speller and Friday afternoon Spelling Matches were the vogue. Mr. Tomlinson taught the principles of the Bible as well as fundamentals of good citizenship.[1]

This same story revealed other forgotten details about Tomlinson Hill.

> The double wedding of R. E. L. Tomlinson and Frank M. Stallworth to the popular Bettie and Billah Etheridge twins December 23, 1891 was the social event of the season. Old Beulah Church was packed with folks from all over the county to witness the nuptial ceremony performed by the popular Baptist preacher Rev. J. R. M. N. Touchstone. . . . Following the wedding an old fashioned In-Fare and recreation was enjoyed by the guests. Tables groaned under the weight of fried and baked chicken and all the trimmings. The festivities even followed the two couples to Marlin, where they made their home.

As a child, I had grasped for evidence of Texan aristocracy. Reading R.E.L.'s obituary as a child had given me pride in my southern heritage, but now the same words made me cringe. In an obituary entitled "Beloved Pioneer and Leader Expires Tuesday," the language was too easy to decipher:

> He was born at Tomlinson Hill Jan. 25, 1862 son of James K. Tomlinson and Sarah Jemima Stallworth Tomlinson, at a time when the star of the Confederate States of America shone in its greatest brilliance. Of a great family of Southerners, with typical devotion to the cause and its leader the young son born during the war, was named after the famous Confederate commander-in-chief.[2]

Recognizing these southern dog whistles as an adult, I knew that my eight-year-old self would likely be disappointed by what I might find as I researched my family. But the investigative reporter in me was even more intrigued.

The obituaries told me that R.E.L.'s father-in-law, W. G. Etheridge, was a well-educated Unionist who had spoken out against slavery and opposed Texas secession. When the Civil War began, Etheridge fled to the North, but afterward he returned to Falls County and served as sheriff from 1875 to 1876 and was elected to the state legislature in 1882.[3] I wondered what Etheridge would have thought about the fact his daughter was marrying into a slaveholding family that supported the Confederacy. I wondered which legacy would have a stronger influence on my family.

Growing up in Texas, I had known many racists, and I understood something of their netherworld. While visiting my mother's parents in another part of East Texas, I had heard Baptist preachers claim that black skin was the "mark of Cain." God's curse, they argued, justified segregation. I listened to the county constable and my maternal grandfather talk about those "damned niggers" who lived across the river in Coffee City. I always knew when white men were talking about black men, because it was the only time they referred to an adult as a "boy." Unless they were talking about a "good ol' boy," which meant the man was white and "dependable." A "boy" could never be forgiven, while a "good ol' boy" could do no wrong.

I remember going to a pool party when I was thirteen and seeing how the wealthy white family that owned the home became annoyed because the school required the parents to invite their daughter's African-American classmates. My classmate complained that her parents would have to drain the pool afterward because of the "oils" they imagined the African-American kids would leave behind.

None of these white people would have dared reveal his or her true feelings in "mixed company." Most would sincerely have denied they were racist. Instead, they would have argued they were realistic. I knew their attitudes were wrong, but I never spoke up. I either felt outnumbered or thought that my protests wouldn't make a difference. I came to accept this was how most of my white friends behaved.

R.E.L. had died when Bob was only two, so he had no memory of his grandfather, nor did he know anything about James, his great-grandfather. The only thing he possessed that was linked to James was a small buckskin wallet with white stitching. The wallet was trifold, with a leather strap used to hold it closed. There were a few handwritten markings on the outside, but they were too faded to make out. But when I opened it, there was another flap over a change purse with three pockets. Using a fountain pen, someone had written in cursive script across the inside cover, "This book is an old heirloom." Across the closure for the change purse, in the same handwriting, was written "R. E. L. Tomlinson." Below that, on the purse itself, someone had written "R. E. L. Tomlinson Marlin, Tex. July 15, 1883." Under the flap of the change purse, the same person had written, "J. K. Tomlinson 1850 Ala." There were a few coins inside, including a nineteenth-century German ten pfennig piece and a buffalo nickel. We guessed that the wallet must have belonged to James K. Tomlinson, who moved to Texas from Alabama. R.E.L. was only four when his father died in 1865, so it appears that when R.E.L. turned twenty-one, his brothers gave him the wallet as a memento of the father he'd never known. R. E. L. had decided to make sure everyone knew the wallet's provenance.

Dad said his father, Tommy, born in 1901, rarely talked about the family's history. "He had the stock line that we treated our slaves so good that they kept the Tomlinson name after they were freed," he told me. "But that might not be the reason they kept the name."

My father then produced R.E.L.'s teaching certificates from the Sam Houston Normal Institute in Huntsville. The first was dated June 10, 1886, and the second was from May 31, 1888. This was how he had become the chief pedagogue. But R.E.L. had started out at the Agricultural and Mechanical College of Texas in 1881, where he received a military education.

My father said Tommy talked about R.E.L. only in fragments. "R. E. L. Tomlinson had done some farming, and from what my Dad said, there were one too many floods on the Brazos," Bob recalled. "The second or third time it happened, that finished him off." "He was pretty prominent, but how prominent do you have to be in a town of five thousand?" Bob said. "Although Marlin was a pretty rockin' town back then."

In the early twentieth century, Marlin was known for its hot springs, and it is still called "the Official Mineral Water City of Texas." Visitors came from across the state to "take the waters," and it was a popular resort destination. Bob said his memories of visiting Marlin, all before he turned ten, were few but vivid. He said his grandmother lived in a wood-framed house with a big porch near the center of town.

"I do remember walking from their house down to the square, and there was a fire station down there. They still had an old horse-drawn fire truck," Dad said. "They weren't using it, but it was still there."

Bob said that reflection was not in Tommy's temperament, nor was Marlin dear to his heart. "He graduated from A&M in 1923 and never looked back. He moved straight to Dallas," Dad explained. "He didn't worry about the past; he was a builder. He wanted to put new stuff up. It if meant tearing down the [family's] Liberty Street house to put in a parking lot to serve a building he had built for another company next door, no problem."

Unlike his father, Bob holds on to history like a precious gem, in particular Dallas's history. He knows the stories of the city's inner neighborhoods and he laments the loss of landmarks from his childhood. He talks about the old Dr Pepper headquarters on Mockingbird

Lane and how angry he was when the historic clock tower was acciden-
tally destroyed during the construction of new condominiums. He told
me stories about the Fretz family going back three generations, but he
claimed to know little about Tomlinson history, and, frankly, he didn't
seem to have much interest in it. He said he had tried to go to Tomlinson Hill only once, but he got lost on the back roads and couldn't find
anyone who knew where it was. Whenever he spoke about his father, he
would take a quick gasp of breath and then his voice would harden.

"He wanted to retire at fifty so he could drive himself bonkers losing
at gin rummy and getting drunk every afternoon at the Lakewood Country Club," Bob finally said. "When he decided he needed to give me a way
of supporting myself, we started a bowling-supply store."

I pressed him, and Bob began to reveal more about my grandfather.

"He was an all-purpose bigot," Bob said, speaking quietly, as if someone else might hear. "At different times, he would go off on anybody, and
when he came to Dallas, the chief of police was a member of the Ku Klux
Klan. That is a known fact. I don't know if my father was ever a member,
but he certainly had some sympathy for them back in the twenties and
thirties. He became slightly more tolerant as time passed, but it was still
right there. R.E.L. was a good southern man always loyal to the cause,
so I guess we know where it came from."

It was hard to hear that my grandfather's racism ran so deep. In
my heart, I wanted my family to be above the fray. There has always
been a liberal intellectual tradition in the South, and I wanted that to
be my heritage, not the desperate and twisted world of racist populism. But I was finished with fantasies; I wanted to know the truth, no
matter how ugly.

Race relations were on my mind when I watched Barack Obama, the
African-American senator from Illinois, clinch the Democratic presidential nomination. When Obama had visited Kenya in 2006, his public speeches had impressed me, but I had dismissed talk of an Obama
presidency because I didn't think the people of the United States would
elect a black man president.

I listened to Obama's victory speech, which was absent of rancor,
full of hope, and reached out to anyone who would join him. He re-

minded me of Nelson Mandela, whom I had met while covering the 1994 presidential campaign in South Africa. In his campaign, Mandela had resisted political expediency and taken the high road; the one that required true leadership to bring substantive change to his country, rather than just transferring power from a white tyrant to a black one. He was not the demagogic African dictator that whites had expected and feared. Mandela's speeches were not filled with sarcasm and vitriol like those of many American politicians. Mandela exemplified grace.

Obama was following Mandela's example, trying to disarm the less committed bigots and win over everyone else. After spending most of my adult life overseas, I found myself comparing race in America to the ethnic massacres I'd observed in Rwanda and Congo. This new political development fueled my desire to delve deeper into the legacy of Tomlinson Hill. If America was ready for a black president, I hoped it was ready to come to terms with its past.

TWO

I am afraid you have got the negroes to like you and not fear you. If it is the case, you cannot get on, nor take care of anything.

—Churchill Jones

I began my research open to finding acts of heroism, dark secrets, and things in between. But investigating events in the mid-nineteenth century is quite different from interviewing witnesses to a recent massacre. What books or resources existed that might help me understand the Tomlinson story, white and black? The only option was to start Googling and digging, to thumb through book indexes, and to search university databases. I sent e-mails to historians, asking for their help in understanding what had happened and why.

The first things I needed were family trees. That led me to Ancestry .com. I filled in a few blanks with R.E.L.'s name, my grandfather's name, and my own, and soon I had my family tree. I gained access to census forms, draft-registration cards, and old phone books. Scrap by scrap, I put together an outline of my ancestors' lives. I searched for LaDainian's family and found a tree started by a "TorshaT," LaDainian's wife, LaTorsha. She had not logged in for some time, but her tree gave me a starting point for the black Tomlinsons.

I found a few books about Falls County. A sentence here and a reference there helped me add to the family tree and create a time line.

I scoured the Falls County Library in Marlin. I spent days in the Falls County courthouse, collecting deed and probate records. Slowly, I pieced together why the Tomlinsons had come to Texas from Alabama.

In 1848, James Kendrick Tomlinson (known as Jim) was living in Conecuh County, Alabama, when the Treaty of Guadalupe Hidalgo ended the Mexican-American War. The peace deal opened a territory four times the size of France to American settlement.[1] It wasn't long before land speculators were visiting Alabama and promoting the virgin lands in Texas, California, and the other territories the United States had acquired at the end of the war.

Newspapers told stories of poor men who traveled west and became fantastically rich by clearing a few acres of land and throwing some seeds on the ground. But Jim wasn't sure Texas was the right place for his family. At the age of thirty-five, he already had a large plantation and owned thirty-three slaves to tend to his cotton and cattle.[2] His wife, Sarah, had borne three sons and a daughter, and while Jim wasn't the wealthiest of men, he had a comfortable life. He had plans to build a steam-powered sawmill on the Conecuh River to diversify his business.[3]

Jim was also close to his elder sister, Susan Tomlinson Jones, who lived nearby. Jim and Susan were born in Georgia, but their parents had moved to Alabama when they were teenagers. That was in the 1830s, when Alabama was the land of opportunity. Jim met his wife, Sarah, in Conecuh County, and her family, the Stallworths, lived nearby.[4]

Susan's husband was Churchill Jones, who had amassed a fortune by developing plantations across the South. Churchill was born on Cherry Walk, his father's tobacco plantation near Bowling Green, Virginia. He graduated from Rappahannock Academy and Military Institute and moved to Evergreen, Alabama, where he became a schoolteacher and developed a cotton plantation. He had a reputation for being "proud and aggressive." He was prominent in the community and had served in the Alabama legislature, representing the Whig party.[5]

Before the Industrial Revolution, entrepreneurs made their fortune buying land, developing it, and then selling it at a profit. Jones had already lived in three states, and when he heard that cheap land was available in Texas, he went on a prospecting tour in the upper Brazos Valley in 1849.[6] He found a virtually untouched territory. The Mexican-American War had discouraged pioneers, but the military activity had driven off most hostile Native Americans. The soil in the valley was rich and fertile. The Brazos is Texas's longest river, stretching more than twelve hundred miles, from the New Mexico border through the middle of Texas, and emptying into the Gulf of Mexico at Freeport. The water is almost always brown with silt. Wide and relatively shallow, the river frequently floods and produces rich alluvial soils perfect for farming. But the violent floods prompted the Spanish to name it Rio de los Brazos de Dios, or the River of the Arms of God.

Churchill wasn't alone in looking for opportunities in Texas. Between 1848 and 1860, tens of thousands of families from Alabama and Tennessee hung signs that said GONE TO TEXAS or simply G.T.T. on their old homesteads, abandoned their worn-out farms, and took their slaves to Texas.[7] But unlike many people moving to Texas, Churchill was not buried in debt. He was looking to expand his empire, and that desire would change the lives of dozens of his relatives and their slaves.[8]

Cheap land and cheap labor were the keys to Churchill's success. Land in Texas cost nearly nothing, and Texas was a slave state. State officials consistently flirted with bankruptcy, and the only way to avoid economic collapse was to attract settlers who could bring capital, grow crops, and pay taxes. As a forty-four-year-old established planter with a fortune and eight children, Churchill was exactly the kind of man Texas wanted.[9]

THE FALLS PLANTATION

During his Texas tour, Churchill saw several properties he liked. His first purchase was Lake Creek Farm in Montgomery County, about forty miles north of Houston. But the land along the Brazos River impressed him more, particularly at the "Falls of the Brazos." The red soil was perfect for cotton farming and stock raising. Most important, the price per acre was a fraction of what he would have had to pay in the Old South.[10]

The falls marked the northern limit of barge navigation on the Brazos. Floating cotton down to Galveston for sale and export would be easy, and Churchill saw a potential business there, too. There was also plenty of room for a water-powered cotton gin to maximize profits. He soon dreamed up a plan to build the largest cotton plantation west of the Mississippi, and the only integrated operation for growing, milling, and selling cotton in the West. Churchill was certain that pioneering Texas would provide a return on investment he couldn't get anywhere else. He returned to Alabama a Texas evangelist.[11]

In July 1850, Churchill met Christopher Sterns on a hill overlooking the falls. Sterns's wife had inherited the land, but they lacked capital. Sterns sold Churchill 28,000 acres on both sides of the river for fifteen thousand dollars. Churchill named it the Falls Plantation and returned to Alabama.[12]

A few months later, Churchill sent his brother-in-law Aylett Dean to Lake Creek Farm with forty slaves, oxen, wagons, and equipment. He gave his eldest son, James Sanford Jones, responsibility for setting up the Falls Plantation. The twenty-two-year-old led an expedition of five overseers and one hundred slaves overland from Alabama. Three of the overseers were Churchill's nephews, including a man named George Daffan. Churchill, meanwhile, traveled by coastal steamship and was waiting for the group when they arrived at the Falls Plantation on February 18, 1851.[13]

Churchill told James and George to concentrate first on getting the farm operational and then to build homes for the family and slaves. Though Churchill spent most of 1851 and 1852 in Alabama, he visited the Falls Plantation each year to inspect his son's progress and buy more land.[14]

By the spring of 1852, James had his first cotton crop in the ground, and Churchill was setting up other enterprises. He applied for, and received from the Falls County commissioners, a license to operate a flatboat ferry to carry travelers across the Brazos. He was authorized to charge twenty-five cents for a man and a horse, 50 cents for a horse and carriage, one dollar for a carriage with two horses, a dollar and quarter for a four-horse wagon, and a dollar and a half for a six-horse wagon. Pedestrians and loose horses were both ten cents. He was allowed to charge double if the river was flooding but was required to give Falls County residents a 50 percent discount. Churchill's slaves operated the boats under an overseer.[15]

That same year, Churchill appeared on the Falls County tax rolls for the first time. He listed eighty-one slaves, valued at $38,050. A good field hand was valued at two thousand dollars at the time. Jones's 28,000 acres were valued at one dollar per acre. In two years, his land had already appreciated 86 percent.[16] Like most planters, Churchill kept most of his wealth invested in land and slaves. He was the richest man in Falls County. With 30 percent of all of the slaves in the county he was one of the wealthiest men in Texas.[17]

During his absences, Churchill wrote long letters to James and the overseers, describing how he wanted the plantation to operate and what he wanted built, such as slave quarters in the river bottom. From a letter to overseer George Daffan, dated July 25, 1853, it is easy to see where Churchill got his reputation for being "proud and aggressive." His letters put to rest the southern mythology about benevolent slave masters:

James said nothing about losing my flat [boat] at the Ferry there. I suppose he was ashamed to name it, as he and you ought to be. It was pure carelessness certainly. George, I am afraid you have got the negroes to like you and not fear you. If it is the case, you cannot get on, nor take care of anything. They must know when you speak they have to obey, and to do this you have to stand square up to them and show yourself master. You cannot coax a negro to do his duty. You have to force him, and if they only like you and not fear you, they will soon hate you and get tired of you. That is the nature of negroes, but to make them fear you and like you both, you can do anything you want with them.[18]

Churchill's tone was not unusual for a man in his position, particularly in addressing young relatives whom he wanted to develop into successful planters. In the same letter, Churchill instructed the men to build a dog-run, a pair of eighteen-by-twelve-foot cabins, which were typical in Texas before 1860. Dog-runs got their name from the porch created between the two cabins by the single roof connecting them. These homes were built from hand-hewn logs, cedar if the landowner was lucky enough to have it. Cedar stands up to the weather better than almost any other wood found in Texas. The state had few sawmills, and the little milled lumber available was usually of poor quality. In rural areas, squared-off logs remained the best building material into the 1870s. The slaves dovetailed the ends of the logs to fit together at the corners.[19]

Builders packed the gaps between the logs with mud, and they fashioned chimneys from mud and sticks. They used clapboard planks weighed down by long poles for the roof. The covered porch, or run, kept leather and iron goods protected from the elements. The run also funneled breezes between the two cabins, cooling both. Hunting dogs usually slept in the shady parts of the run, giving the cabin its name.[20]

Early pioneers cut clearings in the dense scrub that surrounded life-giving rivers and springs. They then set fire to the underbrush to clear the land for planting. For months, or perhaps years, these compounds consisted of tents, crude lean-tos, and simple cabins, with livestock, farming tools, and all manner of trash scattered around. Farmers brought horses, cattle, pigs, and chickens and allowed them to freely roam the woods and meadows. While some early settlers built outhouses, a ditch in the woods provided a perfectly acceptable latrine for most people.[21] Poor subsistence farmers living in rough-cut farms were called "white trash" because of the garbage that piled up around their cabins.[22]

While poor settlers usually had dirt floors, Churchill insisted on wooden ones. He ordered his slaves to build a smokehouse and an outdoor kitchen and to choose a spot for his main cabin not far from a spring. He had James and George build concrete cisterns to store fresh water during the long, dry summers. While family farmers initially concentrated on subsistence crops, Churchill immediately planted revenue-producing cotton. He did grow corn to feed his family, slaves, and pigs, but from the very beginning Churchill saw his new home in Texas as a business. Cotton was a global commodity that allowed planters to inject cash into struggling frontier economies, making the planters not only wealthy but powerful.[23]

Meals consisted of salt pork, corn bread, sweet potatoes, and molasses. Hunters could find deer and rabbit, if they had gunpowder. Beef and honey were available, but these were reserved for special occasions. Most early settlers did not keep a vegetable garden, nor did they keep milk cows. Butter was a rare luxury.[24]

The slave's diet was similar, though on larger plantations, like Churchill's, the slaves tended vegetable gardens for both themselves and the whites.[25] Meals were prepared and served in a communal kitchen managed by an overseer. Slaves were given two sets of clothing a year, and on the Falls Plantation the slaves made them.[26]

There were dozens of white families dotted across Falls County in 1853. Only one in four families held slaves, so they had to do the hard work themselves. Whites formed churches and often joined forces to help build homes and barns. Nevertheless, Churchill's letters suggest that he held many of his new neighbors in contempt, and poorer farmers probably didn't appreciate him very much, either.[27]

Such snobbery was typical of the era. Most of the new arrivals to Texas were Calvinists, who were taught that a person's wealth, or lack of it, was a reflection of his virtue. They respected hard work and considered thriftiness next to holiness. Laziness was a sign of a lost soul, and there were too many of these in Falls County, as far as Churchill was concerned. In his letter to James on August 4, he was adamant that his son not hire any white laborers. He was also anxious for James to finish building the family's cabins before Churchill brought Susan and his younger children to Texas.

> I think you had better let white men alone. I am tired of feeding idle lazy loafers to do nothing and pay them big bills when they leave. Tell George I shall want to see in his books how Tidwell could make a bill of $80 against me, at $25 for every 20 days he worked full. He was to

keep account in his book of every day and piece of day that he
worked.

I sent whiskey, flour, sugar, etc. to you last May. I would like to
hear whether you got all safe or not. The whiskey I sent for medical
purposes and not as an everyday beverage. Take [what you need] of
everything. There was over 400 pounds of sugar. You will use very
little of that quantity by the time we get there. The lard take care of
for your Mother. You have plenty of butter for you all to use. Let me
hear all about the stock, cotton, and hogs, and whether you were able
to get any or not. Write me whether pork will be plenty or not next
winter.[28]

Churchill was planning to move his family to Texas in October
1853.[29] From Evergreen, they would travel by stagecoach eighty-five
miles to Mobile, Alabama. From there, they would take a steamboat
to New Orleans, where they would spend at least one night before taking another coastal ship to Galveston, then the largest city in Texas,
with five thousand residents. From Galveston, it was a 235-mile stagecoach ride on a rutted path along the eastern bank of the Brazos to
Marlin, the seat of Falls County. This part of the journey was by far the
worst, since Texas had no graded roads outside of Galveston. In bad
weather, the dirt paths became quagmires. The Falls Plantation was
another eight miles outside of Marlin by horse or wagon.[30]

TYPHOID AND YELLOW FEVER STRIKE

In September 1853, typhoid struck Alabama hard and delayed
Churchill's departure. The fever killed two of Jim Tomlinson's brothers-
in-law, Nicholas and Calloway Stallworth. The Tomlinsons, Stallworths, and Joneses lived near one another northwest of Evergreen. That
closeness led Churchill to encourage the Tomlinsons and Stallworths to
follow him to Texas to escape the illness. But Churchill was having a
hard time getting his family to Texas. The summer yellow fever season
along the coast was especially bad that year and lasted longer than
usual. Churchill wrote on August 28 to tell his son James that he did

not know when the family could leave Evergreen without risking yellow fever in New Orleans. He also informed James that the Stallworths had contracted typhoid, and they had also lost six slaves on their Alabama plantation.[31]

While there is no doubt that slaveholders brutally controlled the lives of their slaves, those same people represented as much as 50 percent of an average planter's wealth. Slaveholders were always concerned about the health of their slaves and sometimes spent up to eight dollars a year per slave in medical costs, a considerable amount in those days.[32] To lose "valuable negroes" to illness was a major financial loss for any planter, and from his letter, Churchill considered the death of Nicholas Stallworth's slaves a major financial loss for his widow. So it was not surprising that Churchill was upset to learn from his son James that several of his slaves at the Falls Plantation were ill. Churchill wrote on September 5, 1853:

> You spoke of a good deal of sickness which I am sorry to hear, though you say there is no serious case. Give all the attention you can to all the sick. You can manage the cases by cleaning the stomach well first with emetics and then with pills made of equal parts calomel [mercury chloride, a laxative and disinfectant], aloes and rhubarb, and then followed up with bitter teas. That bitter weed you showed me down in the bottom last December is very good. Have a tub full made at a time and make them drink it rapid all the time. After the stomach is well cleaned, should the negroes be taken with dysentery or bloody flux [another term for dysentery], you must not use calomel or blue mass [another mercury-based medicine]. It is perfect death. I wrote you before about this and do not forget. Oil, spirits of turpentine and laudanum [an opiate]—begin with 2 spoons full of oil, 1 teaspoon of spirits of turpentine, and 30–60 drops of laudanum—then small doses of soda and salts. One half teaspoon of carbon of soda and two teaspoons of salts mixed together in sage tea given as the emergency requires. If bad cases, give often, and use astringent teas made of post oak bark, running dewberry briar root. The tea should be made strong. Give anything that will heal the bowel, eat little and

drink no cold water. Give injections of soapsuds and oil with some
laudanum in it.[33]

In a letter dated October 17, Churchill was pleased to hear that the
sickness in Texas had passed, but he was still worried about when
he could safely move his family, predicting it could be late December.
He also noted that James had complained about his letters:

> You seemed to think in your last letter to me that I was grumbling
> a good deal. All I said was intended to bring your and George's minds
> fully to bear on the importance of looking well to the interest of the
> business there generally, and not allow yourselves to be deceived by
> trifling white men. It is your interest more than mine to look well
> into these things and take care.[34]

The illnesses in Alabama and Churchill's enthusiasm for Texas
made Jim Tomlinson reconsider following Churchill and Susan. But
Jim was looking after the Stallworth widows and he was managing
slaves belonging to his sister-in-law, Mary Stallworth Travis, who also
became a widow at thirty-four when her husband died from fever.[35]
Jim and his wife, Sarah, decided they needed to stay close to her family,
and they told Churchill and Susan they would stay put for the moment.
Jim concentrated on his new steam-driven sawmill.[36]

For his part, Churchill closely monitored the yellow fever epidemic
in New Orleans and Galveston. His letters became more detailed, adamant, and angry as he continued to delay their departure. He worried
that after three years of living in frontier conditions, James and George
were not keeping "the negroes under the right management." He feared
they were becoming too friendly with their only real community in
Falls County. Churchill wrote, "Unless they do fear you, they will not
obey promptly; they will parley, twist, and turn about and get you to
believe they are doing all that you wish, and when you come to find out
right, it is all to no avail."[37]

He repeated his concern in subsequent letters:

I am a little fearful George is trying honey [to] coax the negroes to work. If this is the case he had just as well quit. No man on earth can have business done unless he knows how to make negroes move under the proper fear, and go to the top of their speed. A man to be a business man must be a full judge of what hands can do at the different branches of plantation business, and then he must ask them no odds about their doing of it, make them do it at a word, if the whip is needed give it to them in full . . . I want rigid and strict government among my negroes . . . Tell George to recollect his father's management among negroes. He was a little too severe but not much.[38]

But Churchill also believed in positive reinforcement:

The next thing is when you get them to discharge their duty fully and faithfully on all occasions, treat them fairly and with humanity. Allow them all that is right on their part, and they will then like you. When they fear you and like you both, you may do anything in reason that you want, but you must hold a tight rein at all times.[39]

The old slaveholder knew blacks were not happy to be slaves. Some chose to fight back or flee, but few were successful. Instead, most offered passive or subtle forms of resistance. Malingering and conniving were acts of subtle rebellion. They feigned ignorance, pretended to be ill or injured, or, as Churchill feared, tried to manipulate young and impressionable whites in order to get better treatment. The slaves had no stake in the success of Churchill's newest project, but they knew he had a financial stake in their well-being. Many whites didn't recognize the slaves' passive resistance to their orders for the civil disobedience that it was, and instead labeled all blacks as lazy and deceitful, a stereotype that persisted for generations.[40]

Churchill's clan finally left Alabama in December 1853, after the cold weather killed most of the fever-carrying mosquitoes, and they arrived at the Falls Plantation in January 1854. The cabins were built and ready for habitation, and the slaves quickly moved into their own cabins along the river bottom. Churchill's eldest daughter, Sarah, brought her new daughter, Sue, and her husband, George Green.[41]

Susan Tomlinson Jones settled into her new cabin, which was quite a step down from her large, well-appointed home in Alabama. But she'd been through this before as a child and as a young wife. She looked out on the fallow fields, visited the spring, where sweet water flowed from the limestone, and looked down on the wide, muddy Brazos. Susan saw the potential to build a fortune for her children on the frontier. She rode north from her cabin to see the land her husband had purchased, whereupon she came to a rise that offered a view of Marlin to the east. She became the first Tomlinson to stand on what would become Tomlinson Hill.

THREE

Some white folks might want to put me back in slavery if
I told you how we were used in slavery time, but you asked
me for the truth.

—Wes Brady

Falls County was only four years old in 1854, and Marlin was barely
a village. The county's founders laid out the town around a small log
courthouse built from split cedar logs. The one-room structure served
as court, school, and church during the day. And citizens held political
meetings and dances in it at night, when the pulpit was hoisted into the
rafters by a pulley system. A hotel, tavern, lawyer's office, and a few shops
and warehouses made up the rest of the town.[1]

Churchill Jones quickly became one of the most important people
in the county, financing a new courthouse and investing in a sawmill.
He and his wife, Susan Tomlinson Jones, also organized political meetings and social events.[2]

Churchill's son-in-law George Green decided to become business
partners with a young man named Zenas Bartlett, a New Hampshire
native who had panned for gold in California but ended up a shopkeeper in Texas. They bought a log cabin and a two-story frame building on the town square and began Green and Bartlett, the largest general
store in Falls County. Their letterhead declared they were "Dealers in Dry
Goods and Fine Jewelry, Clothing, Boots & Shoes, Hardware & Crockery,

Groceries, Wooden Ware, Ploughs, Iron, Nails, And All Kinds of Plantation Goods."[3]

Importing manufactured goods from the North was a gamble in 1854. Most Texans operated on a barter economy, and there was little paper money in circulation. Most settlers never saw a gold or silver coin. Businesspeople traded promissory notes like currency, but when hard money was needed, Spanish and Mexican silver coins served as the only legal tender in Texas. Prideful Texans would hammer out the Spanish king's profile or the Mexican eagle that marked those coins, but defacing them didn't diminish the bullion's value.[4]

Most Texans made their own clothes, shoes, soap, candles, wheels, harnesses, and crockery. The idea of buying goods manufactured on the East Coast and then shipped through the Gulf of Mexico was beyond most settlers' imagination. Only planters could afford such luxuries.[5]

George and Zenas ordered goods from New York on credit and paid their debts when they visited there. Texas law prohibited banks, so there was little alternative to relying on the credit terms offered by wholesalers.[6] According to their ledgers, Churchill bought most of the goods George and Zenas sold, and he was the only one to pay his bills on time. Churchill's cotton thrived, his herds grew, and he purchased more slaves, or brought them over from his other plantations. He built a large clapboard house so that his family could move out of the dog-run. He ordered almost everything he owned, including the family's clothes, from Green and Bartlett. The store thrived until George fell ill with tuberculosis. After months of treatments and travel to spas across the South, George died in Marlin in 1856. Zenas settled the accounts, then reopened the shop as a sole proprietor. Fourteen months later, Zenas married George's widow, Sarah, and became part of the Jones family.[7]

Churchill's plantation was the largest in Falls County and was populated with scores of slaves. He was also one of the rare men with a private, university-level education. His time in the Alabama State House had left him with a regal bearing. Churchill and other planters like him formed the top tier of Texas society, though he was only a big fish in what was then a very little pond.[8]

Susan wrote to her brother, Jim Tomlinson, describing their beautiful plantation and their profits. About a dozen other wealthy families from Alabama, Georgia, and the Carolinas had moved to Falls County, and they were establishing a planter society like the ones they'd left behind. Susan urged her brother to join her on the Brazos. She even had a plot of land in mind for him.[9]

PLANTATION LIFE

For the vast majority of white Texans, including most slaveholders, every day was spent working on the farm. Even planters with as many as fifty slaves would rarely hire an overseer, choosing instead to go into the fields themselves. The average farmer's life was a drudge.[10]

Wealthy planters, though, were chief executives. Life on Texas plantations with fifty or more slaves followed intricate protocols and manners. The planter ventured into the fields only to inspect the work. A white overseer was responsible for watching to "see that a full day's work is done," as Churchill often said. Planters believed "a gentleman did not sweat." Most wealthy planters managed operations from an office in their homes and would hold daily meetings with the overseer. The overseer might be invited for dinner, but he lived in a dog-run cabin away from the "Big House."[11]

House slaves cooked the meals in outdoor kitchens and cleaned the big house, but they were never allowed to sit down while inside. Such rules maintained the social order and prevented confusion about a person's role. The planter's family members had no obligation to work, and their days were spent socializing, reading, or engaging in a hobby. Horse racing was the most popular sport in Texas in the 1850s, and rich men raised hounds and staged fox hunts. Texans of the 1850s fully embraced the belief that a southern gentleman should be generous, gracious, honest, and brave, though there is plenty of evidence that few wealthy Texans lived up to those standards. The myth of southern aristocracy was strong in Texas.[12] As a child, I fell for it 120 years later.

Churchill's distaste for white laborers exposed his higher respect for slaves, when they were well managed. In general, planters were more likely to accept Jews and Roman Catholics into their homes at a time when both groups were despised by poor whites. But planters didn't think twice about murdering or torturing a black man who would not grovel before them. They defended their "peculiar institution" by arguing that it had always existed, that it was economically necessary, and that blacks were racially inferior.[13]

One of the excuses often made for my ancestors is that they didn't know any better. But planters knew they could not defend slavery on moral grounds, and they almost never used the word *slave*, being embarrassed to do so. They referred to slaves as "negroes" or "hands." They used the word *nigger* in conversation, but they rarely put it in writing. Every slaveholder knew in the 1850s that Europeans and most Americans condemned slavery. They knew Britain kept battleships off the coast of Galveston and New Orleans to intercept slave traders. Southerners understood that most cultures they respected abhorred slavery, yet they practiced it anyway for personal gain.

When Churchill rode his horse along the western bank of the Brazos in 1854, he was painfully aware that slaves outnumbered whites by three to one on his plantation. But this was the life he wanted, to settle new territory and convert wilderness to civilization. His neighbor Benjamin G. Shields, who went by the title General even though he had never served in the military, was improving his land just two miles northwest of the Falls Plantation. Like Churchill, Shields was an itinerant planter. He was born in South Carolina in 1810, but he moved to Alabama to make his fortune in cotton farming. He served as a congressman, representing Alabama from 1840–1841, where he was a close ally to President John Tyler. He was also a close associate of President Andrew Jackson and Vice President John C. Calhoun, a leading defender of slavery. Shields and Churchill were both Whig party members.[14]

In 1844, Shields supported James K. Polk's campaign for the presidency, and Polk rewarded him with an appointment as the U.S. chargé d'affaires to Venezuela. The country profoundly changed Shields's worldview by allowing him to see firsthand what he called "the salutary effects of the abolition of slavery." He wrote that "slavery was not only wrong from a moral stand-point but a curse and blight on the section that maintained it." In Falls County, Shields was surrounded by slave-holders trying to re-create the lives they had enjoyed in Alabama, North Carolina, and Missouri. Despite his views on slavery, he became Churchill's close friend.[15]

In the mid-1850s, when Churchill's daughter Lucinda reached her late teens, her parents wanted to find her a suitable husband. None of the families in Falls County provided reasonable prospects, so they reached back to the families they knew in Alabama. They found Francis Marion Stallworth, the son of Nicholas Stallworth, whose death from typhoid Churchill had lamented in 1853. The Joneses had known Frank since birth. His family shared the same values and social status as the Joneses and the Tomlinsons. At twenty-one, Frank was a year older than Lucinda, and the two had grown up together. To give Frank a step up after losing his father, and confident in the match, Churchill and Susan arranged the marriage. Frank and Lucinda married at Falls Plantation on June 15, 1856. Lucinda gave birth to their first daughter, Martha, two years later.[16] Frank was also Jim and Sarah Tomlinson's nephew. With two sets of relatives writing to say how wonderful life was in Texas, the Tomlinsons began to reconsider their decision to stay in Alabama.

THE SLAVE'S VIEW

Accounts of slavery in the 1850s range from praise for a system that civilized African barbarians to tales of unmitigated cruelty. Based on county tax rolls, there were 48,145 slaves in Texas in 1850, and that number rose to 169,166 by 1861. Federal census data from 1860 places the number at 182,000, a small number compared to that in other slave states.[17] Historians believe that observations by Anglos are better understood as a reflection of their personal attitudes toward slavery, rather than as an accurate view of the world around them. Most slaves couldn't write, so few contemporaneous accounts exist of slave life in Texas. The best accounts, though still imperfect, come from oral histories collected between 1936 and 1938 by the Federal Writers' Project. The Work Progress Administration project set up by President Franklin

Roosevelt during the Great Depression sent writers to collect oral histories from both blacks and whites across the United States.[18] At the time, the writers were encouraged to transcribe the stories phonetically, but to make the narratives easier to read, I've used texts where the spelling and grammar have been corrected.

The white people transcribing some of these accounts clearly influenced them. Realistic accounts of slavery appeared to make some of the interviewers uncomfortable in the 1930s, when whites idealized antebellum Texas. One former slave from Washington County, Wesley Burrell, told a WPA supervisor, "A white lady was here the other night, wanted to know about slavery time and when I started to tell her she said she didn't want to hear that stuff. I told her the half hadn't been told. If she didn't want to hear that, it wasn't nothing to tell."[19]

Many of the accounts start with how a former slave reached Texas. While most wealthy Anglos traveled via stagecoach, steamboat, and railroad, the majority of their property, including slaves, went overland by ox-drawn wagons. They followed a trail blazed by average southerners making the same trip. Usually only personal slaves traveled with their owners by boat and rail. But for most, it was a long, tedious trip by foot or wagon. Eliza Holman described the trip with her middle-class owners:

> Massa and missus argued all the way to Texas. She was scared most of the time, and he always said, "The Lord is guiding us." She said, "It is fools guiding, and a fool move to start." That's the way they talked all the way. And when we got in a mud hole, it was an argument again. She said, "This is some more of your Lord's calls." He said, "Hush, hush woman. You're getting sacrilegious." So we had to walk two miles for a man with a yolk [sic] of oxen to pull us out of that mud hole, and when we were, our massa said, "Thank the Lord." And missus said, "Thank the men and the oxen."[20]

Ben Simpson's owner was fleeing legal trouble in Georgia and was cruel to the slaves:

He chained all his slaves around the neck and fastened the chains to the horses and made them walk all the way to Texas. My mother and my sister had to walk. Emma was my sister. Somewhere on the road it went to snowing, and massa wouldn't let us wrap anything around our feet. We had to sleep on the ground, too, in all that snow.

Massa had a great, long whip platted [sic] out of rawhide, and when one the niggers fell behind or gave out, he hit him with that whip. It took the hide every time he hit a nigger. Mother, she gave out on the way, about the line of Texas. Her feet got raw and bleeding, and her legs swelled plumb out of shape. Then massa, he just got out his gun and shot her, and whilst she lay dying he kicked her two, three times, and said, "Damn nigger that can't stand nothing." Boss, you know that man, he wouldn't bury my mother, just left her laying where he shot her at. You know, then there wasn't any law against killing nigger slaves.[21]

When slaves arrived on a new plantation, they lived under tarps, in tents, or in the back of covered wagons. While a successful slaveholder would live in a cabin only until he could build a better home, the cabin was as good as it would get for a slave. Amos Clark recalled building everything:

Marse and missus found where they wanted the house and we got the axes out and in a few days there a nice log house with two big rooms and a hall between them almost as big as the rooms. We had been on the road about six weeks and Missus was sure proud of her new house. Then we made logs into houses for us and a big kitchen close to the big house. Then we built an office for old marse and made chairs and beds and tables for everybody. Old Miss brought her bed and spindly, little table, and we made all the rest.[22]

The average slave cabin was twenty by twenty feet, with a dirt floor and a fireplace for cooking and heat.[23] The cabin would accommodate a single family, perhaps more depending on the slaveholder and the quality of the plantation. The structures were minimal because slave-holders spent as little money as possible on them. Nails, hinges, and other iron building materials had to be ordered from other states and were expensive. Glass windows did not come to Falls County until the early 1850s. The only piece of furniture the slaveholder would supply was a bed built into the wall. Otherwise, the slaves were left to their ingenuity to improve their quarters and to make their own furniture with the little free time available to them. Sylvia King said most of this work was done in the winter, when days were short and the long nights were spent spinning thread, singing, and smoking pipes.[24]

Henry Broadus, who worked on the Falls Plantation, started his oral history describing my great-great-great-aunt Susan Tomlinson Jones:

Up 'til I was 'bout ten years old, I wore a long shirt like a girl's dress. No pants at all. Used to watch the geese; they would catch me by the shirt. My first pair of shoes had brass on the toe. I thought I was rich with them on. When I got them muddy, I'd wipe them off real care-fully. White mammy made me behave; she used to cut me around the legs with a switch. I was shore a bad young'un. But just let any-body else try to whip me, and I yelled so loud white mammy come running and say "Don't touch that child."[25]

Broadus, who was a child during the Civil War, also recalled Churchill:

Ole Man Jones was good to the pickaninnies on his place. There was a lot of them. Ole man wear a long white beard, reach 'bout to his waist. He used to let us climb around him an' I kin recall 'bout a dozen of us, sitting on his knee and plaiting and twisting on his beard. He shore was a fine ole man.

Marse Jones didn't allow nobody to whip his niggers too hard. Mustn't leave no scars on his black folks, else he going sure roar. We'd all work and no sass, and us got along alright.[26]

For the most part, the slave experience in Texas wasn't appreciably different from slave life in other places, except in a few ways. In Falls County, they had to worry about black bears, wolves, coyotes, cougars, and the five species of venomous snakes, and instead of working in established fields, they cleared new ground, cutting through dense brush to create pasture, and clearing forests to reach rivers, creeks, and springs.[27]

On a big plantation the slave cabins were grouped together, creating a small community. The Falls Plantation was typical, with the slave quarters located in the river bottoms about a mile from Churchill's house. Slaves rarely approached a planter's house unless they worked there, and they would see him only when he inspected the fields or their quarters.[28]

The former slaves' oral histories confirm that most planters followed accepted plantation practices. The workday lasted "from see to can't see." The only day off was Sunday, though some planters gave a half day off on Saturday, or every other Saturday. This free time was used to clean a slave's quarters, and often included an inspection.[29] While slaveholders wanted to protect their slaves from disease, they didn't hesitate to use violence to intimidate them. Slaveholders often publicly ridiculed planters who did not regularly use violence, arguing they were undermining the entire institution of slavery.[30]

Slaves who worked in the fields performed hard labor, often in harsh weather. Summer days in Texas regularly reach one hundred degrees, and sudden thunderstorms can bring lightning and hail. Winter storms can turn a fine winter's day into an ice storm in a matter of hours. But perhaps nothing was more dangerous than the overseer. Wes Brady described working on a plantation in Harrison County:

> Some white folks might want to put me back in slavery if I told you how we were used in slavery time, but you asked me for the truth. The overseer straddled his big horse at three o'clock in the morning, rousted the hands off to the field. He got them all lined up, and them came back to the house for breakfast. The rows were a mile long, and no matter how much grass was in them, if you left one sprig on your

row, they beat you nearly to death. Lots of times they weighed cotton by candlelight.

All the hands took dinner to the field in buckets, and the overseer gave them 15 minutes to get dinner. He'd start cuffing some of them over the head when it was time to stop eating and go back to work. . . . He'd drive four stakes in the ground and tie a nigger down and beat him till he was raw. Then he'd take a brick and grind it up into powder and mix it with lard and put it all over him and roll him in a sheet. It'd be two days or more before that nigger could work again.[31]

House slaves, or personal slaves, developed close relationships with the slaveholders and their families. They worked and lived in much closer proximity to one another, and the house slaves were the most likely to be sexually exploited. In other cases, a mutual affection might develop. Silvia King worked as a cook and described her experience:

I cooked and worked in old missus' garden and the orchard. It was big and fine, and at fruit time all the women worked from light to dark serving and the like.

Old marse was going to feed you and see that your quarters were dry and warm or know the reason why. Almost every night he went around the quarters to see if there was any sickness or trouble. Everybody worked hard and had plenty to eat. Sometimes the preacher would tell us how to get to heaven and to see the ring lights there.[32]

THE TOMLINSONS DECIDE TO MOVE

Wealthy immigrants to Texas in the mid-1850s worked hard to convince their friends and families of the wisdom of moving to the frontier. In their letters, pioneers called Texas the "Promised Land." Churchill and Susan Tomlinson Jones wrote letters to Alabama, describing a Garden of Eden and encouraging family and friends to come see for themselves. Frank Stallworth also wrote to his aunts, Sarah Tomlinson and

Mary Travis. In late 1857, at Susan's urging, Jim Tomlinson decided to start a farm in Texas.[33]

Apparently, Jim didn't need to see Texas before he decided to move there. He took a mortgage from Churchill on January 4, 1857, for ten thousand dollars' worth of land, then traveled overland, taking with him provisions and slaves to begin work on his new plantation. He reached Falls County in early 1858 and found that his brother-in-law was prospering beyond his wildest dreams.[34]

Churchill had accumulated more than 31,000 acres of land, with 1,200 acres under the plow and 120 slaves to work it. He had 27 horses, 350 head of cattle, and he was producing more than three hundred bales of cotton a year. The global cotton market was strong, and the bales that floated down the Brazos on flatboats to Galveston were sold to European buyers for bullion.[35]

Churchill had far more land than he could use himself, and after eight years, the value of his holdings had grown 400 percent. He had already set up Lucinda and Frank Stallworth with a farm. He was ready to do the same for his brother-in-law.[36]

Jim took the highlands north of Churchill's plantation, overlooking the Brazos River to the east and Deer Creek to the north. The ridge was only sixty feet higher than the river bottom, but that was high enough to put his new homestead above the savage floods that came with the spring and fall rains. On March 3, Jim signed the ten-thousand-dollar promissory note to Churchill in return for 6,500 acres. A few weeks later, he took a $392 loan from Churchill to buy materials so the slaves could begin work on his new home.[37]

On April 24, 1858, a late-spring ice storm hit Falls County, covering everything with a half-inch-thick coat of ice.[38] The freeze killed most of the crops, and farmers scrambled to replant. But once the ice melted, Jim returned home to prepare his family for the six-hundred-mile move from Evergreen, Alabama, to Tomlinson Hill.

Unlike Churchill, Jim didn't have a son old enough to start improving the land and building cabins, so he left his sister's family in charge of his slaves. Churchill provided the labor to prepare the Hill for cotton planting the following January. Jim planned to return with his family and the rest of his slaves by then to avoid missing a growing season.[39]

After three months on the road, Jim returned to find his wife Sarah four months pregnant. The couple's third daughter, Sarah Elizabeth, arrived on August 15, 1858. Almost as soon as she was born, the family began packing their belongings. In November, when the yellow fever season ebbed, Jim loaded Sarah and their eight children—whose ages ranged from three months to fifteen years—onto wagons and stagecoaches. Sarah's sister Mary and four of her children were part of the entourage, as well as a half dozen personal slaves. The first leg of the journey was to Mobile, where they would catch a steamboat for New Orleans.

After a few days in New Orleans, the Tomlinson and Travis families boarded the steamship *Matagorda* for Galveston. They arrived on December 22, 1859, following what the *Galveston Weekly News* called "the Coldest Week on Record."[40]

The Galveston paper printed passenger manifests on the front page back then, alongside news of impending war between free and slave states. Dozens of slaveholding families were moving to Texas in the hopes of living in a place where slavery was unlikely to be abolished.

While Jim and his family were making their way to Texas, the state of Virginia hanged the militant abolitionist John Brown, who had led a raid in October on the federal armory in Harpers Ferry, Virginia, to steal weapons for a slave insurrection. Marines led by Lt. Col. Robert E. Lee captured Brown, and a state court convicted him of treason. In the North, many mourned the execution of the antislavery crusader, while those in the South celebrated his death.

Politicians who would later lead the Confederacy were already talking openly about secession and the possibility of war. U.S. senator-elect Louis Wigfall of Texas was a combative politician who believed passionately in slavery. He also held a deep-seated hatred for Texas hero Sam Houston, whom Wigfall criticized openly when Houston ran for governor. The week before Jim and his family arrived, Wigfall gave a speech, which was the main story in the *Galveston Weekly News* the day the Tomlinsons arrived:

The next presidential election decides the all important question of
Union. If a Black Republican [one who opposes slavery] be elected,
our army, navy, forts, treasury and swords are handed over to the
enemy. We must stand firm, and not be broken down by that stupid
song, "The Glorious Union."

Days later, the Tomlinson and Travis families boarded the Houston and Texas Central Railroad and rode 115 miles to its terminus in
Millican. There, they switched to a stagecoach for the long, bumpy
ride to Falls County.[41] The fields still had snow on them from a bliz-
zard that had struck on December 13. They traveled for miles without seeing any sign of human life. The frigidly cold weather and
snow were unusual for Texas, but the scene must have been frightening for the hopeful newcomers from Alabama.[42] When they finally reached the falls on the Brazos, they were carried across the
river by Churchill's flatboat, and three miles later, they were on Tomlinson Hill.

Jim and Sarah concentrated on creating a home for themselves and
their slaves. There were only ten families on the western side of the Brazos, and they were spaced miles apart. The vegetation along the Brazos
is mostly thicket, a tangle of vines and dense undergrowth, with cedar
elm, live oak, and post oak trees rising above it. But there was plenty of
deer and other wild game for meat.[43]

The 1860 census shows that Jim held forty-eight slaves, and Mary
Travis had seven. Among Jim's slaves were Milo and Phillis, as well as
their six-year-old son, Peter. Milo was born in Alabama, and Jim brought
him to Texas when he was thirty-four. Phillis, age thirty-five, listed her
birthplace as Georgia. Milo's father, George, who was born in Africa in
1798, was also a slave on Tomlinson Hill.[44]

Slave marriages, while not legally recognized, were common on large
plantations. Slaveholders encouraged women to have as many children
as possible and gave pregnant women lighter duties. Since slaveholders
often encouraged the enslaved to go to church—sometimes in a segregated part of a white church—blacks practiced some of the same Christian traditions as their owners.[45] Henry Broadus said he "went to

church with de white folks and heard mostly white preachers, though some black folks had the call to preach."[46]

The only story I have about the black Tomlinsons' lives before emancipation was told by Peter and passed down through the generations. Peter said that when he was a boy during the Civil War, Phillis sent him to the fields to gather a few ears of corn for dinner. It was dusk, so when he heard a crashing sound in the cornstalks, he couldn't see very clearly who was there. At first, he thought it was just someone else collecting corn for their dinner, so he walked down to see who it was. After a few paces, though, he saw it was a black bear, standing on its hind legs and turning to face him. Peter said it was the most frightening thing he had ever seen, and that he'd never run back to the cabin so quickly.[47]

There is no doubt that Falls County was still largely wilderness in the 1860s, but that also brought some advantages. Along the western ridge that overlooks the Brazos today, dozens of small springs bubble through the limestone aquifer and create short creeks leading to the river. They provided a natural irrigation system for the river bottom, where most of the cotton was grown. Jim and Sarah picked a spot about twenty-five yards from one of the fastest-running springs to build their compound. The water still seeps out of the gravel there before falling over a four-foot rocky ledge, creating a natural pool just large enough for two people to sit in. The water has flowed nonstop for as long as anyone can remember.[48]

Life on any cotton plantation followed the crop cycle, which varied depending on the climate. In Texas, work began in January, with slaves plowing the fields to prepare the soil for seed. Each cotton field, which could be as large as one hundred acres, was repeatedly plowed to remove all the plant life and to turn the soil so it could weather and make the minerals available to the plants.[49] After the final frost, logs or railroad rails were pulled behind horses or oxen to pulverize the crust created by the rains. The slaves then plowed the land again, this time dropping seeds by hand into the furrows.[50]

Early in the growing season, slaves would cut, or thin, the cotton, using heavy hoes with long wooden handles. They wanted only one cotton stalk to grow from each mound of dirt. This cycle of plowing, thinning, and plowing again was repeated three times during a growing season. In addition, weeding was constantly required.[51]

The last plowing and hoeing was usually done in late July, and after that the cotton was considered to be "laid by." The plants were left alone to grow during August, the hottest month, and on large plantations, the slaves enjoyed a respite from the fields. There was usually light work to be done, but the pace slowed, and many communities staged celebrations or parties on the sultry summer days. Slaveholders would allow slaves to stage their own celebrations and dances, and they were also allowed to fish and hunt for themselves.[52] On smaller plantations with more varied crops, however, August marked the beginning of the corn harvest.

Cotton picking usually began around September 1 in Falls County. One slave would walk on each side of a row, carefully pulling the white cotton from the boll. Early cotton gins did not do a good job of sorting out leaves from the cotton, so overseers put an emphasis on picking "clean cotton," without any detritus mixed in.[53]

The slaves put the cotton in huge bags they pulled between the rows. These bags became heavy as they filled up. The average slave picked at least two hundred pounds of cotton a day, though the best could tally up to six hundred pounds. The slaves loaded these bags onto wagons, which delivered the cotton to the gin for cleaning and baling before sale.[54] The process was usually complete by mid-November, whereupon the slaves began preparing for Christmas and the New Year.

CHAPTER

FOUR

In this free government all white men are and of right ought to be entitled to equal civil and political rights; that the servitude of the African race, as existing in these States, is mutually beneficial to both bond and free, and is abundantly authorized and justified by the experience of mankind, and the revealed will of the Almighty Creator.

—Texas Declaration of Secession

The U.S. Census was critical to American politics in the mid-nineteenth century. The accounting of the country's population determined a state's political representation in Congress, and therefore the electoral college vote for president. The Constitution spelled out that slaves counted as three-fifths of a white man when apportioning seats in the House of Representatives. For that reason, a planter who might hide his slaves when the taxman came by made certain they were counted when the census taker visited.

In Falls County, an assistant marshal took the census by going from home to home, tallying the number of dwellings, the number of families, and the names of all the family members. The marshal recorded each person's age and gender, his or her occupation if the individual was an adult, and where the person was born. They also recorded the family's estate and whether anyone was disabled.

Assistant Marshal J. C. Billingsley visited the west bank of the Brazos on July 23 and 24, 1860.[1] In cursive handwriting, he recorded the Tomlinsons as the forty-seventh family he had visited in that precinct. Jim Tomlinson was then forty-six years old and his wife, Sarah, forty-two.

He counted James Eldridge, seventeen, and William, fifteen, as farm laborers. The rest of the children were Amanda, thirteen; Augustus, twelve; John, ten; Eldridge, five; Sarah, one.

Mary Travis lived with the Tomlinsons. Her children included Mary, who was eighteen; Caroline, sixteen; John, fourteen; Nicholas, twelve. Of the fourteen whites on the plantation, Jim was the only adult male.

Jim listed real estate assets of $25,000 and personal property worth $27,585. This made him one of the wealthiest planters in Falls County, where the average white family might have a few thousand dollars. Mary Travis was more representative, with no real estate and just $2,800 in assets. On the other end of the spectrum, Churchill was the richest man in the county, listing $200,000 in real estate holdings and personal assets of $153,150.

To count blacks, the census included "Schedule 2,—Slave Inhabitants." In Texas, the names of the slaves were not recorded. The census taker put the name of the slaveholder on the first line, and then each slave was listed according to gender, age, and "Color." Blacks were given the letter B. People of mixed race were assigned the letter M, for mulatto.

Jim Tomlinson listed twenty-eight men and twenty women as his property, their ages ranging from one year old to seventy-five. Five had a white father and were listed as mulattoes. Mary Travis held four men and three women, according to the census. With fifty-five slaves, Tomlinson Hill was one of the largest slave plantations in Falls County, and this placed Jim in the top 2 percent of slaveholders in Texas.[2]

Roughly ten families lived in western Falls County at the time.[3] The Tomlinson house was about a mile sorth of Frank Stallworth's farm, where he held twenty-four slaves. The Jones compound was two miles to the south. Ben Shields was their neighbor to the west, about a mile away. Another friend of the Tomlinsons and Stallworths who lived north of Tomlinson Hill was Samuel Landrum, a friend who had arrived a year earlier from Alabama.[4]

Another resident of western Falls County was William G. Etheridge, who had moved to Texas from Arkansas, where he had supervised the construction of a railroad. He lived near Shields's house on Deer Creek, northwest of Tomlinson Hill. These families would come to depend on one another and become intertwined as war loomed and financial ruin came to Falls County.[5]

SLAVEHOLDERS OPPOSE SECESSION

The large planters in Texas wielded economic and social influence beyond their numbers, while the average farmer did not own slaves and survived on subsistence farming. These poor farmers aspired to the wealth and leisure that the planters enjoyed, but they resented how the planters relied on slaves. With blacks making up 47 percent of the population in Falls County, the poor Texan's greatest fear was a slave insurrection.[6]

Poor whites also worried about what could happen if blacks gained equal rights, including the right to vote. White political leaders played on fears of black equality and black retribution to win support for secession. The tactics worked well with the uneducated masses, but it did not hold water with many of the large slaveholders. The wealthiest planters were for the most part members of the Whig party and believed that constitutional arguments were the best way to fight northern abolitionists. Like anyone with a lot to lose, they favored law and order over radical solutions like secession. The more educated planters felt they were protected by the Supreme Court's Dred Scott decision in 1857, which declared no person of African ancestry could hold U.S. citizenship, and therefore could not vote. The Supreme Court also consistently upheld personal property rights. To many wealthy planters, secession was an illogical rush into an abyss.[7]

Abraham Lincoln's presidential candidacy also stoked southerners' fears. His "A House Divided" speech in 1858 made it clear that he felt the disagreement over slavery had to be resolved by abolition. The speech's title comes from Matthew 12:25, "Every kingdom divided against itself is brought to desolation; and every city or house divided against itself shall not stand."

Ironically, Texas revolutionary hero Senator Sam Houston had used the same quote eight years earlier during his speech to Congress supporting the Compromise of 1850, which allowed for the expansion of slavery into the Southwest. Houston was famous for leading the Texas rebel army during the Anglo insurrection against Mexico in 1836. He also served as the first and third president of the Republic of Texas. He had been one of the main architects of Texas's becoming part of the Union and became one of the first two senators from Texas in 1846. Houston left the Senate in 1859 to run for governor as a Unionist. He won by leveraging his connections with powerful plantation owners.[8]

Once in the governor's mansion in Austin, Houston campaigned to maintain the Union, rejecting the premise that an independent South could form alliances with European powers. He knew that Britain, which had passed the Slave Trade Act of 1802, was not going to help the South as long as it allowed slavery. But for all of Houston's reasoning, the average southerner became convinced that John Brown's raid on Harpers Ferry was just the beginning of a northern movement to encourage a slave rebellion and the massacre of pro-slavers. Soon a paranoia swept across Texas and doomed Houston's campaign to keep the Lone Star State in the Union.[9]

SUSPICIOUS FIRES

On July 7, 1860, the Marshall *Texas Republican* newspaper reported that Independence Day celebrations were unusually quiet because of a drought and heat wave.[10] When a fire started at Wallace Peak's drugstore in Dallas on July 8 and ended up destroying most of the business district, the 678 Anglo residents were unnerved. Initially, they suspected the fire was caused by prairie matches, a new kind of phosphorous match that could spontaneously combust in hot weather. But fears of arson appeared confirmed when similar fires erupted the same day in Denton's town square and in Pilot Point. Suspicion turned into conspiracy theory when three more fires broke out in towns across north Texas, including Ladonia, Honey Grove, and Milford, within a week.[11]

One farmer, who'd watched his barn burn before the Dallas fire, interrogated his slaves. He eventually forced one to confess to setting the fire. Other slaveholders followed suit, and more slaves confessed to increasingly outlandish plots. Charles R. Pryor, the editor of the burned-out *Dallas Herald,* spread the panic by writing to other newspaper editors about a statewide plot by abolitionist preachers to foment a slave insurrection. "I write in haste, we sleep upon our arms and the country is most deeply agitated." The Austin, Bonham, and Houston newspapers published the dispatch and subsequent letters describing a plot led by two Methodist abolitionists who allegedly planned to install black men in power so they could exact revenge. Arson was only the beginning, Pryor wrote. "Poisoning was to be added, and the old females to be slaughtered along with the men, and the young and handsome women to be parceled out amongst these infamous scoundrels."[12]

Communities across Texas formed vigilance committees: secret groups formed to bypass normal law enforcement and courts. For the most part, theses groups acted unchecked.[13] A Dallas vigilance committee executed three slaves on July 24 for the fires there. Committees in six more counties executed an unknown number of blacks for their part in what nationally became known as the "Texas Troubles." Though the troubles never reached Marlin and Tomlinson Hill, Falls County residents formed vigilance committees and armed patrols.[14]

Not everyone bought into the conspiracy theories, nor did everyone believe the slaves' confessions. Sam Houston and A. B. Norton, editor of Austin's *Southern Intelligencer,* accused Pryor and his allies of fabricating the plot to win votes for pro-slavery presidential candidate John C. Breckinridge in the August 6, 1860, election. Breckinridge went on to win in Texas.[15]

Historians today agree with the cooler heads in 1860. Prairie matches combusting inside hot and dry wooden buildings during a heat wave almost certainly started the fires.[16] The panic and the lynchings accomplished nothing in terms of justice, but they did prepare Texans for secession.

On September 22, 1860, Sam Houston gave one of the most important and eloquent speeches of his life at a Unionist rally in Austin. He
was sixty-seven years old and ill, and he knew most Texans would condemn him, but he spoke as long as he could.

> The Union is worth more than Mr. Lincoln, and if the battle is to be
> fought for the Constitution, let us fight it in the Union and for the
> sake of the Union. . . .

> Who are the men . . . taking the lead in throwing the country into con-
> fusion? Are they the strong slaveholders of the country? No; examine
> the matter and it will be found that by far the large majority of them
> never owned a negro, and will never own one. I know some of them
> who are making the most fuss, who would not make good negroes if
> they were blacked. And these are the men who are carrying on practi-
> cal abolitionism, by taking up the planters' negroes and hanging
> them. . . . Texas cannot afford to be ruined by such men.[17]

On November 8, 1860, Abraham Lincoln won the electoral college
in a four-way race and became the president. He lost the popular vote
by almost one million ballots and received fewer than 100,000 votes
outside the states he did win. Not a single vote was recorded for him in
Texas. Despite Lincoln's pledge not to outlaw slavery, and his party's
failure to win control of either the Senate or the House, his election
was the last straw for those who supported slavery. South Carolina
moved first, placing a secession bill on the legislature's agenda less
than week after Lincoln's victory. That state was the first to secede on
December 20, 1860.

Houston stalled as long as he could. Initially, he refused to call a
state convention to debate secession. Under enormous pressure, though,
he called the legislature into special session and it authorized an election to select delegates to a state convention. Convention delegates
voted for secession 166–8. Unionists had only one chance at overturn-
ing the decision, and that was a public referendum. Houston and other
Unionists traveled the state, trying to win enough votes to stop seces-

sion before the law took effect on March 2, the anniversary of Texas's independence from Mexico.[18]

Churchill was one of the planters convinced that "he was better protected in his slave property than he could possibly be under any new form of government, as the sentiment of the civilized world was emphatically opposed to this peculiar institution."[19] Shields spoke up at a secession meeting near Tomlinson Hill, where "people were wild with excitement." "Many now living can recall his fervid reasoning and impassioned appeals to friends and neighbors, that they should stick to the grand old Union of Washington and Jackson. The effect of his effort was to partially break up and cut short the meeting."[20]

When Houston came to town, he led a Unionist rally at the courthouse. Shields, Churchill, Jim Tomlinson, and William Etheridge attended. When Houston stepped from the stagecoach, he was clearly in pain and angry. A crowd in Waco had thrown stones when he spoke, and he had blood on his clothing.[21]

Houston's campaign, though, did little good. The adult white men of Falls County voted 215 in favor of secession, with 82 against.[22] The opposition to secession in Falls County was higher than average, surely influenced by the most prominent planters in the county. But an overwhelming number of Texas voters chose secession.

As a child growing up in Texas, I was taught that secession was not about slavery, but about states' rights. Like many of the Civil War fairy tales told to children in the South, that simply isn't true. White Texans were deeply racist and devout believers in white supremacy. They had heard all of the arguments against enslaving other human beings and rejected them. There is perhaps no clearer statement of their beliefs than the declaration of Texas secession. Texans argued they had joined the Union only sixteen years earlier while "holding, maintaining and protecting the institution known as negro slavery—the servitude of the African to the white race within her limits":

> We hold as undeniable truths that the governments of the various States, and the confederacy itself, were established exclusively by the white race, for themselves and their posterity; that the African race

had no agency in their establishment; that they were rightfully held and regarded as an inferior and dependent race, and in that condition only could their existence in this country be rendered beneficial or tolerable.

That in this free government all white men are and of right ought to be entitled to equal civil and political rights; that the servitude of the African race, as existing in these States, is mutually beneficial to both bond and free, and is abundantly authorized and justified by the experience of mankind, and the revealed will of the Almighty Creator, as recognized by all Christian nations; while the destruction of the existing relations between the two races, as advocated by our sectional enemies, would bring inevitable calamities upon both and desolation upon the fifteen slave-holding states.[23]

Texas became independent for the second time on March 2, and the state convention immediately sent a delegation to apply for membership in the Confederacy. They need not have bothered. The Confederacy had admitted Texas before the state applied. Texas became part of the Confederate States of America on March 5, 1861.

All state elected officials in Texas were required to take an oath to the Confederacy. Houston refused, saying it would violate his oath to the United States. The legislature declared the governor's office vacant. Lincoln sent word through a military officer that he would send Union troops to keep Houston in office. But Houston rejected the offer. He didn't want to spark the Civil War.[24]

Lt. Col. Robert E. Lee was commanding the Second Cavalry in San Antonio when Texas seceded, and he pondered his own future. Many of the federal troops in Texas were southerners, and most were heading home while Unionists boarded ships for northern ports. Despite listening to an impassioned plea from Unionist judge Edmund J. Davis in the Menger Hotel, Lee decided that his loyalty belonged with Virginia.

Many Texans felt their obligation was to follow their state, even if they opposed secession. William Etheridge was an exception. He was close to Shields, Jim, and Churchill, but he was a strong supporter of the Republican party, and the pro-slavery residents of Falls County knew he opposed them. The twenty-six-year-old was not about to compromise.[25] Etheridge and his wife, Ellen, rode north, where they remained until the war was over.

Once Texas had seceded, passions grew stronger. Zenas Bartlett may have been born and bred a Yankee, but he had married into the slaveholding Jones family. On March 18, 1861, he wrote his uncle Joe to express his fear and anger:

> I hope the consciences of you people will now be at ease as the sin of slavery is removed. I have no doubt you wonder much at the course the South has taken, but had you lived here as long as I have, you would have been one of the strongest for Secession. How can you forget that your leading men have repeatedly said that this country must either be all slave or all free—that John Brown and confederates invaded our soil with quantities of pikes and arms made in New England to distribute to negroes to murder white men, women and children—that you sympathized deeply that he failed and suffered the just penalty of his crime—that Massachusetts even made a Governor who said [Brown] was right and sympathized so deeply for him that he put on mourning at his death.

> Can we forget that here in Texas the past summer we had to watch over our houses and stores nights for many weeks to prevent the Hellish abolitionists from burning us out, and that some four or five of our most flourishing villages in this region were destroyed. Now is it strange that when we succeeded in catching any of them we should hang them to the first tree we come to? Is it unreasonable that we claim the right to take our property unto territory acquired by our blood and money as much as yours? Is it strange that we quit the Union when you pass laws imprisoning the owner who is in pursuit

of his fugitive slave when the Constitution expressly says he shall be given up?[26]

The first shot of the Civil War was fired at Fort Sumter, South Carolina, on April 12, 1861. Once the fighting began, the question of secession was moot. Everyone knew they had to choose a side. Etheridge chose to leave Texas. But the Tomlinsons, Joneses, and Stallworths stayed with their state and prepared for war.

The dream of a short and active campaign under which I
enlisted has vanished.

—James Jones

The shots at Fort Sumter on April 12, 1861, started a war, but in
Falls County they had little impact on the Tomlinsons' immediate
needs. Clearing the scrub forest that covered the Brazos river bottom
and planting a crop before the spring rains ended required everyone to
work long hours. While Jim still had an interest in his Alabama plantation, his older brother was running that one. The immediate need,
war or no war, was to get a crop in the ground. All of Jim's money was
tied up either in slaves or in the new plantation, and he needed to ensure income for the family at harvest time.

Jim's dependency on a successful cotton crop mirrored the Confederacy's larger economic strategy. Secessionist leaders promised that the
South's cotton exports would make the Confederate States of America
a prosperous independent nation, and that Britain's and France's dependency on the South's cotton would force them to recognize the new
nation. Cotton represented 60 percent of the nation's exports in 1860,
and the South grew 75 percent of the world's cotton supply. Now in full
rebellion, Confederates were putting their "King Cotton" theory to the
test, and growers such as Jim played a critical role.[1]

President Abraham Lincoln and his commanding general, Winfield Scott, understood the South's dependence on exports and responded with a blockade of southern ports.[2] In those early months, most Southerners held out hope that secession would pass peacefully or thought the fighting back east would last only a few weeks. In Texas, two state militia units easily surrounded the Union headquarters in San Antonio, and Maj. Gen. D. E. Twiggs surrendered 10 percent of the Union army. Those prisoners who wanted to remain joined the state militias, and the rest boarded ships and sailed for Union ports. Texas seized three million dollars' worth of federal military matériel.[3] Enthusiastic about secession, Texans volunteered in numbers far larger than the new Confederate army could absorb, equip, or pay.

Texans didn't worry about Union invasion from the east because they knew the Mississippi and Sabine rivers were formidable obstacles, but the state was vulnerable on two fronts.[4] The far superior U.S. Navy could attack the coast at will and slow the export of cotton, and on the western frontier, the Union cavalry's withdrawal meant Apache and Comanche warriors could raid white settlements with impunity. Governor Edward Clark ordered troops to strengthen the defenses around Galveston and sent state militias to man western forts.[5]

In Falls County, white men did little more than formalize the Committees of Safety they had formed to guard against rebellious slaves. Officers who had served in the Texas Revolution and the Mexican-American War took command of the small units. Their main mission was to protect the 1,654 slaves living in Falls County, whose market value was $496,200.[6]

The Tomlinson Hill slaves added value to Jim's real estate holdings by replacing his log cabin with a framed home. They also built new slave cabins about a quarter mile from Jim's house.[7]

In the summer of 1861, Sarah Tomlinson gave birth to her sixth son and last child. Caught in the patriotic fever, they named him Robert Edward Lee, after the hero of the Mexican-American War, who had recently taken command of the Confederate Army of Northern Virginia.[8] A few months later, Jim traveled back to Alabama and began supplying Confederate troops with corn and beef and renting the Evergreen Plantation's grazing pasture for Confederate army livestock.[9]

While almost every planter publicly supported the rebel cause, many still had reservations. Churchill shared his doubts one evening with two Unionist state judges, J. W. Bell and a man named Wheaton, who stopped at the Falls Plantation for dinner and spent the night. Churchill said he "was entirely opposed to the secession policy of the south."[10] Nevertheless, all of Churchill's property was in Texas and Alabama, and he was not about to walk away from it, or the fortune he had invested in slaves. Churchill also began selling supplies to Texas army units, and he even delivered a wagon train of food and clothing to troops serving in Arkansas.[11]

In the late summer of 1861, the newly elected governor, Francis Lubbock, rode to Richmond, Virginia, to visit his friend Jefferson Davis, who had become the Confederacy's president. Lubbock arrived just after the First Battle of Bull Run. The rebels had routed the Northern troops, sending them in full retreat to Washington, D.C., with 2,896 casualties and losses. The Confederates' wounded, dead, and missing totaled 1,982 in a single day.[12] No American had ever witnessed death on such a scale, but commanders knew the Battle of Bull Run was just the beginning of something new: industrialized warfare.

Davis asked Lubbock to raise eight thousand Texans to join the Confederate army. Lubbock knew that wouldn't be enough, and he promised to raise more. While no one will ever know for sure, it's estimated that more than half of white Texan men between the ages of sixteen and sixty eventually served in the war.[13]

DEFENDING THE COAST

In December 1861, Sarah Tomlinson's sister Mary Travis died on Tomlinson Hill at the age of forty-five. Jim probated her will and requested permission to sell her meager belongings, except for the slaves. The list of her estate that Jim submitted to the probate court in February 1862 still exists in the Falls County Court House in Marlin.

Her most valuable possessions were "one negro boy named Frank, $1000 and one negro woman named Betsey, $600." Appraisers valued the balance of her personal property at $46.30.[14] According to the 1860 census, Mary's four youngest children, ages ranging from thirteen to nineteen, were living with the Tomlinsons. The eldest daughter, also named Mary, cared for her younger sister and two brothers until she married in 1867, and then she took them with her to her new home.

Susan Tomlinson Jones died from fever in 1862 at the age of fifty-one. The loss struck both Jim and Churchill hard. Susan had been the first Tomlinson to move to Texas, and she was the first buried in its soil.[15]

In the early years of the Civil War, some units took their names from their commanders and only later received a numerical designation. The smallest unit was a company, then came a battalion, and then a regiment. Most companies and battalions remained parts of their original regiments, which numbered no more than twelve hundred men. A regiment would join or leave a division or brigade as ordered by a commanding general.

In January 1862, Maj. J. W. Speight and Maj. J. E. Harrison recruited volunteers in Marlin and Waco to join what they named Speight's Battalion. The infantry unit was based in Galveston at the time, part of the coastal defense.[16]

Will Tomlinson, Jim's second eldest boy, at seventeen, was the first of the western Falls County men to volunteer. He rode his horse eighteen miles to Waco on January 15, where Harrison swore him in as one of the first enlistees and sent him home to await orders. James Jones, Churchill's eldest son, joined the same unit twelve days later. James Eldridge Tomlinson, Jim's eldest son, suffered from poor eyesight and couldn't serve in the infantry, so in February he enlisted in Company K of the First Texas Heavy Artillery, also at Galveston.[17]

Most Texans joined cavalry units, reflecting the state's tradition of horsemanship. Few volunteers wanted to man artillery around Galveston, a posting that meant spending humid summers on a string of barrier islands endemic with malaria and yellow fever. Galveston was the largest city in Texas, but illness was a constant threat.[18]

Some volunteers didn't get a choice of assignment after artillery-men spotted Union battleships off of Galveston's coast.[19] Volunteers showing up for infantry duty in April 1862 saw their units redesig-nated as Companies A, I, and K of the First Texas Artillery. Will, James Eldridge, and James Jones found themselves all headed for Galveston.[20]

The Union ships formed a blockade, but made no immediate move to come ashore. Thirty-two-year-old James wrote to Churchill about the boredom:

> There is too little excitement and too little to do. I have wished many times I was in more active service. I am aware, too, of the greater hardships attendant upon it, nevertheless in the end it would be more satisfactory if not in the actual performance of such service.
>
> I have thought seriously several times of changing into Cavalry, but am afraid to risk a chance of officers and companions. I am certainly weary of soldiering. Tis the worst problem of my life by far. The dream of a short and active campaign under which I enlisted has vanished, and I can only brood over the present home existence as being length-ened out and the uncertainty of the future. Yet I would have been almost miserable had I never taken part in the great struggle.[21]

Wealthy planters took personal slaves with them, and commanders required planters to supply slave labor for the war effort. Commanders knew they needed strong defenses to protect Galveston, and combat engineers recommended earthen defenses made from mounds of rock and earth, combined with trenches. James Jones guessed almost a quar-ter of the blacks in Falls County were needed:

> I understand Judge Calvert and Major Hannah are empowered to press one-fourth of the negro fellows of Falls County in place of some to be released here. If such is done, a good and attentive overseer ought to be sent with them as a great many of them die here, and mainly for want of good attention. It is true the season is healthier now than it was, but deaths are yet occurring. The negroes, after staying here

awhile, get very homesick, and if they have a chance to get on mainland, runaway [sic] and go home, at which their owners are always
pleased.[22]

Union troops in April 1862 captured New Orleans, the Confederacy's most important port, and they cut off coastal ship traffic between Texas and the rest of the South. The land crossing at Vicksburg
became the only reliable connection. In addition, New Orleans provided Union troops a foothold to fight northward along the Mississippi to Vicksburg.

The Confederacy wanted to press tens of thousands of slaves into
service to help maintain the system that kept them in chains, but
planters did not readily heed the call. They may have wanted to maintain slavery, but keeping their slaves alive was more important. As
early as April 1862, General W. R. Scurry issued a desperate appeal in
Houston's *Tri-Weekly Telegraph*:

> Galveston is comparatively defenseless. In a short time, with negroes
> to work on the fortifications, the Island can be made impregnable,
> and the state saved from the polluting tread of armed abolitionists.
>
> I therefore call upon the planters of the above counties to send at once
> one-fourth of their male negro population, of the ages between 16
> and 50 years, with spades and shovels, to report at Galveston, to Col.
> V[alery] Sulakowski, Chief Engineer.
>
> They must bring with them their bedding and cooking utensils.
>
> Clothing and shoes will be furnished them at cost prices. Comfort-
> able quarters [will be] provided for them. Medical attendance, medi-
> cines and rations furnished free, and thirty dollars per month will be
> paid [to their owners] for their services.
>
> Overseers with 25 negroes will be paid $60 per month. Transporta-
> tion to the Island and back home furnished free.[23]

Sulakowski, the Polish chief military engineer in Galveston, described in an April 1863 report why he needed more slave labor:

> The force of negroes on the island consists of 481 effective men. Of these, 40 are at the saw mills, 100 cutting and carrying sod (as all the works are of sand, consequently the sodding must be done all over the works), 40 carrying timber, which leaves 301 on the works, including obstructions. The whole force of negroes consists, as above, of 481 effective, 42 cooks, 78 sick: Total 601.

> In order to complete the defenses of Galveston it will require the labor of 1,000 negroes during three weeks, or eight weeks with the present force. The work of soldiers amounts to very little, as the officers seem to have no control whatever over their men. The number of soldiers at work is about 100 men, whose work amount to 10 negroes' work.[24]

I feel certain Tomlinson Hill slaves were forced to serve the Confederate cause, but it's difficult to know where they worked, or for whom. Jim Tomlinson might have sent the slave Milo, who, at age thirty-five, could have provided skilled labor. Milo's seven-year-old son, Peter, could have served as a personal servant. They might even have seen combat.

The artillerymen in Galveston got a taste of battle on May 15, 1862, when the federal schooner *Sam Houston* shelled their positions for two days, until the Union commander demanded the city's surrender. But the federal ships did not have enough troops to capture the island and sailed out of the bay when the rebels called their bluff.[25]

The Confederate Congress approved a law in April 1862 allowing for the conscription of any white male between the ages of eighteen and thirty-five. The law exempted slave overseers, government officials, and clergymen. The law allowed the conscription of state militiamen into the regular army to help states meet their enlistment quotas. Texas discharged Will from the artillery in July and sent him to Col. Tom Green's Fifth Texas Cavalry Regiment. Green had led cavalry during the Texas Revolution and the Mexican-American War, and his reputation for courage reached across the state. His men called him "Daddy" Green.

Will met up with the Fifth Cavalry's Company B in the summer of 1862, when Green sent his men home to rest and reequip following a tough campaign in New Mexico. Will joined a group of combat-proven men who had tasted victory, only to see it stolen away by poor logistical planning. Confederate commanders considered the Fifth Cavalry one of the top units west of the Mississippi.[26]

THE INVASION OF GALVESTON

In the fall of 1862, three Union ships attacked Fort Sabine, a post overlooking the mouth of the Sabine River on the Louisiana border. The retreating Texas artillery troops destroyed their fort, burned a railway bridge to slow the Union troops, and retreated along the coast to Galveston, sixty miles to the west, the next Union target.[27]

James Tomlinson's Company K held an artillery position called "the Strand" on the beach just outside of town. James fell ill and was sent home on furlough from July 15 until at least September. A soldier's family could provide better care than the army.[28]

Gen. Paul Octave Hébert, a flamboyant West Point graduate known for his extravagant uniforms and rat-tail mustache, served as the senior Confederate commander in Texas in 1861 and 1862 and brought with him a reputation for arrogance. In Galveston, he felt insufficiently manned or equipped to defend the Texas coastline, the second longest in the nation. Once he looked at the Union flotilla's location and inspected his troops hobbled by yellow fever, he ordered a retreat across the bay and left the island to the Union. He assigned the First Artillery to move all but one of their heavy cannons across the one-and-a-half-mile rail trestle to Virginia Point on the mainland.

Almost as quickly as the rebels evacuated the artillery, the Union gunboat *Harriet Lane* steamed into Galveston Bay. The men at Fort Point, the only battery still equipped with a cannon, fired a single warning shot. The Union warship *Owasco* returned fire and destroyed their fighting position. The commander of the Union flotilla, William B. Renshaw, demanded the immediate surrender of Galveston, but he acquiesced to a four-day truce for civilians to evacuate. On October 8, 150 marines landed and found several hundred civilian men and two thousand women and children too poor or sick to leave the island.[29]

Hébert concentrated several hundred Confederate infantrymen and artillerymen at Fort Hébert to keep Union troops from crossing to the mainland. Their only position on the island was a small post at the railroad bridgehead. With Texas forces blocking all goods from crossing the railroad trestle, Renshaw found himself struggling to feed his troops and the 2,100 civilians isolated on the island.[30]

The Union marines in Galveston stationed themselves at the end of Eighteenth Street, on Kuhn's Wharf. Renshaw ordered his flotilla of seven ships to anchor in the bay to provide cover for the troops. He also warned his troops to be ready to leave Galveston in a hurry because he had nowhere near enough marines ashore.[31]

Renshaw and Hébert reached an understanding, whereby Hébert's men would control the bridge, with a small number posted on the island. The Union gunboats sat anchored within range of the bridge, ready to destroy it should the rebels try to mount a counterattack. But that also placed the *Harriet Lane* within range of Confederate guns at Virginia Point. Since neither side wanted to take down the cedar bridge, which would be useful later, a truce was struck.[32]

The Confederate high command, though, was scandalized at losing Galveston with only one shot fired and relieved Hébert of command. They appointed Maj. Gen. John Bankhead Magruder, a combat veteran, whom Texas fighters called "Prince John," and he immediately began planning to retake the island.

Magruder ordered Green's Fifth Cavalry to move to Virginia Point and wanted the only battle-tested troops in Texas to lead an amphibious assault with artillery supporting them.[33] Texas troops converted two river steamers, the *Bayou City* and the *Neptune,* into gunboats by mounting cannons and howitzers. Magruder's plan called for volunteers from the First Texas Artillery to fire the heavy guns at the troops ashore while the cavalrymen boarded the Union ships.[34]

For James Tomlinson, who had poor eyesight, the artillery was a suitable place to serve. James couldn't make out the enemy looking down the barrel of a rifle, or spot them at a distance in a cavalry charge, but he could load and fire a cannon. A typical artillery team consisted of at least six men per gun in order to fire as quickly as possible. Only the team leader aiming the cannon needed to see at a distance.[35]

Troops stacked cotton bales three-high on the decks of the *Bayou City* and the *Neptune* to absorb enemy fire and protect the artillery teams and the three hundred sharpshooters from the Fifth Cavalry. They also mounted oversized gangplanks on the upper decks to board the Union gunboats. Magruder ordered two tenders, the *John F. Carr* and the *Lucy Gwinn,* to carry follow-on troops.[36]

The plan called for three thousand Confederate troops to overwhelm the much smaller Union force of 150 marines. The Union, though, had superior firepower, with six gunboats carrying twenty-nine naval artillery pieces.[37] The attack became even more risky when 264 infantrymen from the Forty-second Infantry Regiment, Massachusetts Volunteers, arrived from New Orleans on Christmas Day. The fresh troops took over a church and used the steeple as a lookout. The rebels needed to act fast before more Union reinforcements arrived. Unbeknownst to the Texans, another seven hundred Massachusetts Volunteers departed New Orleans on December 29 aboard the slow-moving *Cumbria* and *Honduras* for the three-day trip to Galveston. The Second Vermont Infantry Regiment was also en route with a shipment of one thousand rifles to arm Texas Unionists.[38]

Magruder decided on New Year's Eve to mount a two-pronged attack. Artillery, infantry, and cavalry would sneak across the railroad bridge under the cover of darkness, pushing a rail-mounted eight-inch gun in front of them, and other smaller artillery pieces behind. One of the artillery teams would pass through the town and set up on Fort Point on the northern end of the island and prepare to shell the Union ships. The two rebel riverboats would attack the six gunboats anchored in the harbor. The artillery at Fort Hébert would provide supporting fire.[39]

The rebels began marching at nightfall, crossed the two-mile bridge, and had moved four more miles into the town by midnight. A Union patrol reported hearing artillery wheels in the downtown market at 1:00 A.M., but no one investigated. Once the moon set after 3:00 A.M., the First Texas Artillery formed an arc two and a half miles long and opened fire on the Union gunboats and Kuhn's Wharf.[40] James Tomlinson was manning one of these positions, while James Jones was serving on the *John E. Carr*.[41] In the predawn hours, Magruder's troops fired the first round at the Union ships, which returned fire down Galveston's shadowy streets. A *New York Tribune* reporter described the battle: "At this time it was as dark as Erebus; a black illumined only by the flash of cannon, the blasting of shell, and the quick, intermittent spark of musketry. The sounds at once horrible and indescribable, welcoming this New Year's morning, need not be dwelt upon."[42]

Renshaw's flagship, the *Westfield*, steamed out of the bay, but in the darkness it ran aground. Renshaw signaled the *Harriet Lane* to fire on the town.[43] But just when the Union troops appeared to have gained the upper hand, the Confederate ships entered the harbor at the first peek of dawn. The surprise would have brought a quick victory if the *Bayou City*'s thirty-two-pounder cannon had not exploded when the soldier manning it tried to fire, killing the Company B artillery commander and two of his men.[44] The Union sailors maneuvered away when *Bayou City* tried to ram the *Harriet Lane*, and they spun their pivot gun around and blasted a hole in the side of the *Neptune*, sinking her in shallow water. The cavalrymen aboard the rebel's *Bayou City*, though, maintained withering rifle fire on the *Harriet Lane*, forcing her crew to seek shelter belowdecks. That gave the *Bayou City* a chance to ram her and for Col. Tom Green's men to climb aboard.

With Renshaw's flagship still aground on Pelican Split, he could not see what was happening or issue orders. Absent direction, each federal gunboat made its own decision to stop fighting and withdraw. The rebels watched them steam away, as did the men of the Forty-second Infantry, Massachusetts Volunteers, who were sitting on Kuhn's Wharf. Their commander surrendered when the gunboats passed out of sight. The Union navy lost more than 150 men, while the Confederacy lost 117.[45]

One of the controversies of the Battle of Galveston surrounds how the two senior officers on the *Harriet Lane* died. While one report said rebels mortally wounded the men before they boarded the ship, another account said the Confederate commander, Maj. Leon Smith, summarily shot Cmdr. Jonathan M. Wainwright when he refused to surrender, breaching nineteenth-century etiquette. Wainwright's second in command, Lt. Cmdr. Edward Lea, did live long enough to make it ashore, where his father, Maj. Alfred Lea, was serving as Magruder's engineering officer. The two men had not seen each other since they had chosen opposite sides, crystallizing for a moment the truly destructive nature of civil war. Major Lea was next to his dying son, whose final words were, "My father is here."[46]

SIX

If by chance we should have any children, I will instill in
their minds the love of peace and should they want a bugle,
drum or toy gun I will give them such a thrashing that they
will hate the sound of any of them.

—John W. Watkins

The Confederate victory at Galveston shocked the Union naval
command. Lt. Cmdr. Richard Law, who ordered the withdrawal
following Renshaw's death, was court-martialed. Union Rear Adm. David Farragut ordered another flotilla to retake Galveston at the first
opportunity, but when Commodore Henry H. Bell led five warships to
Galveston, he found that the rebels had removed the channel buoys,
making it impossible for his ships to navigate the silt-filled estuary. Bell
ordered his ships to lob one hundred shells at Galveston, but to little
effect.[1] He eventually reported to Farragut that without an army to support him, there was little chance of recapturing the city.[2]

James Tomlinson's Company K returned to the ocean side of the
island, and the colonel ordered James Jones's Company I back to Virginia Point on the mainland. The men stationed in Galveston with the
First Texas Heavy Artillery never saw significant action again.

The other white Tomlinson boy, Will, left Galveston with the Fifth
Cavalry on January 26, 1863, to prepare for deployment to Louisiana.
Company B was full of Falls County men, and among them was John
W. Watkins, a clerk from Bartlett's store in Marlin. Watkins was popular

with the Marlin men and they elected him sergeant major. Later, the battalion commander made him an adjutant on Col. Tom Green's staff.[3] Writing to his wife, Irene, Watkins realized that the war was not going to be short or easy:

> I wish this accursed war was over so that I could be a free man once more. You have seen the papers and have read all the news and can make your own comments, some think it is a good omen, but for myself I don't think this war will be over for several years, and I expect to see several hard fought battles before it is over. This brigade has been complimented very highly and will be placed in front of the battle. I have a feeling or presentment or whatever you may call it that I will see it safe through and again fold you in my arms to live again in quietness and peace.[4]

Along the way to Louisiana in March 1863, the regiment encountered what any military faces: poor discipline, nonsensical orders, and encounters with exotic locales and people. Watkins described court-martialing a young soldier for having sex with a mule and remarked on the beautiful plantations and women in Louisiana. The Fifth Cavalry soon settled in at Fort DeRussy—ninety miles from the Texas border—on the Red River, near Alexandria, Louisiana.[5]

At the time, Union generals were considering three choices to capture territory west of the Mississippi. The first was to move up the Mississippi River from New Orleans and capture the rebel fort at Port Hudson. Capturing the city, along with Vicksburg, would cut Texas, Louisiana, and Arkansas off from the rest of the Confederacy. But thousands of rebels defended Port Hudson and Vicksburg. The second option was launching amphibious landings in Texas, but the Union had attempted this before and had lost at Galveston and Sabine Pass. The final option was to fight up the Red River, which runs southeast from the Texas-Oklahoma border, across Louisiana, and empties into the Mississippi River at Simmesport.[6]

Gen. Ulysses S. Grant marched his army south from Tennessee with the goal of capturing Vicksburg, and the Union command decided to attack Port Hudson with troops moving up from New Orleans. From April through June 1863, the brigade that included the Fifth Cavalry moved up and down Bayou Teche, a waterway that is parallel to the Red River, skirmishing with Union troops to draw them away from Port Hudson.[7]

In late June, the Fifth Cavalry attacked a Union fort at Donaldsonville, a small town on the Mississippi between New Orleans and Port Hudson. Union troops killed the regiment's executive officer, Maj. Denman Shannon, when he made it over a fortress wall, only to find another one on the inside, this one impregnable. A federal soldier shot him through the head. A Union officer called on the next in command to surrender, and when he refused, the Union officer shot and killed that rebel, too. By the end of the battle, only three out of eighteen officers involved in the attack had escaped without wounds. Green's brigade lost three hundred men and failed to capture Donaldsonville.[8]

At about the same time across the country in Pennsylvania, Gen. Robert E. Lee lost Gettysburg; the next day, July 4, 1863, Confederate troops defending Vicksburg surrendered to Grant after a forty-five day siege.[9] The victory at Gettysburg weakened Lee's army, and Grant's capture of Vicksburg gave Union forces control of the Mississippi River, marking a turning point in the war.

The Union general in command of troops in Louisiana, Nathaniel Banks, was then free to turn his attention to capturing Texas. He sent a flotilla of ships to capture Sabine Pass in September 1863, but the Texans repulsed the attack.[10] A few months later, Banks landed Union troops at Brownsville, the Texas border town used to export cotton to European buyers in Mexico. He sent scouting teams from there northward to Corpus Christi and drove Confederate troops out of emplacements on Matagorda Island and occupied Indianola, a major port.[11]

Magruder sent out a public proclamation on November 27, 1863, warning coastal Texans to remove their valuables, including their slaves, or see them destroyed by Confederate troops:

> The Commanding General has certain information that the enemy
> has brought with him from five thousand to ten thousand muskets,

with which to arm the slaves against their masters. . . . Therefore, he calls upon the citizens of Texas living in the counties bordering upon the navigable portions of the streams, and within fifty miles of the coast, to remove their able-bodied male slaves at once, at any cost and at all hazards, further into the interior, else [the commanding general] will be forced to drive them before him with his cavalry, in haste and without regard to their well-being.[12]

With the war going badly, Jim Tomlinson left Tomlinson Hill and enlisted in Company C, Fourth Cavalry Regiment of the Texas State Militia in Galveston. At fifty-one, Jim was too old to ride with the self-defense units that patrolled the state, but as a planter who held a large number of slaves, he was well suited for another difficult task. Magruder assigned Jim the task of visiting large plantations and gathering slaves to serve the Confederacy. Magruder wanted to build defensive positions up and down the coast, and slaveholders were not cooperating. Jim's job was to appeal to their patriotism, and if that failed, to forcibly take a quarter of their male slaves for military service.[13]

THE RED RIVER CAMPAIGN

As Magruder prepared for a Union invasion, the Union high command was hatching a completely different plan.[14] The newly promoted General Grant ordered Banks to pull his forces off the Texas coast and march up Louisiana's Red River and invade Texas from the east.[15]

Despite thinking it was a bad idea, Banks followed orders and prepared a Red River Campaign to be fought in the Louisiana swamps.[16] Banks gathered 25,000 men and a flotilla of support ships in central Louisiana and convinced the federal commander in Little Rock, Arkansas, to send 15,000 Union troops south, where they would hopefully rendezvous at Shreveport, then the headquarters for the Confederacy west of the Mississippi. Intelligence officers reported that planters had stored 150,000 bales of cotton in Shreveport and nearby Marshall and Jefferson, creating the opportunity to capture a significant prize. Under Banks's plan, once the Union troops captured

Shreveport, the combined army would march west until Texas surrendered.[17]

Magruder discovered the plan in March 1864, when the massive
Union army captured Alexandria, Louisiana. Confederate forces in Louisiana, under the command of Gen. Richard Taylor, son of former President Zachary Taylor, suffered from limited supplies and rampant illness
and stood no chance before the well-equipped federal troops. Magruder
gave Tom Green five thousand men, including the Fifth Cavalry, and
ordered them to reinforce Taylor as quickly as possible. Green's division
reached the front near Natchitoches on March 29. That brought rebel
forces up to eleven thousand, but this was still less than half of what the
Union had in Alexandria, less than seventy-five miles from Shreveport.[18]

The Union force was too large for the rebels to stop in Natchitoches,
so they spent the next week falling back, slowing the Yankee advance
with small skirmishes. The delaying tactics gave three Confederate di-
visions time to create a line just south of Mansfield, the last major
town between the federal troops and Shreveport. The Confederate retreat had also forced the Union army to split into two, with one part
remaining behind to protect the flotilla on the Red River while the rest
marched inland toward Mansfield. When the Union troops reached
the outskirts of Mansfield on April 8, the rebels outnumbered the
Unionists 10,500 to 6,400. Watkins described the ensuing battle:

> We were drawn up in rear of a large farm, extending out two miles
> on each side of the road. We were dismounted and had just got into
> position, when the enemy came in sight.
>
> As soon as they saw us they sounded the charge, and here they
> came with a yell. We gave them a volley which pushed them to turn
> right about. Skirmishers were thrown out and soon the work of death
> commenced. They attempted to drive back our left wing which threw
> our regiment in one of the hottest places it had ever been in. We
> fought them until five o'clock without gaining any advantage. The
> boys got tired of being shot at and concluded to try the charge—
> everything being in readiness—over the fence we went and charged
> their battery.

They became panic stricken and broke. Our boys ran them about
four miles, capturing about 2,000 prisoners, 150 wagons, 50 ambu-
lances and 20 pieces of artillery. Our loss was very heavy. Gen. Mou-
ton was killed in the last charge. So was Capt. Shepard of Gen. Green's
staff. And many other officers.

The next morning, the rebels formed a line at Pleasant Hill and skir-
mished with the Union troops throughout the day. Then at 4:00 P.M.,
the rebels marched one thousand yards toward the Union forces, who
were dug into rifle pits. Initially, the Union troops repulsed the attack,
but when the rebels attacked a second time, the Union line broke and
the men fled in retreat as night fell. General Green's troops pursued
the Union forces the next morning and captured more than one thousand prisoners.[19]

In a report sent to the Union secretary of war after the battle, Banks
described an overwhelming Confederate army that attacked his forces
while his men were still on the march. He described chaos on the roads
as Union supply trains blocked the retreating soldiers. His forces were
finally able to turn and fight at Pleasant Hill after a New York infantry
unit slowed the rebel advance.[20] Union forces lost more than one thousand men at the Battle of Pleasant Hill, while twelve hundred rebels
were killed or wounded.

Nevertheless Taylor, the Confederate commander, was determined
to cut off the Union retreat. On April 12, he ordered Green's cavalry
and a small battery of artillery to engage Union forces at Blair's Land-
ing, where low water in the river had slowed the Union gunboats. A
two-hour artillery duel commenced. Marlin's Company B arrived too
late, Watkins explained: "We went through the swamp and when in a
few miles of our destination, we came upon an impassable bayou,
which prevented us from getting into the fight. Gen. Green made the
fight and was killed. Thus fell one of our best generals. He was in front
of his men standing on the bank of the river, not over 100 yards from
the enemy."[21]

Taylor called Green's death a "public calamity," and it knocked the rebels back on their heels, but they continued pursuing the Union forces down the Red River. When low water grounded Union ships, the rebels destroyed them, and in one case, they forced the Union to destroy its own ironclad. On April 27, 1864, Watkins exaggerated the Fifth Cavalry's victories, but he became emotional when describing the terror wrought by an army in retreat:

> I am getting tired of it and would be glad to have an honorable peace. And should we ever again enjoy peace, and if by chance we should have any children I will instill in their minds the love of peace and should they want a bugle, drum or toy gun I will give them such a thrashing that they will hate the sound of any of them. But I know that all this will be forgotten and if we were to be again imposed upon, we would be as ready to dig up the hatchet and again go into war. But what misery it entails upon a country.

> [Union troops] laid waste the country from Natchitoches to Alexandria. In some places there is not a house standing for 10 miles. In one instance they set a house on fire while the lady and her children were in it. This lady ran out of her house and came screaming into our lines amid thousands of bullets, with a little child in her arms and two that could just run about following her.

> I could mention many instances where they have set houses on fire while women and children were in them without giving them a chance of getting anything out.[22]

Banks headed for Simmesport, where he intended to cross the Atchafalaya River and make good his escape from the Red River basin. Taylor, though outnumbered, wanted to cause as much damage as possible to the retreating Yankees and ordered the Fifth Cavalry to harass the Union's rear guard.[23]

A bottleneck at the bridge over the Atchafalaya slowed the Union retreat, giving the Texas cavalry a chance on May 18 to drive in the

Union pickets near Norwood's Plantation on Yellow Bayou. The Union troops alerted Gen. Joseph Mower, who spun his rear guard around to attack. It was extremely hot and sunny when the battle began at about 3:00 P.M. Company B was ordered to flank Mower's forces on the left, but he had two brigades in reserve to repulse it. Mower ordered his artillery to open fire on the attacking rebels and then had his infantry charge them.[24] Watkins described Company B at the center of the fiercest fighting:

> Most of the cavalry were dismounted and formed in line of battle. They had to move through a field 1,000 yards wide with nothing to protect our men. The enemy were on the opposite side of the timber. Our men moved up sending a very heavy fire and when in 200 yards charged two batteries which had been playing on our men. They got up to 30 yards of the batteries and drove the gunners away when the whole Yankee army raised up out of the weeds and brush and opened such a heavy fire upon our men that they were compelled to fall back, which they did in quick time.
>
> But alas, we lost some brave men—William Tomlinson was killed in the retreat. Horace Young was wounded in the left arm between the elbow and wrist, one bone broken. John Norwood flesh wound in the leg. Jerry Pinson lost his right leg, taken off at the knee. William McCarroll knocked down with a shell but is up and about. This is all the men you know.
>
> William Tomlinson lived to be taken off the field. He said that he did not want his friends to think he was a coward because he was shot in the back. He was a brave and noble boy loved by all who knew him. I know his death will nearly kill his parents but such is the fate of some of our soldiers—and it seems that the best men always go first.[25]

Will's comrades buried him at Yellow Bayou. The Fifth Texas Cavalry never fought another significant battle.

James Tomlinson fared better than his brother Will. His myopia worsened while he was in Galveston, and five days before Will died, on

May 13, 1864, a Confederate surgeon declared James unfit for duty and sent him home to Tomlinson Hill.[26] The first news he received upon his return was that of his brother's death. With his father, Jim, away conscripting slave labor, James managed the plantation and supervised the construction of a separate home so he could start a family.

That left only one Tomlinson still serving the Confederate cause.[27] Jim was based in Galveston in the summer of 1864, which was experiencing one of the worst yellow fever epidemics in the city's history. Magruder ordered the city quarantined and slaveholders stopped sending their most precious property into harm's way, especially after Union forces burned Atlanta and Lincoln was reelected.[28]

Jim returned home in the spring of 1865 suffering from fever.[29] We'll never know exactly what disease Jim carried back to Marlin, but it was most probably malaria or tuberculosis, both of which can drag on for months. He was at home on April 9, 1865, when Lee surrendered at Appomattox. After that, Confederate troops began walking away from their units.

Almost the entirety of the Confederate force in Texas had deserted by June 2, 1865, when Magruder and his commander, Gen. Kirby Smith, boarded the Union steamer *Fort Jackson* in Galveston harbor. Texas was the last state to surrender to Union forces, and Magruder's and Smith's signatures officially ended the Civil War. An estimated 24,000 Texans had died, about two-thirds of them from disease.[30]

Maj. Gen. Gordon Granger and eighteen hundred occupying troops did not arrive in Texas until two weeks later. On June 19, 1865, Granger issued orders declaring Texas within Union jurisdiction and negating everything the state legislature had done since secession. Because Texas was the last Confederate state occupied by Union forces, Texas slaves were the last to gain their freedom, which was granted by General Order Number 3:

> The people are informed that, in accordance with a proclamation from the Executive of the United States, all slaves are free. This involves an absolute equality of personal rights and rights of property, between former masters and slaves, and the connection heretofore

existing between them, becomes that between employer and hired labor. The Freedmen are advised to remain at their present homes, and work for wages. They are informed that they will not be allowed to collect at military posts; and that they will not be supported in idleness either there or elsewhere.

The *Galveston Daily News* published the order on June 21, and distributed it across the state. The order formalized that Union troops were in charge and slavery abolished. But Lincoln's Emancipation Proclamation covered only the parts of the Confederacy that were still in rebellion in January 1863. Technically, slavery was still legal in border states that had never joined the Confederacy. This fact, combined with Lincoln's assassination and the ascendancy of President Andrew Johnson, a devout white supremacist, led a few southerners to suspect slavery might be restored. That Union officers ordered former slaves to remain with their masters bolstered the theory. Some slave plantations in the East Texas interior simply ignored the proclamation until Union troops arrived and forced the slaves' release at gunpoint.

Former slaves told remarkably similar stories about their masters gathering them together and formally releasing them. On Tomlinson Hill, Jim called his slaves together under a giant live oak tree about halfway between the slave quarters and his house. Jim was very ill, so slaves likely carried him to the meeting point. Jim explained the Emancipation Proclamation and assured them that anyone who wanted to remain and work for pay was welcome.[31] Many slaveholders said, "You are now as free as me." Ned Broadus described those early days of freedom:

And then they say de niggers is free. They gave part of the third crop to us. My white folks give me a cow and some pigs when us was freed. We most of us, stayed on the Jones plantation and helped farm it on shares with the owner. Marse Churchill depended on me to see that the rent was paid and he told me to look after the farm. I been called "Jones" 'till freedom, then I took my daddy's name "Broadus."[32]

Just as Ned and his father had used the surnames of their former masters, it appears at least two of the former slave families on Tomlinson Hill took the Tomlinson name as their own. One of the families consisted of Milo and Phillis, along with their children, Peter and Martha, as well as Milo's father, George. Phillis worked inside the Tomlinson home, and George was the white Tomlinsons' closest neighbor.

Jim's slaves had been the collateral on his debts, and he was now bankrupt. Theoretically, Jim and his family were in no better financial position than the former slaves. But the family retained ownership of their land and had some key advantages. The most important was the color of their skin.

SEVEN

The blacks are the most docile, industrious, orderly, free from serious crime, and with all the substratum that goes to make the good citizen.

—Brig. Gen. Edgar Gregory

Just a few weeks after telling the African-Americans on Tomlinson Hill that they were free, Jim Tomlinson died, leaving Sarah responsible for the estate and dependent on her brother-in-law and neighbor, Churchill Jones.[1] She also owed Jones for most of the loans Jim had taken out to establish Tomlinson Hill. Sarah's son Will was buried at Yellow Bayou and twenty-two-year-old James suffered from poor eyesight. Her next two boys, Augustus, seventeen, and John, fifteen, worked the farm, and the youngest son, R. E. L., was only four and had no memory of his father. Amanda had just turned eighteen and Little Sarah was only six. Sarah had a house full of children, very little money, and a workforce of fifty-five newly freed blacks.

The Falls County Probate Court appointed Sarah the administrator of Jim's estate and ordered an independent appraisal of his assets.[2] Jim's friends in Marlin completed the appraisal, and the court ordered Sarah to post a twenty-thousand-dollar bond to cover the estate's debts until she could pay them back. The court provided her a $2,600 yearly allowance to support the family. The court said it would oversee all of her financial transactions to ensure that she repaid Jim's debts as quickly as possible. Sarah had fallen from high-society wife to bankrupt widow struggling to feed her family.

In Washington, President Andrew Johnson granted amnesty to everyone in the South except for those with assets greater than twenty thousand dollars, or anyone who was a Confederate political appointee or military officer above the rank of colonel. Wealthy planters like Churchill needed to take a loyalty oath and apply directly to Johnson to regain their citizenship. Until that time, they could neither vote nor play any role in politics.[3]

In Falls County, though, elections were the furthest thing from anyone's mind in the summer of 1865. Veterans straggled home, malnourished and in poor health, and many turned to crime. Black Texans did not know yet what freedom meant for them, and whites feared gangs of outlaws and Union troops in equal measure. The folks who stayed at home hadn't fared much better, since they'd sent as much food and supplies as possible to the troops. They'd literally emptied their cupboards.[4]

Texas, though, had suffered none of the destruction wrought in other states east of the Mississippi.[5] Texas farms and ranches had continued to produce cotton and cattle throughout the war, and they had product to sell as soon as the Union blockade ended. Cotton farmers in the summer of 1865 saw a healthy crop that could generate a good profit if they could harvest it. The big question was how to make money using emancipated labor. Freedmen didn't work for free, and a quarter of the white men who had gone to war never came home.[6]

Falls County plantation owners had also lost the $800,000 they had paid for their former slaves.[7] While this seems like a crude way to consider the liberation of more than sixteen hundred human beings, the wealthiest whites in Falls County saw their fortunes walk away. That most residents never heard Union artillery fire or witnessed the horrors of war made them even more resentful.[8]

Emancipation also did not change white supremacy and black inferiority as the foundational principle of southern politics. Andrew Johnson, the Tennessean who succeeded Lincoln, believed emancipation did not mean equality, and he was ready to allow southern states to treat free blacks just about any way they wished. Texas Democrats, like most former Confederates, made their primary goal the creation of a legal system to coerce labor from former slaves.[9]

African-Americans, on the other hand, expected the Union to keep the promise of equal treatment under the law. They knew their former masters better than anyone and understood the risks.[10]

Union provisional governor A. J. Hamilton arrived in Texas on July 25 and immediately organized voter registration for a state constitutional convention. Washington expected delegates to nullify the secession ordinance, verify the emancipation of the slaves, and repudiate state debts incurred by the rebellion.[11]

Washington also named Brig. Gen. Edgar Gregory as the assistant commissioner for the state of Texas, Bureau of Refugees, Freedmen, and Abandoned Lands. His primary job was to ensure that slaveholders treated the freedmen lawfully and to establish freedmen schools. Gregory arrived in Galveston on September 5, 1865, amid the buildup of fifty thousand federal soldiers in Texas, most of whom patrolled the Mexican border. Commanders in Texas also expected the bureau to make sure former slaves understood they needed to work for whites to make a living.[12]

Gregory immediately toured southeast Texas to see how whites treated black Americans. Plantations closer to Houston and Galveston were more likely than those farther from the coast to have the legally required written labor contracts. He also found that whites did not believe African-Americans could take care of themselves or would work without the plantation tradition of violence.[13]

When Gregory ventured farther into the Texas interior in late November, where no federal troops had gone since the end of the war, slaveholders had not told African-Americans that slavery had ended. Some whites said they had interpreted Granger's emancipation order to be slavery under a different name. Whites also warned Gregory about rumors of a black uprising on Christmas Day, an old southern myth that seemed to spread every year. Blacks, meanwhile, believed different rumors, including one that said the federal government would give them forty acres and a mule for Christmas. Black farm workers complained that most white farmers refused to pay the wages they owed and re-fused to negotiate new labor contracts.[14]

Adding to the chaos was the churn of refugees on Texas roads. Some slaveholders had moved west to Texas just ahead of federal troops to keep their property safe. After emancipation, many former slaves went in search of family and loved ones left behind. Whites perceived this search for loved ones as aimless wandering and proof that blacks could not handle freedom.[15]

Gregory, as leader of the Texas Freedmen's Bureau, needed to bal-ance African-American civil rights with the needs of the Texas econ-omy. Gregory knew Texans earned almost all of their hard currency by selling cotton to Europe and beef to the eastern states. He also knew former slaves held no property and had no education and therefore had little opportunity to earn money in the short term except by working on plantations. That meant wealthy white men still held the real power in Texas, despite three regiments of black federal infantry in the state. The sight of armed African-American men in blue uniforms might have struck fear into some white Texans, but planters and Gregory knew who controlled the money.[16]

A NEW RELATIONSHIP

Gregory insisted that planters follow federal rules that required work-ers to enter labor contracts voluntarily and forbade landowners from employing violence to manage their workers. Landowners had to pro-vide housing, comfortable clothing, wholesome rations, fuel, medical assistance, schools for black children, and a negotiated salary schedule. Landowners owed half of the wages at the end of each month, with the balance paid upon sale of the cotton or cattle. Laborers agreed to work ten-hour days, five and a half days a week. Landowners could dock a worker's salary and wages for sick days or missed work. They could also reduce a worker's pay if the individual left the farm without permission. Once both parties signed the contract, it remained in force for the rest of the year, with a representative of the Freedmen's Bureau assigned to settle any disputes.[17]

Many whites, though, overcharged the freedmen for farming supplies, deducted pay for every conceivable breach, and exaggerated input costs to reduce the money paid to workers. If the worker complained, the planter took the worker to court, where the local white judge charged the African-American exorbitant legal fees, while the white jury ignored his or her testimony.[18]

Gregory appointed subassistant commissioners to open field offices in counties with the highest black populations and charged his agents with ensuring the fairness of labor contracts. The subagents would also supervise how local governments treated former slaves, while still allowing for the enforcement of vagrancy laws to punish healthy people who refused to work.[19]

Gregory knew he needed to deploy his assistants across the state as quickly as possible if he was going to fulfill any part of his mission. Initially, he asked for fifteen military officers to open the first field offices, but he had difficulty finding white men ready to spend their days fighting for former slaves. Gregory favored officers who had commanded black soldiers, because they tended to show more sympathy to former slaves. From those ranks, Gregory found about half the agents he needed to fill the first twenty-one field offices. For the other half, Gregory relied on scalawags.[20] Scalawags were native Texans who had remained loyal to the Union throughout the Civil War, such as William Etheridge and Ben Shields in western Falls County. Some scalawags fled the state during the war; others remained behind and kept to themselves. With the Union occupation, scalawags sought to right the injustices they witnessed and, in some cases, take revenge on the Confederates who had discriminated against them during the war. Many of these men were ready to serve as subassistant commissioners in their home counties, where they'd have a company of federal soldiers at their side.[21]

Gregory chose Asa P. Delano to serve as the agent in Marlin. Delano had already won an appointment as postmaster and planned to also work as an agent for Ranger & Co., an agricultural firm that ran several plantations and dealt in cotton, wool, and hides. Delano arrived in Marlin in January 1866, took over the Ranger & Co. storefront, and set up a post office and the bureau office in the back.[22]

Delano's monthly reports suggest that he thought the freedmen's morality needed more attention than the whites' respect for civil rights. Delano gave planters free rein to beat African-Americans and hang them from their thumbs as punishment. Falls County planters praised Delano in a letter to Gregory on April 3, 1866, which they also published in *Flake's Daily Galveston Bulletin*:

> SIR—The undersigned citizens and planters of the County of Falls, and State of Texas, take pleasure to inform you that our farms are now in as good a condition, and our crops are as far advanced, as we ever had them in any previous year. The freedmen are making much better laborers than even the most liberal of us anticipated. If they continue in their industry, with propitious seasons, a large, very large crop may be expected from this county. We desire the freedmen shall become good and substantial laborers. We honestly believe that Capt. A. P. Delano wishes to deal fairly and justly with all, irrespective of color or condition.
>
> [The list of forty-seven signees included the name Churchill Jones.]

Gregory's staff, though, found Delano troublesome. They reprimanded him for billing the bureau for guides he continued to use to travel around the county, even after an adjutant had told him to stop. Delano complained that he spent a great deal of his time correcting the freedmen's "many evils" and jailing or whipping those who did not work. He insisted that freedmen marry and form nuclear families, something that many slaveholders had discouraged. He found that when he insisted that black men work to support their families, those men chose to abandon them. His choice of words revealed how he viewed blacks when he wrote, "[I]t is impossible to keep them together, as they have been accustomed thru life to a change of pastures, it's now pretty hard to confine an old Buck."[23]

In other field offices, freedmen swamped agents with wage complaints. Those bureaus seized property from planters who refused to pay what they owed their workers. Delano, on the other hand, reported dealing with only one such complaint.[24] All of the written record comes from whites, but the freedmen were probably disappointed with Delano's protection.

TAKING POWER BACK

As soon as the war was over, Churchill Jones began petitioning to regain his citizenship in this letter dated September 21, 1865:

> It is true I had to give material aid during the war in the shape of money and other means, that I was obliged to do so to save my life, and barely escaped with it anyway. In my most earnest feelings I have never separated from the great and glorious old federal Union and government over which you preside. For safety, at times, I was compelled to dissemble. The Rebellion was a long, dreary and gloomy time with me, but thank God by his inestimable wisdom and justice, the light of truth and liberty appeared again in its season, placing upon that party the seal of his condemnation.
>
> For them to have triumphed in their scheme of an independent southern government and their idea of self-government, it would no doubt in my mind to have been the greatest calamity that could have ever befallen this people. It is true, I did not obey the order of Mr. Lincoln for all loyal persons to leave the south, my age and encumbrance here will explain that.[25]

Churchill then asked for supporting letters, including one from Judge J. H. Bell, one of the visitors to the Falls Plantation shortly after secession. Bell fulfilled Churchill's request and Governor Hamilton received the application, but he did not write his endorsement and forward the application to Washington until March 29, 1866.

Texans also took steps in 1866 to formally rejoin the Union by electing delegates to a constitutional convention. Conservative Democrats, who opposed Reconstruction, ran on their history as slaveholders and Confederate soldiers and won two-thirds of the ninety seats at the convention. A. J. Hamilton, Johnson's appointed provisional governor, reported to the White House that despite the many "violent and impractical men" elected, he felt there was still a chance the convention would pass an acceptable state constitution and take the steps necessary to rejoin the Union.

White landowners, though, didn't like the change the Union was forcing on them and they became particularly frustrated with Gregory and his Freedmen's Bureau agents insisting they treat blacks equally.[26] Gregory didn't help matters with his tone, as seen in a letter to Benjamin Harris, a grand jury foreman in Panola County, who had complained about how blacks were behaving:

> While from by far the larger part of the state, we learn by the most ample testimony that the blacks are the most docile, industrious, orderly, free from serious crime, and with all the substratum that goes to make the good citizen.

> The same incitements that quicken the industry of other men in free societies are felt by them. Such treatment furnishes all the incentive they need though they are not over anxious to work for nominal wages with the prospect of being defrauded even of their wages as has happened to thousands during the year just past.

> In those counties where the people are well inclined toward the Negro when they comprehend that a narrow and unjust policy toward them does not pay, he is rendering faithful Services for wages and doing better work than the lash could whip out of him, the business goes bravely on.

> If in your locality, the laborer refuses to work it may be because though slavery be dead its collateral influences still exist and survive, and new inducements have not taken the place of the lash and the chain. It may be that the planter as well as the Negro has not yet learned what free labor means.[27]

The planters wrote dozens of complaints to President Johnson, who needed white southern planters to win reelection and therefore wanted their voting rights restored as quickly as possible. Johnson relieved Gregory of duty on May 14, 1866.[28]

Gregory was replaced by Gen. Joseph B. Kiddoo, a twenty-six-year-old Pennsylvanian who had fought at Antietam, Fredericksburg, and Chancellorsville. He had served in the Sixth U.S. Colored Infantry and had suffered severe leg and spinal wounds, which left him in chronic pain.

Kiddoo placed a greater emphasis on building schools, and, like his predecessor, sought more military staff and money to expand operations. It didn't take long for Kiddoo to conclude that only force would compel whites to respect blacks. Kiddoo asked Washington for more authority to arrest white men who committed felonies against blacks, because, he said, the local courts were "worse than a farce."[29]

Instead of more resources, though, Kiddoo saw his cadre shrink. Most of his agents were volunteer army officers serving on temporary assignment. In the summer of 1866, the War Department began decommissioning volunteer regiments, and half of Kiddoo's agents faced immediate discharge. With no bureau agents in the field and no troops to back them up, he could do little to stop whites from imposing slavery by another name.[30]

Meanwhile, the white delegates at the state constitutional convention acted to formalize the subordination of blacks, and federal officials openly wondered if the delegates would pass the laws Congress had declared necessary to rejoin the Union. Those included renouncing secession; ratifying the Thirteenth Amendment, which would abolish slavery; repudiating the Confederacy's debts; and granting blacks equal rights.[31] But a new political coalition had formed and became a majority at the convention, putting the whole process in jeopardy.

The Conservative Unionists were mostly men who had opposed secession but had ended up supporting the Confederacy once the war started. They drafted a constitution that limited blacks to testifying only in court cases that involved them, denied state funds for black schools, banned interracial marriages, and prohibited blacks from holding state office. These delegates also didn't want to count blacks when apportioning political districts, denying them equal representation. The new constitution went before voters in an up-or-down vote on June 25, when they would also cast ballots for a new governor and legislature. True Unionists put up a halfhearted campaign for their gubernatorial candidate, Elisha Pease, and called for a no vote on the constitution, although they knew they couldn't win. Everyone knew that the vast majority of Texans still held to Confederate principles.[32]

When the results came in, the Conservative Unionist candidate, James Throckmorton, became governor, winning 49,277 votes to Pease's 12,068. Voters also overwhelmingly approved the new constitution.[33]

The new legislature, dominated by Confederate veterans and Conservative Unionists, took power on August 6, 1866, and swore Throckmorton in as governor three days later. In his inaugural address, Throckmorton set out a strategy for Texas to rejoin the Union, while at the same time avoiding most of the legal reforms that northern Republicans, who controlled Congress, had demanded. He urged lawmakers to do nothing that might anger northerners, but at the same time he opposed any legislation that might satisfy them.[34]

THE PRICE OF OVERREACH

Unusually heavy June rains in 1866 encouraged grass to grow in the cotton fields, where it strangled the plants and reduced output. In past years, slaves had hoed the fields throughout June and July, but by 1866, planters couldn't find enough workers. African-American men were demanding the best-possible contracts with the most trustworthy planters. Whites blamed the workers for the bad crop, insisting that freedmen didn't work as hard as they had as slaves. Planters also accused the Freedmen's Bureau of meddling in their relationships with blacks.[35]

Kiddoo and his agents, however, were actually forcing black laborers to fulfill their contracts and preventing labor recruiters from luring blacks to break their contracts in the middle of the planting season. The state just didn't have enough workers, despite paying the highest wages anywhere in the South. Kiddoo decided to recruit freedmen from other states, encouraging them to move to Texas.[36]

Many freedmen asked to share the crop rather than earn wages, with the portion of the crop depending on how much the African-American brought to the table. If all the black man could offer was labor, then they earned as little as one-quarter of the crop. If they were entirely self-sufficient, they could demand three-quarters. Because many black women wanted a nuclear family and a lifestyle similar to that of white women, their decision to stay home helped shrink the labor pool. For the first time, African-Americans enjoyed a measure of control over their lives. Many whites resented these changes. Landowners hired white gangs to hunt down blacks who left the plantation, and planters started using corporal punishment again.[37] White landowners also demanded the government do something about blacks becoming what they considered "uppity." Texans looked to other southern states for solutions and decided to use the so-called Black Codes. They had no intention of giving blacks equal rights.[38]

Rather than vote against the Thirteenth Amendment, Texas lawmakers simply ignored it. They knew enough states would ratify the amendment and make it law, so they saw no point in rejecting it. The Fourteenth Amendment, on the other hand, violated the Conservative Unionists' most fundamental positions. While in modern times, the amendment is known for the equal-protection clause and the definition of citizenship, in 1866, southerners considered it an attempt to deny power to those who had participated in the Confederate cause.[39] Section 3 of the amendment reads:

> No person shall be a Senator or Representative in Congress, or elector of President and Vice President, or hold any office, civil or military, under the United States, or under any State, who, having previously taken an oath, as a member of Congress, or as an officer of the United States, or as a member of any State legislature, or as an executive or judicial officer of any State, to support the Constitution of the United States, shall have engaged in insurrection or rebellion against the

· AFRICAN-AMERICAN TOMLINSONS IN 1885 ·

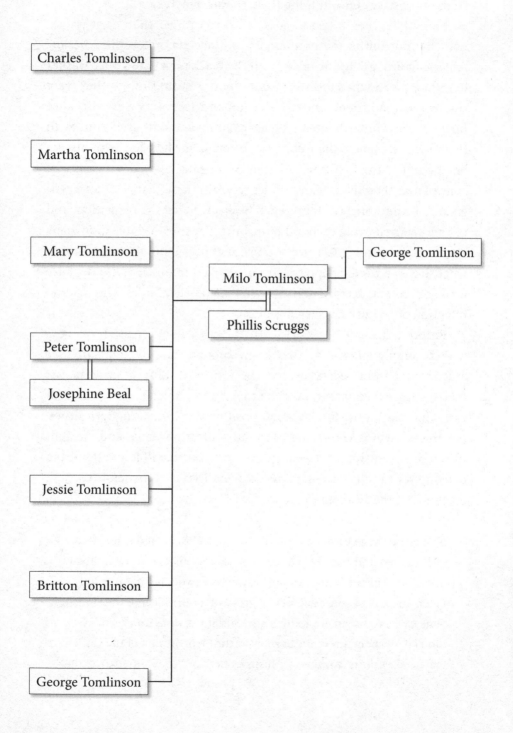

same, or given aid or comfort to the enemies thereof. But Congress
may, by a vote of two-thirds of each House, remove such disability.

The amendment barred politicians who held office in the Confederacy from serving again, unless two-thirds of Congress approved, a
test few of the South's top politicians could pass and none would take.
But by rejecting the amendment, Texas lawmakers fired the first shot
in a protracted battle with the Republican-controlled Congress in
Washington. The legislature's passage of the Black Codes was the second volley.

The first of the Black Codes concerned apprenticeships. The code allowed parents, or the county government, to give blacks under the age of
twenty-one to a white man who could then use the apprentice's labor
any way he chose. An apprenticeship granted the master permission to
use force to compel the apprentice to work and to capture an apprentice
who ran away. County authorities used the law to place teenagers, orphans, or homeless black children on private plantations, where they
provided free labor.[40]

The Black Codes' contract law largely mirrored the regulations
used by the Freedmen's Bureau. Employment contracts lasted at least
a month and employers could set the conditions and establish a code of
behavior, such as no swearing or leaving the farm without permission.
The code allowed employers to deduct pay for disobedience, impu-
dence, or absence.[41]

The most important of the codes, though, was the vagrancy law.
This allowed authorities to arrest anyone who had no visible means of
support or anyone who failed to sign a labor contract. It also allowed
judges to levy fines for vagrancy. In practice, a local justice of the peace
usually placed the vagrant, who was most often black, on a farm to
work off the fine under the same rules as an apprentice.[42]

On civil rights, the legislature guaranteed blacks property rights
and prohibited discrimination in criminal cases. However, it banned
blacks from voting, from serving on juries, from testifying in cases involving whites, and from marrying whites.

Texas lawmakers pronounced their version of the Black Codes a moderate approach, compared to that of other southern states, and passed the package of laws on August 9, 1866.[43]

President Johnson, anxious to guarantee himself the southern vote, declared Texas "reconstructed" on August 20. His order formally declared the war over and set the stage for Texas to return to the Union. But Texas lawmakers in Austin had barely gotten started.

The Conservative Unionists also redrew state political boundaries. Redistricting eliminated any chance for True Unionists to win an elected office and eliminated two district courts where Unionist judges presided. They also passed a homestead law that gave 160 acres of public land to any white man who settled in Texas.[44]

After President Johnson's declaration, Governor Throckmorton argued the federal occupation of Texas was over and demanded that the Freedmen's Bureau leave immediately. Kiddoo and federal officials, understanding that the matter was far from resolved in Washington, said they intended to stay and watch how well state officials protected the rights of blacks.[45]

In September, the bureau headquarters in Washington sent instructions to their agents in the field. While state courts could rightfully assert their authority over most matters, headquarters said contracts and civil matters involving former slaves remained the purview of the bureau. If a bureau agent felt state authorities were not protecting the rights of blacks, the agent was obligated to intervene, using federal troops if necessary. Headquarters authorized subagents to set up independent tribunals that included the bureau agent and two other judges, each chosen by the parties involved in the dispute.[46]

In response to the Black Codes, Kiddoo instructed subagents to stick to the federal rules. Agents in the field were also reporting growing violence against blacks and many cases of farmers cheating their workers.[47]

CONGRESS REACTS

When the four new congressmen and two senators from Texas reached Washington in October, they discovered that northern Republicans were unimpressed with their résumés or the state legislature's new laws. Both senators had supported secession and three of the congressmen had served in either the Confederate Congress or the rebel army. The Republican-controlled Congress, which opposed Johnson, refused to recognize any of the Texas representatives and declared the state's readmission premature.[48]

Texas, though, wasn't the only former Confederate state that Congress considered unreconstructed. Northern lawmakers understood Johnson was trying to save his political career by rushing the South back into the Union. But following a four-year war that left more than 750,000 Americans dead, northerners would not allow a return to the status quo.[49]

SETTLING THE TOMLINSON ESTATE

Sarah Tomlinson reported her progress to the Falls County Probate Court on December 31, 1866. She had sold her cotton but had not raised enough to pay off all the debts. She was not alone in her disappointment with the Texas cotton crop of 1866.[50] Underdeveloped bolls and a cotton-worm infestation cut production by a third, and new cotton plantations in Egypt and India drove down prices by 20 percent, devastating Texas planters.[51]

Sarah owed more than a dozen creditors $17,707, but her farm brought in only $3,000 from 80 bales of cotton, $70 from 500 pounds of wool, and $100 from 150 bushels of corn.[52] That was little more than the $2,600 a year it took to feed her family and pay her black workers. She needed the court's permission to sell some of her property.[53]

The court allowed her to sell a few hundred dollars' worth of goods, and Sarah whittled away at her debt. The bulk was still owed to Churchill and his son-in-law, Zenas Bartlett, who wanted to give her a chance to pay them over time with proceeds from the plantation. Sarah was under no pressure to sell everything at once.[54]

In Marlin, General Kiddoo relieved Asa Delano of his duties as a bureau agent and postmaster in January 1867 and sent F. B. Sturgis not only to replace him but to arrest him for fraud.[55] While in office,

Sturgis took careful notes concerning several violent attacks on freedmen and either sent them to his headquarters in Galveston or intervened with the company of cavalry assigned to him.

Delano's allies in Falls County did their best to stymie Sturgis, but
some whites cooperated and reported attacks on freedmen. A. M.
Hodges described one attack in East Texas after hiring freedmen in
Louisiana and bringing them to Falls County.[56] Other whites remained
paranoid about what was happening in the new black communities
popping up across the county. In March, Sturgis received a letter from
Robert Calvert, who wrote, "From some information I have received
from a freedman I think there is some danger of an insurrection among
the Negroes in our part of the county. He was told that there were
a company organizing at the sound of a horn. This might not be so,
I write this to keep you and others [apprised] on this I heard."[57]

When Sturgis went to the freedmen's colony, he discovered the
black men were creating an armed neighborhood watch to protect their
women from white men assaulting them in their new village.[58]

Sturgis dealt with reports of wrongdoing, ranging from a white
child striking a black child to lynchings. But the biggest problem for the
freedmen were whites not honoring their contracts. The complaints
read like the docket from a small claims court.

One dispute Sturgis adjudicated involved James Eldridge Tomlinson. A freedman, apparently a former Tomlinson Hill slave named Ed
Shields, accused James on April 3, 1867, of failing to pay a debt. Sturgis
sent James a letter: "Sir, Ed Shields makes complaint to this office that
you [have] a mare purchased from him in the summer of last year, please
make settlement with him or appear at this office and show cause why
you do not do it."[59] When James failed to pay, Sturgis held a hearing at
his office on Marlin's main square ten days later. His notes read: "Ed
Shields states that James Tomlinson bought a horse from him in the
summer of 1866 to be paid for in corn 35 bushels in the full, when
made, and he now refuses to pay for him: 35$. Unsettled."

There are no records showing whether James ever paid the debt,
but the Tomlinsons had trouble dealing with their former slaves. On
May 23, 1867, Sarah Tomlinson asked Sturgis to order the freedmen

on Tomlinson Hill to work. While the details are sparse in Sturgis's records, Sarah filed a complaint against twelve men representing the freed families on the Hill. Among those listed are Milo Tomlinson and "2 freed boys," one of whom may have been his eldest son, Peter, who was eighteen years old. The reason for her complaint is listed as "contract," which presumably means she didn't think they were living up to their part of the bargain.[60] Sturgis did not record how he settled the dispute, but Milo's family remained on Tomlinson Hill for another 150 years. The other freedmen's families in the complaint, the Magees, Baileys, and Johnsons, still lived on the Hill in 2014.

Most white planters took the economic crisis of 1867 as an excuse not to pay their black employees or they looked for any excuse to argue the freedmen had broken the contract. If the white landowner could make a convincing case, local officials would declare that the worker must forfeit his or her pay. Some planters hired white gangs to show up at the plantation after the harvest and threaten to kill any black person who did not leave. The landowner could then claim the workers left without permission and shouldn't receive their pay. Other landowners simply refused to pay the black workers and threatened to kill them if they complained. Whites also attacked black schools or any institution that attempted to fight for the workers' rights. In those rare instances where a worker convinced a court to hear a complaint for lack of payment, state law forbade blacks from testifying in cases involving whites, or from serving on juries. The whites always won in civil court, but they usually lost before the bureau agent's tribunal.[61]

Sturgis intervened in a case involving Churchill Jones. He sent an order to Jones in April to pay his laborers or face arrest, and Jones complied. But then, on June 15, 1867, the freedmen sharecropping on Falls Plantation complained that Jones had refused to provide the former slaves a way to protect their share of the cotton, and as a result, they lost everything. Sturgis logged the results of his investigation:

I went to the plantation of said Jones on the 23rd June to examine this case and find the cotton as stated rotting in the pens, but upon examining the evidence find that it is the fault of the Freedmen, they having drawn from the planter surplus of money to nearly the amount of their crop. [They then] came into Marlin and traded for it a second time giving a mortgage upon it for the same, when it really didn't belong to them.

I further find that there were two gin stands on the Falls place, all the time at their service, and one put upon the Blackman place, before they had got through picking, all of which were at the service of the Freedmen. And that those Freedmen who wished to ginned, picked and deseeded their cotton with [it]. The planters and their complainants could have done the same.

My impression is that I ought to punish the Freedmen for obtaining goods under false pretenses upon complaint of the merchants.[62]

The merchants, though, were not necessarily innocent victims. Whites set up shops on the larger plantations to sell blacks shoddy provisions, poor livestock, and useless goods at high prices. These store owners, colloquially called "buzzards" because of how they exploited blacks, provided cash advances and credit at outrageous interest rates. The store owner usually worked with the landowner to make sure the debts were deducted from a worker's pay and the two would share the profits, while leaving the worker with next to nothing. While this may not have been the case on Jones's plantation, it was a common practice.[63]

Sturgis reported at least one success in helping planters better appreciate the bureau and the freedmen's labor. He convinced 257 freedmen to move from South Carolina to Falls County and supervised one-year contracts between fifteen of them and Sarah's nephew, Nicholas Stallworth. While Sturgis had to intervene in April to force Stallworth to pay wages on time, he reported on June 30, 1867, that he had settled up the contracts and both Stallworth and the freedmen were happy:

I today made settlements with the South Carolina hands and what they thought at first was in me a very arbitrary order [that one half of wages each month be held until the end of the contract by the planters so that they might have some money at the end of the year] as it accommodated. Each month they begin to realize its advantages and some be more interested in how much they were to reserve.

Since my return from Austin I have visited a number of plantations on which these people are employed. When they first came here they were badly clad, poor, half starved-looking creatures, I now find it just the reverse and all contented and happy, though they have to work hard. But they came here for that purpose.[64]

Freedmen filed on average one complaint a day against white planters, and Sturgis was perpetually issuing orders for whites to stop misbehaving. He had a company of black cavalrymen in Marlin for protection and enforcement, and he used them constantly. Sometimes he threatened to send troops if a planter didn't shape up.[65]

For the most part, though, bureau agents like Sturgis could do little but document abuses. Most planters used the Black Codes and state law to legally avoid paying their workers in spite of the bureau. White Texans may not have won the war or maintained their slaveholdings, but within a year of the Civil War's end, they had created a new system for cheap labor and social control over blacks.[66]

EIGHT

The murder of Negroes is so common as to render it impossible to keep an accurate account of them.

—Gen. Joseph J. Reynolds, 1868

Northern Republicans realized that Texas and other southern states could not be trusted to protect the civil rights of blacks. On March 2, 1867, Congress passed the Reconstruction Act, which declared none of the new governments in the former Confederacy legal. Republicans had lost patience with President Johnson's strategy for Reconstruction and were imposing their own plans. Congress placed Texas in the Fifth Military District, along with Louisiana, and Gen. Philip Sheridan took command. He put Gen. Charles Griffin in charge of implementing in Texas what southerners came to call Radical Reconstruction.[1]

Griffin's first order of business was to supervise the election of delegates to yet another state convention in order to write a Texas constitution that would conform with the U.S. Constitution. Congress also required the state legislature to ratify the Fourteenth Amendment before Texas could rejoin the Union. To accomplish this, Griffin excluded high-ranking officials in the Confederacy from voting, or serving in political office, unless he provided special dispensation.[2]

At first, Griffin allowed state and local officials to remain in their posts as long as they cooperated. He didn't trust any of the former rebels, though. He set new rules ending the widespread and common abuse of civil rights and giving Union officers the power to intervene in any legal case where they observed injustice. Griffin also required prospective jurors to take the "Ironclad Oath," pledging that they had never voluntarily aided the Confederacy, and he required that freedmen begin serving on juries.[3] Many state judges simply closed their courts rather than comply.[4]

Griffin also set new voting rules and placed Unionists in control of voter registration. This cleared the way for the Republican party to counterbalance the Democratic party, which was controlled by former Confederate leaders. Texas Unionists who had fled at the war's outset returned to the Lone Star State to build a biracial party that could defeat the Democrats and ensure a state government loyal to the Union.[5]

Sturgis supervised the division of Falls County into four precincts, which at the time were called "beats." He appointed three Union soldiers, two recently returned white Unionists and one African-American to the voter-registration board representing Marlin. In western Falls County, he named Benjamin Shields, the old Alabama Whig, and William Etheridge, who had fled his farm near Tomlinson Hill. The last representative for western Falls County was Churchill Jones, whom Sturgis initially listed as an "unconditional Union man." But Sturgis later struck through that designation with his pen and left Churchill as a voting official even though he still did not have his citizenship. Sturgis's appointees registered 366 whites and 794 blacks for the election to send delegates to the new state constitutional convention.[6]

Republicans sent Union League organizers to Texas to recruit blacks into the party, and league chapters across the state produced Texas's first African-American political leaders. White and African-American Unionists met in Houston on July 4, 1867, to organize the new Republican Party of Texas. The party platform promised to reform homestead laws to protect blacks and guarantee black children access to public schools. To attract white members, the party promised to drive all former rebels from state government, but Unionists knew that Republican power relied primarily on black voters going to the polls.[7]

On July 19, Republicans in Washington helped Texas Unionists by passing the Third Reconstruction Act, which gave local military commanders the power to remove elected officials if they did not cooperate with martial law. Griffin removed Governor Throckmorton eleven days later and replaced him with Elisha Pease, who had lost the 1866 election. Pease asked Griffin to replace every officeholder in the state with Unionists, but Griffin insisted on handling each case individually. By September, he'd replaced dozens of judges and city officials and eventually removed all of the state's principal officeholders.[8]

Another yellow fever epidemic in Galveston, though, took Griffin's life on September 15. Washington replaced him with Gen. Joseph J. Reynolds, who continued the political purge until ordered to stop by higher authorities.[9]

White planters reacted to the purge by stepping up attacks on blacks and Unionists, focusing on slowing black voter registration and the Union League's expansion. Even with military officers spread out across the state, Union troops remained too few to prevent attacks and could only react after the fact. Republicans could do little to stop the violence against African-Americans, as pro-Confederacy whites controlled most of the wealth and social authority in Texas.[10]

A disappointing cotton crop in 1867 added to white aggravation and violence. The cotton worm had returned and a wet fall kept workers out of the fields, allowing weeds and grass to choke the plants. The rain caused a devastating portion of the crop to rot on the plant before freedmen could harvest it. White landowners took out their frustrations on the black workers, claiming that the low yield proved again that blacks belonged in chains and required corporal punishment. Farmworkers suffered murder, rape, mutilation, and beatings. Landowners also attacked white Republicans, whom they blamed for organizing blacks and making them "uppity." Planters warned black workers that if they joined the Union League or voted Republican, they'd never work again.[11]

INTIMIDATION CAMPAIGN FAILS

The state registered 60,445 whites and 49,550 African-Americans to vote, or about 50 percent of the white voting population and 89 percent of the black. White voters outnumbered blacks by eleven thousand, but twelve thousand of them were Unionists, giving the Republican party a clear advantage if they could turn out the vote. Where blacks were the majority or where the Freedmen's Bureau held sway, blacks registered in higher numbers and whites in lower. In northern counties, where white planters dominated, few blacks registered.[12]

General Reynolds ordered an election for delegates to the constitutional convention from February 10–14, 1868. Throckmorton, the former Democratic governor, argued that whites should vote against the convention because martial law was preferable to accepting equal rights for blacks. Other conservative Democrats argued that whites should attend the convention and write another constitution, one that rejected black equality. Both factions agreed the North would eventually grow tired of military rule over Texas and relent in trying to change Texas's white culture.[13]

Democrats, though, suffered a massive defeat. Roughly 89 percent of registered black voters turned out and cast 36,392 votes, along with 7,750 white Unionists. Democrats mustered only 10,623 votes. Unionists filled eighty-two of ninety-three seats at the constitutional convention. Of the eighty-two Republicans, sixty-four were Unionist Texans. Only nine African-Americans served as delegates, eight of them former slaves. The remaining nine delegates were whites who had moved to Texas after the war.[14] The convention began in June 1867, and Republicans splintered between conservatives and radicals. Despite their majority, Republicans couldn't even agree on a presiding officer. The process of drafting the new Texas constitution dragged on until February 6, 1869, when the convention dissolved in failure.[15]

THE KU KLUX KLAN COMES TO TEXAS

National Democrats wanted to win the 1868 presidential race, so the party made opposition to Reconstruction and black suffrage their key issues. To draw blacks away from Republicans, Democratic leaders offered jobs and protection from the rising violence. They held barbecues for African-American farmhands, and in return for joining a black Democratic political club, the Democrats promised to give them written certificates that would protect them from white violence as long as they didn't vote Republican. Blacks who did not join faced harassment, intimidation, beatings, and robbery. Democratic newspapers encouraged local businesses to place Republicans on blacklists. Editors proclaimed that allowing blacks to vote would lead to the "Africanization of Texas" and give former slaves power over their masters.[16]

As these Democratic clubs spread across the state, the Ku Klux Klan followed. The Klan had suppressed black political participation in other states, so its arrival in Texas had only been a matter of time. While no records directly connect Democratic clubs with Klan activities, circumstantial evidence is strong. The *Galveston News* proclaimed early on that Democrats needed a secret organization to counteract the Union League and to establish "a purer social atmosphere and as the last hope for the maintenance of the supremacy of the white race in this Republic."[17]

According to John Hereford, a Texas Klansman who testified in Washington about a disputed congressional race, the Klan supported the Democratic party:

> There were two objectives, one was a political object, in order to defeat the radical [Republican] party, that was the first. The second was, the people of that county did it for self-defense and the majority of good men of the county belonged to it. . . . It had a name. I don't remember the name it was called by the organization, by outsiders it was called Ku-Klux, those who called it so were principally woman and children and negroes.

The object was not to vote for any except a Democrat of the first water. The organization was in part, so that each man could know his neighbor, and whether or not he was a white Democrat, and to establish a concert of action among the Democratic Party.[18]

William Lewis, a former slave who campaigned for the Republican ticket, testified that whenever he stopped in a town to speak to freedmen, they warned him that his life was in danger. Lewis, who worked as a city policeman in the town of Jefferson, described escaping from a white mob in Denton County:

As near as I recollect about 25; they were generally armed with revolvers. The first I saw of them they had Col. Stokes [a Republican] surrounded. The first I heard they say were ordering him to leave town, that no damned Radical should stay there, and that if he did not leave immediately, they would kill him. . . .

I heard one say, "What will we do with the damned nigger that came from Jefferson?" Another one replied, "Tar and feather him and burn him."[19]

In Millican, a town north of Houston, Klansmen marched through the black part of town as a show of force on July 15, 1868. The freedmen fought back and drove the whites away, at least for a while. When the Klansmen returned, they killed twenty-five black men, including George Brooks, a Methodist preacher who had established the local Union League. When blacks didn't show up for a Democratic party barbecue in Jefferson on July 4, three hundred whites attacked black residents and white Unionists until they fled the town. Groups identified as Klansmen also attacked Freedmen's Bureau schools in Anderson, Fort Bend, Harrison, and Red River counties, driving away the teachers. Local authorities did nothing to stop the violence or to prosecute those responsible.[20]

That summer, Freedmen's Bureau agent Charles Haughn reported that two Klan gangs, known locally as "the Families of the South," roamed the Waco area in McLennan County. At least one of the groups also operated in Falls County.[21] In reading the *History of Falls County*, written in 1947, I was shocked to see the Klan's activities explained like this:

> In the confusion, ignorant Negros, not knowing how to use their new freedom, further confused economic conditions by failing to work, looking to the government for "forty acres and a mule" or something else and controlled by radicals. They thrust themselves obnoxiously into activities where they were of no use or actual hindrances. The Ku Klux Klan showed up in Texas, although, apparently not connected with similar organizations east of the Mississippi. The Texas bands existed briefly and were about the only means the white people had to making it known they had a few rights in the land. The bands depended for effect by appealing to the superstitions of the Negroes, more than upon violence.[22]

But in 1868, General Reynolds took a very different view and warned his headquarters in Washington of the growing problem:

> Armed organizations, generally known as Ku-Klux Klans exist, independently or in concert with other armed bands, in many parts of Texas, but are most numerous, bold, and aggressive east of the Trinity River.
>
> The precise objects of the organizations cannot be readily explained, but seem, in this State, to be to disarm, rob, and in many cases murder Union men and negroes, and as occasion may offer, murder United States officers and soldiers, also to intimidate everyone who knows anything of the organization but who will not join it. The murder of Negroes is so common as to render it impossible to keep an accurate account of them.
>
> Many of the members of these bands of outlaws are transient persons in the State, the absence of railroads and telegraphs and great length of time required to communicate between remote points facilitating their devilish purposes.

These organizations are evidently countenanced, or at least not discouraged, by a majority of the white people in the counties where the bands are most numerous. They could not otherwise exist.

Free speech and a free press, as the terms are generally understood in other States, have never existed in Texas. In fact, the citizens of other States cannot appreciate the state of affairs in Texas without actually experiencing it. The official reports of lawlessness and crime, so far from being exaggerated, do not tell the whole truth.[23]

Republicans knew that if the violence didn't stop, black civil rights had no hope in Texas. They sent a delegation to Congress, asking it to give Governor Pease more authority to replace local officials who did not enforce the law. Congress did not act, but it did exclude from the presidential election any state that was not reconstructed, including Texas.[24]

SARAH TOMLINSON AND HER FAMILY PROGRESS

Sarah Tomlinson took the final steps to settle her husband's estate in the fall of 1867, more than two years after his death. She asked the Falls County Probate Court on October 28 for permission to settle her land debt with her brother-in-law, Churchill Jones. Churchill agreed to take back six thousand acres of land that was adjacent to Falls Plantation, settling the balance owed on the original $10,000 mortgage, as well as the $412.34 debt she owed on two smaller loans.

A week later, she sold twenty-five cotton bales to John Dean and Co. for $858.72. She then sold fifty-five bales to a trader named Holeley for $2,209.85. Her sheep produced 490 pounds of wool for $70.75 and the farm produced 153 bushels of corn that sold for $97.40. Yet this was still not enough to pay off the remainder of her debt. She and her attorney, J. D. Oltorf, went back to court on November 23.[25] The court could not compel her to sell her land under the state's homestead laws. Sarah also asked the court to allow her to keep some other assets:[26]

Five mules	$80.00 each	$400.00
One mule wagon		$120.00
Three horses	$60.00 each	$180.00
One carriage		$175.00
Farming Utensils		$100.00
One Gin stand		$100.00
One gun		$10.00
2,000 barrels of corn	40 cents each	$800.00
Cash		$1115.00
		Total:$3,000.00

To pay her debts, she asked the court for permission to sell sixty head of sheep and goats, one damaged corn mill, three oxen, one ox wagon, four mules, one mule wagon, one horse, two looms, one bed, one-half league of land, and a box of books. The court scheduled an auction for December 10.[27]

Few people showed up, but those who did made sure Sarah's debt was settled. Her eldest son, James, bought two mules, three oxen, all of the sheep and goats, the books, the loom, the wagon, and the mill for $222. Her next eldest son, Gus, bought the other two mules and the ox wagon for $186. Churchill bought back half a league of land for $6,500. Everything stayed in the family. Oltorf took the proceeds and paid off what remained of the forty loans that Jim had taken out during the Civil War. County Judge W. M. Reed declared the estate settled on Sept. 29, 1868.[28]

During this time, James fell in love with a scion of a historic Texas family, Emma Diantha Perry. She was born in 1845 in Grimes County, which was named after her great-grandfather Judge Jesse Grimes, a signer of the Texas Declaration of Independence. James and Emma married on October 1, 1868, when he was twenty-five and she was twenty-three. They built a home on the north side of Tomlinson Hill, near Deer Creek. Their first son, William Augustus, bore the names of two of James's brothers. The couple had two more sons, James Eldridge Tomlinson, Jr., born in 1871, and Albert Perry Tomlinson, born in

1872. A daughter, Mary Eliza, was born in 1875. James and Gus helped their mother, Sarah, keep the plantation going, employing their former slaves to raise the cotton and care for the cattle.[29] Tomlinson Hill remained one of the most valuable properties in Falls County, worth at least ten thousand dollars. Two years after bankruptcy, Sarah's personal wealth was set at $2,200, a respectable sum for the period, and enough to increase production.[30]

Zenas Bartlett, Churchill's son-in-law and a cousin of the Tomlinsons, wrote to his sister in New Hampshire that life in Falls County was going well. The letter reveals the widely held disdain the former Confederates felt for the northerners who moved to the South to ensure the civil rights and education of the freedmen:

> You probably do not see this matter in this light, but had you been living in the South and suffered as we have, then lost all Negro property, had taken away the honest hard labors of a lifetime,—and then had Bureau Agents and "Carpet Baggers"—the off-scourings of the Northern States—to rule with a harsh tyranny over you, you would have understood this better.
>
> But as God brings good from evil, so now we are doing very well, for the above class has lost all control over the Negroes, who have gone back to their old masters, as a general thing, and are behaving as respectfully as old. And we treat them in the same kindly manner as we used to. 'Tis true we cannot punish them by whipping as we used to, but we can drive them off from our plantations, which is a greater punishment and quite as effectual. The Freedmen are working tolerably well. I am farming with my old slaves, and doing as well as when I owned them.[31]

The 1869 crop was bountiful, but Churchill was growing frail and remained saddened because the White House had still not answered his appeal to restore his U.S. citizenship. Churchill died on October 25, 1869, and his 54,000-acre plantation was divided among his heirs.[32]

ABANDONED

Gen. Ulysses S. Grant won the 1868 presidential election, putting a Republican in the White House who would cooperate with the Republican-controlled Congress. But the congressional mandate for the Freedmen's Bureau expired on December 31, 1868, and there was no interest in extending it. Across the state, bureau agents packed up their offices and sent their files to Washington. African-Americans no longer had federal agents to protect them.

Republicans at the state constitutional convention weren't keeping their promises, either. The caucus fractured into two main groups. Radicals believed in equal rights for African-Americans, included all the black delegates, and enjoyed the support of Grant and the national Republican party. Moderates opposed equality and formed a majority coalition with Democrats that promised to limit the rights of blacks. The Republican schism caused the convention to fall into disarray, resulting in an inability to finalize a new constitution. Gen. E. R. S. Canby, the new military commander in Texas, told his men to gather up all of the convention's documents and piece something together that Texans could vote on.[33]

The new constitution would radically change Texas politics. The first article declared state law subordinate to federal law and gave the legislature power to suspend judges and release people from jail for lack of evidence, while creating stronger roles for the governor and powerful state agencies. The governor would also appoint state judges.[34] It granted equality to all persons before the law and prohibited "any system of peonage whereby the helpless and unfortunate may be reduced to practical bondage." The right to vote was granted to all male citizens over twenty-one years old who were not disqualified under federal law. The right to vote was a double-edged sword for Republicans, though, because it did not exclude white men who had served the Confederacy. If the Republicans wanted to hold power in Texas, they would need to attract conservative whites.[35]

The Klan became even more active before the constitutional vote in

1869. While they claimed merely to punish lawless blacks, their unspoken goal was restoring white conservatives to power. They played on the fears of average whites, claiming that blacks were going to take power and steal their property. Klansmen demanded the support of whites in return for protection against a promised war between the races.[36]

The November 30, 1869, election pitted the two Republican factions against each other, as well as against a Democratic splinter group. Moderate Republicans and conservative Democrats tried to prevent African-Americans and radical Republicans from voting, while secret militias, including the Klan, warned blacks to stay home or be killed.[37]

In Falls County, landowners took their black workers to the polls and gave them ballots marked for the moderate Republican ticket. Whites ripped the ballots out of the hands of any black trying to vote for the radical ticket. In neighboring Milam County, an army officer attempted to escort one hundred African-Americans to the polls, but a group of white men attacked the polling station, forcing it to close before the blacks could vote. Similar violence occurred throughout East and Central Texas.[38]

Despite the interference, the radicals won by 39,838 to 39,055 votes, with the Democratic ticket taking only 445 votes. The radical Republican candidate, Edmund Davis, became governor, and voters approved the new constitution. The moderate Republican and conservative Democratic coalition failed to turn out more than forty thousand registered white voters. Most whites could not bring themselves to vote for the new constitution.[39]

The voter intimidation campaign took a toll, though. Only 66 percent of registered blacks voted, down from 76 percent in 1866. The biggest drop-off was in northern counties, where the Klan was particularly active. In Collin County, black turnout dropped 70 percent between 1866 and 1869. In the race to elect a state senator to represent Falls County, 267 fewer blacks voted than whites, allowing a Democrat to win that seat.[40]

There was no doubt, though, that Davis owed his victory to black voters, since fewer than five thousand whites voted for him. Democrats said this was proof that the Republican party was only for black people.[41]

On January 8, 1870, General Canby appointed the winners of the election to their offices and called the legislature to meet in Austin to carry out the final steps for Texas's readmission to the Union. Lawmakers ratified the Thirteenth, Fourteenth, and Fifteenth amendments, and on March 30, Congress voted to allow the Texas delegation to take their seats in Washington. From the point of view of northerners, Texas had finally elected a legitimate government. But the majority of white Texans despised the Republican leaders, whom they felt were being unjustly imposed on them.[42]

William P. Ballinger, a prominent lawyer and Democrat, wrote to former Lieutenant Governor Fletcher Stockdale on December 20, 1869, with an ominous prediction: "The Radicals will never be able to establish themselves here without military force. Their manipulation and control of the Negro will turn the people against them. It will only be a matter of time before the people will rise up and turn them out."[43]

NINE

[The blacks] were overbearing. I remember how when the men went to vote . . . at Marlin, they had to march between rows of Negro guards. How they were all set to win their men and how the white men came armed in order to fight, if need be, for their right to vote.

—R. E. L. Tomlinson

Texas's Twelfth Legislature convened on April 26, 1870, and Governor Edmund Davis took the oath of office two days later. He made law and order his top priority, not only to cut the high crime rate but also to end racial and political violence. His second priority was economic development. The enormous state held many natural resources, but the population was too small and the infrastructure too weak to exploit them.[1] Davis proposed a state police force to enforce the law in places where the sheriff was either too weak or uninterested in stopping crime. He also intended to prosecute gangs, primarily the Klan.[2] The new governor believed public education was key to achieving both law and order and economic development. Davis also wanted to encourage railroads, but he didn't want lawmakers spending too much taxpayer money subsidizing them. Few Texans could disagree with these programs, but Democrats demonized Davis and denounced everything he said or did.[3]

While Republicans controlled both chambers of the legislature, Davis didn't know who belonged to what faction. Few carpetbaggers won election, which meant almost all of the lawmakers were native Texans.

In the state senate, two of the thirty senators were black, as were twelve out of ninety representatives. Davis knew that despite their sparse representation in the legislature, blacks were the majority of his supporters and he had to address their issues.[4] The first few votes made it clear Davis could count on a majority in the house, but the senate was a problem.[5]

Davis set up the state police, issued railroad bonds, and began opening new public schools within his first year in office. Democrats claimed he hired criminals to serve as police and called his railroad deals corrupt. Democrats generally disliked the schools because Davis required a standardized curriculum, but they complained the most about how much the schools cost, particularly to educate blacks. To pay for all of this, the legislature passed a new tax plan, which gave counties the power to raise property taxes, resulting in a 300 percent spike in taxes in some parts of the state.[6]

Education for blacks was not opposed by all whites, though. In Falls County, Henrietta Gassaway, the wife of a major planter near Marlin, established in 1870 the first school for blacks on her property, two miles up Little Deer Creek from Tomlinson Hill. Shortly afterward, James Tomlinson and Nicolas Stallworth opened a school for African-Americans at the base of the Hill; it was called the Tomlinson Negro School. Nicolas initially taught the former slaves himself, but later he hired a black man from Marlin. The Tomlinson Negro School was surprising because it preceded the first white school in western Falls County. White mothers generally taught their children at home.[7]

The plantation business was also changing, with landowners forced to diversify their products. In the 1860s and early 1870s, a combination of weather and labor problems kept cotton production in Falls County from returning to levels seen in the 1850s. The increasing cotton production in India and Egypt, combined with the opening of the Suez Canal in 1869, meant lower global prices. The U.S. Department of Agriculture pleaded with farmers to focus on self-sufficiency, but large-scale planters were deep in debt and needed a cash crop.[8]

The main alternative to cotton was cattle. Falls County has an abundance of springs and streams feeding into the Brazos River and there was no fencing, so cows could graze far and wide on plentiful grass. Prairie fires were still common at the time, and they burned back shrubs and trees, so there was even more grass and less forest then than there is today. Cattle speculators bought huge herds in Texas and drove them overland to the railheads in Kansas and Missouri to meet high demand in the East. More than 700,000 head of Texas cattle went north in 1869, and these cattle drives gave birth to the American cowboy.[9]

The inhabitants of Tomlinson Hill always had cattle, but Sarah, James, and Gus quickly recognized the potential of developing their herd, since much of their land was prairie. Yet cotton, even at depressed prices, remained king, bringing Texas ten million dollars for 84,485 bales exported from Galveston in 1869. In 1873, Galveston exported 333,502 bales for $32 million.[10] Cotton production built Texas, not the lonesome cowboy herding cattle on the range. But the cattle kept many planters, including the Tomlinsons, afloat.

AN ACTIVIST JUDGE COMES TO FALLS COUNTY

Governor Davis made many enemies in Falls County by appointing John W. Oliver in July 1870 to serve in the new Thirty-third Judicial District, which included McLennan and Limestone counties. A thirty-five-year-old Mississippian, Oliver held true radical Republican views, and Davis asked him to replace a white Waco judge who was treating blacks unfairly. The district ended up with an overenthusiastic young man ready to stir up trouble, particularly when it came to elections.[11]

The 1871 election gave Texans their first chance since the war to choose leaders without military supervision. National Democratic leaders adopted a platform called the "New Departure," which required Democratic candidates to run on a shared party platform supporting state's rights and dropping their opposition to African-American civil rights.[12] Texas Democrats embraced the platform and relentlessly criticized Davis for everything but black suffrage. They established a statewide newspaper in Austin, the *Democratic Statesman,* to provide the party a single voice; the paper condemned rising taxes, corrupt rail-road deals, and the squandering of taxpayer dollars.[13]

Davis made an easy target. Before 1869, the state had never spent more than $100,000 on any single program, but Davis had created doz-ens of schools, hired teachers, and begun instruction in less than a year, costing taxpayers in 1870 more than $1.2 million. Democrats, mean-while, argued that mandatory school attendance infringed on personal liberty, claimed that school employees earned too much money, and said that the whole undertaking was intended to brainwash children.[14]

While the Democratic party and its official mouthpiece remained quiet on racial issues, disguised men on horseback terrorized black communities and letters to newspapers expressed seething resentment toward blacks. Klansmen attacked black churches and schools across the state.[15]

Republican leaders focused their message increasingly on the econ-omy and less on civil rights, mostly because they knew they could no longer afford to be identified as the "black party." Candidates became less pro-black and more pro-business.[16]

Davis scheduled the 1871 congressional elections for October 3–6 and, anticipating violence, placed all police in the state under his direct authority. Police required all voters to return home immedi-ately after casting their ballots and ordered guards to disperse large gatherings.

Before the first ballot was cast, violence raged across the state, with some of the worst of it in Oliver's Thirty-third District. A riot broke out in the Limestone County seat of Groesbeck on September 30 after Oliver ordered state police to arrest a white man for publicly threaten-ing to kill Republicans. A white man was shot during the riot, forcing the police to retreat into the mayor's office until reinforcements ar-rived. Once they left their safe haven, the police fled Groesbeck and the armed white mob took control. Rumors spread that the town's blacks were planning to attack. Davis declared martial law, but the order did little to help the election. The mob seized the ballot boxes and the re-sult was 97 percent for Democrats.[17]

The violence was probably unnecessary. Conservative whites turned out in huge numbers, dominating the balloting and crushing the Republicans. Democrats won all four congressional seats, with landslides in three districts. Both Republicans and Democrats recognized that despite six years of Reconstruction, white conservatism still dominated Texas politics. The stage was set for the 1872 general election.[18]

Trying to save their careers, Republicans in the legislature turned on Davis and slashed funding for his most important programs, security and schools. Republicans joined with Democrats to take away the tax authority granted to counties for public roads and buildings. Many Republicans denounced Davis, but he managed to retain control of the party and it endorsed him for reelection.[19] Democrats, meanwhile, promised tax cuts and smaller government.[20]

In Falls County, Judge Oliver did everything he could to guarantee that African-Americans and white Republicans could vote in 1872. But his efforts to protect blacks and enforce Davis's policies turned him into a villain among conservative whites, who were still railing against him in their 1947 history of Falls County. The book, compiled by Roy Eddins and published by the Old Settlers and Veterans Association, reflected generations of hatred perpetuated by oral and official history. Eddins quoted from a short book by Tom McCullogh, *Memories of the Hills of Home and Countryside*:

> Even in Falls County, the monstrous effrontery of the carpet-bagger seriously challenged the peace and order of society. Judge J. W. Oliver of Waco was a carpet-bag judge . . . and allowed a liberal contingent of soldiers or militia and these were usually illiterate Negroes, who liked to wear a blue uniform and carry a gun. These attended his court and executed his orders, not only in judicial matters but in many matters of administration, or tax assessment and collections, as well as in political activities. Judge Oliver was of keen intellect but of overbearing and unscrupulous methods of domination of the people and the province.[21]

Eddins described Election Day in October 1872:

The voting place in Marlin was the Bartlett building (now Marlin's City Hall). It was protected by soldiers under orders of Judge Oliver "to assure a fair and impartial election." Through two rows of soldiers, most of whom were Negroes, voters were about to pass to cast their ballots.

Some of the county's leaders saw through the scheme, which was to intimidate some voters and encourage others. They saw the gross injustice to fair-minded people and remonstrated, taking their appeal to Judge Oliver. The judge was adamant and insisted the soldiers were necessary for a "fair election." Some of the citizens walked quietly away and, one by one, returned and, unobserved, mounted the roof of the court house, armed with rifles and pistols. From their position they held a commanding view of the voting place.

By pre-arrangement, a few citizens, including J. D. Oltorf, an attorney, called upon Judge Oliver and asked that the soldiers be withdrawn. The judge insisted they were necessary and offered explanations—much to the exasperation of the citizens. Mr. Oltorf, after listening patiently, replied calmly in words to this effect: "All right Judge, if you persist in keeping the soldiers there, somebody is going to get hurt, perhaps killed. It is not known who will be the first to get killed, but you'll be the second!"

The bold action produced the desired result. The judge realized he was dealing with people whose tempers had been imposed upon too long. He withdrew the soldiers—and the election proceeded peacefully.[22]

My great-grandfather, R. E. L. Tomlinson was ten years old and at the courthouse that day. In 1936, he would recount what happened in starker terms to a woman from the Federal Writers' Project who was collecting oral histories during the Great Depression:

[The blacks] were overbearing. I remember how when the men went to vote . . . at Marlin, they had to march between rows of Negro guards. How they were all set to win their men and how the white men came armed in order to fight, if need be, for their right to vote. There was a comparatively peaceful election before someone began shooting up near the square and most of the Negroes fled to the Brazos bottom, and the white men went on with their voting. After it was over, they held a celebration that night over their success. Bonfires were lit and great was the rejoicing over the return of the white man to his right to vote.[23]

Democratic candidates swept the election at every level. They took control of the state house of representatives and obtained a one-vote majority in the state senate. Republicans held on only where either African-Americans or German immigrants made up the majority. Oliver left office on January 1, 1873.[24]

Davis had one year left on his term, but the writing was on the wall. The Republican party, and the North's attempt to reform Texas, was over. Confederates had returned to power.[25]

TEN

You talk about slavery, it never begun until after we was supposed to be free.

—Dave Byrd

In 1872, Sarah Tomlinson's health failed and she died at the age of fifty-three. Her children Gus, John, Eldridge, and R. E. L. were still living at the family home, while James and Emma lived in a cabin nearby. Her sons decided to keep the farm operating as a single unit, with each of them taking a share of the profits.[1]

Later that year, James and Emma had a second son, Albert Perry Tomlinson, and Gus married the daughter of a planter who lived just down the road, Elizabeth Jane Landrum. Elizabeth's father, Benjamin Landrum, had also moved from Alabama and operated a general store and post office. As a wedding gift, Benjamin gave the newlyweds land not far from Tomlinson Hill. The couple had their first daughter, Minnie Augustus, on September 9, 1873.[2]

Whites were back in total control of Falls County, even though Davis remained governor. The Freedmen's Bureau was gone, and a conservative Democrat had replaced Judge Oliver. Race relations were back to where whites liked them, according to local historians in 1947:

There had been no great animosities engendered between the whites and blacks, because slave-owners and slaves understood each other. Frequently there was a deep affection between them. As far as known, there were no cruel and unfair slave-owners here. They realized their responsibilities to the slaves and treated them accordingly.

Most of the Negroes continued to work for their masters. Albert Perry Tomlinson said Churchill Jones, one of the largest slave-owners, provided land for his ex-slaves, either giving it to them outright, or selling it to them on very easy terms.

During the Reconstruction naturally the votes of Negroes were appealed to in many and, sometimes, unholy ways. They were given many wild and impractical promises by "carpet baggers" and schemers, most of whom were more interested in personal profit than the welfare of Negroes. Most of the Negroes, however, with confidence in their "white folks," remained loyal and good citizens.

Falls County's problems with the Negroes were not extreme and white people, as a whole, cooperated to help them make the most of their opportunities. A few Negroes thrust themselves forward, impolitely, and prematurely, without respect to social aesthetics.[3]

This so-called history has little basis in truth, but it was the predominant perspective held by the dominant race at the time. I have included it to demonstrate how a bigoted history can survive for generations. In an official history of Marlin, the Chamber of Commerce published the same myths in 1976:

Carpetbaggers from the North joined scalawags at home to make life difficult. Reconstruction governments were established in the former Confederate States, which were governed as occupied territories. Agents of the Freedman's [sic] Bureau were stationed in each county. E. J. Davis, the radical Republican governor of Texas, appointed Judge J. W. Oliver to preside over the district in a harsh and high-handed manner.

[The county's] large negro population, which became less involved in politics than in most counties, became a large, peaceable, and industrious part of the population.[4]

Freedmen's Bureau records, though, report dozens of attacks on blacks and identify the former slaveholders who abused them after emancipation. But local historians, who took pride in their slaveholding ancestry, had no interest in reviewing the records compiled by "carpetbaggers."

I learned early in life that whites abused African-Americans in the decades following slavery, and I knew that my ancestors most likely participated. But reading the Freedmen's Bureau docket assigning names to both perpetrators and victims made it feel more concrete. Many of the African-Americans I've met in Falls County tell me that my ancestors didn't know any better. But history tells me otherwise. The whites of Falls County read newspapers, which laid out the debate over civil rights, and yet chose to remain oppressors. The Declaration of Independence says civil rights are God-given, but after Reconstruction, Democratic lawmakers argued that states' rights allowed them to deny civil rights to African-Americans. They claimed this authority by majority rule.

Once in power, Democrats in 1873 eliminated the state police, the only organization that reliably protected African-Americans.[5] Then Democrats unified the state militia and segregated the units, limiting the role of blacks, who were seldom called to duty.[6]

The next step was to abolish the state school board and return authority to local boards. Democratic lawmakers banished the common curriculum and reduced the mandatory school year from ten months to four. Conservatives said teachers who worked other jobs for eight months of the year would become better educators. State lawmakers cut all general revenue funding for schools and took away the counties' authority to levy school taxes.[7]

To complete their task, the Thirteenth Legislature rewrote election laws to give authority for voter registration to county clerks, giving them the power to keep African-Americans from voting. Legislators also redrew the state's political districts to keep blacks from winning elections.[8] Conservatives also passed a law disqualifying anyone who could not read or write from serving on a jury, thereby giving the elite control of the civil justice process.[9]

All executive and legislative offices expired in April 1874, so lawmakers set an election for December 1873. Four constitutional amendments proposed to take away the governor's authority to declare martial law, make the county tax assessor an elected official, increase the state supreme court from three to five seats, and prohibit the legislature from passing laws on local matters.[10] For governor, Democrats nominated Richard Coke, a lawyer from Waco, a Confederate veteran, and a former state supreme court justice.[11] The campaign began in September 1873.

On the campaign trail, Davis painted the Democrats as unreconstructed secessionists and racists who wanted to take Texas back in time. He accused conservatives of kowtowing to the railroads and big corporations that exploited the poor, no matter the color of their skin. He promised to protect the civil rights of all Texans against oligarchy, corruption, and discrimination.[12]

Richard Coke sounded all of the traditional themes of conservative Democratic politics. He called Davis and other Republicans traitors to Texas and scalawags. Coke said they had become tyrants over the state's true citizens, imposing oppressive laws imported from the North. He called the state police an instrument of oppression and the public schools a patronage system to reward corrupt whites and ignorant blacks. He pounded home how taxes rose under the Republicans and fell when Democrats took back the legislature. Newspaper editors repeatedly portrayed Davis as the black man's candidate, and therefore a threat to whites everywhere. They equated equality with the creation of a mixed-race, mongrel society.[13]

When Texans went to the polls in December 1873, they voted without federal troops or state police. Black turnout dropped and white turnout increased. Coke won the election with 85,549 votes to Davis's

42,663, and Democrats won every statewide office and took control of the legislature. The counterrevolution was complete.[14]

MARLIN BECOMES A CITY

Marlin grew rapidly in the late 1860s and early 1870s. Zenas Bartlett's general store, Bartlett and Watkins, got new competition from another mercantile firm, Scruggs and Company. Visitors also had their choice of two, two-story hotels. The Outler House was built from hand-sawed boards and had a veranda across the front. Thomas Read built a new, fancier hotel on the northeast corner of Court Square. Both served as stagecoach stops until the Houston & Texas Central Railroad arrived in 1871.[15]

In 1873, James D. Oltorf, the Tomlinson family attorney and Democratic crusader against Judge Oliver, became mayor. Oltorf was old friends with Coke, the new governor, both having practiced law in Falls and McLennan counties before the Civil War. Now that Democrats were back in control, they began devolving power back to local authorities.[16]

Oltorf, who owned the biggest mansion in the city, set out to impose order on Marlin with new city regulations. In September 1874, the city council passed an ordinance imposing a five-dollar fine on anyone who played baseball within the city limits because it was "detrimental to the peace and quiet of people." Oltorf's nineteen-year-old son founded a weekly newspaper called the *Moving Ball,* which later became the *Marlin Ball.*[17]

What bothered Oltorf the most was the condition of the city's main square. A decade earlier, a mysterious fire had destroyed the old log courthouse. A new one was planned to replace it, but in that time the square became populated with bars and businesses that Oltorf despised. He issued a proclamation in 1875 to restore decorum:

Whereas many of the old stone houses fronting on Court Square are occupied by a class of people who are wicked, filthy, ignorant, immoral, immodest, unchaste, miserably depraved and altogether reckless as to the rights of others . . . and a shame and disgrace to our otherwise respectable and growing city . . . I call upon the citizens to assist in making the owners remove the terrible nuisance and stigma of disgrace that hangs over the Public Square of the city.[18]

The city council, made up of the town's wealthiest residents, passed a requirement that only the owners of buildings on the square could occupy them, unless they received written permission from the mayor. Once the city had cleared the riffraff, the county began work on a new brick courthouse.[19]

Marlin also saw schoolhouses begin to pop up. In his role as the Falls County historian, Roy Eddins wrote:

It is known that soon after Reconstruction, a revival of interest in education arose dramatically. Children, young and old—and parents— flocked to available schools. Many new people arrived in the county and educational demands skyrocketed. The free Negroes posed problems, because they are unaccustomed to "going to school" and were reluctant to go. This discouraged people in providing schools for them. However, by 1875, education in the county was receiving it's [sic] just attention and schools arose rapidly."[20]

Eddins again showed his bias. Modern historians know that one-third of black families sent at least one child to school, if one was available.[21] But most schools were private and expensive. In a brochure, the Marlin Male and Female Academy advertised that school would open January 14, 1874 for the following fees: spelling, reading, and writing at two dollars per month; intermediate classes at three dollars per month; Latin, Greek, algebra, science at four dollars per month; and additional incidental charges for music, piano, and guitar lessons at fifty cents per session. The city's elite did not bother with such "subscription schools" and sent their children to boarding schools back east or in Europe.[22]

The state's wealthiest residents did not mind paying for a quality education for their own children, but they objected to paying taxes to educate other people's children, particularly blacks. State law, however, required counties to provide public schools, and Falls County announced it would open one in 1875. William Shelton, the owner of the Marlin Male and Female Academy, shuttered his private school and announced his building was for rent or sale. County commissioners hired Shelton, who helped them apply for funding from the Peabody Foundation to set up a new school system that rented his own school. The Marlin schools were still not completely free, but they were cheaper than before. Shelton went on to serve as mayor.[23]

As the western Falls County community grew larger, whites established churches and schools in the 1870s, but the Tomlinson Negro School was the only one for African-Americans. The Tomlinson Hill cotton gin was on a hill above the school, and the children would collect surplus seed for their parents to plant on their private plots the following season.[24]

Communication could be difficult for white teachers in African-American schools. Folklore tells a story about a young teacher who found her black students confused by simple math. A boy finally interpreted what she was trying to say, suggesting that instead of saying, "bring down your one, and carry your two," tell the children to "bring down your one, and tote the two."[25]

After the success of her black school, Henrietta Gassaway established the Beulah School for whites in 1870 on the other side of Tomlinson Hill. The small one-room log cabin doubled as a church. Billy Magee, the son of a local Baptist preacher and cotton planter, taught during the week and preached on Sundays. The Magees were the Tomlinsons' closest white neighbors.[26]

Benjamin Shields operated a general store in western Falls County, far from Marlin, in the early 1870s, selling basic supplies, clothing, and shoes. In 1870, twenty-eight landowners, including William Etheridge, established Masonic Temple No. 330 and began holding routine meetings, which the Tomlinson men joined.[27]

On Tomlinson Hill, Gus Tomlinson built a home for his wife, Elizabeth, and their children. Elizabeth inherited sixty-three acres from her father's estate, and they managed the black workers on that land as well, raising cotton and cattle. They lived on Tomlinson Hill until 1883, when Gus purchased a large farm near Lott, five miles away.[28]

Gus's younger brother, John Nicholas Tomlinson, married Christian McPherson in 1872. The two had their first child, Mary, the same year. They lived in the main house with James's growing family and the youngest Tomlinson boy, R. E. L. In 1874, John and Christian had a second daughter, whom they named Sarah, after John's mother, but they called her Sallie. James met "an untimely death" just before Christmas 1875, at the age of twenty-five.[29] History does not record the cause.

A NEW KIND OF SLAVERY

With control of the legislature, the governor's office, and the state supreme court, Democrats rewarded their supporters by passing the Landlord and Tenant Act, which gave planters the first claim on a tenant farmer's crop. The law allowed the landowner to have the sheriff seize a sharecropper's property to pay for debts.[30] Democrats also passed laws requiring segregated schools and allowing local school boards to operate African-American schools any way they wished.[31]

Democrats also wanted a new constitution. They organized a third constitutional convention in the fall of 1876 to further decentralize power by creating more elected offices and giving more authority to county officials. They also cut the governor's salary, ensuring that only the wealthy could afford to hold the post, and diminished the office's patronage powers. The new constitution limited the authority of the legislature to tax and issue debt and required judges to run for election. Lastly, the constitution of 1876 made it almost impossible to make a significant change to state law without voters approving a constitutional amendment. Voters approved it 136,666 to 56,653. The Texas Democratic Party retained unmitigated control over the state for the next one hundred years, and the constitution of 1876 continues to govern Texas today.[32]

FINDING REFUGE

While white Texans rebuilt their communities following Reconstruction, African-Americans built new ones from scratch. Many continued to live in the same one-room cabins and shacks they had built while enslaved, but now they paid rent for these dilapidated structures, which often housed seven or eight people in two small rooms. Others established villages on the outskirts of white areas, knowing that white society would not accept them. Small villages with churches, shops, and other services sprang up in river bottoms, along property lines, or in places where white landowners tolerated them. These places became known as "freedom colonies," where African-Americans could develop their own American culture.

In 1870, only 1.8 percent of Texas blacks owned land, and Reconstruction did little to advance the freedmen's economic independence. The conservative backlash eroded the few civil rights African-Americans possessed following emancipation, but while African-Americans understood the reality of their plight, they slowly and steadily worked to improve their lives just out of sight of whites. By 1890, 26 percent of African-Americans owned land, and by 1900, that would reach almost one-third.[33]

Two freedom colonies developed near Tomlinson Hill and became known as Gravel Hill and Cedar Valley. Another, called China Grove because of the many chinaberry trees, popped up on the Falls Plantation where Jones Creek intersected what is now Farm to Market Road 2027.[34]

Because these communities were African-American, white authorities never officially recognized them and rarely entered them. Each was located along a creek and centered on a church, and they developed into thriving communities. But they remained largely invisible to outsiders. Passersby might see a few old slave cabins, a couple of new black homesteads, a church or a school, and maybe a fire pit or some kiosks scattered in the trees. They didn't look like much, but they could exist because they went unnoticed by whites.[35]

Blacks who did not own land, or live in separate villages, lived on the plantations and were nominally self-employed under the share-cropping system. The white landowner provided a black family with a twenty- to thirty-acre plot of land, seed, horses or oxen, farming equipment, a house, and whatever they needed to survive through the growing season. The supplies of food and clothing were called "furnishings." The landowners collected the cotton after the harvest, sold it, and deducted the African-Americans' expenses from the profits, then handed over the remaining cash. Based on the landowner's accounting, though, there was often nothing left at the end of the year. It was not uncommon for a black family to end a growing season in debt, and once in debt to the landowner, the sharecropper could not leave until the debt was repaid.[36]

Sharecropping, though, was better than working as contract labor, which was scarcely different from slavery. Black families lived in former slave quarters, and a pistol-carrying "pusher," who behaved much the same as an overseer, regulated the workers' lives, with the sole goal of producing a crop.[37]

Larger plantations along the Brazos incorporated aspects of both systems. The families technically sharecropped the land, but they worked with other families to cover a huge field. This "through-and-through" system meant all of the sharecroppers worked as a team, and there were no distinct land leases. Everyone's crop was combined, and the landowner determined who got what in the end. There was no challenging the white landowners' word, since they controlled the sheriff and the courts.[38]

Many former Texas slaves felt life had been better during slavery. Whites no longer saw a reason to care about their workers' health or well-being. Former slave Dave Byrd said:

> You talk about slavery, it never begun until after we was supposed to be free. We had to work farms on the halves, very little to eat, and no clothes except what we begged. Then after we got a crop made, it would take every bit of it to pay our debts. We had no doctors when we got sick, and from the day we was turned loose, we had to shoulder the whole load. Taxes to pay, groceries to buy, and what did we get? Nothing.[39]

The larger the plantation, the worse the abuse. For landowners, replacing a sharecropper was easier than replacing a mule. Many blacks moved away from their old slave quarters to find homes of their own. In some cases—such as on the Tomlinson, Jones, and Stallworth plantations—planters set aside land for former slaves who chose to stay and work. While not officially deeding over parcels, they did provide a more private life.[40]

When African-Americans got plots of their own, they felled trees by setting slow-burning fires at the bases of the trunks. They used those logs to build two-room cabins, sometimes with a loft, homes like what they had built for their masters during slavery. They swept the dirt floors clean and kept a bare-dirt boundary around the cabin to protect against snakes and wildfires. The men fashioned picket fences from logs split along the grain to keep livestock away. Sometimes they made split-rail fences.[41]

In the winter, they cooked meals in a fireplace made from mud and straw. A long pole was always kept outside in case the chimney caught fire and needed to be pushed over before it set the house on fire. Women rose before dawn and cooked biscuits in large three-legged black pots known as "Dutch ovens." They made "hoe-cakes" by spreading corn-meal batter on the blade of a large cotton hoe and holding it above the flame. Others simply made "ashcakes," by brushing away the hot coals from the hearth and pouring batter directly on a hot stone, then covering it with ashes. In the summer, women prepared meals in outdoor fire pits.[42]

Farmworkers used their cotton hoes to plant their first crop of corn and vegetables. They hunted for wild game, which was still plentiful in the hardwood forests of the Brazos river bottoms; notched the ears of their hogs and cattle and allowed them to graze freely in communal pastures; marked their chickens and turkeys and let them roam during the day, while luring them home with corn in the evening. These free-range methods continued into the 1940s.[43]

In areas where blacks built their churches and schools and set up cemeteries, freedmen built simple structures and lived close enough to white planters so they could sharecrop or work for a monthly wage.

They acquired mules, oxen, and horses and made plows out of old trees and scrap iron. This eventually allowed them to plant a cash crop on their own land while still working for white landowners. But subsistence crops came first: sweet potatoes, peas, peanuts, corn, melons, vegetables, and syrup cane. Sweet potatoes fed the family year-round, and corn not only fed humans but also domesticated animals. If either of these crops failed, a farm family could lose everything, and, in the worst case, starve. On the other hand, a sign of prosperity was a full corncrib, a plentiful supply of potatoes, and a smokehouse full of pork.[44]

The freedman's goal was simple: avoid the discrimination and humiliation that came from interacting with whites. The more self-sufficient a black family became, the less they suffered. African-Americans who owned their land had the best chance for success, even if they lived on the worst land in the most distant corners of the county. But it also required exceptional frugality and resourcefulness never to waste anything, especially money.

In 1877, there were only 678 black schools in Texas, and, even if a school was nearby, most children couldn't go because they worked.[45] Child labor was always part of subsistence farming, and black children performed chores at home until they were big enough to harvest crops or wield a hoe. Farm labor was intense and primitive: "Planting was done by sowing the seed by hand and cultivating with eye-hoes and mules, behind which were cast-iron plows and a man or woman, walking four times down each row—from sun to sun. Work was hard, almost backbreaking, and there was little rest or relaxation."[46]

Boys and young men raised hunting dogs and spent their free time chasing rabbits with sticks, rocks, and slingshots. But they more often hunted at night, catching possums by hand. Black hunters developed ingenious traps for everything from ground-dwelling birds to white-tailed deer. Baked possum with sweet potatoes was a popular dish, and raccoon and squirrel provided variety in the diet.[47] Hunting and fishing provided not just food but also recreation. Sometimes black men arranged large social events to catch fish to celebrate Juneteenth, the day Texas slaves were emancipated. The majority of the meal would come from fried catfish, foraged greens, and wild blackberry pies.[48]

As much as these communities strived to be self-sufficient, the inhabitants still needed to purchase some manufactured goods, such as needles, spices, and kitchenware. They could visit a friendly white shopkeeper, or, more frequently, a white traveling salesman would stop in the village. In the larger freedom colonies, a black man would likely run a store from his home.[49]

Based on the household numbering system used by census takers, Milo and Phillis Tomlinson lived a short distance from the white Tomlinsons. Milo was a sharecropper and the couple had three children born before emancipation: Peter, in 1857; Martha, in 1863; and Charles, in 1864. Hylland and Bird were born in 1868 and 1869, respectively.[50] Milo and Phillis formalized their marriage at the Falls County courthouse in 1869 after a wedding ceremony performed by the Reverend Calvin Magee at the Gravel Hill Baptist Church.[51] Milo, Phillis, and Peter were illiterate and owned no real estate; they had two hundred dollars in personal property, well below the average even for black families in western Falls County.[52]

Other African-American families working for the white Tomlinsons included the Baileys, Magees, Jacksons, Johnsons, and Davidsons. Each household averaged six or more people, sometimes with more than one family sharing a single cabin. The Baileys still live on the Hill and hold a family reunion every year. They were among the wealthiest black families in the county, with four hundred dollars in assets, more than many white farmers in the late nineteenth century.[53]

Three black churches served the Tomlinson Hill area: the Gravel Hill Church, nestled among African-American homes; the one at Cedar Valley, which was a half mile to the north; and the one at China Grove. All were Baptist churches built on land donated by the Tomlinson, Stallworth, and Jones families, who were also Baptists.[54] The participatory style of the services appealed to many blacks, most of whom had grown up with white Baptist preachers during slavery.[55]

Each Baptist church was governed by seven deacons, who managed the church's finances and hired the minister. Church deacons settled disputes and passed judgments in their communities, since white lawmen generally didn't get involved in disagreements or crimes involving only blacks. Banishment was the ultimate punishment.[56] Under white oppression, opportunities to hold formal political leadership positions dwindled, but the church offered black men the chance to lead their communities with little interference from whites. This led to a varying degree of commitment to religious duties, with some using the church only to gather power over others.[57] In addition to Saturday-night suppers and Sunday-morning services, churches held revivals in the summer, usually in August, when there was little agricultural work. These lasted from two to three weeks, and frequently brought together congregations from several churches.[58]

Before her death in 2012 at the age of eighty-six, Pinkie Taylor Price described China Grove and Cedar Valley in an oral history interview. She talked about her grandparents Milo and Martha Travis, who were born into slavery on Tomlinson Hill. Taylor described how Milo chose the name Travis and discussed their life in Cedar Valley:

> They told all the slaves to go to . . . the county seat, to register and be citizens of the United States because they were free then. And so on the way there, my grandfather was riding whatever vehicle they had to ride in, a wagon or whatever. He just decided he just didn't want to be named for his master. So when he was going in, he saw a sign and it had, Travis, T-R-A-V-I-S, but nobody knew how to pronounce it or not, but he remembered it. So when he got to the courthouse and they asked him, "What's your name?" instead of saying Milo Tomlinson, he said Milo Travis. And that's the only family I know, down in China Grove or in Falls County, that was named Travis. And I wondered why we didn't have nobody else, you know, named Travis. But I found out that's why, 'cause he took on his own name.[59]

Pinkie's grandmother, Martha, married a man who was also independent and had saved enough to buy his own farm. He insisted that she stay at home with their children. They spent most of their time growing subsistence crops, including vegetables, berries, grapes, peanuts, and watermelon, but also raised hogs and cotton for cash.

Pinkie remembered how as a little girl she saw Martha still living in the one-room log cabin that Milo had built in the woods near Cedar Valley.

Pinkie explained how sharecroppers had almost no control over their finances and recalled how the white Tomlinsons promised three-fourths of the crop to the tenant farmer, only to keep all of it to repay the loans for the furnishings:

> He would lend you enough money to raise that, and then he'd tell you what store to go to and buy your groceries. And the owner of the store would keep all the records of what you buy and he'd keep track. And he would tell the man that lent you the money what it is. You're not supposed to keep no kind of records for yourself. You're sup-posed to let those two men decide how much you took up and how much you didn't.
>
> And then they had a store in town where your people go and get them some clothes on credit, but that man and the man that you're working for kept that record. You didn't keep it.
>
> By October or November, I know 'cause my cousin's family lived close to us and they worked for Tomlinsons, they would get upset every fall 'cause they would owe the Tomlinsons all the money [ac-cording to the records].

There were other options, but few good ones. Some landowners of-fered different contracts, but all seemed to end with the black farmer owing the white landowner whatever money the crop brought at mar-ket. Owning your own land brought in more revenue, but there was always the chance of a failed crop. One bad year and a farmer would likely lose his land, because the land was almost always the collateral for the seed money. Black farmers suffered because 59 percent of them worked fifty acres or fewer, and 83 percent worked fewer than one hun-dred acres. By comparison, white landowners cultivated an average of 425 acres and enjoyed an economy of scale. Whites also negotiated with different stores and suppliers to get favorable loans.[60]

The Convention of Colored Men protested the sharecropping system and lobbied for reform, and black activists created the Colored Farmers Association and the Colored State Grange, an advocacy group that helped form black cooperatives. Black farm workers organized strikes against large plantations, but none of these efforts created any significant change.[61]

African-Americans in Texas, already suffering from the depression of 1877, recognized that whites had constructed enormous barriers to keep them from prospering. African-Americans had also watched white Republicans abandon any real attempt to enforce civil rights. As a result, approximately twelve thousand African-Americans left in the exodus of 1879 for Kansas, after rumors spread that they could acquire free land. But no free land existed, and about 10 percent of the migrants returned.[62]

Other black Texans enrolled in the American Colonization Society's program to ship blacks to Liberia, a new African colony established by freedmen. Twelve Texans traveled to Africa in 1879, and the society's agent continued to promote the colony into the 1890s, but no large-scale emigration took place.[63]

Yet there was some progress for blacks in Texas. The white-controlled legislature established the first black land-grant college in 1878 near Hempstead, naming it Prairie View Agricultural and Mechanical College. The college was placed under the Texas A&M board of directors and began with eight students. The state government converted it into a normal school to train teachers the following year. Enrollment shot up to sixty, with every student appointed by either a legislator or a member of the board of directors. The only other colleges admitting blacks were private church schools, including Paul Quinn College, in Austin; Wiley College, in Marshall; and the African Methodist Episcopal Church's normal school, in Denison. In 1881, church groups opened four more colleges for African-Americans, most of them dedicated to training teachers.[64] African-Americans made up 25 percent of Texas's population in 1880.[65]

The black Tomlinsons, though, were primarily concerned with the spring rains, unpredictable Brazos floods, and the cotton boll weevil. Milo and Phillis had eight children under their roof, while their eldest son, Peter, and his wife, Josie, had two boys and one girl.[66] They all worked a portion of Tomlinson Hill, hoping their share would exceed the debt owed to the white Tomlinsons.

ELEVEN

The votes of the Negroes were to be reckoned with, since most of them followed leaders. There arose a general adverse feeling against them, because of this—a feeling, which perhaps lingers, to the present.

—Roy Eddins

Mayor J. D. Oltorf launched a campaign to beautify Marlin in 1878, and the city council ordered those guilty of misdemeanors to clean the streets of horse dung. When city convicts refused to do the work, Oltorf and the city council drafted a new ordinance:

> It shall be the duty of the Marshall of said city to tie such convict or convicts by the thumbs and with their hands raised over their heads, tie them to the ceiling of the roofing inside the calaboose, and keep them in that position until they shall consent to comply with the terms of said ordinances; and if any convicts . . . use profane, vulgar or obscene language in the hearing of the citizens of said city, it shall be the duty of the Marshall, if necessary, to prevent the use of such language, to gag such convict.[1]

African-Americans made up more than 50 percent of the state's prisoners at the time, and cities across the state used vagrancy laws to jail blacks and force them to work. City marshals prosecuted African-Americans much more aggressively for petty crimes, including using "abusive language," which was often nothing more than speaking back to a white person. Since blacks had little money, they couldn't post bail and were forced to occupy Oltorf's calaboose. The mayor's use of torture to force African-Americans to work was not unusual. Many towns still used whippings to punish minor offenders when they could not pay a fine, and, again, blacks made up the majority of those who suffered.[2]

Cattle drives from Marlin up the Chisholm Trail reached their zenith in the early 1880s, less than twenty years after they started. Popular fiction then, and Hollywood films later, glamorized the Texas cowboy, but the former slaves who picked cotton and raised the cattle on places like Tomlinson Hill contributed more to the state's economy. Milo's family helped raise the Tomlinsons' cattle, which bore the "7" brand.[3] When cows were ready for market, blacks helped the white Tomlinsons herd them to northern markets. A quarter of all cowboys were African-American, but when white authors wrote the folk history of the West, they omitted blacks.[4]

In 1880, Eldridge Tomlinson left Falls County to seek his fortune as a cowboy. He made his first cattle drive to Kansas for Beal and Shankle, a large ranching operation. After he returned, he enlisted in Company C of the Frontier Battalion of the Texas Rangers on July 15, 1881. His commander was Capt. George Washington Arrington, another immigrant from Alabama and a Confederate veteran.[5] Arrington, however, was not the captain's real name.

Arrington was born John C. Orrick, Jr., and he was escaping a dark past. Orrick's father was an Illinois doctor who joined the North when the Civil War broke out, while his son, then only sixteen, joined the Confederacy. Orrick junior ended up with the Forty-third Virginia Cavalry Partisan Rangers under John Mosby, known as the "Gray Ghost" and considered the father of modern guerilla warfare. Orrick junior scouted for Mosby and frequently went undercover as a spy. When the Civil War ended, Orrick fled to Mexico, but he returned to Alabama in 1867, where he killed a black businessman. He fled prosecution to Central America and gradually worked his way to Texas in 1870. He joined the Texas Rangers' Frontier Battalion using his mother's maiden name.[6]

The governor promoted Arrington to captain in 1878 and his company moved into the Panhandle to fight Comanche, who were stealing horses near present-day Crosbyton. When Eldridge joined the unit, Arrington was launching long-range patrols into New Mexico to map Indian hideouts and water sources. The Rangers often angered U.S. Cavalry commanders patrolling the same areas.[7] That the cavalrymen were African-Americans, known as "buffalo soldiers," contributed to the tensions. The white commander of one unit called Arrington a "notorious hothead, with a particular feeling of disdain for the army, and Negro troopers especially."[8]

The Rangers broke up a major rustling ring and made Arrington a hero among local ranchers. He resigned in the summer of 1882, became a rancher, and ran for sheriff.[9] Eldridge resigned with Arrington and worked for him as a ranch foreman.[10]

While Eldridge was riding the plains with the Texas Rangers, R. E. L. turned twenty years old and received an appointment to Texas Agricultural and Mechanical College, the first land grant college in Texas. The college, now known as Texas A&M, had opened in 1876 and there were only 250 students on the campus in 1882. The campus was all male, and the school required students to participate in military training. R. E. L. made the sixty-mile trip by stagecoach to Bryan–College Station to enroll.[11]

While R. E. L. was learning basic military and farming skills at the college, James and Gus built new, larger homes for their growing families and focused their attention on raising cattle. They left the farming to sharecroppers. From 1880 to 1885, beef prices reached new heights and cattlemen, including the Tomlinson brothers, filled up their unimproved fields with cows. This led to overcrowding and encroachment on cropland. Farmers started fencing their land, and that led to skirmishes with ranchers. Despite fierce opposition and a lot of fence cutting, ranchers eventually accepted farmers putting up barbed wire. The days of letting your cattle wander on the open range were over, but the greater demand for beef led entrepreneurs to open a packinghouse in Waco, ending the need for driving herds to Kansas. The cowboy era was over.[12]

STOKING WHITE FEAR

In the late 1880s, whites became increasingly concerned about racial mixing, probably because more and more people were moving into urban areas, and whites more frequently encountered African-Americans they didn't know. Fear of miscegenation grew even though lawmakers had banned mixed marriages in 1858. The state legislature outlawed interracial sex in 1882.

The Convention of Colored Men protested in 1883 that prosecutors never used the law against white men. They filed dozens of complaints against white men for visiting black prostitutes and, in some cases, living with their African-American children. But prosecutors refused to apply the law equally.[13]

White politicians and newspaper editors also stoked white fears of "negro domination" with weekly stories about black men assaulting white women somewhere in the state. The papers approvingly described white mobs lynching the suspects rather than waiting for a trial that might embarrass the victim. Many conservatives considered this speedy, violent retribution to be chivalric.[14]

Whites saw no problem with treating African-Americans unequally because the vast majority considered blacks intellectually and morally inferior and felt that a mixture of benevolence and violence was all they understood.[15] White landowners in western Falls County treated their African-American neighbors in the 1880s just as Churchill Jones had treated them during slavery. To white Texans, their racial superiority was a natural law as obvious as gravity. They could not understand why blacks could not accept it as fact.

Most African-Americans spent their time trying to better their lives, and in rural areas, segregation meant little. In 1880, twenty-six-year-old Peter Tomlinson lived in a cabin in Cedar Valley with his wife, Josie, their two children, and Josie's mother, Becky. Next door, Jede Tomlinson lived with his mother and sister, both named Annie. Peter and Jede were sharecroppers for the white Tomlinsons. Ten of eleven households in Cedar Valley belonged to black families. Around the

Stallworth and Tomlinson plantations, there were forty-two whites and fifty-eight blacks.[16]

On the western side of the Brazos, black schools operated as part of the Lott school district, and the children of sharecroppers attended the single-room Tomlinson Negro School. The district built another school in 1880 for the children at China Grove, called the Perry Creek School. The Stallworths and Tomlinsons hired a twenty-nine-year-old, New York–born mulatto man named J. S. Murmer to teach at the Tomlinson school.[17] In addition to his Texas-born wife and two-year-old son, Murmer had three adopted children between the ages of nine and twelve living in his cabin on Tomlinson Hill, next door to James Tomlinson and his family.[18] Though attendance for the older black children varied depending on the phase of the cotton season, most children received four months of education a year. By comparison, white children attended school for six months.[19]

When it became clear that the Tomlinson Negro School was too small to accommodate all of the black children, F. M. Stallworth and other white landowners opened two more small schools near the Landrum store west of Tomlinson Hill, and the Beulah Church, located on Deer Creek, just a half mile west of Tomlinson Hill. All three schools operated under the same set of trustees. In 1886, Benjamin Shields donated land for the white Shields Academy. White Baptist preacher J. R. M. Touchstone was the first teacher there.[20]

The proliferation of schools and civic development in Falls County can partially be attributed to the harvest of 1882, probably the best year in the county's history.[21] Gus Tomlinson finally made enough money to start his own farm. He kept a share of Tomlinson Hill but bought a new farm near Lott in 1883, where he could build a substantial and elegant home for his wife, Lizzie, and their three children. He leased much of the new land to sharecroppers to grow cotton and corn, while he built a feedlot for cattle, a more profitable undertaking.[22] In June 1883, R.E.L. returned home with his degree from Texas Agricultural and Mechanical College. Gus, James, and Eldridge—R.E.L.'s surviving older brothers—gave him a wallet that had belonged to the father he'd never known. The buckskin trifold was hand-tooled with a simple pattern and was sewn along the edges with tan thread. A thin strap wrapped around it to keep it closed. Inside was a coin purse and three compartments. R.E.L. recognized the significance of the gift and wrote on the inside cover with a fountain pen, "This Book is an old heirloom."

R.E.L. stayed on the farm for a year before deciding to become a schoolteacher, which required two more years of training. He left for Huntsville, one hundred miles southeast of Tomlinson Hill, to attend the Sam Houston Normal Institute, or teacher's college, to earn a teaching certificate. The white Tomlinsons built their fortune just as their father and grandfather had done—by leveraging cheap black labor to produce cash crops on large acreages. Like most Texas whites, the Tomlinsons had recovered from the Civil War and Reconstruction with their way of life largely intact. R.E.L was breaking this tradition by working in the city.

BLACK TEXANS ORGANIZE

Barred from joining most white trade associations, African-Americans formed their own organizations. L. C. Anderson formed the Texas Colored Teachers' Association in 1884 to promote the education and protection of black teachers, and black doctors created the Lone Star State Medical Association in 1886, with Benjamin Bluitt becoming the first black surgeon in Texas when he arrived in 1888. The following year, R. L. Smith created the Farmers Improvement Society of Texas to help black farmers get better prices and learn better farming techniques. Cotton pickers went on strike in 1891 and black longshoremen struck in 1893, both times failing to win concessions.[23] The National Negro Protective Association fought at the federal level, complaining when the postmaster general said that blacks could not serve as postmasters in white communities.

African-Americans in Texas turned out to vote in record numbers in 1890, casting 100,000 ballots. Despite the odds stacked against them, blacks continued to win seats in the legislature as Republicans. But the more that blacks participated, the more whites resented them, as shown in this account from the 1947 history of Falls County:

> For a long time, even to the 1890s, intense rivalry over the Negro vote existed. The votes of the Negroes were to be reckoned with, since most of them followed leaders. There arose a general adverse feeling against them, because of this—a feeling, which perhaps lingers, to the present (1946).
>
> Conservative thinking people did not lay all the blame for the evils at the feet of the Negroes.
>
> The commissioners' court records show that Nelson Denson, a Negro, was elected Falls County commissioner and served on the court. His service was satisfactory, despite the prejudices of the day. Later Denson was elected alderman of the city of Marlin, but refused to serve "in the interest of harmony."[24]

That "general adverse feeling" against blacks was not limited to places like Marlin. Southern whites did not want African-Americans to feel equal, and as educated blacks and black associations began to assert themselves, the greater the need many whites felt to separate themselves. Old conservative Democrats, who had tried for years to pass laws denying blacks equal treatment, developed new strategies for passing racist laws. The first came in 1889, when the legislature allowed railroads to supply separate coaches for black and white passengers. Two years later, they made segregated railway coaches mandatory.[25]

Black Texans watched helplessly as what little political influence they'd enjoyed in the legislature slipped away and the Republican party embraced segregation. In 1883, blacks made up 90 percent of Republican voters, and party delegates elected African-American N. W. Cuney, a member of the Republican National Committee, to lead the party. Republican president Benjamin Harrison appointed Cuney the customs inspector of Galveston in 1889 in order to secure black support. However, the move split the Republican party, with conservatives forming a bloc known as the "lily whites." While Cuney attended the National Republican Convention and became the most powerful African-American in Texas, Democrats used his leadership to politically bludgeon Republicans among whites. Democrats won nearly every race in the state by 3–1 margins.[26]

Many in the Republican party had worked tirelessly to create a coalition of blacks, liberals, and poor whites to create a majority against the conservative Democratic machine. But by the 1890s, white Republicans questioned the strategy, and even African-Americans started leaving the party. In 1892, more than 50 percent of blacks voted for James Hogg, a progressive Democrat who promised better public education and an end to lynching.[27] African-Americans soon discovered that national Republican leaders were slowly withdrawing their support for black leaders, and by 1906, the Republican party was firmly in white hands.[28]

Outside of party politics, Booker T. Washington and W. E. B. DuBois emerged as national African-American leaders advocating education and self-sufficiency. Washington ran the Tuskegee Institute, in Alabama, which trained young African-Americans to teach farming and skilled trades as well as academic subjects. He became a national advocate for black colleges, and the *Marlin Democrat* regularly ran stories about the institute. Washington gave his most important speech in 1895 to a mostly white audience at the Cotton States and International Exhibition, which became known as his "Atlanta Address." Washington was concerned that whites might turn to European immigrants for cheap labor and stop employing African-Americans. He was ready to accommodate white bigotry in return for patronage:

> To those of the white race who look to the incoming of those of foreign birth and strange tongue and habits for the prosperity of the South, were I permitted, I would repeat what I say to my own race, "Cast down your bucket where you are." Cast it down among the eight millions of Negroes whose habits you know, whose fidelity and love you have tested in days when to have proved treacherous meant the ruin of your firesides. Cast down your bucket among these people who

have, without strikes and labor wars, tilled your fields, cleared your forests, built your railroads and cities, and brought forth treasures from the bowels of the earth, and helped make possible this magnificent representation of the progress of the South. Casting down your bucket among my people, helping and encouraging them as you are doing on these grounds, and to education of head, hand, and heart, you will find that they will buy your surplus land, make blossom the waste places in your fields, and run your factories. While doing this, you can be sure in the future, as in the past, that you and your families will be surrounded by the most patient, faithful, law-abiding, and un-resentful people that the world has seen.

The wisest among my race understand that the agitation of questions of social equality is the extremist folly, and that progress in the enjoyment of all the privileges that will come to us must be the result of severe and constant struggle rather than of artificial forcing. No race that has anything to contribute to the markets of the world is long in any degree ostracized. It is important and right that all privileges of the law be ours, but it is vastly more important that we be prepared for the exercises of these privileges. The opportunity to earn a dollar in a factory just now is worth infinitely more than the opportunity to spend a dollar in an opera house.[29]

Washington's speech was the public affirmation of an informal deal known as the Atlanta Compromise, which he and other black leaders had reached with the white elite attending the exhibition. African-Americans would submit to white political rule and not seek the vote, equal rights, or integration. In return, they expected southern whites to guarantee due process of law and a public education. Washington was convinced that only by co-opting Southern moderates could African-Americans expect to succeed, and he was ready to delay the fight against racism to concentrate on literacy and self-sufficiency. Not all blacks agreed, and many continued the civil rights struggle. But Washington's fame and influence persuaded many African-Americans to back his cause, and the white community embraced the Atlanta Compromise, even if they didn't plan to honor the deal. The following year, the U.S. Supreme Court heard arguments in *Plessy v. Ferguson*. The case originated with lawmakers in Louisiana who passed a law requiring railroads to provide separate cars for blacks and whites. A civil rights group in New Orleans called the Comité des Citoyens, or the Citizens Committee, convinced Homer Plessy to buy a first-class ticket and take a seat in the whites-only car. The committee had made arrangements ahead of time with the railway, which didn't want to accommodate the new law, and it hired a detective with arrest powers to charge Plessy with violating the Separate Car Act. When Plessy appeared in court, attorneys for the committee immediately argued that the Louisiana law violated the Constitution's equal-protection rights in the Thirteenth and Fourteenth amendments. The court rejected the arguments, fined Plessy twenty-five dollars, and the case began its journey to the Supreme Court.

The Supreme Court justices, by a 7–1 majority, rejected Plessy's arguments that the separate accommodation discriminated against him. Justice Henry Billings Brown wrote that separating the races was simple public policy and that, since the railroad supplied both white and black rail cars, asking members of different races to ride separately was nondiscriminatory. Brown's ruling became the "separate but equal" doctrine, which would condone racial segregation for the next fifty-eight years. Justice John Marshall Harlan wrote the sole, scathing dissent, calling the ruling a violation of the Fourteenth Amendment. He had long condemned the violence of the Ku Klux Klan and similar groups, and Harlan found the law utterly ridiculous because it discriminated only against blacks, not other minorities. In his dissenting opinion, he argued the policy would allow whites to ride in the same rail cars as Chinese, a race many considered equally inferior.[30]

The *Plessy* decision opened the door for state legislatures across the South to pass countless segregation laws, as long as separate facilities existed. Lawmakers gave little concern to whether they were truly equal. The Texas legislature created a second black college as quickly as they banned African-Americans from attending the state's best public universities. They just didn't fund construction of the second black college.[31]

COMPLETE DISREGARD

Texas's leadership became increasingly bold about doing whatever it wanted regarding African-Americans. The publisher of the *Marlin Democrat*, J. M. Kennedy, complained in an editorial about someone stealing a ballot box from the African-American community of Sutton during an election in 1897. The loss of black votes guaranteed that a white Confederate veteran, Col. W. R. Blackburn, won a state house of representatives seat over the African-American candidate, Alexander Asberry. Kennedy was shocked that no one else in Falls County seemed to care.[32]

A stolen ballot box, though, was nothing compared to what happened in other Texas towns. Two white teenage boys in Leonard, 140 miles northeast of Marlin, went to a black church on Sunday, August 15, 1897, and began acting up. Services were under way, and several black men told the boys to go away, but they refused. One black man called one of the white boys "a very vile epithet." When the white boys tried "to resent it," a fight broke out, leaving one of the boys, Earl Meadows, badly injured. Constable J. H. Albright arrested a black man for the assault and sent him to the next county to keep him from being lynched. The boy died that night. The *Dallas Morning News* quoted Albright's description of what happened next:

> At first a few gathered in knots and discussed the matter, and in the course of conversations the remarks were made that they, meaning the white people, clean the town of the negroes. This was carried to the negroes, who began to leave the neighborhood in a hurry. We have learned here that a number went to Bonham (the county seat) and reported the matter to the authorities there.
>
> Sometime last night a note was dropped in the front yard of Mike Yeager, a negro. It does not have anybody's name signed to it and it reads as follows: "To the negroes of Leonard: You must leave this place; don't let the sun set on you in Leonard tomorrow. This means all of you."
>
> This gave the negroes another great scare and they have left hurriedly today. Only a few are left in town now.[33]

The next day, the *Dallas Morning News* reporter confirmed that all of the African-Americans had left Leonard except for one of mixed race, whom whites called, pejoratively, a "Guinea negro":

> The small hours came and grew larger until the sun came up, but it shone on no dusky faces, and today with the exception of John Browning, the village "Guinea negro," not one has been seen on the streets.
>
> "Old Uncle John" has come and gone at will: the children have listened to his bear stories, the boys around the grocery stores have not forgotten to give him a slice of watermelon just as usual; he has shown the same inclination to "argify 'ligion," [argue about religion] in fact he has the freedom of the town. He knows that Mike Yeager got a warning and that it said, "This means all of you," but Uncle John prides himself on being an "ole time niggah," and says it didn't include him.[34]

The news reports from Leonard spread across the state and the nation. Newspapers condemned the residents and the constable for the ethnic cleansing. One resident of Leonard wrote a letter to the *Dallas Morning News,* complaining about the stories describing the incident. J. A. Thomas claimed that "there was no real threat of violence" against the African-Americans living there, and said that the white residents only wanted justice and the black community was responsible for the boy's death. In the *Marlin Democrat,* Kennedy called those responsible by their proper name:

> This act of the Ku Klux shows that community to be possessed of a gang of hoodlums that would disgrace the most disreputable community in Texas. It is an everlasting shame to Texas that such people reside within her limits. This is a free country and every person, no matter how humble has a right to live here.[35]

Kennedy's tirade against the racial injustice in Leonard was just the beginning of a fifty-year career campaigning for equal rights as the publisher of the Marlin paper. But the fiery Irish-American usually found himself in the minority among his fellow newspapermen, who more frequently supported the white mobs, most of whom were customers.

The government's inaction in Leonard sent a clear message to whites across the state and, the following week, whites distributed leaflets in Mineral Wells, High Island, Cleburne, and several other Texas towns, ordering all the African-Americans out. They all left.

LEAVING THE PLANTATION

R. E. L. graduated from Sam Houston Normal Institute on June 10, 1886, and returned to Tomlinson Hill with a teacher's certificate of the first rank. His brothers had the farm under control, and Eldridge was planning his marriage to Ella Louise Landrum. Ella was the little sister of Lizzie Landrum, who had married Gus. Double in-laws were not uncommon in small towns during the nineteenth century.[36]

R. E. L. got a job teaching at the Busby School, a white school near Little Deer Creek, not far from Tomlinson Hill. He eventually became chief pedagogue.[37] He taught English, using the *Blue Back Speller,* and the school held Friday-afternoon spelling bees.[38] A former student described what school was like in that era:

> During recess periods we played tag, wolf-over-the-river, stealing chips and mumble peg. We had no school band, but did have a little organ which had to be pumped by hand that we used for our exercises in the rooms. It was moved from room to room. I played for singing hymns and marching. Bessie Owens and Mrs. Tom Clampet, wife of a local attorney, also played for the school—had no Parent Teacher Association in those days—the girls wore hats and sunbonnets to keep their white and fair skin—students took buckets and baskets filled with buttered biscuits, boiled eggs, fruits and other goodies. Students started at nine in the morning and closed at four in the afternoon—hour for lunch and two recesses of 15 minutes—teachers applied the "hickory" and required stay-ins after school as

punishment for misbehaving—usually a few "tough bullies" in schools—usually conquered by a razor strap.[39]

R.E.L. taught for five years before the area's white children started attending a new, larger school. He moved to Marlin, where he got a job as a deputy county clerk and spent his days recording deeds and marriages. R.E.L. lost another brother on April 29, 1888, when James died suddenly at the age of forty-five, leaving his forty-three-year-old wife, Emma, a widow with four children, who ranged in age from thirteen to nineteen.[40] Emma remained on the Hill, and later that year her eldest son, William, married Harriet People, the daughter of a Confederate veteran from Arkansas. The couple lived with Emma until William and Harriet could build a home of their own nearby.[41]

Down the hill in Cedar Valley, Milo Tomlinson's son, Peter, celebrated the birth of his seventh child. In 1895, his wife, Josie, gave birth to Vincent in the family's two-room cabin. Peter's children attended Tomlinson Negro School, and the white Tomlinsons and Stallworths continued to serve as patrons. An African-American teacher named Annie Hodges ran the school in 1897. A school report in the *Marlin Democrat* said, "The patrons are taking a great deal of interest in the school and where we find cooperative patrons we will always find a good school. Attendance was good, very little tardiness."[42]

In 1891, R.E.L. began wooing Bettie Etheridge, one of William Etheridge's twin daughters. Etheridge, the old Unionist, had just finished a term in the Texas house of representatives and taken over the county prison camp, where he leased black prisoners to local farmers. Whatever political differences the Tomlinsons and Etheridges may have had before the war did not carry over to their children. R.E.L. was thirty years old, but that didn't matter to twenty-three-year-old Bettie. The two went on double dates with Bettie's twin sister, Billah, and R.E.L.'s cousin, Frank Stallworth. Frank had also moved to Marlin to work at his father's shop with his brother, the Marlin postmaster. On December 23, R.E.L. and Bettie, as well as Frank and Billah, married on Tomlinson Hill:

The double wedding of R. E. L. Tomlinson and Frank M. Stallworth to the popular Bettie and Billah Etheridge twins on December 23, 1891 was the social event of the season. Old Beulah Church was packed with family from all over the county to witness the nuptial ceremony performed by the popular Baptist preacher Rev. J. R. M. N. Touchstone. F. M. Boyd, Sanford Tomlinson, Mary Liza Tomlinson, Lena Etheridge stood with the two couples. Following the wedding, an old fashioned In-fare and reception was enjoyed by the guests. Tables groaned under the weight of fried and baked chicken and all of the trimmings. The festivities even followed the two couples to Marlin, where they made their home.[43]

After Frank won election as city marshal, R.E.L. decided to enter politics as well and won election as Falls County clerk in 1892, serving one, two-year term. Afterward, he returned to teaching and began selling real estate in addition to helping manage the family farm. R.E.L. joined the Masonic Temple and became a deacon in the First Baptist Church, helping the Reverend Touchstone build a new chapel in downtown Marlin. R.E.L. taught Sunday school, and Bettie joined the church's women's auxiliary.[44]

Marlin was thriving, too, so much so that in 1890 the editor of the *Marlin Ball* released a special edition on October 23 for the ten thousand people living in Falls County. Thomas Oltorf wrote the opening article, welcoming all of the men moving to Marlin, "whether he served under the Star Spangled Banner or followed the Bonnie Blue Flag" carried by Texas troops in the Civil War. He said the special edition was to celebrate Marlin's businessmen and farmers because he felt "a just and pardonable pride in their marvelous growth and general prosperity."

Marlin's rapid growth meant that water was in short supply. The nearest surface water was a small creek that ran into the Brazos River six miles away. In 1891, the Marlin city council issued $25,000 in bonds to drill an artesian well that could supply the entire town with fresh water.[45] The contractor drilled to two thousand feet and struck nothing, so in 1892, the council asked him to drill to three thousand feet.

On the way down, the city struck hot mineral water, which stank of sulfur and, while drinkable, tasted sour. The water gushed to the surface, but residents demanded sweet water. So the city council decided to drill deeper, until on March 31, 1893, the city ran out of money. That summer, they asked the contractor to keep drilling deeper, running up $4,125 in debt. The contractor got down to 3,350 feet, where he broke the drill bit and couldn't continue drilling.[46] Marlinites pledged to pay the city's debt and convinced the contractor and the council to develop the mineral-water well. The council ordered a network of pipes throughout the city so at least the fire department could use it, thereby driving down insurance rates.[47]

The council tried to sell the mineral water and built a public bathhouse. They sprinkled streets to keep dust down and offered the mineral water at a lower price than fresh water. But there was still more mineral water than demand required and the excess ran down a gulley out of town.[48] Residents who used the water, though, noticed it had strange qualities. Ill People and animals who bathed in the water benefited from its properties, and their chronic skin problems healed. Those who drank the water claimed to feel healthier. A black man bathed his mangy dog in the gulley, and the dog was cured. One day a man from Houston with a horrible skin disease passed through town, and Marlinites got an empty barrel and started soaking the man daily. In six weeks, he was cured.[49]

Local doctors had read about healing waters in other places and ran tests on the Marlin water. They determined the mineral content was curative for both internal and external diseases, mostly bacterial problems. Several doctors and businessmen formed the Marlin Natatorium Company and built a bathhouse in 1895. That company transformed into the Marlin Sanitorium Company and began offering a course of healing baths for a fee. Local businessmen, including J. M. Kennedy, organized the Marlin Commercial Club to pool their money and buy national advertising promoting Marlin as a health resort. The club convinced the county commissioners to improve the road between Marlin and Waco and build a new bridge over the Brazos at Tomlinson Hill to attract customers.[50]

Bizarre medical treatments, snake oils, and quackery ran rampant in the 1890s. The vast majority of ads in the *Marlin Democrat* were testimonials for some sort of mail-order remedy. Before the discovery of penicillin in 1928, there was no treatment for bacterial infections, but the sulfur in hot mineral wells was a natural antibiotic.[51]

Once word got out, Marlin's growth went into overdrive. By September 1896, there were between fifty and one hundred visitors a day seeking "the cure," and the existing bathhouses and hotels couldn't meet the demand. Local investors built more baths and hotels. Gus Welle won a license from the city to build the county's first electric power plant and string transmission lines throughout the city. On January 9, 1897, the owner of the Marlin Opera House turned on electric lights for the first time, replacing the oil lamps he'd used for years. A few weeks later, his troupe performed *Faust* for an audience that included many tourists who had come to town for the waters.[52]

Economic growth was always Marlin's priority. Frank Stallworth's uncle, Dosh Stallworth, repainted the interior of his general store and fitted it with oak-finished cigar cases and fixtures, promising that his store would be "the very latest and most up-to-datest place in this progressive burg."[53]

Ever the contrarian, Kennedy noted that while Marlin progressed, Texas was still a backwater: "The per capita (GDP) in Massachusetts is $264, while that of Texas is $8. We need factories." Kennedy also reported in the same issue that the mayor fined three ladies with excessive makeup one dollar each for "vagrancy," a sign of Marlin's prosperity.

LEST WE FORGET

As Marlin grew and filled with enterprising businesspeople, Civil War veterans reached middle age and worried about their legacy. All of the Tomlinsons who had fought in the war had died by 1897, and the majority of Texans were too young to remember the war. The old veterans saw their numbers dwindling and worried that no one cared anymore about their sacrifice for the Confederacy. Frank Stallworth's father, Nick Stallworth III, was the adjutant of the United Confederate Veterans' group in Marlin, Will Lang Camp No. 299. He wrote a letter for the March 4 edition of the *Marlin Democrat*, calling on veterans to start showing up for meetings, to rally in memory of their dead comrades, and to remind Falls County residents of their sacrifices.

UCV members elected Stallworth to represent them at a national convention and declared the last Tuesday of April as "Decoration Day of the Camp," when they invited students from white schools to march with them through downtown to honor the lost cause of the Confederacy. At their August 29 meeting, the Marlin UCV decided public school history books also needed to reflect their version of the "War of Northern Aggression":

> We offer no apology for the interest we now take in this matter, nor for the zeal with which we expect to urge this change. We have been patient under the misrepresentation, and often slander, that has been taught our children in the public schools. In the name of our dead comrades, in the name of those who survive, we demand that the truth be taught.[54]

African-Americans also remembered the Civil War, but for entirely different reasons. Black leaders organized a club in 1896 to plan Juneteenth celebrations. In the March 18, 1897, edition of the *Marlin Democrat*, they called on the black community to organize that year's celebration. The paper reported that the celebration went off well:

> Emancipation Day was observed in Marlin by the colored citizens of the city and vicinity.
>
> The day was ushered in by the booming of anvils. About 11 o'clock the procession passed through the principal streets to the fairgrounds where the celebration was held.
>
> A feature of the parade was a float upon which a miniature cotton field was represented. In the field were a number of darkies dancing and playing the banjo. The music for the occasion was furnished by a Waco band.

The speakers of the day were Rev. S. W. R. Cole, Marlin; Prof. I. M. Burgen, president of Paul Quinn College, Waco; Prof. Blackshear of the Prairie View Normal.

The colored citizens deported themselves with dignity befitting the occasion. There were no disturbances during the day and everything passed off pleasantly for those celebrating the anniversary of their freedom.[55]

African-Americans in Marlin still hold a parade on Juneteenth and offer special sermons to mark the day. On the first Juneteenth after Barack Obama's election, one family built a float with a miniature cotton field and wooden shanty. In place of a banjo player, they placed an Obama poster and a banner that read FROM THE OUTHOUSE TO THE WHITE HOUSE.

Across the South in the 1890s, freedmen watched both Union and Confederate veterans organize social groups that transformed into political action committees. Veterans lobbied Congress to give them and their widows pension benefits. As with all wars, many of the veterans returned home handicapped, while others developed physical and psychological problems later in life. The former slaves, who had spent much of their lives physically abused, also demanded a pension for their years in slavery. Specifically, they wanted the forty acres and a mule that many thought the government should have given them at emancipation. While sympathetic whites in Congress introduced bills to provide some compensation, the measures never passed. That didn't stop white con men from visiting black families and, for a small fee, certifying them as former slaves so they would qualify for a pension that didn't exist.[56]

TWELVE

If taking from the hands of an officer in the dark hours of night a helpless prisoner and swinging him to limb is not murder in the coldest, bloodiest, and most brutal form then the law is a travesty and Holy Writ a mockery.

—J. M. Kennedy

When most adult men were away during the Civil War, crime was rampant in Texas, and vigilantes routinely hanged murderers and thieves. Most of the victims were white, and the mobs wanted speedy justice for their communities. Lawmen rarely made any effort to punish those responsible, or even to record the lynchings. While most went unreported, a few small newspapers recorded these slayings and the editors shared their stories on the Associated Press telegraph wire with larger newspapers in Galveston, San Antonio, and other cities. Much of the information about Texas lynchings comes from these newspaper reports.

Almost all of the victims of reported lynchings before 1865 in Central Texas were white. This is not to say that people did not kill African-Americans before emancipation; they just didn't make it public. While slaveholders illegally killed some of their workers, such slayings were not the result of mob justice. There was also a taboo against killing another man's slave, because it was the equivalent of stealing another white man's property.[1]

The amount of information known about lynching in a community also depended on the editor of the local paper. Before J. M. Kennedy began publishing the *Marlin Democrat* in 1890, there were no reports of lynchings in Falls County, while newspapers in neighboring counties reported dozens of slayings.[2] Thomas Oltorf, publisher of the *Marlin Ball,* did not report on vigilantism in Falls County, and his paper's silence certainly implies that the Marlin mayor's son was more interested in boosting the county's image than committing journalism.

Kennedy, on the other hand, moved to Marlin from neighboring Limestone County with a mission to start an aggressive newspaper. He and his brother had started the *Mexia Democrat* and wanted to expand their business.[3] The Kennedys joined the Associated Press news agency, which meant they received news from across the country via telegraph, and in return, they transmitted their stories to other newspapers. Both the *Waco Daily News* and the *Dallas Morning News* were also members of the AP and printed news from Marlin.

The first newspaper report of a lynching of a black person in Falls County came on January 2, 1891. The attack took place in the Lang community, about two miles from Tomlinson Hill. The *Dallas Morning News* carried two accounts from different newspapers:

Two o'clock yesterday afternoon Charles Beall, a negro 20 years of age, entered the residence of Mr. James Fisher, a farmer near Lang, Falls County, and finding Mrs. Fisher alone subjected her to the vilest indignities and cruelly broke her skull with a hammer. He then looted the house and left, taking away a small sum of money and a few articles of value.

Neighbors called and found Mrs. Fisher still alive. She rallied enough to tell her story and describe the assailant. A party of young men well armed and mounted on fleet horses took the trail and at 3 o'clock this morning they had the negro captive. He was caught not far from Cameron, Milam County.

The lynchers took him to the residence of the victim, who identified him, upon which he confessed. After this Beall got the shortest shrift. He was taken to a grove and allowed time to pray, after which a three-quarter inch manila rope was noosed to his neck and he was dragged to a tree and hoisted to a bough upon which he dangled until this morning, when an inquest was held by Justice Hedrick of Lott. The verdict was hanged until dead by unknown parties.

Mrs. Fisher was alive at noon, but there was no hope of recovery. Her skull is shivered and a portion of the brain was spilled upon the floor. After striking the lady with the hammer the negro chopped off part of her cheek and one ear with a hatchet. Mr. Fisher was absent at a neighbor's helping to build a house, and the little children were at school.

Charles Beall, the negro, was raised by Mr. Fisher, and was a trusted servant in the household.[4]

The judge's conclusion that the perpetrators of the lynching could not be identified points to the conspiracy of silence that often surrounds mob violence. Reporting breaking news can be difficult, since witnesses and authorities often twist the truth to appease the community. This later account of the lynching included further details:

Mrs. Joseph Fisher, the victim of the outrage at Lang, Falls County, last Wednesday, rallied yesterday and gave the full recital of the assault made upon her. She stated that Squire Beall and his son, Charles, the latter being the negro lynched the next day, Monk Johnson and William Paul, four negroes, all assaulted her in turn. Afterward they beat her with a hatchet, a coupling pin and a hammer. She became insensible under the blows. One of her ears was cut off and her skull broken. She was also beat over the body.

When the lady told her story Sheriff John Ward and Constable Dick Tucker were present with a squad of deputies. They immediately seized the negroes and started with them for Marlin, ten miles distant. Sheriff Ward, with one of the negroes, had no difficulty, but Constable Tucker with the other was closely pursued by lynchers that he took to the chaparral and arrived with the prisoner safe.

It will be remembered that Squire Beall, the old man, was removed to Marlin the day his son was lynched.

This morning more mounted and well-armed men passed through

Lott, headed for Marlin obviously bent upon storming the jail and lynching the three negroes.

A dispatch from Marlin says Sheriff Ward put all three on the [rail]cars and sent them to Galveston for safekeeping so that the lynchers will be baffled after all.

When the house of Squire Beall, the old man, was searched his shirt was found soaked in blood, rolled up and hid in a crevice in the wall.

A startling feature in the case is that Monk Johnson and William Paul are said to have encouraged the lynching of their confederate Charles Beall. Yesterday they vociferously proclaimed their own innocence to Sheriff Ward and Constable Tucker and with equal vehemence accused old Squire Beall of participation.[5]

That report, too, had errors. The sheriff put only Squire Beall on the train to Galveston. He sent the other two to the McLennan County Jail in Waco. The jail there was made of stone and brick, with an iron cage to hold prisoners. McLennan County's sheriff, Dan Ford, doubled the guard, fully expecting a lynch party to lay siege. Ward and his deputies patrolled the roads to Waco the night of January 4 to head them off.[6] Based on the numbers and the geography, some of the Tomlinson men likely joined the mob.

All of the suspects had connections to Tomlinson Hill. Peter Tomlinson had married Josephine Beall in 1877, and she was related to Squire Beall. William Paul's family was one of the largest in China Grove, and the Johnsons had worked for the Tomlinsons since emancipation, though Monk Johnson's family lived on the Fisher farm at the time.[7] The attack, the lynching, and the attempt to lynch the other suspects angered the residents of China Grove, which was less than a mile from the Fisher farm. The lynching mobilized the freedmen:

Last night the negroes along the Pond creek gathered near the Lang schoolhouse and held some sort of ghost dance. They built a big fire and were seen brandishing old cap and ball shot guns and sawed-off army muskets. They adopted a resolution that the four negroes are innocent or justifiable and that Charles Beall was infamously murdered by the whites. While they were in their pow-wow, the farmers came upon them and they fled.

RIDDLED WITH BUCKSHOT

A Chilton correspondent states that Mr. George Taylor, a young farmer who had been accused by the negroes of leading the lynchers in the hanging of Charles Beall last Thursday, was riddled with buckshot last night at a late hour just as he entered his door.

"This," says the correspondent, "aroused the farmers and ranchmen to the highest pitch, and they gathered in Lott and Lang by hundreds. The three negro leaders fled and a posse is pursuing them, believing they shot young Taylor. The negroes at Cameron, a town south of Lang, met and appointed a committee to go to Lang and investigate the lynching of Charles Beall. The committee arrived near Lang and saw a troop of longhaired Texans galloping toward them, and abandoning their ponies, they took to the chaparral. They were caught and after an explanation were warned not to return to the vicinity anymore.[8]

Governor Lawrence Sullivan Ross, known as "Sul," cabled the McLennan County sheriff and recommended that he send Paul and Johnson to the capital for safekeeping at the Travis County Jail. Ford was more than happy to oblige and he placed them on a railcar for Austin without the lynch mob noticing.[9] Taylor later died of his wounds.

The mob's attempts to intimidate the black community clearly were not working. The fact that African-Americans armed themselves, demanded justice, and lynched a white man themselves proves they were prepared to defend their freedom colonies from white terror.

No action was ever taken against the lynch mob. Texas law enforcement and politicians knew their legal responsibilities to prevent lynching, but they also knew that the mob had the support of the white public.

Editors, meanwhile, needed to sell newspapers, and the 1890s saw the rise of yellow journalism. Editors knew reports of black men "committing outrages" against white women drove sales. These stories almost always assumed the black man's guilt, cited white eyewitnesses, and frequently ended with a white mob lynching the black suspect. Between three hundred and five hundred black Texans were lynched in the late nineteenth century. Most cases involved the murder or rape of a white person.[10]

Between 1860 and 1929, there were sixty-four lynchings in the counties surrounding Marlin. In twenty-two cases, the underlying crime was unknown. But of the forty-two cases where the motive was clear, seventeen involved a white woman and fifteen lynchings were in response to murders. Most of those lynchings took place in the 1890s.[11]

White Texas men during that time grew up on their fathers' romanticized stories of forming posses to hunt down and kill criminal gangs or Indian raiders. They fundamentally believed the myths about southern chivalry and the South's noble fight for "the Cause" during the Civil War. Secret societies became popular, each offering its own mystical purpose. Marlin had a Masonic Temple and chapters of the Knights of Honor, Knights of Pythias, and the Ancient Order of United Workmen. Texas society taught men to admire those who were violent and self-sufficient, so when young men found an excuse to kill, they got "excited," to use the newspapers' parlance, and took action, believing they were following in their fathers' footsteps.

There is also no doubt that some victims of mob violence were probably guilty, and their crimes held symbolism. When one member of a community rapes a member of another, the act takes on a special significance, not only for the victim but also for the community. Rapists subjugate and terrorize their victims, taking away their sense of security and autonomy. Warriors throughout the ages have marked their victories by raping the wives, mothers, sisters, and daughters of their enemies. Rape is a profound demonstration of power, and the ultimate biological conquest is to spread your DNA and to dilute your enemy's.

In an opinion piece about lynching on March 1, 1893, the *Dallas Morning News* recognized that rape elicited a very different response based on the perpetrator's race. The editors made a perversely racist argument for lynching white rapists, not blacks:

> Why not lynch with despairing regularity all white ravishers? Why not indeed? Why should it be the rare exception and not the rule for white violators of women and children to undergo mob execution? If this crime is beyond the law and above the law when perpetrated by a negro is it not made, if possible, more horrible when perpetrated by a white man?[12]

In the South, a black man raping a white woman eroded the white man's perceived superiority and dominance in a place where whites and blacks lived in close to equal numbers. So white Texans made swift and unequivocal punishment of African-Americans who broke this taboo their highest priority. Some reasoned the more horrible and terrifying the execution, the greater its deterrent powers.[13]

THE DANGER OF BACK TALK

Sex and violence were not the only things that could get an African-American in trouble; merely standing up to a white man could end in death. One black man's defiance in 1895 ended with what the *Dallas Morning News* depicted as the first terrorist bombing in Texas history.

Abe Phillips was a leader in the black community in northern Falls County, had a reputation for fearlessness, and feuded with the Arnold family, whites living on a neighboring farm. Abe was the only sharecropper who lived in the area; the rest of the African-Americans worked as hired hands. Phil Arnold had taken in two black orphans under the apprenticeship law and expected them to work in return for room and board. But the children kept running away and showing up at Abe's house, asking for protection. When Phil and his brother Ed Arnold confronted Abe and his stepson Wesley Bragg and demanded they turn over the children on April 17, 1895, the men drew their guns.[14] Abe fired the first shot at Phil Arnold and missed. Phil returned fire and killed Abe instantly. Bragg then shot Phil in the back with a shotgun, fatally wounding him. Ed Arnold then shot and wounded Bragg, whom the sheriff arrested.[15]

A jury acquitted Bragg in Phil Arnold's death because he acted in self-defense. That led some white neighbors to decide they needed to make an example of the entire Phillips family. White men harassed the family over the next three months, poisoning their livestock and shooting randomly at their property, trying to convince them to flee. But the Phillips family kept on farming. The intimidation escalated on July 18, when a child living in the house died, apparently from eating poisoned meat from the family's smokehouse.[16]

In the early hours of July 20, 1895, a group of men crept up to the Phillips home, twenty miles north of Marlin. The black family lived in a cottage surrounded by elm trees, a corncrib, and the smokehouse. The cottage was a one-room log cabin, with three lean-to sheds built along the outer walls and a porch on the front. On that night, Abe Phillips's widow, Fannie, was asleep inside the sixteen-by-eighteen-foot main room with her three sons and a granddaughter. Fannie's brother, Ben Harrison, and a hired laborer named Kid Taylor were sleeping in the shed on the west side of the cabin. Fannie's son-in-law Henry Hill, his wife, and their infant lived in the east lean-to.[17]

That night, someone crawled under the cabin, which was built on stone blocks, and planted fifteen pounds of dynamite under the kitchen floor. At 2:00 A.M., the attackers triggered the blast. A *Dallas Morning News* reporter described the scene:

> Tourists arrive and gaze at the hole in the ground and the elm trees, the boughs of which are hanging with the odds and ends of a negro household, the thrifty accumulations of fifty years, which on that sad morning went off in a blast and littered a farm of 600 acres as evenly distributed as if the successful design was to distribute the fragments as a means of fertilizing crops. The house stood on blocks and one of the blocks flew with the force of a cannon ball in a horizontal line nearly a mile making a tunnel through the cotton plants in its flight. The wheels of the sewing machine flew in all directions, one of the larger wheels descending like a [ring] on a corn stalk, 300 yards away.

Henry Hill's wife owned an organ and one of the keys of this instrument was found a mile down the county road. . . . In Mart, the nearest town, it shook the houses and some of the merchants donned their clothes in haste and rushed to their stores thinking their safes had been cracked by burglars. Others thereabouts thought it was an earthquake.

[When rescuers arrived] they found an appalling spectacle. In the light of the early morning, Henry Hill's wife was wandering around with the baby in her arms, partly singed. Kid Taylor, the hired hand, was leaning against the crib enclosure bleeding and inarticulate, and the corpses of Fanny Phillips, her three sons and Hannah Williams, her granddaughter, were scattered about the yard wrapped in flames which afforded a horrible light by which the three [rescuers] were able to survey the uncanny environments. They could not immediately rescue the bodies from the flames because of exploding cartridges which went off in successive volleys like musketry. The five-gallon can of oil which occupied the corner in the kitchen had been sprinkled over the bodies and over fragments of bedding and wardrobing.[18]

The attack horrified both the white and African-American communities. Murdering an African-American following a crime was one thing, but blowing up a home filled with women and children was going too far. Black leaders organized a strike in the cotton fields, demanding the sheriff track down and prosecute the perpetrators.[19] To appease their angry laborers, on whom they depended just as cotton picking was set to begin, whites held public meetings, denouncing the attack and pledging to help the survivors. Between the governor and the black and white communities, they offered a fifteen-hundred-dollar reward for information that would lead to the arrest and conviction of those responsible. The people of Mart also passed a resolution condemning the attacks and promising an investigation.[20]

The *Dallas Morning News* reported that dozens of private detectives combed through the blast site and tried to find evidence that would lead to those responsible. But the bombers were never caught. And as shocking as the bombing was, the lynchings in Falls County did not stop. There was a rash of vigilantism in the summer of 1897, and one case turned the whole idea of chivalric murder on its head.

AN INTOLERABLE INDIGNITY

Freedman Columbus Fendrick lived in a log cabin in western Falls County with his wife, Hattie, and worked for Robert H. Boyd, a white cotton farmer who owned land six miles from Tomlinson Hill. When Fendrick came home from the fields on April 25, 1897, his wife told him that Boyd had come looking for him. Finding the young five-foot, eighty-five-pound woman alone, Boyd had asked her for sex in return for money, which she had rejected.[21]

Fendrick sat at the dinner table, staring silently at his food. Hattie grew nervous as she watched her husband become more and more angry. Eventually, Fendrick went to his friend Abe Sanders and asked if he had any cartridges for a Winchester rifle. Sanders said he didn't know where they were, but Sanders's uncle, Arthur O'Neal, had a few. The three men then went to Boyd's house.[22]

Standing out front, Fendrick called Boyd outside. He told Boyd what Hattie had told him about the incident and wanted to know why Boyd had insulted his wife. Boyd threw his hand behind him in a threatening manner and said, "I will fix you, you." Fendrick pulled the rifle's trigger, shooting Boyd in the stomach. Boyd's wife, Ruth, ran out of the house and saw the three black men running away. Boyd survived about two hours, long enough to tell Ruth that Fendrick was the shooter, and that he had accused Boyd of propositioning Hattie.[23]

Fendrick ran about three miles to the village of Travis, where he stopped to sleep. In the morning, Fendrick turned himself in to a constable and asked for protection. The constable testified that another officer warned Fendrick that he didn't have to say anything, but Fendrick immediately confessed.[24]

The Falls County sheriff, D. R. Emerson, put Fendrick on a train to Waco for safekeeping and four days later arrested Sanders and O'Neal as accomplices. When the white men of western Falls County heard the suspects were in custody, two hundred men formed a lynch mob on Tomlinson Hill:

> Sheriff Emerson noticed a number of men, whose homes are in the vicinity of the scene of the murder, lounging about town that afternoon and became suspicious of their actions. Advices were received later to the effect that the main body was marching on Marlin. City Marshal Coleman ordered the fire alarm turned on about 9:30 o'clock and the hideous screams of the whistle soon had the entire population of Marlin aroused.
>
> Within a remarkably short space of time the public square was thronged with men. The prisoners had been taken from the jail to the third story of the courthouse. About 10:30 they were taken to the depot by Sheriff Emerson and Marshal Coleman and taken to Bremond and upon arriving in Bremond they were put into a box car by officers and brought back through Marlin to Waco.
>
> The Democrat has it from good authority that no body of men were nearer Marlin than Beulah Church six miles from Marlin, where it is reported about two hundred armed men assembled to hang the negroes previously referred to. However they returned to their respective homes as soon as a courier carried the news that the prisoners were gone.[25]

All three men returned to Marlin weeks later to face trial individually. Abe Sanders was released for lack of evidence. O'Neal was sentenced to ninety-nine years in prison for supplying the ammunition. After twenty-four hours of deliberation, the jury sentenced Fendrick to life in prison. Onlookers began shouting for a lynching.[26] Attorneys for both men appealed the convictions, without success, and the men went to prison.

If a black man had propositioned a white woman, there is no doubt a lynch mob would have delivered swift punishment. In the twisted world of Texas justice, society was ready to forgive any husband for defending the honor of his wife, unless that man was black. This double standard would be put to the test in Falls County only a few weeks later.

Early on the morning of May 12, 1897, seventeen-year-old Lillie Coates awoke to a hand on her shoulder and a man standing over her bed. The Coates family lived about thirteen miles southeast of Tomlinson Hill. Lillie screamed, and her parents tried to enter the room, but the door was locked. The mother ran onto the porch to get to her daughter's window and saw an African-American man running away. Lillie said she saw a black man climb out her bedroom window, while a second man held it open for him. The two men ran in opposite directions, but both mother and daughter said they looked familiar. Rosebud constable Roe Owens went to the black neighborhood and arrested several men the next day.[27]

That afternoon, Owens decided to leave town, and after nightfall a mob formed outside the Rosebud city jail. The deputies and constables on duty tried to move the suspects to Marlin, but they didn't make it. Kennedy wrote in the *Democrat*:

> The dead bodies of the three negroes lay stretched in a row on the floor. It was a gruesome, almost sickening spectacle, one that could not be contemplated with indifference. The first corpse one came to was that of Sabe Stuart, alleged to have been the negro who entered the room and laid hands on the young lady. He was below the average size, about 22 years of age, and he had an intelligent expression. On the side of his neck was a small indention made by the rope. His neck was broken and the muscles were very rigid. He was dressed in a grey undershirt, jeans pants and brogan shoes.
>
> The next of the bodies in the row was that of Berry Williams, a lad of 16 or 17 years old. His neck was also broken and bore the marks of the rope. He is said to have been the negro who held the window while Sabe Stuart entered the room.
>
> The other negro, Dave Cotton, presented a horrifying appearance. The limb on which he was hanged gave way and his neck was not broken. He slowly strangled to death and his features were distorted

as though his agony had been worse than the most awful torture imaginable.

The bodies lay on the floor all day long and were viewed by hundreds of people. About six o'clock they were taken to Wilderville, their late home, for burial.

The men were probably innocent, the lynchings based on a coerced confession:

This alleged confession was secured on Wednesday night, the night before the lynching, from Berry, by coercion. On that night, Berry and his brother Nelson, were taken from the calaboose at Rosebud and conveyed to a pasture two miles southeast of town and each were swung up to a limb for the purpose of forcing a confession.

Nelson, who is older than Berry, stoutly denied any knowledge of the crime, although he was hanged twice by the neck and severely beaten with an inch rope doubled. As Nelson was separated from Berry, no one, except his persecutors, knows what Berry did say in the way of a confession. He stated after being taken back to town, that the men only swung him up once, but also beat him up with a rope. Just what he really did say after being swung up will always remain a mystery unless somebody "peaches."

After it was reported that the confession was made Sabe Stuart and Dave Cotton were re-arrested and again placed in the calaboose.

It is stated that some of the mob were not much in favor of lynching Cotton, as they were not altogether clear as to his connection with the crime, but they were very few.[28]

Kennedy added an editorial in the *Democrat* that week:

From the facts that have so far developed there appears to be no excuse for the lynching of the three negroes, Stuart, Cotton and Williams, near Rosebud Friday morning. There is no excuse for mob law under any circumstances. Every criminal, of whatever nature, should be accorded a fair and impartial hearing in the courts of the land, and whenever he is denied this the Constitution is trampled upon and the majesty of the law set at naught.[29]

The *Democrat*'s editorial criticizing the lynching sparked outrage from the editors of the *Rosebud News,* the paper in the town where the lynching took place, and the *Lott Clarion.* Kennedy was happy to engage these editors in a debate over the merits of lynch law. On May 25, he addressed the question posed by the *Rosebud News*:

> *The News* would like to ask the DEMOCRAT what excuse, if any, would satisfy it for the lynching of the three negroes?—*The Rosebud News.*
>
> Brother Warrock, there is no excuse for mob law under any circumstances. Does the laws of Texas sanction it? Does the constitution endorse it? Does the Book of books excuse it? Does not the law say that he is guilty of murder who willfully takes the life of a human being? Does not the constitution guarantee to all citizens the same protection accorded to every other citizen and does not the Bible, that Law upon which all other laws, say "Thou shalt not commit murder?" Now, if taking from the hands of an officer in the dark hours of night a helpless prisoner and swinging him to limb is not murder in the coldest, bloodiest, and most brutal form then the law is a travesty and Holy Writ a mockery.

Three weeks later, Kennedy replied again when the Lott paper condemned the lynching of a white man in Tyler, Texas:

> *The Lott Clarion* evidently believes that "consistency is the virtue of fools only." It thinks the Rosebud lynching was a Christian act but denounces the Tyler affair as "murder, premeditated and with malice aforethought." The *Clarion* would make a distinction where there is really no difference. If the shooting to death of the white man Bill Jones at Tyler was "murder, premeditated and with malice aforethought" the hanging of the three negroes, Cotton, Stuart and Wil-

liams near Rosebud was triple "murder, premeditated and with malice aforethought" and is the greater crime because three men were murdered instead of one as at Tyler.

WHITECAPPING

The *Marlin Democrat* soon began a campaign to record every incident of vigilante justice, not only lynchings but also whitecapping, where mobs used corporal punishment to keep blacks in line.

White terrorism against blacks came to a quick yet brief halt when in 1896 Judge Samuel R. Scott, the district judge for McLennan and Falls counties, ordered a grand jury to investigate the whitecapping of four men in Hillside, a farm community near Waco. A masked group of white men attacked five African-American farmworkers in the middle of the night, killing one and severely beating the other four before ordering them to leave the county. Scott called it "the worst stain on the fair name of the county," adding that "the men who did the whitecapping were ten times worse than the victims of their wrath." The all-white grand jury became the first in Texas history to indict whites for mob violence against blacks. The jury named ten men, but a yearlong search did not turn up the four black victims to testify, so Scott was forced to drop the charges. But the case sent a clear message that white vigilantes were no longer immune to prosecution.[30]

The white community struggled to maintain a balance between violence and benevolence, much as they had during slavery. Whitecappers tried to strike this balance, targeting black leaders and intimidating the rest of the community. In many ways, whitecapping was a more insidious activity, less spontaneous, and more calculated than lynchings, which normally took place during a bloodthirsty frenzy.

Many would like to believe that those in the mob were uneducated dolts addicted to violence. But in many of the lynchings in Falls County, the mobs were so large that nearly every white adult male must have ridden with the vigilantes or joined the crowd at the kill site. These people were far from ignorant, since more than 80 percent of white Texans could read and write. Marlin had two well-edited newspapers, in which residents read long stories about the massacre of British diplomats in Guinea, an explanation of Islamic jihad, and the role that religion played in the battle for Armenia.

The white people of Falls County were also very religious. There is little doubt Protestant teachings at the time belittled African-Americans, but they also taught benevolence.

There is no way to know for sure that my ancestors rode with the lynch mobs of Falls County or joined the whitecappers in their enforcement of white dominance. But R.E.L.'s obituary described him as part "of a great family of Southerners, with typical devotion to the cause." He and his brothers were respected leaders in their community, and R.E.L. defended lynchings in the oral history he gave to the American Folklore Project in 1936. The degree to which he was guilty of participating in the relentless racial violence in the 1890s will never be clear, but I find it difficult to believe that he and his brothers were not involved. Even if he did nothing, he allowed others to maintain the power and privilege he enjoyed in the community by employing terrorism. And my opinion is not solely that of a twenty-first-century citizen. In August 1897, the editors of the *Belton Reporter* wrote:

> The newspapers fairly reek with the revolting incidents of lynching after lynching. And still, many of our newspapers and prominent citizens attempt to excuse and mitigate this terrible wave of lawlessness which is sweeping over the land by abusing the courts in our country and inveighing against what they term the delay of the law. It is hoped that all who have the good of the country at heart and are sincerely in favor of the enforcement of laws will realize there can be no compromise with mob law, which is nothing more nor less than red handed murder and anarchy.

THIRTEEN

The Brazos has again proved its claim to a treacherous stream. The channels and its currents are constantly shifting. Its caprices are weird, peculiar and tragic.

—*Marlin Democrat*

On June 29, 1899, a massive thunderstorm formed just northwest of Waco and a torrent of rain began falling over the upper Brazos River. The valley was the state's largest agricultural producer, with cotton and corn accounting for most of the crops. Farmers along the river knew it was prone to spring flooding, depositing the soil that makes the valley so fertile. The soft red silt banks easily erode in a heavy rain and the river constantly changes course, creating oxbow lakes along Texas's longest river. R. E. L. was born in a house overlooking the river, and he and his brothers understood its fickle ways better than most. But no one in Falls County was ready for this freakish torrent.

The storm built up over Waco and inched its way down the river toward the Gulf of Mexico, dropping hail on Marlin for five straight days. The National Weather Service reported that an entire summer's worth of rain fell from June 29 to July 15. Meteorologists called the storm one of the most remarkable weather phenomena in the state's history.[1] The river, normally twenty-five yards wide, broke its banks and stretched twelve miles wide along some reaches. At Tomlinson Hill, the water lapped at the family homestead almost a mile away, fifty feet above the normal waterline. On the low-lying east side of the river, the water spread out over five miles, reaching within a few hundred yards of the courthouse in Marlin.[2]

The few crops that survived the hail perished under the floodwaters, leaving many farmers broke, including the white Tomlinsons. African-American tenant farmers lost everything, and farm laborers found themselves without jobs. The floodwaters also drowned thousands of cattle, horses, hogs, and other livestock. Groups from across the state donated money to buy seed for grain and vegetables that could grow in the remaining months of the season, but there was nothing the farmers could do for their cotton and corn.[3]

R. E. L., who still owned a share of Tomlinson Hill, joined dozens of Brazos River farmers in asking the governor to give them a break from paying taxes, at least until they recovered their losses.[4] The governor provided relief, but the weather did not. On April 27, 1900, another thunderstorm dumped a huge amount of rain directly over western Falls County, sending Deer Creek and Pond Creek beyond their banks, with floodwaters rising even higher than the previous year. Deer Creek, the northern boundary of Tomlinson Hill, Perry Creek, to the south, and the Brazos, to the east, all overflowed their banks in a flashflood that turned Tomlinson Hill into an island. Pond Creek, at its closest point to Tomlinson Hill, was six feet higher than during the record-breaking flood of 1899. The rushing water destroyed the steel highway bridge over Deer Creek that connected the Hill to Marlin and washed away the railroad trestle. The floodwaters poured into Peter Tomlinson's shack on Deer Creek, sending the black Tomlinsons scrambling for higher ground.[5]

The devastation of R. E. L.'s cotton crop for a second straight year was more than he could take. He hadn't lived on the Hill since he'd gotten married, and his two older brothers did most of the farming. So he decided to get out of farming all together, sold his brothers his land, and concentrated on brokering real estate.[6]

Despite the challenging weather, the new century held much promise for Marlin businessmen. Hundreds of visitors came by train every week to partake of the mineral water, pumping money into the economy. Marlin was also a rail center, with connections to Austin, Dallas, Houston,

A keepsake photograph from 1862 showing
Sarah Jemima Stallworth Tomlinson holding
her infant son, R. E. L. Tomlinson, in her arms.
Sarah was born in Conecuh County, Alabama,
in 1918 and married James K. Tomlinson in
1843. R. E. L. was her eighth and final child,
born in 1861. Her husband returned from
the Civil War ill, and he died shortly after
Emancipation Day, leaving Sarah to keep the
farm running during Reconstruction.

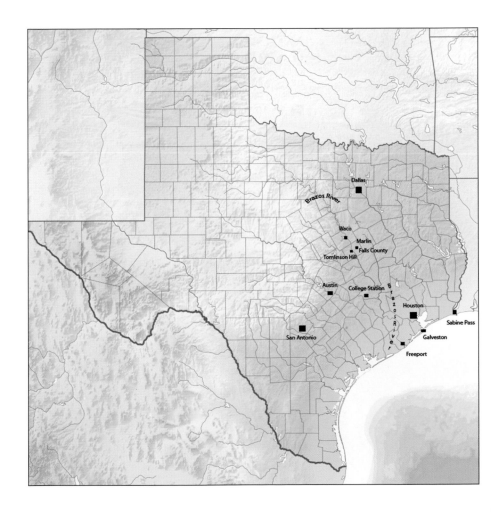

MARLIN, THE "HOT SPRINGS" OF TEXAS
Deepest And Hottest Artesian Well In The World

THE WATER CURES		ANALYSIS OF MARLIN HOT MINERAL WATER
Catarrh, Eczema, Malaria, Constipation Rheumatism. All Blood And Skin Diseases		*By E. Everhart, P. H. D. University of Texas*

Insoluble Matter 1.88
Alumina Sulphate.... 12.20
Magnesium Sulphate, 16.15
Sodium Bicarbonate..11.66
Calcium Sulphate.....3.95
Calcium Carbonate...34.10
i. on Sulphate...........3.02
Pota. sium Sulphate.....80
Sodium Chio 112.39
Sodium Su.'phate....312.32
Total grains per gal.508.47

Free carbonate acid gas per gallon, 360 cubic inches

Temperature of well, 147o Fahrenheit.

For Further Information Address, JOE LEVY, Marlin, Texas

MARLIN HOT WELL.

An advertisement for Marlin's hot mineral water baths printed on the back of an envelope in the early 1900s. The Marlin Chamber of Commerce aggressively marketed the mineral baths around the country, drawing comparisons with some of the most famous healing mineral baths in the world. The baths allowed the Marlin economy to boom and made the town a resort destination in addition to an agricultural hub.

Family photo courtesy of Cynthia Montgomery.

Augustus and Lizzie Landrum Tomlinson stand outside their home in Lott, Texas, circa 1925. Augustus was the son of James K. Tomlinson, the founder of the Tomlinson Hill plantation, and came to Texas from Alabama when he was eleven years old. Lizzie's father was Benjamin Landrum, who also established a slave plantation in western Falls County in the 1850s. Landrum gave Augustus and Lizzie land as a wedding gift, and the two moved off of Tomlinson Hill in the 1870s and built a home in Lott, about ten miles away. Augustus was one of the founding members of the Old Settler's Association and helped build the reunion grounds that now mark Tomlinson Hill.

A postcard from the 1930s of the Arlington Hotel in downtown Marlin. The Arlington hotel was the city's grandest hotel before the Great Depression, with a large ballroom and the ability to accommodate hundreds. But by the 1920s, the hotel was showing its age, so the city council and chamber of commerce recruited Conrad Hilton to build a new, more modern hotel. The Arlington was later torn down and its materials used to build a new school gymnasium.

The formal portrait of William G. Etheridge as a representative in the Texas Legislature in 1883. He helped settle Falls County, but fled during the Civil War because of his Union loyalty. He returned to Falls County after the war and was a Unionist leader during Reconstruction, serving one term as sheriff. Etheridge's daughter, Bettie, married R. E. L. Tomlinson.

A color photo of the Falls Hotel on a postcard from the 1950s. The Marlin Chamber of Commerce wanted to modernize the town in the 1920s to maintain the city's status as a top resort destination. All of the major hotels had been built prior to 1900, so the chamber asked Conrad Hilton to build a modern hotel in downtown. He agreed to build his ninth hotel in Marlin, if the chamber provided a ten-percent down payment on the construction cost. Hilton finished the hotel in 1929, just weeks after the stock market crash that triggered the Great Depression. He was forced to sell the hotel and it was renamed the Falls Hotel.

The buckskin wallet that has been passed down through the white Tomlinson family that James K. Tomlinson brought from Alabama. James died when his youngest son, R. E. L. Tomlinson, was only four years old, and R. E. L. did not remember him. His older brothers gave him the wallet after he graduated from Texas A&M College. He wrote inside that it was an "old heirloom" and detailed who owned it and its origin. He passed it down to his son, Tommy Tomlinson, and it now belongs to the author.

The cover of *Southern Bowler* magazine, featuring Bob Tomlinson after he bowled a perfect 300 game in 1959. Bob started bowling when he was fourteen years old and he took to the game quickly, bowling his first perfect game just four years later. Bob dropped out of Texas A&M and entered the bowling supply business with his father, Tommy. While Tommy grew up a racist in Marlin, Bob's childhood in Dallas took him in a different direction and he embraced the civil rights movement.

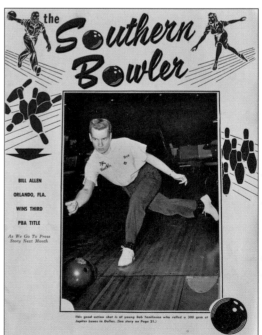

A family photo of Beth and Bob Tomlinson's wedding in 1963. From the left, Leon and Mary Jane Ward, Beth and Bob Tomlinson, and Mary and Tommy Tomlinson. Bob met Beth on a blind date to a Texas A&M University football game. They married just weeks after she graduated high school in Arlington and they lived in Dallas, where Bob operated a bowling supplies dealership with his father.

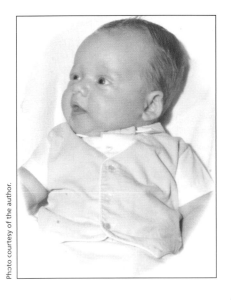

A family photo of Chris Tomlinson as an infant. Chris was born in July 1965 when his father Bob operated a bowling supply store and was trying to break into the Professional Bowlers Association. Chris grew up in Dallas and did not visit Tomlinson Hill until he became an adult.

Tommy Tomlinson holding Chris at his home in Dallas in 1965. Tommy was a stern man, but proud to have a grandson to carry on the family name. Tommy's full name was Albert Edward Lee Tomlinson, carrying on the tradition of honoring the Confederate General Robert E. Lee. Tommy named his son Robert Lee Tomlinson, and Bob named his son Christopher Lee Tomlinson.

Beth and Bob Tomlinson pose for a family portrait holding Chris in Dallas in 1966. Tommy was a successful home builder and Bob's mother inherited money from her father, who was a successful Dallas businessman. But Bob wanted to pursue his passion for bowling, a blue-collar sport. Despite Tommy's and Bob's best efforts, their bowling supply business went bankrupt following Tommy's death in 1973.

Chris Tomlinson's family at Christmas in 1976. From left, Dana, Bob, Chris, and Beth, taken by the author's grandmother. Dallas schools were undergoing court-ordered busing in order to end decades of segregation and inequality. Every year in the mid-1970s, Chris attended a different school as the city worked to comply with the court order. Teachers gave lessons on the civil rights movement and Chris first heard Martin Luther King's "I Have a Dream" speech played in class.

Chris Tomlinson's fourth-grade class picture from the Richardson Independent School District in 1975 before Dallas schools began to bus students to desegregate schools. Despite living in the Dallas Independent School District, officials allowed Chris to attend the suburban school because it was closest to his home. Court-ordered desegregation forced school officials to strictly enforce district boundaries, and the following year Chris attended Dallas schools.

Chris Tomlinson's sixth-grade class picture from the Dallas Independent School District in 1977 after busing had begun to desegregate schools. Note the more diverse and larger class size. Between 1970 and 1980, more than 100,000 whites moved out of Dallas and into the suburbs, many of them wanting to avoid sending their children to integrated schools. Dozens of businesses also relocated outside the Dallas city limits for the same reason.

White Tomlinsons

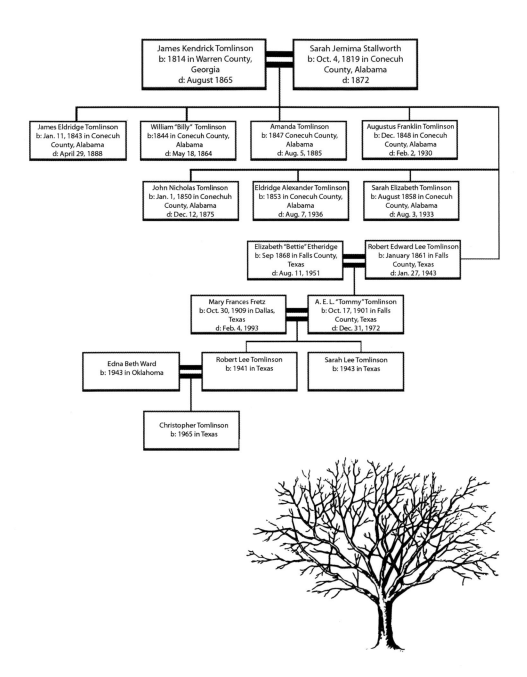

James Kendrick Tomlinson
b: 1814 in Warren County, Georgia
d: August 1865

Sarah Jemima Stallworth
b: Oct. 4, 1819 in Conecuh County, Alabama
d: 1872

James Eldridge Tomlinson
b: Jan. 11, 1843 in Conecuh County, Alabama
d: April 29, 1888

William "Billy" Tomlinson
b:1844 in Conecuh County, Alabama
d: May 18, 1864

Amanda Tomlinson
b: 1847 Conecuh County, Alabama
d: Aug. 5, 1885

Augustus Franklin Tomlinson
b: Dec. 1848 in Conecuh County, Alabama
d: Feb. 2, 1930

John Nicholas Tomlinson
b: Jan. 1, 1850 in Conechuh County, Alabama
d: Dec. 12, 1875

Eldridge Alexander Tomlinson
b: 1853 in Conecuh County, Alabama
d: Aug. 7, 1936

Sarah Elizabeth Tomlinson
b: August 1858 in Conecuh County, Alabama
d: Aug. 3, 1933

Elizabeth "Bettie" Etheridge
b: Sep 1868 in Falls County, Texas
d: Aug. 11, 1951

Robert Edward Lee Tomlinson
b: January 1861 in Falls County, Texas
d: Jan. 27, 1943

Mary Frances Fretz
b: Oct. 30, 1909 in Dallas, Texas
d: Feb. 4, 1993

A. E. L. "Tommy" Tomlinson
b: Oct. 17, 1901 in Falls County, Texas
d: Dec. 31, 1972

Edna Beth Ward
b: 1943 in Oklahoma

Robert Lee Tomlinson
b: 1941 in Texas

Sarah Lee Tomlinson
b: 1943 in Texas

Christopher Tomlinson
b: 1965 in Texas

and Waco. The population swelled to ten thousand people, with four hotels and four hospitals offering the healing waters. If R. E. L. and his wife,
Bettie, wanted to take in a show or a concert, they could choose the Marlin Opera House, the New Opera House, or the Kings Opera House. R.
E. L.'s cousin Zenas Bartlett operated Rush, Gardner and Bartlett Co., a
new, three-story hardware store on Live Oak Street, a business that remains a landmark more than a century later. Marlin voters elected Zenas's son, Churchill Jones Bartlett, to serve in the state legislature from
1906 to 1910. Also in the 1906 election, R. E. L.'s cousin and brother-in-
law Frank Stallworth won the city marshal's race a second time. A young
lawyer named Tom Connally also won election as county attorney, beginning a political career that would include eleven years in the U.S.
House of Representatives and twenty-four years in the U.S. Senate.[7]

J. M. Kennedy, the *Marlin Democrat*'s progressive publisher, was
mayor, and residents began to put an emphasis on public education for
white and black children.[8] Communities in Falls County operated one
hundred schools in 1900, serving 33,342 residents.[9] Across the state,
black illiteracy fell from 75.4 percent in 1880 to 38.2 percent in 1900.[10]

That didn't mean, though, that all children liked to go to school. On
the eve of the first day at the white high school, September 2, 1900, "one
or more headstrong boys" set fire to the Victorian structure, burning it
to the ground. The city council rented a warehouse downtown as a temporary school building and sold the destroyed property to investors.
They built the Marlin Cotton Compress, which brought every cotton
trader in the region to the city. Students remained in the warehouse for
three years, until the city raised enough money for a new school.[11] The
Tomlinson Negro School continued to operate into the first half of the
twentieth century, and in 1903, Miss Fannie Steen taught reading and
writing to sixteen students there.[12]

MARLIN ENJOYS PROSPERITY

I. J. Nathan bought two electricity plants in 1902 and created the city's
first electric utility. He ran transmission lines to any home owner willing to pay for the service. His generators also powered a cooling plant

to make ice, which a team of black men delivered door-to-door in wagons and wheelbarrows. One man, Son Jones, worked for the plant for fifty years, becoming a fixture in the community. That same year, Nathan also brought the first automobile to Marlin and published his driving schedule in the *Marlin Democrat*, warning that his loud, smoke-belching, two-cylinder Oldsmobile was going to pass through town. The notices often read "Be prepared to hold your horses. I'll be out in my auto from four to five, Sunday afternoon."[13]

Nathan's favorite drive was to the Falls Club House, three miles from town and on the Brazos across from Tomlinson Hill. Locals called the romantic single-lane lined with huge willow trees "Lover's Lane" because young people drove their horse-drawn carriages along it on dates. Marlin also had a racetrack for harness racing.[14]

Within ten years, though, young lovers could go to the Old Lyric on Live Oak Street to watch silent movies or listen to soloists sing along with hand-colored slide shows projected on the screen. The Peacock Bottling Company began selling Café Kola, Koca Nola, Peach Blow, and Tart Tasty Pomay, drinks the opera houses served ice-cold. Albert Levy operated the Arlington Opera House and Electro-Theater, promising "high class and refreshing pastime and pleasure for the theater-goers of Marlin."[15]

Whites could not have been more secure in their power. A Confederate veteran of the Fifth Cavalry was governor and the state was unabashed in its hatred of the North. When Confederate Generals John B. Gordon and James Longstreet died in January 1904, Confederate flags flew along Marlin's main thoroughfare in a sign of mourning.[16] Planters made their money on cotton, just as they always had, and the crop was still profitable thanks to cheap African-American labor. In Texas, landowners employed 35,000 farm laborers at seventy-five cents a day in 1900 and rented land to 45,000 sharecroppers. About 20,000 African-Americans owned their own land, while 57,000 blacks worked on farms. Among those were 38,000 unskilled laborers.[17]

Falls County, though, was more than just an agricultural community, thanks to mineral water. In 1908, Dr. John W. Torbett, Sr., built the Torbett Sanatorium next to the hot springs pavilion, starting Marlin's first general hospital, and the First State Bank opened later that year.[18] The healing waters and bucolic setting attracted major-league baseball teams who needed a southern locale for spring training. Charlie Comiskey brought his Chicago White Sox in 1903, and the Philadelphia Phillies, Cincinnati Reds, and St. Louis Browns soon followed, all staying at the New Arlington Hotel, practicing in the mornings and taking baths in the afternoons. In 1908, the New York Giants made Marlin their permanent spring-training camp and built a large ballpark, complete with grandstands.[19]

To shore up their power, local governments in 1900 began using white-only primary elections. The U.S. Constitution guaranteed blacks the right to vote in general elections, but primaries were run by the individual parties, which gave them the authority to decide who could participate. Since Republicans stood little chance of winning the general election, the Democratic primaries almost always decided who would win on Election Day. Blacks could vote in the federal election, but since the Democratic nominee would always win, they essentially had no power.[20]

Just to make sure blacks couldn't influence the general election, though, Texas voters, by a 2–1 margin, gave counties the power to impose poll taxes. Supporters believed that eliminating poor people from voting would help pass Prohibition and reduce the influence of recent immigrants from southern and eastern Europe. Whites also argued that a poll tax would reduce voter fraud, but mostly it disenfranchised blacks.[21] Voter turnout across Texas plummeted, never breaking 50 percent from 1900 to 1950.[22] Black voting dropped from 100,000 in the 1890s to just 5,000 in 1906.[23]

Racist whites continued using violence to maintain power, but newspaper reports sparked a backlash among the majority of whites, who grew frustrated with their politicians' empty rhetoric against vigilantism. Lawmakers soon introduced laws to stop lynchings, and in Texas they dropped from about eighteen a year in the 1890s to ten a year between 1900 and 1903.[24]

Simultaneously, though, the same whites who abhorred lynching wanted segregation. In 1907, state lawmakers made it legal for theaters and private amusement parks to segregate whites from blacks, or to ban nonwhites all together. The legislature segregated state prisons and required railroads to build separate waiting rooms in 1909. Every other public accommodation not governed by the legislature took their cues from these new laws, and soon there were white and black entrances to businesses and separate water fountains.[25]

BUILDING A BETTER FUTURE

African-Americans did not fight back, but neither did they sit idle. In Marlin, parents elected P. A. Stamps as the principal of the black school in 1906, and he expanded it to ten grades, for the first time offering more than just an elementary education. Teachers taught classes at the black Davis Chapel Church on the south side of town until the city agreed to build a black high school in 1916 at the corner of Samuel and Aycock streets.[26] The new school included facilities to teach home economics, carpentry, and music for the first time and included space for athletics and clubs. The better building and course offerings led black parents to form a parent-teacher association, and more African-Americans sent their children to school than ever before. To accommodate the new students, Stamps rented the Providence Baptist Church and the black Masonic Lodge. In 1925, they named the school after Booker T. Washington.[27]

There were still few college-level facilities for blacks in Texas. In those that existed, much of the time was spent teaching remedial classes to get students up to a high school–level of education. In 1914, only 129 African-Americans enrolled in college-level coursework.[28]

Booker T. Washington's National Negro Business League opened chapters in Dallas and Galveston in 1904, following Washington's doctrine of developing black communities and avoiding confrontation with whites. R. L. Smith founded the league's state chapter in Dallas three years later. By 1911, the black business community in Dallas was so robust that it hosted the National Negro Bankers Association's national convention. Middle-class blacks in Houston and Dallas organized the Negro Protection Congress of Texas in 1906 to enforce law and order when white police would not. Black churches, still the center of the community, counted 396,157 members in 1916.[29]

Houston blacks formed the first Texas Chapter of the NAACP in 1916, and by 1919, there were thirty-one chapters and seven thousand members across the state, making it the largest state chapter in the South. White authorities opposed the organization's confrontational approach, shut down their meetings, and refused to register the group.[30] When the NAACP's white executive secretary, John R. Shillady, met with blacks in Austin, Travis County judge Dave Pickle was waiting. He had warned the Irish New Yorker against "inciting negroes against the whites," but Shillady held the meeting anyway. Pickle, Constable Charles Hamby, and Ben Pierce found Shillady and beat him unconscious, causing injuries that led to his death in 1920. Pickle said, "I told him our negroes would cause no trouble if left alone. Then I whipped him and ordered him to leave because I thought it was for the best interest of Austin and the state."[31] Local police arrested no one, and the governor, William P. Hobby, said the attack was justified.[32]

ENTERTAINERS AND ATHLETES

Paradoxically, African-Americans became prominent in popular culture. A Texas musician became nationally famous in 1901 for a new style of syncopated, or "ragged," piano playing popular in red-light districts: ragtime. After writing the "Maple Leaf Rag," this composer and songwriter, Scott Joplin, moved from Texarkana to New York and became known as the "King of the Ragtime Writers." In 1905, black cowboy Bill Pickett joined the 101 Ranch Wild West Show and gained fame as a trick rider.[33]

Jack "the Galveston Giant" Johnson, an African-American stevedore from Galveston, made history in 1908 by defeating Canadian Tommy Burns in Sydney, Australia, to become the first black heavyweight champion of the world. Boxing promoters immediately began recruiting white boxers to take back the championship, billing each as "the Great White Hope." Johnson defeated four of them in 1909 alone. The following year, Johnson scheduled a fight with retired heavyweight champion James Jeffries, a match billed as the "Battle of the Century," mostly because whites desperately wanted to see Johnson defeated. On the Fourth of July, before twenty thousand people in Reno, Nevada, the fight lasted fifteen rounds before Jeffries threw in the towel to keep a knockout from blemishing his record.[34]

Johnson's victory sparked race riots in fifty cities in twenty-five states, particularly in Texas. Whites felt Johnson had humiliated the entire race, and police scrambled to stop several lynchings that night. African-Americans celebrated with parades and prayer meetings, recognizing a dramatic validation of their equality.[35] A team of filmmakers shot extensive footage of the bout and turned it into a film, *Jeffries-Johnson World's Championship Boxing Contest*. The Texas legislature banned that film and all future movies that showed Johnson defeating white contenders.[36]

Earning huge sums of money, Johnson lived extravagantly, owning fancy cars and tailored clothes. His wealth and fame allowed him to break the biggest taboo of all by openly dating white women, marrying three of them, and prompting white supremacists to call for his lynching. A month after his first wife committed suicide, Johnson was arrested on October 18, 1912, for violating the Mann Act, a federal law that punished the interstate transport of women for immoral purposes. Johnson was traveling with Lucille Cameron, whom some alleged was a prostitute. Cameron refused to cooperate with police and married Johnson six weeks later, making the charges moot. They remained married for twelve years.[37]

That didn't keep federal authorities, though, from arresting Johnson again in Illinois on the same charge, this time involving another alleged prostitute, Belle Schreiber. She did testify against him and an all-white jury convicted him in June 1913. Johnson posted bail and fled the country with Cameron, living in exile for seven years. In a fight in Havana, the Galveston Giant lost his title in 1915 to Jess Willard, a white boxer from Kansas. Johnson returned to the United States in 1920, surrendered to federal authorities, and spent a year in prison. Many believe racist federal authorities framed Johnson, and in 2009, Congress passed a resolution calling for a presidential pardon, which has not been granted.[38]

BEYOND COTTON, CORN, AND CATTLE

R.E.L. celebrated the birth of his first and only son, Albert Edward Lee Tomlinson, on October 17, 1901. Albert, who was nicknamed "Tommy," in many ways came of age with modern Texas. He was born the year the state's most famous oil well, Spindletop, came in outside of Beaumont, unleashing 100,000 barrels of crude a day. That salt dome became the most productive oil field in the world, giving birth to Gulf Oil, Texaco, and Chevron. Suddenly, Texas had more to sell than just cotton and cattle.[39]

Tomlinson Hill was becoming more divided with every generation of white Tomlinsons. The family's penchant for naming their children after their brothers and cousins makes telling their story difficult, so I will not try to give a complete accounting of all of them, or where they went. But by 1900, the sons of James Tomlinson, William Tomlinson and Albert Perry Tomlinson, were comanaging the farm on Tomlinson Hill. Albert Perry's wife was Bennie Etheridge, the younger sister of R.E.L.'s wife, whose twin was married to Frank Stallworth.[40]

The white Tomlinsons spent most of their time managing sharecroppers and the black workers on the land they had retained for themselves. They kept track of what the tenants owed in seed, fertilizer, and equipment and checked on their crops about once a week, because a failed crop would hurt the planter and tenant equally. The whites devoted most of their effort to livestock and land trades, where they made even more money.[41]

In 1908, Gus was the oldest living Tomlinson, at the age of sixty, and worked his farm in Lott. He and other early settlers watched the modernization of Falls County and worried that the younger generation would soon forget their work transforming the prairie. Gus was ten years old when he arrived from Alabama and first saw the Texas savanna filled with deer, bear, and snakes. Now automobiles whizzed past him as he rode horseback, and he recognized fewer and fewer people when he went to town. So on the Fourth of July 1902, he and thirty-one other men founded the Old Settlers Association of Falls County. They appointed committees to write bylaws and to organize a reunion of old settlers the following year on July 3. They announced the group's purpose was to "brighten and quicken our interest in the history and traditions of our county."[42]

Membership was open only to white residents who had settled in the county prior to 1887, but that was soon expanded to include "all white persons who have been citizens of Falls County ten years and all native born, female white citizens who have arrived at the age of 18." At the 1909 reunion, the local chapter of the United Confederate Veterans made a strong showing and were invited to attend all future meetings as full members. The Marlin and Lott chapters of the United Daughters of the Confederacy participated in the 1910 reunion, and soon membership in the UDC automatically meant membership in the Old Settlers Association. In 1911, the association changed its name to the Old Settlers and Confederate Veterans Association.[43]

The association initially declared itself nonpartisan, and forbade all talk of politics, but when it filed its charter with the state in 1911, the group added a new purpose: to support an educational institution "to teach the rising and younger generations the true history of the South and the perpetuation of the memory of those who engaged in the Civil War; and of the early pioneers who underwent hardships in the settlement of Texas."[44]

From the very first year, the Old Settlers wanted a plot of land of their own for the annual reunion. Albert Tomlinson offered to donate some land and sell more to the association at the geographic center of Tomlinson Hill, near a highway intersection less than a mile from the Brazos River. The association agreed to Albert's offer of seventeen acres, and members raised money to buy the tract. R.E.L. and William Tomlinson joined Albert, along with Harry Stallworth, Pete Landrum, George Gassaway, and a half dozen other members of the Old Settlers to clear the land, build a shed, and construct barbecue pits. The Old Settlers and Confederate Veterans held their first reunion on Tomlinson Hill in 1912. An open tabernacle, built by members in 1914 from rough-hewn posts, still stands today.[45]

The summer reunions attracted people from across the region, and the early membership constituted a Who's Who of Falls County. Albert, whom everyone called "Uncle Albert," was one of the most active members and often served as an officer of the association. The group hired blacks from the Tomlinson and Stallworth farms to help at the reunions, which were basically huge picnics. The organizers established a tradition of saying a special prayer for the early settlers and Civil War veterans who had died since the last reunion.[46]

TOWN LIFE

R.E.L. and his family attended the First Baptist Church in Marlin, and as conservative churchgoing folk, they supported Prohibition and welcomed the 1917 local election that banned alcohol sales in Falls County.[47] The ban did little to slow the sale of beer and whiskey, though, as an underground market quickly emerged, and cafés resorted to speakeasy tactics or simple bribery to keep the alcohol flowing. A farmer named Bozeman diversified from roses and honey to keeping a still behind the hives, a tactic to discourage the law from snooping around. He delivered the bottles hidden in bunches of roses.[48]

R.E.L. expanded his realty business and specialized in royalty and lease agreements for oil prospecting and tenant farming. But he remained interested in education and served on the Marlin Independent School District Board of Trustees while Tommy was in junior high and high school. He helped negotiate the financing for a new white high school, and his name was on the cornerstone when construction began in May 1917. Tommy was one of the first students to enter the new school at the corner of Capps and Oak streets that fall.[49]

Tommy was a typical teenager, playing baseball at Rimes Park with his cousin John. When he was a junior and John was a sophomore at Marlin High, they played one another on class teams, Tommy in the outfield and John as a pinch hitter. The juniors won in 1918.[50] Tommy also kept score at the school's basketball games. He and his friends would sometimes sneak out in the middle of the night and shoot at the school bell with a .22 rifle, waking up everyone who lived nearby, or sometimes they'd tip over an outhouse with someone inside.[51]

World War I made headlines in the *Marlin Democrat* from 1914 onward, but not until German submarines sank seven U.S. merchant ships in early 1917 did President Woodrow Wilson join the fight. Congress declared war on Germany on April 6 and instituted a draft a month later. The president activated 116 Marlin men serving in the National Guard and transferred them to the Thirty-sixth Infantry Division. By July, more than 3,800 Falls County men had registered for the draft. The War Department conscripted 402 whites and 80 African-Americans.[52] About 25 percent of the 31,000 men conscripted from Texas were black, even though African-Americans made up only 16 percent of the population. Many whites opposed conscripting blacks, who largely supported the war, because they objected to giving African-Americans weapons.[53]

R.E.L. was too old to fight, and, at sixteen, Tommy was too young. But they participated in dozens of patriotic rallies and fund-raisers. The Marlin High School band played concerts of patriotic music and sold Liberty Bonds to raise money for the Red Cross. About 115 local men organized a home guard using their hunting rifles and became Company H of the Texas National Guard, known locally as the Tom Connally Rifles, after their congressman.[54]

The first Falls County soldier to die in combat was Irby Curry, nicknamed "Rabbit" for his speed on the football field. Curry was Tommy's cousin from the Stallworth side of the family. Rabbit had played football at Vanderbilt University, where the stadium is still named after him for his battlefield heroics. The First Baptist Church held a memorial service for him, but his body was buried in France.

The warring nations signed an armistice on November 11, 1918, with the fighting ending at 11:00 A.M. Like people in most American small towns, Marlinites took to the streets in a giant, joyful procession and afterward went to their churches for prayer services.[55]

Tommy was in his senior year, and after the armistice his final semester was especially festive. He had a great year playing football and was named a letterman.[56] For their senior play, the class of 1918 performed *The Yokohama Maid* to a standing-room-only crowd in the school auditorium, and Tommy donned Oriental makeup to sing in the chorus. Tommy's commencement ceremony took place on May 26, and the *Marlin Democrat* ran portraits of all of the seniors in the newspaper that afternoon. As a school board member, R.E.L. sat proudly on the stage when Tommy collected his diploma. R.E.L. convinced Tommy to follow in his footsteps and attend Texas A&M. While more than two million American men were taking off military uniforms, Tommy put one on as a member of the Corps of Cadets.

R.E.L.'s minerals royalty and leasing business was going strong in the late 1910s and early 1920s, a period of crazed oil and gas speculation. Wildcat oilmen drilled wells all over the state, hoping to strike it big. R.E.L. drilled two test wells on Tomlinson Hill and struck both oil and gas. He founded the Deer Creek Oil and Gas Company, and he ran ads in the *Dallas Morning News* in October 1918, announcing that he had six thousand acres leased, and offered an "attractive proposition to driller with rig who can move at once." R.E.L. had big dreams of making a fortune, but the deposits ultimately turned out to be insufficient to make money.[57] Oil wells dotted Falls County, but none of them became fortune-making gushers.

Marlin businessmen formed a Chamber of Commerce in 1919, and among its most prominent members were the Levys, who ran a general store, a retail grocery store, and eventually a wholesale grocery operation. Marx Levy was a Jewish traveling salesman originally from Poland who arrived in Marlin with the first railway in 1870. He was one of the first Jews to settle in the county and built his business near the train station. Marx was instrumental in building the hotels and bathhouses for the mineral-water tourism business and had several sons, including Moses Levy, who expanded the family's businesses.[58]

Frank Stallworth, R.E.L.'s cousin and brother-in-law, was elected mayor in 1921, defeating W. E. Hodges by only ten votes. Stallworth had served two terms as city marshal and one as the alderman for Ward 2.[59] After Frank became mayor, he made R.E.L. a census enumerator and an election judge in 1922.[60] Their cousin Sanford J. Stallworth, a grandson of Churchill Jones, joined them in city and county politics.

One pressing political problem was the county's roads and bridges, which had not kept up with Marlin's rapid growth. The rail lines to and from Marlin were excellent, but the roads remained largely unpaved and subject to flooding. The banks of the Brazos River eroded easily and the river cut a new path after every major flood. The Falls Bridge, which connected Marlin to Waco at Tomlinson Hill, constantly needed work.

Heavy rains in May 1922 made the Brazos run high and fast, cutting away at the bridgehead and loosening the bridge's piers.[61] No one was surprised that the old one-lane bridge, made of iron and wood, was near collapse, and county engineers closed it until they could make repairs. Mayor Stallworth convened a meeting of the town's top businessmen and asked for their help to cover the costs. They agreed on a plan and the county workers, along with volunteers, drove out to start pouring sand and cement to shore up the bridgehead. Stallworth led the volunteers, along with Walter Allen, the town's most prominent physician and one of its wealthiest men. The normally placid and muddy Brazos roared, with millions of gallons a second flowing under the bridge. The men set to work on the western side of the bridge, at the foot of Tomlinson Hill. They drove two cars and a truck loaded with tools and cement onto the span. A seven-year-old African-American boy, who had followed his dad to work that day, was sitting in one of the cars. At about 2:30 P.M., the workers heard a huge snap and the main pier collapsed beneath them and the western span dropped and twisted, sending seventeen people into the rapids below. People standing on the eastern span had about ten seconds to run onto the shore before the water swept the three hundred feet of twisted iron and splintered wood downriver fifty yards to the western bank.[62]

The victims who survived the thirty-foot fall grabbed onto debris or swam for the shore. Witnesses saw two African-Americans floating down the river on a plank of wood. Stallworth and Allen apparently struck some of the wreckage. Witnesses said they saw Stallworth with a deep gash across his face as he floated away, apparently unable to swim. Another witness saw Allen, who appeared similarly injured. The boy in the car, B. J. Briggs, apparently drowned inside it. Three other people also died that day. Rescuers found Stallworth's and Allen's bodies a week later. The *Marlin Democrat* reported: "The Brazos has again proved its claim to a treacherous stream. The channels and its currents are constantly shifting. Its caprices are weird, peculiar and tragic. In this horrifying instance it has more than maintained it gruesome history."[63]

Falls County commissioners sent a telegram to Fort Sam Houston, near San Antonio, asking the Army Corps of Engineers to install a pontoon bridge across the river. A week later, the Corps of Engineers arrived and assembled the pontoons. Soldiers manned it for months until the county could build a new bridge.[64]

A PARALLEL UNIVERSE

The turn of the century in the Gravel Hill freedmen's colony brought months of hard work as farmers and laborers rebuilt their homes and prepared their fields for another planting after the floods of 1899 and 1900. Peter Tomlinson may have rented his home and farm on Tomlinson Hill, but he was a tenant, not a laborer, which meant he had a contract, not an hourly wage.[65] The distinction is important because Peter had more autonomy than a hired hand, but he also assumed more risk. He made a greater effort growing his crop than a worker paid by the day, hoping to put away a little extra money by bringing in a better harvest. He and Josie were active in the Gravel Hill Baptist Church, where they had been married and took their seven children.[66]

The only black Tomlinson subject to the World War I draft was Peter's son Vincent. He was twenty-one and he had attended the Tomlinson Negro School, placing him among the first generation of black Tomlinsons to have a formal education. When the war started, he registered for the draft on the first day of selective service. The registrar described Vincent as a medium height, slender black man working on Albert Tomlinson's farm and stated he claimed no exemptions from service. Despite the young man spelling his name Venson, the registrar signed the form on his behalf as Vincent. His draft number never came up.

Four days after the armistice was signed, Vincent married his sweetheart, Julie Ward, at the Gravel Hill Baptist Church. The Reverend Tom Broadus, one of the few black landowners and a leader in the community, presided over the ceremony on November 15, 1918. Julie was eighteen years old and had been born in a cabin in Falls County to Nathan and Emma Sorillas Ward. The Wards also lived on Tomlinson Hill, where they rented a house a short distance from the white Tomlinsons. Unusual for the era, the Wards could read and write, though Nathan was only a farm laborer. The Wards sent Julie to school, so she, too, was literate.[67]

Though supposedly equal to that of white schools, the education at black schools was anything but. The Texas Education Survey in 1924 found that 75 percent of black schools had no librarian, industrial rooms, or playground equipment, and at least 38 percent had no textbooks, while 11 percent had no toilets. In 1925, the state counted 150 black high schools, but only 34 were accredited. To help black education, the Julius Rosenwald Fund built schools across the country and completed 130 new rural schools in Texas, where, surprisingly, the state's lawmakers appropriated more matching funds than any other state.[68] The foundation built one of the schools in Marlin, where the school district couldn't keep up with the growing population.[69]

In 1920, Julie gave birth to her first child, Lizzie Mae, in the cabin she shared with Vincent on Deer Creek. They lived next door to his older brother James and his wife, who already had a full house with a five-year-old son, a brother-in-law, and a niece, all of whom shared the two-room home. Another brother, Ellie, and his seven children lived nearby also, as did members of the other African-American clans, the Scotts, Travises, Baileys, and Broaduses. All of the families were related by marriage and formed the nucleus of the Tomlinson Hill black community. Julie became a leader in the Gravel Hill Baptist Church, and the couple had four more children by 1930.[70]

Vincent earned Albert Tomlinson's respect through hard work and loyalty, and Vincent's clean-living habits increased his stature in the black community, where the black Masons in Lott welcomed him into their ranks. African-Americans saw the advantages that white men enjoyed by forming fraternal orders, and black chapters also saw rapid growth in the 1900s. The Masons counted 30,000 black members, while the Knights of Pythias had eight hundred lodges, with 35,000 black members in 1921.[71]

These organizations became important for an increasingly mobile population. The number of blacks working in agriculture was dropping by 1920, and farms employed less than 48 percent of black laborers. Low commodity prices and a boll weevil plague destroyed cotton crops in the 1920s and encouraged many blacks to move to the cities. Tractors started showing up on Falls County farms at about the same time, and they became commonplace by 1930, reducing the need for black labor.[72] But Vincent loved the land where he was born and enjoyed living in a community that shared his name. He had no plans to go anywhere.

FOURTEEN

Now as to the Klan. I have watched the order grow from its infancy to its present period of greatness, and I want to say that so far as I know, the criticisms that have been made of it have been without foundation.

—Dallas mayor Louis Blaylock

White Tomlinsons celebrated their heritage at the Old Settlers reunions on the Hill every summer. At the 1922 reunion, Dr. J. W. Torbett, whose father had founded the general hospital in Marlin, gave a speech entitled "Inventions: Past, Present and Future." The association also invited Marlin's congressman, Tom Connally, to speak. The *Marlin Democrat* recapped the event:

A reading entitled "Marse Robert's Asleep," by Miss Alice Summers received merited applause and brought tears to the eyes of many of the old veterans who followed the Great Robert E. Lee, who said that the sublimest word in the English language is "duty."

The forenoon exercises were closed with a great address by Miss Decca Lamar West, president of Texas Division of the United Daughters of the Confederacy, in which she called to mind the great achievement of those who wore the gray, and called attention to the fact that history has not done justice to the great name of Jefferson Davis, the president of the Confederacy.[1]

The old settlers were indeed passing away at a quickening pace. R. E. L.'s father-in-law, William Etheridge, died two months after the 1922 reunion at the home of one of his twin daughters, Billah Stallworth. The death of Billah's father, just four months after that of her husband, was devastating for the whole family. Sadly, Etheridge probably never attended the Old Settlers reunions, because while he was one of the earliest of settlers, he'd fled Texas rather than serve the Confederacy. To him, men like Jefferson Davis were traitors and unworthy of praise.[2] But after generations of revisionism, Etheridge was in the minority in Texas, where the effort to portray the fallen South as a noble, lost cause found fertile ground in the early twentieth century. Within a few years, white southerners would embrace white supremacy in a new wave of terrorism.

State and federal authorities had cracked down on the Klan following Reconstruction, and the gangs had dissipated. White supremacy groups didn't disappear entirely; they just became ad hoc vigilante groups at the turn of the century because blacks posed no threat to white power. But as African-Americans gained greater cultural visibility and educated blacks formed professional organizations, white conservatives saw a slow erosion of their authority. Perhaps nothing angered a poor white man more than the rare encounter with an African-American who had a higher education or more money than he did.

Many upper-class whites despised how the races mixed in poor parts of the state or in red-light districts, and they condemned white men who took black mistresses. There was a growing number of mixed-race children in the South, and white men favored mixed-race women as mistresses. African-Americans had a folk song about these women:

> *A yaller gal sleep in a bed*
> *A brown skin do the same*
> *A black gal sleep on de floor*
> *But she's sleepin jes de same.*[3]

Despite countless Sunday sermons and numerous laws banning sex between the races, whites and blacks socialized across the South, and white supremacists felt a need to stop this.

THE KU KLUX KLAN REBORN

A Baptist preacher from North Carolina named Thomas Dixon, Jr., released the second part of his fictional trilogy about the Ku Klux Klan in 1905. *The Clansmen* portrayed members of the KKK as well-organized, noble, and chivalric keepers of white, Christian, and American values. They were exclusively Anglo-Saxon Protestants, and the author considered all other races and religions inferior. Dixon hoped his book would inform northerners about the fiction of racial equality, writing that if given freedom, blacks became savages. The novel is set during Reconstruction and the plot involves a Yankee Speaker of the House trying to place African-Americans in control of the South in order to subjugate whites. When northerners try to give blacks equal rights, the Klan rises up to defeat the northerners and return blacks to second-class status, under the watchful care of benevolent Klansmen. Dixon wrote a play with the same plot. Northerners protested both the novel and the play, but in the South, the play incited even more nostalgia for all things antebellum.[4]

D. W. Griffith's film *The Birth of a Nation* was adapted from the play and was originally called *The Clansmen*. The film became a phenomenon in 1915 because it pioneered advanced filmmaking techniques and glorified slavery and the Klan, while denigrating African-Americans, Unionists, and Reconstruction. The Kentucky-born filmmaker amplified Dixon's portrayal of the federal government oppressing the civil rights of white southerners. Griffith himself understood southern culture and white poverty well, having grown up on a farm that failed shortly after his father died, when he was ten years old. His mother moved her children to Louisville and he quit school to support the family. As an adult, he became a film actor in New York, which led to his directing films.[5]

The film and play validated a romantic view of southern history, where noble whites provided for inferior blacks. Confederate veterans applauded the film's portrayal of the cause. The play and film inspired a Georgian named William J. Simmons to form a new Ku Klux Klan, modeled not on the original Klan, but on Dixon's and Griffith's fictional group. The only connection to Reconstruction-era Klansmen was the founding document, "The Prescript." The Klan's robes and burning crosses came directly from the costumes and practices imagined for Griffith's film.[6]

Simmons loved secret societies and had joined dozens of fraternal organizations, so he based the Klan's organization on the groups he liked best, such as the Masons and Knights of Pythias. The Klan's rules called for secrecy and anonymity, since the KKK performed their "good deeds" under cover of the night, with credit going to the organization as a whole. As a result, almost no membership records survive, and while rumors circulated about who was in the Klan, members faced expulsion if they revealed themselves without a grand dragon's permission. The Klan ran announcements in local newspapers, but it tried to keep the location of its meetings secret. Many members referred to the local Klan chapter merely as "the Lodge" to throw off anyone who might be eavesdropping, since all fraternal organizations referred to their meeting spaces as lodges.[7]

Fraternal societies were incredibly popular, and not so secret. Marlin had two Masonic temples, the order of the Eastern Star, the Knights of Pythias, the United Confederate Veterans, the United Daughters of the Confederacy, the Odd Fellows, Rotary Club, Lion's Club, the Old Settlers and Confederate Veterans Association, and, after World War I, the Veterans of Foreign Wars. Many men and women joined multiple lodges and one could go to a different meeting every night of the week and probably see the same people. Some groups attracted the same membership, and the UCV and UDC shared the same values as the Klan. In 1916, a UDC chapter president in California wrote a book called *The Ku Klux Klan* to promote the new group. Annie Burton Cooper wrote:

Every clubhouse of the United Daughters of the Confederacy should have a memorial tablet dedicated to the Ku Klux Klan; that would be a monument not to one man, but to five hundred and fifty thousand men, to whom all Southerners owe a debt of gratitude; for how our beloved Southland could have survived that reign of terror is a big question.

The very name Ku Klux shows that the order was formed among men of letters. It is a Greek word meaning circle. Klan suggested itself; the name complete in turn suggested mystery.[8]

The rest of her history of the Klan, which she dedicated to her father, is as fanciful and hyperbolic as Dixon's novel. But for a white male southerner taught simultaneously to fear and oppress African-Americans, the organization offered the chance to join a mythical, paramilitary organization that purported to be doing God's work on earth.

In Texas, white vigilantism was already routine, and the modern Klan offered a veneer of respectability, since many Texans already held the historical Klan in high esteem. The 1906 Texas A&M yearbook features a photo of ten men in Klan robes and with swords, calling themselves "the K.K.K.'s." In the summer of 1918, reports of secret organizations tarring and feathering people for immoral acts began popping up across the South. In Texas, a group of teens called the Ku Klux Kids in Wharton covered one of their members with sorghum molasses and rolled him in sharp cotton hulls as punishment for telling their club's secrets. Rumors of a Klan chapter forming in Beeville led four hundred residents to hold a town meeting and approve a resolution opposing the Klan to keep vigilantism out of their town.[9] But by 1920, dozens of Klan chapters began to pop up openly across the state.

Another impetus for the Klan came from a spike in immigration that brought thousands of foreign-born people to Texas. Most past arrivals had come from northern Europe, but more and more new immigrants came from eastern and southern Europe, as well as from Latin America and Asia. By 1920, 54.4 percent of immigrants arriving

in Dallas came from these places, compared to less than 16 percent in
1900. White Texans saw more people who did not look like them than
ever before, people who did not speak English fluently and who practiced different religions. These new immigrants were also poor and
lived in slums upon arrival.

Wealthy whites with northern European heritage wanted distance
between themselves and anyone not Anglo-Saxon. In 1916, Dallas passed
the first formal residential segregation law, allowing the Deere Park
Improvement League to develop a new subdivision exclusively for whites.
The city council justified segregation by declaring that blacks posed a
risk of infectious disease.[10] Real estate men challenged the law, and the
state supreme court overturned it in 1926. But the legislature passed a
law the following year that allowed cities to use building permits to
segregate cities.[11]

The Klan began to influence Texas politics in 1921 when Klan members paraded through towns and their leaders gave public speeches. The
organization was made up primarily of lower- and middle-class whites
who resented immigrants, Jews, Catholics, and African-Americans. The
Klan's secret nature rubbed many established politicians and businessmen the wrong way. In dozens of editorials, *Marlin Democrat* publisher
J. M. Kennedy railed against anyone who refused to put their name to
their ideas, but particularly those who wanted to take rights away from
others.

Protestant preachers formed the early leadership of the Klan and
cloaked it in religious propaganda that provided a moral justification
for its actions. Politically, the Klan supported Prohibition and attracted
support from the Women's Christian Temperance Union and similar
groups. The first head of the Women of the Ku Klux Klan was a former
WCTU president in Arkansas.[12] While today the Klan is taboo, in the
early 1920s, most whites saw the Klan as a conservative Christian patriotic group fighting against immorality and the dilution of white
Protestant society. The Klan played on white fears by making protection
of white women its highest, and most noble, priority. By cloaking themselves in chivalry, religion, patriotism, and anonymity, they hoped to
put a positive face on vigilantism.[13]

The national Republican party found southern lynchings revolting, and if local law enforcement would not prosecute the mobs, they wanted the federal government to do it. In 1921, President Woodrow Wilson fought for an antilynching bill, which all Texas congressmen opposed. One of them called the bill a political payoff for blacks:

> During the discussion yesterday afternoon, Finis J. Garrett, Democratic leader, denounced the bill as a further effort to destroy the constitution, 'The bill ought to be labeled "A bill to encourage rape,"' he declared.
>
> Garrett said that its passage is a "Republican pretense to pay political debts" and that the Republicans are compelled to vote for the bill "by their Republican overlords."
>
> Garrett charged the negroes were responsible for the Republican victory "and now they demand payment of political debt."[14]

THE KLAN IN DALLAS

The Klan claimed 100,000 members in Texas by 1921 and ethnic violence was on the rise, with attacks on blacks, Catholics, Jews, immigrants, and allegedly immoral whites. To announce their presence in Dallas, Klansmen invited a *Dallas Times Herald* reporter to accompany them for the April 1 kidnapping of a black elevator operator who worked at the downtown Adolphus Hotel. The Klansmen took the man, whom they accused of having sex with a white woman, beat him, and used acid to brand the initials KKK into his forehead. They took him to the Adolphus and ordered him to walk half-naked and bleeding into the hotel.[15] The *Times Herald* carried a front-page story the next day, but both the Dallas police and Dallas County sheriff Don Harston refused to investigate. Both the sheriff and the police commissioner were Klan members. "The Negro was guilty of doing something which he had no right to do," Harston said.[16]

Six weeks later, on May 21, hundreds of men wearing Klan robes marched behind an American flag and a burning cross through downtown Dallas. They carried placards that read GAMBLERS GO; GRAFTERS

GO; WE STAND FOR WHITE SUPREMACY; FOR OUR MOTHERS; FOR OUR
DAUGHTERS; and THE INVISIBLE EMPIRE THERE TODAY, HERE YESTER-
DAY AND HERE FOREVER. The group timed their march for 9:00 P.M. on
a Saturday night, when downtown theaters and department stores
emptied out and traffic snarled. The march lasted an hour and thousands watched as the Klan passed without saying a word. A story ran
on the front page of the *Times Herald,* along with a proclamation from
the group:

> That this organization is composed of native born Americans and none
> others.
>
> That it proposes to uphold the dignity and authority of the law.
>
> That no innocent person of any color, creed or lineage has just cause
> to fear or condemn this body of men.
>
> That our creed is opposed to violence, lynchings, etc. but that we are
> even more strongly opposed to things that cause lynching and mob
> rule.
>
> That this organization stands for the enforcement of all laws without
> fear or favor. It recognizes, however, that situations frequently arise
> where no existing law offers a remedy. It hopes to see such conditions
> remedied by the power of public opinion and the enactment and en-
> forcement of proper laws.
>
> That this organization does not countenance and it will not stand for
> the co-habitation of blacks and whites of either sex. It does not coun-
> tenance and it will not stand for social parasites remaining in this
> city. It is equally opposed to the gambler, the trickster, the moral de-
> generate and the man who lives by his wits and is without visible
> means of support.
>
> This organization further believes that the certainty of perpetuating
> American liberties lies in the solid support of our public school sys-
> tem, adding thereto love of country and veneration for the Deity. With
> this in view, it wants to see an American flag raised each day with
> appropriate ceremonies over every public school house in the state
> and each pupil in those schools instructed in the principles of moral-
> ity. We believe in the enactment of a statute to that effect.[17]

The *Dallas Morning News* immediately opposed the Klan. The day after the march, editorial-page editor Alonzo Wasson wrote a piece entitled "Dallas Slandered," in which he did not hesitate to mock the city's newest fraternal organization:

> The spectacle of eight-hundred masked and white-gowned men parading the streets of Dallas under banners proclaiming them Knights of the Ku Klux Klan and self-appointed guardians of the community's political, social and moral welfare has its ridiculous aspect. To this none can be blind, unless it be the Knights of the Ku Klux Klan. Their sense of superior righteousness may have had the effect of dulling their sense of humor. But also it has a serious significance which will not be lost on the minds of men who cherish the community's good name and have the intelligence to understand how well-designed that exhibition was to bring it under reproach.
>
> It was a slander on Dallas, because the only conditions which could be given to excuse the organization of such a body do not exist. This exhibition bore false witness against Dallas to everyone who has heard of it. White supremacy is not imperiled. Vice is not rampant. The constituted agencies of government are still regnant. And if freedom is endangered, it is by the redivivus of the mob spirit in the disguising garb of the Ku Klux Klan.[18]

Wasson wrote the editorial on a Sunday, and he did not ask permission before running it. The paper's publisher, English immigrant George Dealey, paid a visit to Wasson the day the piece ran to discuss his paper's new editorial position. Dealey was angry with Wasson for not conferring with him, but he congratulated him on a job well done. The editorial set off an almost decade-long battle between the *Dallas Morning News* and the Klan. Wasson's swift and eloquent response to the Klan is yet another sign that the old excuse we southerners use for our ancestors—that they didn't know any better—doesn't hold water.[19]

In September 1921, the *Morning News* and the *New York World News* combined forces to run a lengthy investigative series on the Klan. The reporters dug into the Klan's finances to see how it was spending the millions of four-dollar membership fees it collected. Simmons had built a $1.5 million Imperial Palace in Atlanta, taken over a defunct university, and bought expensive homes for the group's officers. The newspapers also exposed how the Klan was recruiting members of the military. In Marlin, Kennedy ran the story in the *Democrat*:

> The Klan organizers go out instructed by headquarters to make their first drive to secure city, town and village authorities as members, and to center their efforts also on judges of local and circuit courts and the police forces. In the weekly news letters sent out from Atlanta by Imperial Kleagle [Edward] Clarke [the chief recruiter] for circulation among Klansmen, the success achieved along these lines is boasted as the reason why in so many places the Klan has ventured to work openly without fear of interference, and as an incentive for pushing forward the work of setting up an invisible, Klan-controlled super-government throughout the country.[20]

No one could call the stories about the Klan balanced. The papers relentlessly attacked the organization as violent, subversive, and anti-American. The papers compiled a detailed list of the invisible empire's illegal activities since its founding on Stone Mountain in 1916. The reporters gathered many secret Klan documents, outlined its rituals, and interviewed Klansmen. Most of all, the reporters showed the Klan's hypocrisy, noting that the group's actions differed dramatically from the leaders' words. But it did little to change the Klan's popularity, and the Klan continued to grow, a phenomenon that gave more and more political business leaders reason to consider the organization a threat to democracy and their authority. Martin McNulty Crane, the former lieutenant governor, organized many of Dallas's top business leaders in 1922 to form the Dallas County Citizens League, primarily to oppose the Klan.[21]

Despite their pledge against violence, Dallas Klansmen castrated a light-skinned African-American doctor for allegedly dating a white woman, and hooded men raided the offices of Houston's *Informer* and Dallas's *Express*, black newspapers. By November 1922, Democrats elected an admitted Klan member to the U.S. Senate, Earle B. May-field. Nationally, the Klan claimed more than four million members by 1922, a number that would reach six million in 1924.[22]

As the Klan's popularity grew, the leaders made an aggressive effort to recruit the most powerful people in Dallas to join them. One delegation visited Edward Titche, the owner of the successful Titche-Goettinger Department Store and one of the city's wealthiest citizens. When they asked him to join, he told them that would be impossible because he was Jewish. The Klan delegation politely agreed.[23] Nevertheless, Alex Sanger, the Jewish owner of the Sanger-Harris Department Store, agreed to sit on the dais next to Klan leaders when they opened a Klan-sponsored children's home. Sanger and his family secretly financed the anti-Klan Dallas County Citizens League. This provides an idea of how difficult even wealthy and powerful Dallasites found it to navigate the city's politics. The Klan boycotted businesses that did not support the group and insisted that some businesses require their employees to join the invisible empire or face a boycott. Yet many Klan members dropped their anti-Semitism stance when their businesses required them to work with Jewish merchants. Ultimately, all sides placed profit making over their feelings about the secret brotherhood.[24]

A TOMLINSON GOES TO DALLAS

Tommy Tomlinson graduated from Texas A&M with a degree in civil engineering in May 1923 and took a job in Dallas. He didn't want to return to small-town life and decided to make a name for himself in the Big D. Tommy was tall and thin, with a country accent that left the impression he was not well-educated, but he knew enough about engineering to get a job with the most prestigious residential real estate developer in the city, Flippen-Prather.[25] The firm designed and built the toniest subdivisions in Dallas, beginning with Highland Park in 1908. Tommy wanted nothing more than to become wealthy and to live in one of the mansions his new company built. When he first got to Dallas, he made sure to meet the most important people in the city, especially politicians and businesspeople. Tommy was a Mason, like his father, and used that fraternal organization to build connections. He also attended Dallas's First Baptist Church.[26]

Tommy spent much of his time on construction sites, supervising white, black, and Mexican laborers. He fit the engineer stereotype, socially awkward and always certain in his calculations. He was unfriendly and aloof on job sites, and he considered anyone who was not a white Protestant like himself inferior. He used racial and ethnic slurs casually against the people who worked for him and harbored a hatred for both Catholics and Jews. There is no direct evidence of Tommy joining the Klan, but his sympathies certainly rested with the group, and he associated with many men who made their Klan affiliation known, including the Dallas police commissioner and the pastors of the largest Protestant churches. His son Bob, my father, thinks Tommy may have joined the Dallas Klan:

> This is strictly hindsight, but I wouldn't be at all surprised if my father had been a member of the Klan when he came to Dallas, or joined right afterwards, because the Klu [sic] Klux Klan was so entrenched in Dallas in 1923 when he came here. That would have been the quickest way for a guy to get ahead and he certainly had the requirements as far as his attitude was concerned . . . it would almost be surprising if he weren't, but he never mentioned it.[27]

My father didn't know at the time that Tommy's father, R.E.L., was almost certainly a Klansman in Marlin, giving Tommy even more reason to join in Dallas. In the mid-1920s, an estimated 40 percent of eligible American white men joined the Klan. In Dallas, nearly 50 percent became Klansmen between 1921 and 1924, the highest per capita Klan membership in the country. Klansmen controlled city hall and most elected county offices.[28] The Klan's strategy to recruit the elite was intended to impress and attract the working class and young professionals like Tommy.[29] Tommy probably never physically attacked anyone—the average Klan member didn't—but as a young man steeped in racism and looking to establish himself in Dallas, he very likely spent at least some time with those who did.

The exalted cyclops of Dallas Klan No. 66 was Hiram Wesley Evans, who was also a Thirty-second Degree Mason. Evans orchestrated a Klan coup and overthrew founder William Simmons as the national leader in November 1922 to become the new imperial wizard. While Evans was one of the Klansmen who had branded the Adolphus Hotel elevator operator, he publicly denounced violence in 1922, arguing that it would only bring government attention and distract from his goal of making the Klan a powerful political party.[30] Evans blatantly lied about Klan vigilantism to the *Dallas Morning News* in a 1923 interview: "In no single instance has the Klan been involved in such a proceeding. The greatest mistake the press of the country has made is in assuming that the Klan has had anything to do with those outrages."[31]

Evans's charisma attracted many new members, and he used contemporary scientific theories about racial superiority to justify the Klan's goal of a permanent white Protestant ruling class in America. The Klan's leadership included Dallas's police commissioner, Louis Turley; criminal district judge Felix Robertson; the county's Democratic party chairman; the county tax assessor; the local superintendent of Ford Motors; four Dallas Power & Light Co. executives, and the *Dallas Times Herald*'s managing editor, Phillip Fox, who later quit to become the national Klan's publicity director. Regular members included Dallas County State Bank president and future Dallas mayor Robert L. Thornton, and several top-ranking Dallas police officers. The Klan's puritanism won support from high-profile clergy, including Dr. C. C. Selectman of the First Methodist Church and the pastors of Westminster Presbyterian and the First Presbyterian churches.[32]

The Klan's enforcers turned the Trinity River bottoms, which run through the center of Dallas, into an open-air torture chamber, abducting and bullwhipping suspected sex offenders, bootleggers, African-Americans, supposedly immoral women, and anyone else they felt violated their code. Historians have documented at least sixty-eight victims of Klan floggings along the river.[33]

To demonstrate how mainstream the Klan was, Evans pushed for a special Klan Day at the Texas State Fair in Dallas, one of the state's most important events. The monthlong carnival and rodeo included livestock and crop competitions, educational displays, and plenty of rides and food. Certain days were designated for different groups, such as high school or elementary days. In 1923, fair organizers declared Klan Day on October 23, and the Dallas chapter planned a Klan initiation ceremony at the fair that evening, complete with a fireworks display. City and county offices closed and the Union Pacific Railroad booked eight special trains to deliver Klan supporters from across the state and Oklahoma. Thousands of Klansmen marched through downtown in full regalia to Fair Park, marking one of the largest-ever Klan gatherings. That morning, Dallas Klan No. 66 opened a home for abandoned children with a ceremony attended by the mayor, Louis Blaylock, who said, "Now as to the Klan. I have watched the order grow from its infancy to its present period of greatness, and I want to say that so far as I know, the criticisms that have been made of it have been without foundation."[34]

More than 151,000 people went to the fair that day. At 1:00 P.M. Evans gave a speech entitled "Immigration Is America's Big Problem." He hoped to rally working-class whites by blaming their low pay and unemployment on immigrants from non–northern European countries. In Evans's world, whiteness was far more limited than we might imagine today. He pronounced that people of Latin, Greek, Balkan, or Slav descent could not follow the rule of law like people from western Europe, and therefore the United States should ban them. Jews and Catholics represented a special threat, he warned, because they plotted to control the world. Evans cooked an anti-Semitic, racist, and anti-immigrant stew that he flavored with populism and trade unionism. He denounced industrialists for making people work on Sundays and condemned the wealthy for instituting slavery to ensure a cheap workforce. Now that slavery was banned, he argued, those same capitalists imported inferior workers from overseas because they were cheaper than white men. "Do our overlords of industry realize what they are doing to America?" Evans asked the rapturous crowd.[35] The Klan's national leaders swore in 5,631 new members after the speech, while the drum and bugle corps from Dallas Klan No. 66 performed for

75,000 onlookers in the Fair Park grandstand.[36] Evans felt triumphant.

For many Dallas elites, though, the *Dallas Morning News*' repeated warnings against the Klan appeared prescient. When Evans took this more populist tack, he revealed to Dallas's elite that Klansmen were not chivalric, patriotic Protestants protecting antebellum southern values, but urban working-class vigilantes empowered by demagogic leaders. The city's most powerful residents decided to stop the Klan.

For the next six years, the Klan's battle with the *Morning News* continued, with ever-increasing support from businessmen, and editorial writers railed against the Klan's secrecy and pandering to poor whites. The Klan denied any wrongdoing and pointed to its charity work. The group called on its members to boycott the paper and threatened any business that advertised in it. The paper's circulation plummeted and the parent company sold the *Galveston News* to keep the Dallas paper afloat. Dealey later called the paper's stand against the Klan "perhaps the most courageous thing *The News* ever did."[37]

The Dallas Klan owned a meeting hall at 421 Harwood, across the street from the First Presbyterian Church and a block from the Scottish Rite Mason Hall, which Tommy attended. The Klan held fundraising parties for the children's home, Klan Haven. At Christmas, the group handed out food baskets and used clothing to needy families.[38] While the Klan worked hard to give off the appearance of a charitable and honorable organization, internal schisms in 1924 began to break the invisible empire apart.

THE KLAN EMERGES IN MARLIN

Hatefulness is not an attractive quality, and most people share their deeply held bigotry only with those whom they know agree. Klan anonymity allowed people to hate in a safe environment. Keeping their numbers secret also led the general public to overestimate the Klan's size, giving it more influence than it deserved. Therefore Klan membership was a closely guarded secret. Even in a small town like Marlin, most people did not know with certainty who was a Klan member until they went to a meeting. And even then, they wouldn't learn the full scope of the local Klan's operation until they underwent initiation.[39] Klansmen used secret handshakes and coded language to identify one another. For instance, a man may say "a.y.a.k." or "A-YAK" to inquire "Are you a Klansman?" The proper reply was "a.k.i.m." or "A-KIM," meaning "A Klansman I am."[40] Many of the most powerful men kept their membership secret from low-ranking members to avoid implications for their businesses or political careers. But even if someone did not publicly proclaim their membership, it could be inferred, and I have found evidence that R.E.L., my great-great-grandfather, was a Klansman.

When R.E.L. joined the Marlin school board in 1916, he took over a seat vacated by William Daniel Kyser, a prominent farmer and businessman who had moved from Alabama after the Civil War. Both men were active in the First Baptist Church and the Masonic Lodge. Kyser grew cotton and raised cattle, the same as R.E.L.'s family, and Kyser built the first cotton gin in Marlin. In 1892, he joined other Marlin businessmen to start the Marlin Cotton Oil Company Mill, which he managed for twenty-eight years. R.E.L. grew up with Kyser's son, William Earnest Kyser. The two men lived ten blocks from each other and both speculated in oil and gas leases. R.E.L.'s peer and business colleague William Earnest Kyser established the local chapter of the Ku Klux Klan and became its cyclops.[41]

Marlin Klan No. 107 made its first public appearance on September 13, 1921. Using the group's standard tactic, 206 men wearing head-to-toe white masks and robes marched behind an American flag and a burning cross from Rimes Park through Marlin's downtown streets. Rumors of the Klan march had spread throughout Falls County, so large crowds lined Live Oak, Walker, and Coleman streets as the men silently passed. The Klansmen made a point of marching down Wood Street, Marlin's black main street:

> In the parade were a number of public officials, some from Marlin
> and some from other towns. On account of the lights being turned

off our lynx-eyed reporter could not read all the signs on the banners, but they were of the usual strong character carried by the Klan in other towns, with an addition or two. One of these favored the freedom of speech and of the press.[42]

The *Marlin Democrat* reported that Klansmen from Waco, Mart, Rosebud, and Chilton joined the procession, with some apparently going to the wrong park and arriving late.[43]

Two weeks later, the Klan tried to announce their presence with a similar march in Lorena, a town twenty miles to the west. McLennan County's sheriff, Bob Buchanan, asked to see the Klan leaders while they were putting on their robes to inform them that marching anonymously violated state law. They refused to see him and marched anyway. The sheriff confronted them:

> A wild scene ensued. Ten or 15 pistol shots were fired in rapid succession. The sheriff and Deputy Burton, who with Deputy Wood had accompanied their chief to the scene, were seen dashing about the road.
>
> Buchanan had been knocked down at the beginning of the trouble by one of the paraders, but arose knife in hand. He said someone took his gun away from him while he was down, Buchanan soon cleared a space about him with his knife. In a few minutes, however, he was seen to fall again and was carried to a nearby store for treatment.
>
> All of the wounded men were immediately given first aid and ambulances rushed from Waco and bore those seriously hurt back to hospitals in that city.
>
> "I begged, and I pleaded, and I begged and I pleaded with them to halt," [Buchanan] said wearily, "but they wouldn't hear me."[44]

Buchanan and eight other people suffered gunshot and knife wounds. Buchanan took two rounds in his chest and thigh, but he remained conscious until he reached the hospital in Waco.[45] The following day, eight hundred Lorena citizens signed a letter denouncing Buchanan.

They said they did not believe the Klansmen had violated any laws and had implored Buchanan not to interfere.[46]

In an editorial, Kennedy explained that the Klan parade violated the Texas penal code, which makes it a crime to threaten or intimidate someone anonymously. The Klan also violated federal law, he added, which bans two or more persons from oppressing, threatening, or intimidating someone from the free exercise of their rights under the Constitution. Kennedy warned that the Marlin Klan members who had participated in the Lorena march could face prosecution.

Two days later, Waco businessman Louis Crow died from wounds he had suffered after taking his family to see the parade. The riot and murder of a bystander made front-page headlines across the state. Governor Pat Neff offered to send Texas Rangers and asked the attorney general to issue an opinion on whether the Klan had broken the law. Lt. Gov. Lynch Davidson called on the Klan to dissolve.[47]

Texas attorney general Calvin Cureton concluded that if Klansmen used threats, intimidation, or violence—even for a moral reason—the entire chapter could face prosecution for conspiracy. Cureton said the anonymous threatening letters and flyers carrying the Klan's name clearly violated the state's penal code and that Klansmen also faced prosecution if they violated a person's civil rights. Governor Neff forwarded the opinion to sheriffs across the state, urging them to prosecute Klan members who made threats or used violence.[48]

BLACKFACE AND WHITE ROBES

Racial awareness was a fundamental part of life in rural Texas, where entertainment during this era often revolved around stereotypes. African-Americans routinely performed as jesters or musicians, and these minstrels inspired white actors to put on black makeup and mimic them. During the 1920s, seniors at all-white Marlin High School put on "negro minstrel shows," calling themselves the "Marlin High Burnt-Cork Artists," a reference to how they blackened their faces. The songs they performed included "Massas in de Cold, Cold Ground," "Polly-

Wolly-Doodle," "Jim Crack Corn," and "Old Kentucky Home." In 1922, R. E. L.'s nephew smeared blackened cork on his face to play in a show the *Marlin Democrat* pronounced "a big hit."[49] That same year, the high school seniors hosted a Kriss Kross Karnival to raise money.[50]

Poll taxes and the all-white Democratic primary meant that African-Americans had no political power. When Falls County officials announced how many people had paid the poll tax in 1922, the *Marlin Democrat* ran the headline POLL TAX RECORDS BROKEN—ONE THOUSAND QUALIFIED IN THE CITY OF MARLIN—NINE-TENTHS ARE WHITE. Of those who paid the tax, 821 were white men, 576 were white women, 66 were black men, and 62 were black women.[51]

After marching through Marlin, the Klan moved to smaller Falls County towns. The *Dallas Morning News*, of March 8, 1922, reported a parade near Tomlinson Hill:

> It was estimated that 2,000 people were on the streets when the lights were turned out before the parade started. Many people came from Marlin, Rosebud, Chilton, Travis and other Falls County towns to witness the parade. No demonstration was made and scarcely a sound was heard during the parade.
>
> About thirty automobiles parked outside the city limits earlier in the evening and the occupants were seen to clothe themselves in white robes in a grove of trees.

Klan chapters also formed in Chilton and Rosebud, aggressively recruiting members and threatening those who opposed them. In an open letter, the Klan ordered one critic "to improve his conduct and cut out your activities."[52]

Dozens of citizens wrote open letters, asking political candidates to state their views on the organization, with the authors providing their names and registering their opposition to the invisible empire. Many prominent Marlinites issued statements in the *Marlin Democrat*, promising that they had never joined the Klan and held no alliance to the group. No Tomlinson or Stallworth made such pledges.

George Carter, a local Democratic party leader, attended public meetings across Falls County for two years, explaining why the Klan was dangerous. In Marlin, he was usually welcome, but in Chilton and other villages, the *Democrat*'s reporter called the meetings "cordial." Carter wanted voters to minimize the influence of known Klan members at precinct meetings, hoping to keep them from becoming delegates to the Democratic party's county convention.

Voters in Marlin's northern precinct elected three Klansmen to serve as Democratic party delegates in 1922. A newspaper report did not name who the Klan members were, only who were not:

> On the matter of selecting delegates a motion was made by W. E. Hodges that a committee composed of S. J. Stallworth, L. J. Davis and B. J. Miller be elected to recommend a list of delegates to the county convention. J. W. Spivey offered an amendment that Frank Oltorf and N. J. Llewellyn, who are not members of the Klan, be added to the committee. This amendment was promptly voted down.[53]

W. E. Hodges, the author of the Klan list, was an officer in the Old Settlers and Confederate Veterans Association. Sanford J. Stallworth was Churchill Jones's grandson and R.E.L.'s second cousin. The report clearly implies that at least Sanford was a Klansman. In Marlin's South Precinct, the chairman named the delegates to the convention "without regard to Klan membership" and placed R.E.L. on the list.[54] But it was clear that the paper believed that the majority of the city's delegates were Klansmen, and R.E.L.'s appointment and his relationships with known Klansmen makes his membership pretty clear. The Klan's success in Falls County was not unusual:

> In the counties in which are located Houston, Beaumont, Port Arthur, Dallas, Waco, Fort Worth, Wichita Falls and others the Klan ticket swept nearly everything before it. The visible membership strength of the Klan appears to be almost entirely in the cities, and the invisible methods used are such that non-members do not know who the members are, or who the Klan candidates are for the reason that the Klan candidates in nearly every instance deny that they are mem-

bers, the law of the Klan suspending them automatically the moment they are asked the question.[55]

The 1922 election was a wake-up call for Democrats, who witnessed a racist club take control of their party. Klan members saw nothing wrong with endorsing candidates or in Klansmen running for office. Critics, though, refused to believe Klansmen when they denied using violence and intimidation, and they worried about a secret society wielding so much hidden influence. Those opposing the Klan did not necessarily denounce white supremacy; most supported segregation and the ban on African-Americans voting. They worried only about their power and privileges.

The *Marlin Democrat* of the early 1920s did not report any of the signature attacks the Klan carried out in larger cities. No stories exist about masked men lynching anyone, or tarring and feathering people for alleged immorality. Considering his anti-Klan editorials and his extremely thorough coverage of the Klan elsewhere in Texas, Kennedy is unlikely to have looked the other way. In fact, the *Democrat* took a slightly mocking tone toward the KKK:

The Ku Klux Klan entertained a large crowd on the Falls County courthouse lawn Thursday evening regaling the audience with several speeches before treating them to a watermelon feast that had been prepared.

The melons, which had been in cold storage for several days, proved delicious and the supply was abundantly sufficient for all.

A number of out-of-town Klansmen were on the speaker's platform. Also in the audience.

The meeting was called to order by W. E. Kyser, Cyclops of the Marlin Klan.

"We are gathered here for three purposes," Mr. Kyser said:

"First, that we might mix and mingle together in friendship for the cause of high citizenship and Americanism, and we hope that we shall not in any way offend any race or nationality; second, we are here to hear some addresses, and third, for the watermelon feast."

"The Knights of the Ku Klux Klan is a patriotic, fraternal, benevolent organization. It has been accused of fighting the Jews and the
Catholics. That, we deny. If I had to belong to an organization that
would bar me from association or business with my Jewish friends,
that organization would be without me."[56]

Kyser then handed the dais over to the Reverend T. J. Slaughter, a
Baptist minister from Killeen, who gave a speech that strikes twenty-
first-century notes. He accused northern liberals of imposing their
values on the South, declaring Baptist marriages void and their children bastards. He mixed traditionally conservative values with his
bigotry to make the latter more palatable:

When I went into the Klan, I thought there was a strong probability of
it being a whipping bee, or a tar and feather party. But soon after-
wards, I learned differently. That is not the purpose of the organization at all.

The men who started the Klan on Stone Mountain in Georgia
have since aroused many hatreds unintentionally and have assumed
responsibilities of which they never dreamed.

Today, the Knights of the Ku Klux Klan is the most misunder-
stood, the most abused institution in the country, but in spite of this,
it has grown, thanks to the men who met on Stone Mountain and
dedicated their lives to Christian ideals and everything for which
our country stands.

There are people in this country who declare your children were
born out of wedlock because they did not sanction your marriage.
Our homes would be declared violators of the law, if we did not stand
up in our own defense.

Every Klansman believes in the tenets of Christianity as taught in
America. I love to preach Klan principles, just as I love to preach the
gospel. The time must never come when we cannot talk out plainly
about our ideals. God forbid that you and I shall ever see such a time
in America. Religious liberty is a gracious thing.[57]

The next speaker was Garland Adair, editor of the *Mexia Daily News* in neighboring Limestone County. He was publicly coming out as a Klansman and compared the group to the American Legion. He said the Klan's disguises followed the tradition of the Boston Tea Party in 1773, when antitax protesters dressed as Native Americans: "There are many members of the Klan who do not believe in the robe, but if you condemn this in principle, you condemn the men who conducted the Boston Tea Party as the first act of the American revolution, and you condemn the [Klansmen] of the 1860s."[58]

That fall, the Klan began advertising its meetings in the *Marlin Democrat*. They met every other Tuesday "at the usual place."

Twenty-four years later, members of the Old Settlers and Veterans Association still struggled to explain the Klan. In its official 1947 history, the authors briefly mention the group:

> What the modern Ku Klux Klan signified, its objectives and what its "inner" activities were, only members knew. Those on the "outside" came to understand that the Klan stood for a self-defined American-ism, excluding certain races and setting up a code in variance with tolerance, religious freedom, and moral ethics, not adjusted by legal processes. They thought of the Klan members as people wearing long white robes, concealing their identities on parade, or at, or going to, meeting places. They saw fiery red crosses, marking and dramatizing assemblies in some exclusive and guarded place.
>
> The Klan stirred differences in opinion in many sections of the nation, resulting in hatreds, even outbursts of violence. In the county the Klan was short lived and in 1946 references to memberships in it were in lighter vein.[59]

The decision to allow those on the inside to believe what they wanted, and simply to describe what outsiders perceived, is a curious editorial decision. The Klan played a tremendous role in Texas politics between 1921 and 1926, and it certainly dominated headlines in the *Marlin Democrat*. In 1976, the all-white Bicentennial Committee of the Marlin Chamber of Commerce, led by a member of the Oltorf clan, compiled another history of Marlin and Falls County, still struggling with whether to condemn the Klan in full:

> In Marlin, the Klan had three different meeting places. The first was upstairs above the building on the northwest corner of Commerce and Wood Streets. J. M. Kennedy, editor of the Democrat, strongly opposed the Klan and published the names of those attending the meetings in his paper. The Klansmen thought it was an inside job of reporting and planned to "tar and feather" the traitor if he was discovered. Mr. Kennedy's employees did not attend another meeting, but the names continued to be published. Years later it was learned that Skeeter Levy [grandson of Jewish merchant Marx Levy] sat in an unlighted office behind Bill Bowdon's garage and listed each Klansman as he attended the meeting.
>
> The Klan also met at the barn on Anders Street behind E. E. (Bud) Kyser's home. The governing body of the Klan was the Klo Kouncil, which met at Conyer's Barn at the foot of Bean Hill.
>
> One night in August of 1924, the Klan announced they were going to parade down Main Street and then have a mass meeting on the front lawn of the Kyser home on Anders.
>
> The streets were lined with spectators, as row after row of white-robed figures with white-robed horses rode silently through the down town section of Marlin. The Klansmen at each side of the column carried huge burning torches.
>
> As soon as the last rank of Klansmen had passed, the townspeople got in their cars and drove over to the Kyser's to see the assemblage. Three huge crosses on the law were lighted from the torches and these burned furiously throughout the meeting.[60]

I was unable to find either the lists of members or any report of the Klan marching to Kyser's home, but the *Democrat* archives are incomplete. Kennedy did take a hard line against the Klan and denounced any organization that relied on anonymity. He believed a healthy democracy relied on people who put their names to their opinions and participated in public debate. He refused to run any anonymous submissions in his paper.[61]

DEMOCRATS ORGANIZE AGAINST THE KLAN

The Klan did its best to make the 1924 gubernatorial election about Prohibition. Governor Jim Ferguson could not run again because he'd been impeached, so he convinced his wife, Miriam, to run as his surrogate. The couple was known as "Ma and Pa Ferguson" and everyone knew a vote for the ever-popular Ma was really a vote for Pa. Running against Ma was Judge Felix Robertson, a Dallas County criminal judge who was an open member of the Klan and supported Prohibition.[62]

The Fergusons and mainline Democrats made Robertson's Klan membership the main issue, pointing out that unknown assailants had flogged or tarred more than sixty people in Dallas County without Robertson's court indicting anyone for those crimes. Ferguson supporters openly questioned whether Robertson's secret oath to the Klan was more important than the public oath he had taken as a judge. Kennedy wrote an editorial every week to explain how Robertson and his Klan allies opposed Prohibition until he decided to run for governor. He also remarked on how Ma Ferguson did not drink and banned alcohol from the governor's mansion.[63]

In a five-way primary, Robertson won the most votes, but Ma came in second and forced a runoff. In Marlin, the Klan celebrated at a meeting on August 6.[64] But the loss terrified mainstream Democrats, and they mobilized their supporters for the runoff and minimized Klan influence at the 1924 state convention.[65]

Ma Ferguson won the Democratic nomination and became the first female governor of Texas. Houston's grand cyclops, Sam McClure, promised the Klan would get out of politics and transform into a strictly fraternal organization, open to any Christian gentleman.[66] The following year, the people of Marlin elected Kennedy mayor a second time, and he served three terms, ending in 1933.[67]

Klan membership reached its peak in 1925, when Indiana authorities arrested and convicted grand dragon David Stephenson for the rape and murder of a young white teacher. In Alabama, the group launched a violent terror campaign that garnered national media coverage, and dozens of Klan leaders across the country faced prosecution for fraud and embezzlement, along with federal investigations.[68]

The anti-Klan movement gained steam when major Protestant clergy began denouncing it and civic groups like the Dallas Citizens League openly opposed it. The NAACP and the Anti-Defamation League publicized the Klan's illegal activities and lobbied Washington and statehouses to pass legislation against it. The white middle class came to see the Klan as a group of low-class, uneducated individuals running amok, and they turned against it. Texas membership in the Klan dropped from a peak of 97,000 in 1924 to only 18,000 in 1926 and the Klan closed its Dallas headquarters on Harwood Street in 1929.[69]

The majority of whites may have lost interest in the Klan's secrecy and violence, but they remained convinced that God had created them superior to other races and that their Protestantism was the single true faith.[70] The seeds of the civil rights movement were just beginning to be sown.

FIFTEEN

You must allow some type of sedative, a safety valve, you know, to avoid an explosion.

—Frank Wyman

Urbanization and economic progress defined African-American life at the turn of the twentieth century. Black preachers and politicians taught parishioners that they could succeed, but they needed to be ten times better than any white man. The poorest parents worked hard to ensure their children went to school and saved as much money as they could manage. But they also celebrated life, and for many, that meant going out on Saturday night.

Black cotton pickers mostly spent Saturday night on their corner of the large plantations with picnics, music, dancing, and some drinking. These celebrations, along with Sunday church services, produced skilled black musicians in the late 1890s who sang gospel music on Sundays and gave birth to the blues on Saturday nights.[1] Performers used their voices as an instrument, accompanied by an acoustic guitar. They started with a spoken story and wove a narrative about the troubles of a black person's life, gathering rhythm until it grew into a full-throated song. Gospel music praised the spiritual, while the blues centered on the flesh.[2]

Many African-Americans moved to segregated cities at the turn of the century. Black entrepreneurs established restaurants, hotels, and red-light districts, where the beer and liquor flowed, a gambler could pick up a game, and a lonely man could hire a companion for the night.[3] The red-light district in Marlin emerged on Wood Street, one block south of Marlin's main thoroughfare and safely out of white society's sight. The stretch of mostly single-story redbrick buildings—only 650 feet long from the railroad tracks to Island Street—became an entertainment destination for African-Americans within a hundred-mile radius. Whites described it as "the street where blacks find inexpensive entertainment in the beer joints, pool halls, liquor stores and cafes," and because Wood Street saw so many fights and "cuttings," Marlinites nicknamed it the "Bloody Butcher."[4]

In an age before jukeboxes and cheap amplification, live musicians and dancing attracted people to the cafés and bars on Wood Street, and famous black musicians made it a stop on their southern circuit. Henry "Ragtime Texas" Thomas, an itinerant Texas blues and gospel singer, traveled the state by hopping freight trains that delivered him to Wood Street among other stops. He recorded twenty-three songs for Vocalion Records between 1923 and 1929, and at age fifty, he was one of the oldest blues musicians recorded, providing the earliest examples of Texas blues.[5] More than forty years later, the Loving Spoonful, Taj Mahal, the Nitty Gritty Dirt Band, and the Grateful Dead recorded his songs.

Thomas made a more immediate impact in Wood Street bars, where aspiring musicians listened to him. He usually invited onto the stage anyone who thought they could keep up. One of the more promising musicians, fourteen years younger than Thomas, was Huddie Ledbetter, later known as "Lead Belly." Lead Belly was born on the Jeter Plantation, near Mooringsport, Louisiana, but his family moved to Texas when he was five years old. Lead Belly learned to play the guitar, piano, harmonica, violin, and mandolin at a young age and at fifteen performed on Shreveport's equivalent of Wood Street. He played Marlin frequently. Many believe Thomas influenced Ledbetter's blues playing before he went to prison in 1918 for murder, where he acquired the name Lead Belly. Explanations for the name range from buckshot lodged in his gut to a simple play on his last name and fat stomach.[6]

Before he became famous, Lead Belly befriended Blind Lemon Jefferson, a child of sharecroppers, who grew up near Falls County. Jefferson performed on street corners in Marlin for donations dropped in his tin cup. Like most black musicians, he could sing gospel music in church or minstrel songs for whites on the sidewalk. He learned to sing the blues on Wood Street by listening to Thomas and Lead Belly play. Jefferson traveled with Lead Belly around East Texas and to Dallas's Deep Ellum district from 1910 to 1915. While performing with Jefferson, Lead Belly learned to play the twelve-string guitar, which became his signature instrument. The two men influenced each other's styles until Dallas police arrested Lead Belly for carrying a pistol in 1915, and he was sentenced to serve on a chain gang.[7]

Lead Belly returned to Wood Street after serving seven years in prison on a 1918 murder change. He won clemency in 1925 and worked odd jobs until he was convicted of attempted murder in Louisiana five years later. While in Angola Prison, he attracted the attention of Texas folklorist John Lomax. After Lead Belly was released from Angola in 1934, Lomax took him to New York, and they began recording hit records such as "C.C. Rider," "Jail House Blues," "Ballad of the Boll Weevil," "Midnight Special," and "Irene Goodnight."[8]

While Jefferson was performing at a Baptist picnic in Leon County in 1919, an eight-year-old boy joined the blind man on stage. At first, Jefferson barked when the child played off-key and only realized he was a boy when Sam Hopkins spoke up. Jefferson then showed Hopkins a few things on the guitar and allowed him to play in the background. By the late 1920s, Sam was playing piano on Wood Street, using the nickname Lightnin'.[9] Other black musicians who likely played Marlin while traveling the blues circuit included Alphonso Trent, Troy Floyd, Teddy Wilson, Oscar Moore, Henry "Buster" Smith, and Budd Johnson.[10]

Jefferson was playing in Deep Elum in 1925 when recruiters from Paramount Records asked him to record in Chicago. The small recording company specialized in country blues, but at first they paid Jefferson to record gospel songs under the name Deacon L. J. Bates and only afterward recorded his distinctive brand of Texas blues. Jefferson's extraordinary guitar skills and two-octave vocal range brought a new complexity to traditional blues recordings, and he was an instant hit. His records also captured a very early stage in the genre's history.[11] One of his songs was "Blind Lemon's Penitentiary Blues," which was about Groesbeck, a town twenty-five miles northeast of Marlin.

> *Take Fort Worth for your dressing and take Dallas all for your style.*
> *Take Fort Worth for your dressing, Dallas all for your style.*
> *If you want to go the state penitentiary, go to Groesbeck for your trial.*
>
> *I hung around Groesbeck, and I worked in hard showers of rain.*
> *I say I hung around Groesbeck, I worked in hard showers of rain.*
> *I never felt the least bit uneasy, till I caught that penitentiary bound*
>   *train.*
>
> *I used to be a drunkard, I was rowdy everywhere I go.*
> *I say I used to be a drunkard and rowdy everywhere I go.*
> *If I ever got out of this trouble I'm in, I won't be rowdy no more.*
>
> *Boys don't be bad, please don't crowd your mind.*
> *I said, boys don't be bad and please don't crowd your mind.*
> *If you happen to get in trouble in Groesbeck, they going to send you*
>   *penitentiary flyin.'*

Jefferson was the biggest-selling blues artist in the country from 1926 to 1929, and, by some accounts, he lived well. His records made him famous and he toured the South as the "King of the Country Blues." But by 1929 his heavy drinking and womanizing were catching up with him, and in December police found his body in a snowdrift in South Chicago, the cause of death a mystery. That afternoon he'd visited the Paramount offices and was scheduled to play a house party that night. Explanations range from a heart attack to murder.[12]

Thirty-five miles southwest of Marlin, Willie Johnson grew up in Temple, where his stepmother, angry at Johnson's father for beating her, threw lye in the seven-year-old's eyes and blinded him. Johnson learned to play a homemade guitar and became a street musician who sang gospel songs. In the early days, Blind Willie Johnson played on a Marlin street corner across from Blind Lemon Jefferson, competing for tips. Later in life, he settled down in Marlin, performed at the Church of God in Christ on Commerce Street, and married Willie B. Harris. In 1927, Johnson went to Dallas and recorded gospel songs for Columbia Records. His first record sold 15,400 copies, better than most blues records of the day. In 1930, he recorded his last songs in Atlanta and sold only eight hundred records. Johnson played the streets, bars, and churches of Texas, anywhere he could make a buck. He divorced Harris in 1932 and moved to Beaumont, where he married again and became a preacher. He died in 1945, at the age of forty-eight, possibly from malaria.[13]

In the 1960s, Johnson's music was rereleased as part of the *Anthology of American Folk Music* and profoundly influenced folk revivalists. Bob Dylan recorded Johnson's songs, and rock guitarists, including Eric Clapton and Jimmy Page, copied his slide guitar playing. When NASA searched for sounds to place on a recording to blast into space on the *Voyager* spacecraft in 1977, one was Blind Willie Johnson singing "Dark Was the Night, Cold Was the Ground."[14]

THE BLOODY BUTCHER

Booze, gambling, and women attracted most of the customers to Wood Street, and white authorities left it alone for the most part, even during Prohibition. Whites really didn't care what blacks did as long as whites didn't get hurt. City marshals hired black officers to police the street on their behalf. Many of the city's businessmen profited from renting the buildings or selling black businessmen wholesale goods. White farmers made the cheap beer and moonshine, and some Marlinites alleged the county sheriff and city marshals sold it to black barkeeps.[15]

Churchgoing African-Americans stayed away from Wood Street and parents taught their children that the bogeyman spent time there. Vincent Tomlinson's eldest daughter, Lizzie Mae, said she would peek down the street when she went to town with her parents, but they forbade her from even walking down it, saying only sinners visited Wood Street. Lizzie was also afraid of a legendary woman, more than six feet tall and heavyset, who could beat down most men.[16] Treetop Georgia was the queen of Wood Street in the late 1930s, running a gambling den and at least one bar. She carried a straight razor, though she didn't need it. The big, powerful woman could fight equally well with her fists or a broken bottle. She dealt directly with the law and the businesspeople who ran the street. She kept the chaos to a minimum and sorted out problems when they arose.[17]

Gamblers on Wood Street preferred dice, usually craps. All they needed were a pair of dice and a hard surface, and they could shut down a game quickly if trouble started. During a visit to Marlin, Frank Wyman, a retired professor and a cousin of the black Tomlinsons, told me how professional black gamblers would wait on Wood Street for the farmworkers on payday, and how small a town Marlin could be:

> I was named after my father's brother, and this man was a professional gambler. He womanized throughout the week, and on Friday evening he would put on his fancy clothes and go down to Wood Street and wait for those who worked in the cotton fields with his dice. And that's how he spent Friday, Saturday, and Sunday—he threw dice with field workers—and then Monday when they went back to the field, he just womanized until the next weekend.

> At any rate, one of the women he was womanizing with was also the mistress of what I think must have been a sheriff's deputy, and when he arrived, seeing my uncle drinking his liquor and eating his food and sharing the same woman, they got into a fight. [Frank] actually hit him to the head with an ax, with the side of the blade. My uncle Frank hit a white sheriff upside the head with an ax!

> [Sheriff L. O.] Hay told my dad that because Frank's mother had been the deputy's nanny and had nursed him, fed him all his life, that was the reason that Frank wasn't dead. That is the only reason. Other than that, he'd have been like any other black man in Falls County, and he'd been dead the next day.[18]

The end of Prohibition in 1933 boosted business on Wood Street, and its reputation as a place for African-Americans to have fun. After the draft began for World War II, black soldiers from Fort Hood made the fifty-mile bus ride to Wood Street while on weekend passes. White businessmen certainly profited, but Wyman told me Wood Street, like Beale Street in Memphis and dozens of other streets across the South, played an important role in maintaining white dominance:

> You must allow some type of sedative, a safety valve, you know, to avoid an explosion. And Wood Street was a safety valve. It got people who would chop cotton all day in this type of heat for five dollars and see their families working with them. And on Friday night they'd get as drunk as possible for anyone to get. And Monday morning at 6:30 [they'd] get back on the cotton truck. So it became necessary, because if that was shut down, pretty soon it would be the beginning of a revolution.[19]

Jukeboxes replaced the blues singers on Wood Street in the 1960s, and illicit drugs became more prevalent. When the district attorney brought murder charges in 1961 against Tom Webb, one of the black officers who patrolled Wood Street, for shooting and killing a suspect, Webb used Wood Street as his defense: "His attorneys emphasized that he was a good man in a tough job, keeping order in Marlin's Negro section. Attorneys Robert Carter, Robert Peterson and Tom Bartlett Sr., all of Marlin, labeled the area "as tough a district as you could find anywhere." People who want it to operate "wide open" would like to see Webb out of the way, said Carter.[20]

The all-white jury acquitted Webb.

FORTUNE STREET

In the 1920s, R. E. L. lived on Fortune Street, six blocks from Wood Street. He was scaling back his business and easing into retirement. His Victorian home sat on a one-acre lot, and his wife Bettie oversaw a vegetable garden covering a quarter of it. They hired a black woman to work inside the house, and a black man to tend the garden.[21] Bettie won the prettiest yard contest in 1928.[22] The following year, the city granted a contract to McElwrath Paving Company to pave the city's streets, the cost split between the city and residents. Fortune Street, stretching from the county courthouse to the white cemetery, was among the first finished.[23]

R. E. L. and Bettie also saw the completion of their favorite community project, a new brick neo-Gothic chapel for the First Baptist Church on the northeast corner of Coleman and Oaks streets. Col. Harry Barton, founder of the Dy-N-Shine shoe polish company, donated a pipe organ.[24]

The silent-movie theaters installed sound equipment in the late 1920s, and the arrival of "talkies" ended the community opera house. Only schools and community groups kept producing live theater.[25] The Marlin Chamber of Commerce looked at the aging Victorian-style hotels that ringed the hot springs and wrote to Conrad Hilton, a New Mexico native who'd just finished building hotels in Dallas and Waco. Hilton agreed to build a $375,000 modern hotel if the chamber could raise a $50,000 down payment. Construction began in 1929, and Hilton hired a French firm to paint and decorate it.[26]

The hotel was half-finished when stocks on Wall Street plummeted in October 1929. The crash had little immediate effect on rural Texas, where money was tied up in land and crops, not stocks and bonds. Hilton opened his ninth hotel on May 27, 1930, with a gala banquet, and he invited U.S. Senator Tom Connally and Amon Carter, publisher of the *Fort Worth Star-Telegram*. The ballroom accommodated three hundred people, the largest in the region, with a hardwood dance floor in the center. A fight broke out after dinner, and Hilton called the celebration to a premature end, which turned out to be a bad omen.

During the first two years, the hotel booked big bands, including Lawrence Welk's, but the Depression slowly shrank Marlin's mineral-water tourism. Hilton sold the building to the National Hotel Company, which changed the name to the Falls Hotel.[27] The nine-story building remains the most prominent structure in Marlin, but it sits vacant, having never reached its potential.

The financial shock wave of 1929 eventually trickled down to Marlin's farmers and merchants. White unemployment in Texas rose from 4.2 percent in 1920 to 5.4 percent in 1933. African-American unemployment jumped from 4.8 percent to 8.8 percent.[28] When one of Marlin's banks collapsed, the Chamber of Commerce and Senator Tom Connally bought it, while other Marlin banks struggled. President Franklin D. Roosevelt's Agricultural Adjustment Administration ordered Falls County farmers in 1933 to plow up as much as a third of their cotton crop in the face of a global glut. Many farmers grumbled about destroying crops they had worked hard to cultivate, and the following year, ranchers begrudgingly followed a similar order to reduce their herds of hogs and cattle.[29]

To fight unemployment, Roosevelt established the Works Progress Administration to hire millions for government projects. White farmers watched with dismay as many of their workers left the fields for government construction jobs. Townspeople, though, welcomed the new schools, streets, roads, and, ultimately, the new Falls County Courthouse in 1939. Farmers didn't complain quite as much when the Rural Electrification Administration delivered power to their homes for the first time.[30]

Marlin hosted the East Texas Chamber of Commerce in April 1931, and with high school football's growing popularity, Tom McQueen donated land for Marlin High School's first gridiron. The city continued to grow, and the first Safeway store opened the same year, the first grocery not owned by a local businessman. Business was even good enough that the Scheiblich family opened a second grocery on Coleman Street in 1936, later calling it Kash Way.[31]

OLD SETTLERS

The Old Settlers and Confederate Veterans Association reunions continued to grow in popularity, even during the toughest years of the Depression. Marjorie Rogers, a Marlin-based journalist for both the *Marlin Democrat* and the *Dallas Morning News,* wrote a feature story about the 1937 renunion, providing a glimpse into Falls County society.

Since tradition dictated that everyone take an elderly person to the reunion, Rogers took ninety-year-old Granny Maxwell:

> Granny Maxwell's eyes sparkled as we completed our journey and
> drove up to the tabernacle just as the meeting was being called to
> order by President Tomlinson. A hush fell over the crowd as Tomlin-
> son's rich voice boomed out the opening announcement:
>
> "Ladies and Gentlemen the Old Settlers' and Confederate Veter-
> ans' reunion of Falls county will now begin its annual reunion.
> Chaplain Asbury please give the invocation."
>
> Minutes of last meeting were read by a son of one of the commu-
> nity's pioneers. The minutes were virtually the same as those of pre-
> vious years, for there is little formal business transacted at these
> reunions.
>
> President Tomlinson arose and launched immediately into his
> welcoming address. Occasionally he paused to greet some old timer
> entering the tabernacle.
>
> "Well here is Uncle Ed Smith. Come on in Uncle Ed. Sit down here
> with the rest of your old friends. We are mighty glad to have you here
> with us."
>
> Then he stepped down from the platform to help Uncle Ed find
> a chair, near the front, where he could hear better. Several other late
> arrivals claimed the president's attention before he finally concluded
> his remarks with the announcement that "now we are going to have
> some mighty fine music."
>
> McCreary's Music-Makers struck up a lively tune. There was a
> mixture of old and new melodies from piano, fiddle, saxophone,
> bass-fiddle, banjo and guitar. The players, all country-bred, played
> tunes nearest to the hearts of their audience. Wrinkled, sun-burned
> countenances smiled as the music filled the air. Some patted their
> feet and there was tremendous applause as McCreary sang "Eliza
> Jane."
>
> Three-minute talks by old settlers followed. The oldest were called
> first. Most of the audience had heard the same stories for years, but
> loved to hear them again. Tales of travel to Texas in early days, con-

ditions of the country, Indian fights and carpet-bag rule—all related with as much animation as ebbing strength would permit.

Several ex-slaves were asked to tell of their trips to the war with "ol' massa." They told of swapping tobacco to Yankee soldiers for coffee, dodging Yankee bullets and shells, how they lived on sow-belly and parched corn during the long struggle. These colorful stories by the feeble old darkies drew hearty applause.

"General Hooks," who was a member of Forrester's Brigade brought the house down with his fiery oratory. He ended by singing "That Old Time Religion." At last President Tomlinson announced the meeting would adjourn for dinner.

[After dinner] as the crowd formed a huge semicircle around the tabernacle, the pageant opened and from a wooded section of the hill there emerged an old woman sitting erect in a saddle mounted upon a beautiful spirited horse. She rode like a veteran. Following her was a covered wagon, bearing a pioneer family heading for the promised new land. An iron pot and chicken coop were fastened to the rear of the wagon. Dogs preceded the wagon followed by a cow and a calf.

Presently a band of savage Indians, with bloodcurdling war-hoops, dashed out of the brush and attacked the frontiersman and his family. A terrible fight ensued. The frontiersman, of course won out and the crowd went wild. A large covered wagon drawn by oxen and driven by a man dressed in rawhide clothes ended the pageant. The crowd now moved toward the tabernacle as McCreary's music signaled the opening of the afternoon session.

"Professor" Eddins was first on the program with a Brazos Bottom folklore tale for the children. A mortuary was read by one of the prominent U. D. C. ladies of the county and taps were sounded by a great-grandson of one of the early settlers. A member of the county bar, standing behind a large wreath of flowers delivered a memorial address. Handkerchiefs found their way to [the] moist eyes of some of the audience—relatives and close friends of those whose names had been listed in the mortuary report.

Next came one of the most popular features of the entire reunion—an

old fashioned sing-song. President Tomlinson announced that
Brother Kirkpatrick would lead a few numbers from the Sacred Harp
song book. The community's best singers were grouped near the
front of the tabernacle. Brother Kirkpatrick pitched his voice to do,
re, me, fa, sol, la, his hand going to right, center and left as he kept
time to the music. Everybody took the pitch and the woods rang
with harmony of old-time notes, triangle, circle, square and the like.

Square dances and [a] Virginia reel closed the day's program.
Young and old joined in the dancing, the young boys and girls catching on quickly to the stately figures of the Virginia reel. An hour before sunset the music lagged, as did the hot and tired dancers.
Tomlinson urged them all to come back the next day with well-filled
dinner baskets.[32]

Farmers faced a lot of hardship, and social events like the reunion
helped provide a sense of community. World cotton prices had dropped
as Britain promoted cheaper cotton production in their colonies, while
in the United States, the boll weevil destroyed cotton crops.

SHARECROPPING STRUGGLES

African-American tenant farmers faced a compounded threat during
the Depression. When white farmers made little on the crop, they paid
little to the sharecropper. White farmers also hired machines to replace workers.[33] Historians debate whether black flight to cities sped
mechanization or whether the reverse is true, but the two trends took
place in tandem. At the depth of the Depression, in 1935, 90 percent of
black farmworkers in some parts of Texas were unemployed and the
Falls County population was shrinking.[34]

To understand what life was like for the African-American Tomlinsons, I sought out the last two of Vincent and Julie Tomlinson's
children still living in 2012, Lizzie Mae and Charles. Lizzie Mae was
ninety-two years old and living with her daughter Sandra Tryon in
Houston. Sandra explained that Lizzie suffered some dementia, but she
agreed to let me interview her mother, since she still remembered much

of her early life. Sandra put me in touch with Charles and his wife, Zelma, who lived in Wichita, Kansas. I arranged for them, Sandra, and Lizzie Mae to meet me on Tomlinson Hill. We walked the Hill together and they showed me the places of their childhood, and we paid our respects to their ancestors buried there. They shared with me their life stories.

Vincent and Julie had worked their rented farm, raising hogs and vegetables, doing their best to remain self-sufficient as they raised their children. They lived at the intersection where the roads to Lott and Chilton merged into a single highway to Marlin.[35] Vincent took in his father after he lost his vision, and Peter spent most of his final days sitting on the front porch of the family's two-room shack, listening as his granddaughter Lizzie Mae and the other children played around him.[36] Peter died from prostate cancer at the age of seventy-seven, in 1926, and was buried in the black cemetery in Lott.[37]

Julie gave birth to Vincent Tomlinson, Jr., in 1930, John K. in 1932, Charles in 1933, and Oliver Terry in 1935. While Charles went by his proper name, John was known as J.K., and Oliver went by O.T.[38] Large families were normal on the farm, since mortality rates remained high for African-Americans. In 1936, 1,321 black children died for every 100,000 births, compared to 961 deaths for whites. A black woman was twice as likely as a white woman to have a stillborn child or to die during childbirth.

In addition to their eight children, Vincent and Julie took in at least three others. At one point, fourteen people lived in the twelve-hundred-square-foot cabin that Vincent built on Deer Creek, and Julie fed and cared for them all. Lizzie Mae said the children didn't mind; it just meant more kids to play with and to do chores, like gathering firewood or drawing water from the well.[39] Vincent and Julie had their own bed, but the children had to share theirs, divided up between boys and girls. The entire house was used for sleeping, except for a corner used as the kitchen. Charles described it:

> You had to go up about one, two, three—about four steps up to the porch. We called it the gallery back then. That's the only place we had

to gather. It went from one end of the house to the other end of the house. And then you had that one entrance to the front and had one entrance to come in through the back door.

But when you come in the house, you come into a bedroom in them days. And then the stove, we got heat by, was in the bedroom and that's where we'd sit during the day.

There were four rooms. Because every room was a bedroom, there wasn't just a room by itself for a living room; you didn't have that. Just had a place to sleep.[40]

Vincent and Julie rented one hundred acres from Albert Tomlinson, and in addition to the cotton field, they put in a vegetable garden, a pigsty, chicken coop, a smokehouse, a tool shed, and a small barn for a mule, a horse, and a few dairy cows. Vincent took care of the hogs or the cows, and he sold surplus hogs for cash. Julie took care of the chickens and the vegetable garden. Every winter, Vincent would slaughter a hog, and Julie made pork sausage to hang in the smokehouse alongside the bacon. When they had extra vegetables, usually turnips, Vincent and Julie's children sold them at a roadside stand. Vincent also liked to hunt rabbits and squirrels.

Lizzie Mae and the other Tomlinson children attended the Tomlinson Negro School in the late 1920s, when conditions were desperate. The Tomlinsons and Stallworths had moved the wooden two-room shack to a safer place after the Deer Creek flood, placing it in Cedar Valley. The school did not have electricity or running water, and the students used an outhouse. The rough-hewn structure, with one classroom and a small office, was thirty years old when Lizzie Mae started school, and the building doubled as a church on Sundays.[41]

Julia Ann Taylor and Mabel Tyler divided the forty children, one teaching first through third grades, and the other fourth through seventh. While one group listened to the teacher, the other worked on assignments or played outside. Classes lasted from 8:00 A.M. to 4:00 P.M., with a one-hour lunch break. The Tomlinson children took peanut butter and jelly sandwiches and some crackers for their lunch.[42] The schools themselves were physically uncomfortable, and middle and high schools were far away. The teachers struggled to pay their own bills. To make money on the side, Taylor operated a speakeasy out of her house on the Hill.[43] After seventh grade, the children attended a junior high in Lott and high school in Marlin, if they hadn't already dropped out.[44]

Two-thirds of black schools only had one room, with one teacher who taught all ages. Tax records show that white school property was valued at three times that of black school property. School districts paid African-American teachers $92 a month, compared to $121 for white teachers and the student-to-teacher ratio was 39–1 for blacks and 30–1 for whites. But Texas was actually a bright spot in African-American education, with the state spending forty dollars a year on each black student, the highest in the South, while it spent forty-seven dollars per white student. African-American children valued what little education they received, though, and black illiteracy in Texas plummeted to 13.4 percent by 1930.[45]

Sharecroppers needed the entire family to help plant, chop, and pick cotton, so black schools synchronized their calendar with the farmwork. When the cotton was ready to be harvested, everyone went into the fields. New mothers took their infants and kept them on cotton sacks while they pulled the fuzzy white balls off the shrubs. Charles recalled women giving birth in the fields.[46] Lizzie remembered putting on bonnets, long-sleeved shirts, and pants to keep her skin from blistering:

> I know we had to go to the field every day. I'd lay down on the porch and sleep and I'd hide up under there when it was time to go to [the] field and they would look for me and they'd say that's where she was, trying to hide to keep from working, but we had a good time. We had to pick cotton. We had to chop cotton. We had to pull the corn off of the stalks.

> We had to pick that cotton you know in a big sack. My brother [Ellie] could pick about twelve hundred pounds a day. He was a proud picker.[47]

Life for the black Tomlinsons always teetered on the edge of disaster. Charles told me that one bad crop or a boll weevil infestation could leave the family in dire straits. In those years, Vincent signed the family up to pick cotton in West Texas or near Corpus Christi later in the year. The children would miss school when it started in September and not get back to Marlin until the first week of December.[48]

Lizzie enjoyed going to school, but she told me her younger brothers, particularly J.K. and O.T., would disappear into the woods when class started. The teachers would report them to Vincent, who'd punish them, but the boys never liked sitting in the stuffy wooden schoolhouse, crowded together with the other children.[49]

But J.K. and O.T. also fought, and at least one bout ended with a trip to the doctor. When J.K. was losing, he pulled a knife and swung it at O.T., cutting open the base of his ring and pinkie fingers. The doctor offered O.T. a choice of having his fingers either curled up or pointing out straight. He chose them curled up so he could box, one of his favorite sports.[50]

Charles said he knew that white society didn't really care if he got an education. He'd seen the white schools, with their fancy buildings and new books. Some black children saw no use in going to school when the odds were that they were never going to be more than farmworkers. Most didn't make it to graduation. Charles finished high school, partly because he was determined, and partly because the teachers helped him:

> The teacher wouldn't put too much pressure because she knows what you've been doing. She'll give you time to catch on and get it right. I appreciated that part, too. They was awful good to us all.
>
> I didn't have a reason for making a life out of schooling. I just got my lessons so I could finish school so I would have something. I could read and write. That's what my dad said you are going to learn in school anyway, read and write and knowing to subtract so the white man will not cheat you out of everything you got.[51]

The black Tomlinsons celebrated Juneteenth to mark the end of slavery, but Charles said Vincent and Julie never spoke about the family's slave history, except to say their grandfather Peter was freed from slavery on Juneteenth. Charles said he never thought twice about sharing a last name with Albert until his early twenties, when a neighbor explained how most of the black families in Falls County took the surnames of former slaveholders.

Albert visited Vincent about once a week to see how the cotton was growing. He would pull up to the gate outside Vincent's house, and Charles would run down to open the gate for Albert, who would drive his car up to the cabin and get out, carrying his walking stick. Charles said Albert never entered the black family's house, but he would walk into the field with Vincent, and they'd talk for about an hour:

> He furnished the seeds and everything. If he got two bales of cotton, my daddy would get the third bale.
>
> Albert would just come to talk to Daddy. He wouldn't talk to nobody else. Nobody else was in that conversation. He just come to talk to Daddy because he wanted to know about how's he doing with the crop, you know, how's everything working out. [Albert] told him that Daddy had too much garden, that [Albert] needed some of that land for cotton. My dad said, "Well, we got to eat." I forget the answer, but anyway, he still had that same amount of garden for years.[52]

Julie worked for Albert and his wife, cleaning their house, churning their butter, and milling their grain. Lizzie and Charles said they would go to Albert's house to see their mom, but they always used the back door and never entered past the kitchen. No white family in that era allowed African-Americans to use the front door. The wood-framed Victorian house intimidated the children, and they knew Albert didn't want black children in the house at all.[53]

The black community installed a bell on the Tomlinson Negro School to call children to school, parishioners to church, or to alert the entire community in case of an emergency. When someone needed help, or someone died, they usually sent a teenager to ring the bell. Vincent always responded when the alarm rang and organized whatever help was needed.[54]

If someone got sick, African-Americans could rarely afford a doctor,

so they relied on home remedies or community healers. Traditional-
ists talked about malevolent spirits and used magic potions. Charles
came down with typhoid when he was a child and missed his first two
years of school as a result. When he cut his foot so deep that the
blood spurted out with each beat of his heart, his mother immersed
the wound in coal oil, a type of kerosene, to disinfect it, and then ban-
daged it herself.

At the Gravel Hill Negro Baptist Church, the congregation elected
Vincent a deacon, and he spent much of his free time doing church
work or attending Masonic meetings. Vincent helped organize tent revivals in the summer that brought together African-American Baptist
preachers from across the county. Lizzie Mae said her father made all
the children attend. "It would be about two or three weeks. . . . We'd all
go to church at night and get out about ten, but we had to go to church
because my dad was the deacon and we went. I went to church many
days in a wagon, with my legs hanging off the wagon. Sitting back in a
wagon, you thought you was in a Cadillac."[55]

The Tomlinsons and another family, the Whites, were the most
prosperous African-Americans on the Hill. Vincent bought a used
Model-T Ford, which he drove to Marlin on Sunday mornings to pick
up the church's preacher. After the service, the minister followed Vincent home for a Sunday dinner of fried chicken, fresh-baked rolls, beets,
and collard greens. During the week, when Lizzie Mae and her friends
started attending high school, they piled into the Whites' Hudson for
the daily trip to Marlin:

> They called the Whites and the Tomlinsons big shots. We were well
> brought up and eating. We didn't want for things. I tell you, we had a
> beautiful mother and father.
>
> We weren't real poor. I didn't think so. I thought we were up there.
>
> They were nice families, two families, Tomlinson and the Whites.
> They would can their food. We did corn, peas, all that. . . . We had
> everything that we should have. Sometimes it was hard, just like it is
> now. There are hard times and good times and everything, but I had
> the beautiful life, best, I thought, in the world.[56]

Christmas was a quiet time for farmers. Lizzie and the other children spent those cold months waiting for Santa Claus to bring oranges and fresh apples, a rare treat in those days. Julie would cook six or seven cakes.[57]

At Easter, all of the families wore their best clothes, and women put on special bonnets. Church ladies brought food for a picnic and the one hundred African-American families living on Tomlinson Hill and in China Grove shared the feast. The community also celebrated Juneteenth, gathering at the Old Settlers and Confederate Veterans' reunion grounds for a barbecue. Albert often made a brief appearance to wish his family's former slaves well. For the African-Americans in Falls County, Juneteenth was more important than July 4.[58]

When the crop came in between September and October, Albert collected the cotton as it was picked and sold it in Marlin. Albert would decide how much money to keep to pay off Vincent's debts, then give Vincent whatever was left over. Albert didn't allow Vincent to keep his own records; Vincent had to take whatever Albert gave him. Vincent grumbled that he didn't get all that he deserved, but he kept working for Albert.[59] Not all African-Americans complied with the practice.

Milo Travis, the freedman who had rejected the Tomlinson name, owned his own land and valued his independence. His granddaughter, Roberta, moved back to Tomlinson Hill in 1930 after working in the Dallas area and marrying Hezekiah Taylor. They brought her two children and settled next to Milo and his wife, Martha. One of those children, Pinkie Taylor Price, described their life on the Hill in the 1930s:

> We used to go and pick berries for Albert [Tomlinson] and Willie S. Hayward. And those people would have us picking. If you know anything about blackberries, those vines are full of stickers. But you had to get there and pick them. You didn't have no gloves, and pick a gallon of berries for five cents. And it was quite a few children in my family, and we would go there and we would try and pick as many as we could. And we would cook berries and we would pick more than twenty gallons, and the man would cheat us out of it. He didn't want you to make no dollar.

He's say you didn't pick too many yourself. I tried to argue with him; sometimes you'd get your money; sometimes you wouldn't. You didn't have no "I'm going to court."[60]

Pinkie described what happened when Hezekiah tried to negotiate a different kind of sharecropping arrangement with one of the Stallworths:

My father went to Stallworth and asked him for some land, and he was going to raise his crop like that.

[Stallworth] told him, "Say now, you just go down to the [store], or whoever and all this, and you just get what you want for your people. You can get all the groceries you want, and you go to town and buy some [clothes] and we'll keep all the credit here."

[My father] said, "No, what I want you to do, let me have the money and I'll go to the man and take up the groceries and everything. And then at the fall of the year, I owe you so much money and I pay you what I owe you."

[Stallworth] said, "No, I tell him. Let me go and take it up."

My father said, "I got a name just like you. I can use my own name."

[Stallworth] said, "I'm not going to do that."

My father said, "Well then, I'm not gonna work for you."

He didn't work for Stallworth. Stallworth told Albert Tomlinson, and he absolutely told whoever owned enough land what happened. They got together and said, "Don't let Hezekiah have nothing, because he's smart."[61]

When none of the whites in western Falls County would rent him land, Hezekiah considered asking for work by the day, but they refused to hire him. Hezekiah knew he could find work if he went to West Texas, where farmers paid cash, but he didn't want to leave his family.

A few months after his falling-out with the white planters, Hezekiah joined a Works Progress Administration road crew a few miles away. His family remained in the house they rented in China Grove, and Roberta and the children cultivated the family's vegetable garden, tended to the hogs, and worked on the white farms. But the Taylors never again relied on tenant farming.[62]

ABANDONING THE FIELDS

Vincent accommodated Albert and became the informal mayor of Cedar Valley and Gravel Hill, negotiating with white landowners on behalf of the others.[63] Vincent's house was a little larger than most and was raised off the ground, a desirable feature that kept snakes from getting in. A few hundred yards down the road was John White's house. No one was surprised when John's son Winston started dating Lizzie. She dropped out of Booker T. Washington High School in the eleventh grade to marry him in 1937. Lizzie moved in with the Whites and could see her parents' house across the cotton field. Lizzie and Winston lived with his parents for two years before they saved enough money for their own house.[64]

Lizzie gave birth to her first two children on Tomlinson Hill in 1940 and 1942. Then her mother-in-law moved to Corpus Christi, Texas, and sent word there was indoor work available. Winston and Lizzie followed. They had visited the beach town before, and Lizzie was excited to get away from village life and cotton picking. In the fall, Lizzie's aunts, uncles, and brothers stayed at her house on the coast, hiring on with any farmer who needed pickers that day. Lizzie's eldest daughter, who had never worked in the fields, decided one year she would make some money and go with her relatives. "She went on out there, and, well, my cousin brought her back home. She said she didn't do nothing but sit up under the wagon and drink water. She wasn't used to no picking no cotton. She didn't want to go back anymore."[65] None of Lizzie's children ever worked the cotton fields again. They went to city schools, worked city jobs, and several went to college. They were the first of the black Tomlinsons to abandon the cotton fields since their ancestors had landed as slaves in the United States.

SIXTEEN

Nobody can play music that beautifully and not be a good person, and Miles could. The music really opened up a world for me that I hadn't realized I was missing.

—Bob Tomlinson

In the 1920s, Edgar Flippen and Hugh Prather's firm was becoming Dallas' premier builder and seller of residential and commercial real estate, with my grandfather Tommy Tomlinson as one of their lead engineers. These weren't tract homes; buyers purchased plots and hired builders to construct custom homes. Flippen-Prather built hundreds of them, sometimes selling the land, often just connecting buyers with sellers. Tommy's role was prominent enough for Flippen-Prather to include his name on advertisements in the *Dallas Morning News*.[1]

Wealthy housewives living in the company's Highland Park development often complained in 1928 about fighting traffic to go shopping in downtown Dallas. American shops at the time generally occupied individual buildings along major streets, but Flippen-Prather wanted to build something different closer to their growing residential neighborhood. They traveled to Spain, visiting Barcelona and Seville for inspiration.[2]

Flippen-Prather, with Tommy as the chief engineer, spent the next three years transforming ten acres of north Dallas pastureland into Highland Park Village, a Spanish Revival town square, designed by architects Marion Fresenius Fooshee and James B. Cheek. To accommodate cars, all of the stores faced inward toward a parking lot. Flippen-Prather retained ownership of the property and rented out 200,000 square feet of floor space to all kinds of merchants. They constructed what the National Register of Historic Places calls "a pivotal point in the evolution of the shopping center as distinctive building type in 20th century American architecture."[3]

Having started as a trading post, Dallas was the natural place to give birth to the American mall. The city was home to some of the earliest experiments in national department stores, including Neiman-Marcus and Sanger-Harris, and many of the city's merchants rented space at Highland Park Village. The nomination of the village to the National Register of Historic Places reads:

> Thus the complex provides an excellent representation of the role of the shopping center in facilitating the decentralization of the downtown commercial core of cities across the United States. In this particular case, the Highland Park Shopping Village contributed to the decentralization of downtown Dallas and the northern expansion of commercial and residential development that continued into the late twentieth century in Dallas.[4]

Tommy, meanwhile, was still single and getting older. He attended the First Baptist Church's mixers and bridge parties and was an excellent golfer. He traveled to Paris, Texas, in 1928 to attend the wedding of his college friend and star Texas A&M quarterback Robert Berry. One of Tommy's golfing buddies was Dennis C. Chapin, a junior executive at the Sun Oil Company, and Dennis's wife, Margaret, was part of Dallas' high society. The Chapins introduced Tommy to Mary Frances Fretz, who also enjoyed golf and competed in tournaments at the Lakewood Country Club, the same club where Tommy played.

Mary's grandfather had arrived in Dallas from Switzerland in December 1870. Jacob Fretz and his son Emil opened one of the first barbershops when Dallas was, according to Emil, "a collection of sorry shacks on a sandy foundation around the courthouse square." He built his shop on Lamar Street, between Main and Elm, where the Bank of America Plaza stands now.[5] Emil took advantage of those early days to purchase downtown real estate and build his business into E. A. Fretz and Company, a statewide distributor of barber and beauty supplies, which became Revlon's exclusive agent in the state.[6] Emil was a founding member of the Dallas Commercial Club, which became the Dallas Chamber of Commerce.

Emil led the development of the city's parks and was known in his time as "the father of Dallas parks and recreation."[7] When the Dallas Zoo opened, Mary was pictured on the front page of the *Dallas Morning News* holding a baby cheetah. A city park was renamed in Emil's honor.

Growing up, Mary enjoyed the best that Dallas had to offer, attending the private Ursuline Academy, an all-girl's Catholic school, and graduating in 1928 from Saint Mary's School for Girls, an Episcopal high school. She loved to play the piano and started a citywide pianist's club in 1931.[8] When she and Tommy started dating, young couples watched movies at the Texas Theater in Oak Cliff and the Majestic Theater downtown, where Mary had held her graduation party just a few years before.

The Fretz family announced that Mary and Tommy were engaged at a tea party on April 23, 1933. Mary's house was decorated with bluebonnets and pink rosebuds, the colors she'd chosen for her wedding. She was surrounded by her friends, and Tommy's sister Ruth drove up from San Antonio. They set the wedding for June 8, at the chapel on the St. Mary's campus.[9] Over the next six weeks, the *Morning News* reported that the daughters of the Dallas elite organized six wedding parties for the couple, including one hosted by the Chapins.

George Rodgers Wood, the dean of St. Mary's College, performed Mary and Tommy's wedding ceremony at noon at an altar decorated with lilies and palms. Mary wore a white French crepe suit trimmed with white fox fur and handmade lace. Tommy's sister Ruth was her maid of honor, and Mary's brother Emil Fretz, Jr., was Tommy's best man. R. E. L. and Bettie Tomlinson, along with some Stallworth cousins, took the train from Marlin to attend the wedding. The Fretzs hosted a reception at their home with a ring-shaped wedding cake. The young couple's honeymoon took them to the world's fair in Chicago, where nightclubs on the Midway featured fan dancer Sally Rand and future singing stars Judy Garland and the Andrews Sisters. From there, they traveled to Canada.[10]

WILDFLOWERS ALONG THE FALLS

Mary had a special love for flowers, including bluebonnets, the state's official flower, which grow wild in the spring and carpet Central and East Texas meadows. They grow particularly well in Falls County cow pastures, and in April 1937, Marlin organized the first Bluebonnet Festival for amateur photographers. The festival was headquartered at the Falls Hotel, where organizers signed up photographers and assigned them a young woman to serve as a model, usually dressed as a southern belle. At the end of the competition, judges gave awards for the best photos in a dozen categories and national photo magazines published the winners.[11] Tommy was interested in photography and Mary loved the flowers, so they often made the drive to his hometown for the festival.[12]

Mary continued to participate in Dallas society events and regularly scored near the top in women's golf tournaments at Lakewood Country Club.[13] Tommy started his own general contracting business, often working for Flippen-Prather. Dallas County's population reached 398,564 people by 1940 and showed no signs of slowing down. Tommy built homes across north Dallas and, together with architects and real estate agents, advertised them in the *Morning News*. He built a home sponsored by *House & Garden* magazine in 1940 in a promotion that was unusual for its time. Flippen-Prather built the property and the Titche-Goettinger department store furnished it, calling it a "Wishmaker's House." The "revolutionary development" they offered was the chance "to be your own decorator": "Wishmaker is a wide assortment of everything to furnish your home. More than 1,600 individual items—so skillfully coordinated in color and design—that no matter how you may ensemble them, the result is absolutely perfect. You simply cannot make a mistake! Never before has this been possible in home furnishings. It is truly amazing."[14]

Mary and Tommy wanted to have children, but had trouble conceiving. In October 1941, when Tommy was forty and Mary thirty-three, they adopted a blond baby boy born in Fort Worth, whom they named Robert Lee Tomlinson, nicknamed "Bob."

ANOTHER WAR

A few months before Bob was born, the U.S. government bought 116 farms and ranches just west of Texarkana, on the Arkansas border, to build an ammunition factory and storage facility. The situation was worsening in Europe, so much so that a year earlier, Congress had required young men to register for a possible draft. Tommy won a bid to help construct the Red River Ordnance Depot, one of the biggest projects of his career. He spent a great deal of his time after adopting Bob at the fifty-square-mile site, which grew over the next year into one of the largest arms depots in the United States.[15] Matériel traveled by barge down the Red River to New Orleans, where the U.S. government could ship them anywhere in the world.

Marlinites kept close tabs on international affairs, since Tom Connally, their hometown political hero, was chair of the Senate Foreign Affairs Committee. He made regular visits and often spoke about global affairs. Americans knew trouble was brewing in October 1941 when Connally moved to overturn the nation's Neutrality Law. Debate ended on December 7, 1941, when the Japanese bombed Pearl Harbor and the United States declared war.[16]

The onset of war came as J. M. Kennedy, who had started the *Marlin Democrat* in 1890, was honored as one of the state's most respected editors and publishers. After fifty-two years in the business, he had earned the title "Dean of Texas Journalists." Kennedy had crusaded against lynching when most citizens considered it swift and simple justice. He'd opposed the Klan when almost 50 percent of eligible Texan men paid membership dues. His fellow Marlinites had elected

Kennedy mayor three times and state representative once. He worked at the *Democrat*'s office, and never missed an issue until March 1942, when he fell ill and checked into the hospital. Four weeks later, he was dead at age seventy-three.[17]

R.E.L. had recently turned eighty and was senile when the war started. Tommy and his sister Ruth had planned a big celebration for their parents' fiftieth wedding anniversary on January 22, 1942, but after the declaration of war, they scaled it back to a family reunion at the house on Fortune Street.[18] The following January, R.E.L. passed away at Marlin's Torbett Clinic.[19]

Mary gave birth to a daughter in May 1942. They named her Sarah Lee and called her "Sally." Mary and Tommy moved into a new house on Fairfax Avenue in Lakewood, a wealthy Dallas neighborhood.[20] But Dallas experienced wartime deprivations like any other American city, and key materials like iron, fuel, and nylon were rationed. In 1943, the city experienced a polio epidemic and officials closed public swimming pools and movie theaters. Dallas's racial makeup also changed. World War II nearly doubled the number of black Texans working in cities. There were nearly 300,000, yet African-American unemployment remained at 11 percent, 4 percent more than that of whites.[21]

Mary's father died unexpectedly of a heart attack at his home on July 3, 1944.[22] Mary's mother sold the barber-supply company to its employees, and Mary and her brother inherited a substantial amount of money, including stock in the National Bank of Commerce. Mary's new wealth, in addition to Tommy's small inheritance, guaranteed an upper-middle-class lifestyle for the family.[23]

Mary hired an African-American woman named Gladys to clean the house and run errands. Mary cared for the children and cooked meals, preparing meat loaf, spaghetti and meat sauce, steaks, fried chicken, and chicken and dumplings. Her only work outside the house was volunteering at Saint Matthew's Episcopal Cathedral, but religion divided Tommy and Mary. She had loved the Episcopal Church since her school days, but Tommy was a lifelong Baptist. To appease him, the family attended Wilshire Baptist Church when it opened in North Dallas. Eventually, though, Mary took Bob and Sally back to the local Episcopal church.[24]

Mary's parents had employed an African-American named Wash Harvey to maintain their yard, and he would also help Tommy and Mary. Wash took care of the peach and fig trees in the backyard, planted asparagus and other vegetables, and grew strawberries.[25] Sally remembers Gladys and Wash well:

> I loved Gladys and, well, we called him Wash, Washy. The people that worked for the family—I mean, they were just family—I just adored them. And as a kid, it was never pointed out to me this person's black and you're white. It just . . . it wasn't. And we knew that the white people went to school here. There was certainly a dividing line. I mean it was a difference, black and white. But it was before integration.[26]

Mary and Tommy differed when it came to their treatment of minorities. Mary had grown up in a Swiss-German family and spent much of her childhood around progressive Europeans who found Anglo bigotry distasteful. She also remembered firsthand how Anglos had treated the German-speaking community and people with Germanic last names during World War I, when the city council changed the name of the street where the Fretzs lived from Germania to Liberty. Mary discouraged her children from using coarse language, particularly Tommy's hate-filled racist slurs. She often used a phrase that I remember used to describe both of my grandfathers: "He doesn't know any better." I remember thinking, But you do? Bob described their approaches:

> I've heard him cuss blacks, Mexicans, Jews, Catholics, take your pick. He was an equal-opportunity hater.
>
> My mother, on the other hand, was—I guess she would be described as kind of a benign racist, in that she separated black and

white, but it was more a matter of "Be nice to those people; they are less fortunate than we are."

I think that had a mellowing effect on my father, as well.[27]

Unlike her brother, Sally did not see her parents as racists, but she admitted that Bob spent more time with Tommy:

I guess if either one of them would have been more inclined to be— and I don't want to say racist, but more aware of it—it would have been Daddy probably.

I guess because of his age, the way he was brought up, and it was just separate. Blacks and whites were just separate. And I think it would have been hard for him to see the integration, because that's not how he was brought up. It's not how he was raised. Not to be racist, but just it's like here's white and here's black. If that makes any sense.

Mother loved everybody. I mean, she was a real people person. And it didn't matter to her if somebody was green, or blue, or purple.[28]

The family often went to Marlin to have Thanksgiving with Tommy's mother. Many gray-haired couples sat at the dinner table, but Bob was too young and saw them too infrequently to know how they fit into the family. But he said Tommy didn't like Marlin. As a kid, Bob loved the town:

My strongest memory—figures, for a little kid—was visiting the firehouse down there, the old firehouse, not because of anything dramatic like a call or anything like that, but they had an old horse-drawn fire engine in the back end and I just thought that was a wonderful thing.

I remember the baths, the bathhouses. My father always went for the waters down there when we were in town visiting, and I just thought that was strange. I remember when we were driving there we would go to Waco and turn off on Highway 6 and we'd be desperately looking for the Falls Hotel sign, a big FALLS on top of the hotel, because that's when we knew we were just right there. In spring, it was blue-bonnet wildflower country, gorgeous.[29]

THE GOOD LIFE

In Dallas, the Fretz and Tomlinson families regularly went to the country club, and the children often saw Mary's parents there. Mary's mother, Minnie, enjoyed punching nickels into the club's slot machines while holding Bob on her lap. She'd puff on a cigarette and let the ash grow until it fell to the floor. Sally relayed some of the memories Minnie shared with her:

> She could be absolutely the epitome of grace and the total lady, and then in the next breath she could just rip you to shreds. So you just didn't want to get on her bad side. But she was wonderful. I loved her.
>
> I can remember her talking about when she was a young girl growing up in Dallas, and the dirt streets downtown. And when you're talking about the racial issue, I can remember her describing when she was just a young, young child, and one of her earliest memories in downtown Dallas was just a dirt road. And the black people being tarred and feathered. I remember her describing that once, that she had seen that as a child.[30]

From Bob and Sally's bedrooms in their two-story brick home, they could see across the city. Bob often wore western-style clothing and a cowboy hat, while Sally wore stylish dresses. Bob described Dallas's public schools:

> It was a concrete block house, Robert E. Lee Elementary School. Stonewall Jackson was right up the street. The dividing line between Stonewall and Lee was the alley that ran behind our house. My cousin went to Jackson. At that time it was basically all Anglo, all white, obviously no blacks, but Mexican-Americans.
>
> Mexican kids were able to attend school with the rest of us and we had at least one set of brothers in my class and, yeah, they were just

as accepted as they could be. I didn't realize that there was any discrimination against Hispanics until years after I was out of school. It
just . . . they were always part of our classes. I went from there to J. L.
Long Junior High, Woodrow Wilson High School. Same story.

There were probably twenty-five to thirty-five kids in each class.
There were a lot of amenities that I don't think the elementary schools
have now, like music programs. You could start studying piano in
the second grade and instruments in the third, and I thought that
was great. I did it. I carried my violin for the next ten years, sawing
away on it.[31]

Tommy bought a television in the early 1950s, a large round-screen
Zenith, and the family watched Dallas's two stations. The family's Lakewood neighborhood had its own shopping center with a movie theater,
ice-cream parlor, and everything a young family could want.

The Tomlinsons made their last trip to Marlin in August 1951, when
Tommy's mother, Bettie, died. Her obituary made the front page of the
Marlin Democrat. Bettie had been ill for some time and was in the hospital when she passed away at eighty-two. The Reverend Lloyd Chapman led the funeral rites inside the chapel that she and R. E. L. had
helped build. She was buried next to him at Marlin's Calvary Cemetery,
just a few blocks down Fortune Street from their house.[32] Tommy never
felt the need to visit Marlin again.[33]

In 1952, Tommy constructed a one-story office and warehouse in
the Trinity industrial district to the specifications of the Ford Metal
Moulding Company, a New York firm that agreed to lease the property
to manufacture aluminum rods and bars. Thanks to that deal, and to
the sizable Fretz inheritance, Tommy achieved his ambition of retiring
at fifty. His only obligation was his duty as a board member of the National Bank of Commerce. In 1955, that board made history by appointing the first woman to lead a bank in Dallas. Tommy was one of
six directors when the board elected Maurine Jacobs, who had worked
at the bank for twenty-three years. The appointment was big news for
Dallas's fifth-largest bank.[34]

Tommy spent much of his time at the Lakewood Country Club,

drinking Four Roses bourbon. When his drinking became a problem is unclear, but Bob remembers tense evenings as a child when Tommy came home from the club drunk, expecting a formal dinner. He'd sit glumly next to his quiet children at the head of the table while Mary waited on him. Sometimes, though, he'd return home in a darker mood, screaming and scaring Bob and Sally. On one occasion, Mary took the children into the garage, climbed into the car, and locked the doors until Tommy passed out. Bob said Tommy never physically abused his family, but they often feared him.[35]

Tommy built his dream home in 1956 on a half-acre lot just a few blocks east of White Rock Lake. The ranch-style four-bedroom house with all the amenities was in one of Dallas's newest neighborhoods, Lakewood Heights. Tommy had always liked to walk along White Rock Lake, and now he was a short distance away.

The civil rights movement was gaining momentum in the mid-1950s, and the Democratic party's support for it did not sit well with Tommy. He switched to the Republican party, becoming one of a tiny number of Republicans in Texas at the time.[36]

Bob was an adolescent and beginning to explore the world around him. In the 1950s, high school students observed an annual Ditch Day, when they did something fun instead of going to school. One year, Bob's friends suggested going bowling at Lakewood Lanes:

> That was the first day I ever bowled, but I had been watching it on television. And from watching Buddy Bomar, I knew I should take four steps, hold the ball like this, swing it, and roll at the second arrow. The second frame I ever bowled, I got a strike. I probably got thirty for the game, but the second frame I bowled, I got a strike. I thought it was great fun, and they had a junior league there on Saturday mornings, and I wound up joining that. Basically, I was a nonathlete, but I found out that bowling was something that the jocks couldn't do a whole lot better than I could, if at all. . . . The summer after my senior year of high school was the last junior league that I bowled, and I tied for high average in the house for the summer, 180. I tied with a woman that threw a ten-pound ball like a rocket.[37]

Bob joined teams and had a natural talent. During his high school years, he spent as much time at Lakewood Lanes as he spent at Tommy's new house.[38] He also loved music but wasn't satisfied with the show tunes and light classical pieces he played in the high school orchestra. In his junior year, he discovered another kind of music, one that would become a lifelong passion, while visiting Hi-Fi Incorporated, a record store at Mockingbird and Abrams:

> The man handed me an album and said, "Why don't you listen to this? Maybe this will be something you like."
>
> I took it back into the room and put the needle on, and I had found my home. The first track I played on the album was "Round Midnight" and it was Miles Davis playing it. From that time on, I have been a jazz fan. I was before then, I guess, in a way, but not the same. It's such black music. Nobody can play music that beautifully and not be a good person, and Miles could. The music really opened up a world for me that I hadn't realized I was missing.[39]

MR. SMITH GOES TO THE FAIR

The end of the Klan did little to improve conditions for minorities in Texas; it only made open discussion of white supremacy impolite and racial violence less acceptable. Whites relied instead on Jim Crow laws and all-white juries to maintain social control, not vigilantism.[40]

Racists despised the mixing of the races and insisted a biracial child took on the worst qualities of both parents. Texas law said one drop of African-American blood made a person black and no amount of money or number of college degrees could change that. By treating all blacks the same and discouraging those who tried to pass for white, Anglos kept the black community together and laid the foundation for vibrant, economically diverse communities.[41]

With Jim Crow laws in place, African-Americans for the most part followed the teachings of Booker T. Washington and established businesses and tried to prove wrong all of the stereotypes that whites held about them. Antonio Maceo Smith, though, wanted to bring real change. Smith may have been born in Texarkana, but he'd earned a master's degree in business administration from New York University and was a successful businessman back east. He came home to attend his father's funeral in 1933, and the indignities he witnessed inspired him to move to Dallas and join the civil rights movement. Smith helped resuscitate the Dallas Negro Chamber of Commerce in 1936, establishing himself as a major black leader. He later created the Texas Negro Chamber of Commerce and became head of the Texas NAACP.[42]

When Dallas officials organized a world's fair in 1936 called the Texas Centennial Central Exposition, Smith saw an opportunity to highlight the contributions of African-Americans. He wanted to build a Hall of Negro Life, the first exhibit dedicated to blacks at a world's fair.[43] The Centennial Committee, however, refused to provide any funds, since they had decided the overarching theme of Texas's centennial celebration would be how white Europeans had brought civilization to Texas.[44] They planned to portray people of color as either impediments to civilization or the tools of their white masters.[45] When President Franklin D. Roosevelt visited the exposition, city leaders asked him to unveil a monumental statue of Robert E. Lee riding his famous horse, Traveller.

Smith, though, convinced a white oilman, Walter D. Cline, to lobby for federal funds in return for selling fifty thousand dollars' worth of bonds for the centennial. Cline convinced Congress to appropriate $100,000, and Smith built the ten-thousand-square-foot hall in Dallas's Fair Park, just past a monument to the Confederacy at the park's main gate. The hall opened on Juneteenth.[46] Jazz musician Cab Calloway performed at the ceremony.[47] The exhibit ultimately attracted more than seventy thousand blacks.[48]

The *Dallas Morning News'* coverage of the Hall of Negro Life dripped with ridicule and sarcasm. The writer led off his story with fictional minstrel characters and called all blacks the sons and daughters of Ham, people in Genesis cursed by Noah to be "servants of servants":

Mammy wasn't there when Dallas sat down to cold supper Friday night for with Rastus, and thousands of care-free members of her race, she was busy putting in a glorious Juneteenth at the magic Texas Centennial Exposition. Attendance totaled 46,116. Joining in with the city negroes were other thousands of dusty county merrymakers who had deserted catfish streams and left fiddle-faced mules to munch contentedly in idleness, farm work forgotten, to celebrate Emancipation Day amid the wonders of Dallas' $25,000,000 world fair.

Rolling eyes and flashing white teeth dominated exhibit halls, the Midway and various places where special negro programs, ranging from the dedication of the $50,000 Negro Hall to the highly entertaining hi-di-hoing as performed by Cab Calloway and his Cotton Club Orchestra which was hotter than the blazing afternoon sun.

Laughter and carefree happiness comes easy to the sons and daughters of Ham and with the many wonders and attractions of the magic city at their disposal they made this Juneteenth a Christmas, July Fourth and Thanksgiving all rolled into one.

Another high spot of the day's more serious side was an address to thousands of negroes in the Amphitheater Friday evening by Dr. L. K. Williams, Chicago, pastor of the largest Negro church in the world. Dr. Williams who is vice president of the World Baptist Alliance, was introduced by Dr. George Truett, who heads the organization. A massed chorus sang.

While these more dignified observances of the occasion attracted many thousands, hordes of merrymakers stormed the purified Midway, its strip shows deleted for the day. There they saw the wonders of the freak world, screamed when Snakeoid swallowed a reptile and then regained normalcy by pushing black faces deep into slices of watermelon and welcome ice cream cones.

Friskier members of the race whooped it up while dancing to the ho-di-ho rhythm of Calloway's band at intervals through the afternoon and night in the Amphitheater and had a great time of it, entirely oblivious to the stares of hundreds of white onlookers.

There was plenty of entertainment for both whites and colored in the arena during the afternoon when dusky belles disporting neat curves set off by tight silk suits which obviously were not intended to go too near the water, pranced before an audience of rolling eyes. Contestants in the high brown bathing beauty review were vying for audience applause and the lure of a trip to Hollywood for possible selection for a part in Cab's next picture.

The dusty beauties got plenty of optical attention but they had to share the entertainment angle of the proceedings with a crew of male and female truckers [dancers] whose twinkling feet and widely swayed bodies blended almost to perfection with the sizzling, jungle tomtom rhythm of Calloway's hotcha artists. The truckers, proving once again that shaking the dogs comes as natural to a Negro as swimming does to a fish, brought down the house.[49]

Reporting on the Hall of Negro Life continued with the same tone throughout the duration of the fair, but those who visited the hall saw a presentation of black progress that filled African-Americans with pride. The first statue they encountered depicted a black man breaking chains from his wrists. A mural depicted African-Americans building the United States and contributing to the nation's music, art, and religion. The hall drew 400,000 visitors, the majority of them white, and many of them aghast at the challenge to their narrative of American history.[50]

JUSTICE DELAYED

African-Americans usually only saw such positive depictions of their race at church, where black preachers taught that God would provide in the long run, despite the injustices the congregation witnessed on a nearly daily basis. The church provided a physical and moral center for black society, but African-American church leaders did not escape corruption. White leaders recognized the leadership role preachers played and tried to control the clergy. In larger cities, such as Dallas, black preachers accepted white patronage and, in return, made sure their congregations did not challenge white rule.[51]

Segregation benefited African-American newspapers, often the only source of information about the black community. The *Dallas Express* gained a wide readership in a city where 93 percent of the black community was literate. Not only did the paper report on daily developments but its editors encouraged African-Americans to get involved in politics and offered black history lessons.[52]

Whites, meanwhile, delayed civil rights whenever possible, and Marlin's Tom Connally filibustered the AntiLynching bill of 1937.[53] But there were bright spots among Texas's congressional delegation. That same year, U.S. representative Maury Maverick wrote, "I do not hate colored people; neither do I claim greater knowledge of them than Yankees." That was enough for black Texans to name him one of the few white Texans contributing to race relations.[54] Maverick's support for Roosevelt's New Deal and his progressive approach to race, though, led to a primary challenge, where a conservative white Democrat ousted him.

While black supporters couldn't help Maverick because of the whites-only primary, in nonpartisan city elections, blacks could legally vote if they paid their poll tax. In Dallas, A. Maceo Smith organized the Progressive Voters League to raise money for poll taxes and recruit black voters.[55] The League registered five thousand voters for the municipal election of 1937, the year white politicians split into five competing factions and were surprised to learn that the black vote would choose the winner. Smith convinced all the candidates to commit to building a second black high school, hiring of black police officers, and creating more city jobs for blacks. Smith then backed the Forward Dallas Association, which won five of the nine city council seats. The whites kept every promise, except the hiring of black police officers.[56]

Even progressive whites, though, often treated blacks as second-class citizens and insisted on segregation. When blacks began moving into Dallas's Exline neighborhood, one not racially zoned, assailants detonated eighteen bombs to scare away black home buyers between December 1940 and November 1941. Police never identified any suspects, and African-Americans learned that cooperating with the white community would deliver only so much.[57]

In statewide elections, the Democratic party's dominance left many African-Americans disillusioned, and only fifty thousand blacks voted in the 1940 general election. During the congressional vote two years later, blacks cast only 33,000 ballots. That changed when the U.S. Supreme Court struck down the whites-only primaries in 1944 and ordered political parties to give African-Americans a chance to vote.[58]

The NAACP membership chairwoman in Dallas, Juanita Craft, became the first black woman ever to vote in the Dallas County primary. She spent the next two years recruiting African-Americans, and by 1946, the local chapter numbered seven thousand members.[59] The need for more activism was exemplified in Marshall, Texas, when the leaders of the East Texas town activated the National Guard to stop blacks from voting. African-American leaders and protesters faced down the troops, and city leaders allowed them to vote. The 1946 gubernatorial race was the first since Reconstruction where the top white candidates actively sought the black vote. More than 75,000 African-Americans voted in that election, despite the poll tax, but this still represented less than a 14 percent turnout of eligible black voters.[60]

A 1948 poll showed that 66 percent of whites opposed equal rights for blacks, and in 1950 the Texas legislature expanded segregation by banning joint facilities in state parks. State agencies did little to help blacks, with the highway and education departments offering only menial jobs. Until the 1960s, the Texas Employment Commission maintained a policy of cutting off unemployment benefits to African-Americans who applied for jobs normally held by whites. Nevertheless, African-Americans built successful businesses, including nine statewide insurance companies by 1947.[61]

African-Americans in Texas remained divided on whether to push for integration or to accept continued segregation with truly separate but equal facilities. Many black professionals, such as doctors and teachers, feared that integration would lead to whites taking their jobs, while others worried that desegregation would destroy African-American communities.[62]

Whites resisted any attempts by blacks to move out of the slums of

West Dallas, a nine-square-mile shantytown where fewer than 10 percent of dwellings had indoor plumbing and typhus and tuberculosis were pandemic. In the early 1950s, blacks again tried to move into the Exline neighborhood south of Fair Park, but after blacks bought twelve homes, bombers destroyed them. This time, though, Dallas police made arrests and a special grand jury investigated. Despite testimony implicating prominent white citizens, the grand jury indicted two Hispanics. Prosecutors took only Pete Garcia, a light-skinned Mexican-American living in Exline, to trial, where he claimed white status. Allegedly, he had joined the bombers to solidify his standing in the white community, and a white jury acquitted him. The bombings, though, failed to stop African-American families from moving into the neighborhood, and soon most white families had moved out.[63] Exline became one of Dallas's most impoverished neighborhoods.

REBRANDING

At the Texas State Fair in 1952, organizers unveiled a fifty-two-foot mannequin called "Big Tex." Organizers bragged that Big Tex wore size seventy boots and a seventy-five-gallon hat. The following year, they mounted a moving jaw and a loudspeaker so he could welcome guests to Fair Park with a hearty "Howdy Folks!" Big Tex was perhaps the most transparent attempt by Texans to move away from their history as a southern state with Confederate heroes and transform Texas into a western state, the home of cowboys and oilmen. Interstate 35, which splits Texas on a north-south line from Dallas to Laredo, represents an informal division between the old and new Texas. Almost every county courthouse east of I-35 has a memorial to Confederate veterans, while few to the west do. The rebranding was remarkably successful, and fifty years later many people are surprised to learn that Texas was a slave state.

Texas conservatives, who always had a tumultuous relationship with the national Democratic party, remained publicly opposed in the 1950s to equal rights for African-Americans. In the 1952 presidential race, Governor Allan Shivers endorsed the Republican candidate, Gen. Dwight D. Eisenhower, over the Democratic contender, Adlai Stevenson. African-Americans voted overwhelming for Stevenson and opposed Shivers in the 1954 primary, but Shivers won renomination for a third term.[64]

The *Brown v. Board of Education* decision in 1954 triggered real panic among conservative Texans, and Shivers promised to fight the order by all legal means. In Mansfield, near Fort Worth, 250 white students stopped black students when that district tried to integrate in 1956, and Shivers sent Texas Rangers to remove the blacks.[65]

In 1955, the state legislature cut off funding for any school in Texas that integrated without voter approval and issued a list of excuses a district could use to remain segregated, such as space, transportation, psychological effects, and morality. Lawmakers passed a law that automatically shut down a school if federal troops tried to enforce integration and absolved children from attending school if their parents opposed it.[66]

White conservatives used propaganda to tie the civil rights movement to communism, and they made the Dallas school board their central battleground against liberals, desegregation, and communism for the next twenty years. The chairman of the English Department at Dallas's Southern Methodist University inspired a resurgence of anti-Semitism in 1951 with a best-selling book entitled *The Iron Curtain Over America*. Author John Owen Beaty denied that Eastern European Jews were Jewish and claimed they were a mongrel race descended from Satan that sought world domination. Beaty's book sold very well in Dallas and inspired modern white supremacist groups like the Aryan Nations. Anti-Semitic groups in Dallas linked the NAACP to secret Jewish groups plotting global dominance and the oppression of whites, including the forced breeding of white women with nonwhites.[67]

SEVENTEEN

I'm not the maître d' to the Pearly Gate, so who He lets in is
His business. But I am not going to open the side door to
heaven to one of these racist hypocrites that come up to me
talking about how we loved you all, when I know better.

—Julia Taylor

Albert Tomlinson decided to sell off part of the Hill in 1946 and
gave first dibs to the African-Americans living on it, offering to
sell Vincent the one hundred acres he worked for $45,000. Vincent
didn't have that kind of money, and no bank was going to give a mortgage of that size to a black man, so he was going to have to move his
family, along with all of the sharecroppers on Tomlinson Hill.[1] But
Albert knew he was pushing a hundred people out of the only homes
they'd known, so he set aside a plot a few hundred yards from Vincent's
house for a black neighborhood. The government was offering veterans
coming home from World War II low-cost loans to buy homes through
the Veterans Administration, and Albert wanted to take advantage of
the housing boom. He drew up a plat of one-acre home sites called the
A. P. Tomlinson Development.[2]

Albert gave lots to the African-Americans who had spent generations on the Hill and arranged to build eighteen-hundred-square-foot
bungalows if the black families agreed to pay a third of the cost up
front. After years of paying them their "share," Albert knew how little
cash the families had, so he loaned them the remainder of the building

costs. Vincent chose a lot just off the highway and arranged for his relatives and children to get adjoining lots.[3]

After the years they had spent living in a sharecropper's shack, the new bungalow transformed the black Tomlinsons' lives. The simple house had a pier-and-beam foundation that lifted it off the ground, the walls were insulated, and it had a tin roof. Since it was next to the highway, the house came with electricity, which pumped well water into the house. Vincent bought a propane tank, so the children no longer had to chop wood for heat. Charles told me he loved the new house:

> We bartered and we got us a TV later and already got electricity and all that. We was the only one got a refrigerator up here on the Hill. And the other kids would come by and look at it. You could keep your ice cream in there and put it in the freezer and it would still be hard. With an ice box you would buy your ice cream and put your ice in there, it'[d] get soft. But them ice trays, them cubes, you know, that was something. That was something to see. First time they'd seen it, first time I'd seen it.[4]

Vincent let everyone in his family know land was available at a reasonable price, and soon all the cousins joined the Tomlinsons. Albert sold lots to a dozen other black families, and land ownership instilled pride in the community of 107 people. A new store even opened up along State Highway 7.[5] But the move also signaled less welcome changes.

Albert moved the sharecroppers into a village because the new landowners planned to use machines to work the land, not people, and they planned to grow more corn and raise cattle, both of which require less labor than cotton. Albert was laying off the sharecroppers, and without any farmwork, Vincent found himself unemployed for the first time in his life. His children began looking for jobs, but there were fewer and fewer of those in Falls County. Mineral-water tourism declined once antibiotics became widely available.

People moved off the farm and into towns, while the county combined school districts and bought buses to bring farm children into town for classes. By 1950, the Lott Independent School District had annexed the Tomlinson Negro School, shut it down, and had started busing black children to a segregated elementary school in Lott.[6]

AN OLD-FASHIONED SHERIFF

Falls County residents elected Brady Pamplin sheriff in 1946 for his first of many terms in office. Pamplin had spent a decade as a Falls County deputy, two years as a Texas Ranger, and had served in the Air Force during World War II.[7] He was an old-fashioned sheriff who wore a Stetson cowboy hat and carried a big revolver. Pamplin stood over six feet tall, weighed two hundred pounds, and made a point of knowing everyone's business, both in the black and the white communities. Frank Wyman told me about the first time he saw Pamplin in western Falls County. Six black churches had organized a Sunday school conference in Chilton and a church in Waco had chartered a Greyhound bus to transport those wishing to attend. Frank said he was impressed to see blacks riding in the front of a bus in 1955, but soon trouble started:

> A group of teenage boys, as they would do, went to the downtown area probably to buy a package of cigarettes or something like that. They went into the store and as soon as they walked in the man told them to get out because he didn't serve niggers. One of them mumbled something in response. Under the guise that he just simply didn't take any cursing from anybody, the storekeeper started chasing the boy.
>
> [The store owner] picked up a pipe and chased him, and the boy ran back to the church and it was during a break period. There were people selling dinners. They had little stands out. There were refreshments and all of that. People were mingling, a lot of people from the different churches, and this boy ran down the middle of the crowd with this white man. He had an apron on [and was] carrying a large metal pipe and he ran through the crowd and I rushed to the front just to get a bird's-eye view of it. The bus driver told one of the ministers if they could go in and get the boy and put him on the bus that

he would pretend that the boy was a customer. Then they informed him that he indeed was a customer, that he had come down with the group from Waco.

[The driver] said, "Well, if you can get him on the bus I guarantee nothing will happen to him." . . . The boy had crawled under some-one's house and he came out and they put him on the bus.

The man who was chasing him went back to his store and in just a few minutes showed up with a friend of his in a car. . . . I picked up the pipe and was pounding it in my hand and this elderly deacon walked up to me and gave me a sermon about not having hate in my heart. I said, "This sounds familiar; please don't tell me I should pray for him."

They did get the boy back to the bus. The store owner was driving the car. The passenger, his friend, opened the door of the car before he displayed this huge knife. He turned to the crowd and said, "You all might as well just leave [the store owner] alone, let him do what he has got to do."

[The store owner] went over to the bus and the Greyhound bus driver told him that if he stepped one foot on the threshold of the bus that he would blow a hole through him big enough to drop an egg through. He pulled out this drawer and displayed this huge pistol that he had.

But Reverend Weber sat down in the door, and he was big enough to occupy the entire thing. Reverend Weber was about a four-hundred-pound man. He sat down on the steps of the bus and they were almost to the point of an argument of the bus driver telling him to move. The bus driver cursed like an angry black man: "You know if he's so bad, let him bring his ass up on this bus, let him step up on the bus."

So the preacher, not wanting any bloodshed of anybody, he re-mained sitting on the bus, saying that: "If you're going to get on the bus, you're going to have to come over me."

The sheriff walked up, and they explained the things on both sides to the sheriff. And the sheriff told him, "I'm fixing to go back to Mar-lin and have my Sunday dinner. And I am praying right now that nothing causes me to have to come back over here, because I will put my boot ankle-deep up your ass, do you understand what I'm saying? Excuse me, Reverend."

That ended the confrontation, and the white store owner left. Frank said everyone knew what was coming next when Pamplin said, "I don't like violence, but . . ."[8]

Frank's college-educated father, Charles Wyman, was a schoolteacher, and many African-Americans came to him for advice. The white community also recognized Charles as a leader in the community, and Pamplin often asked Charles for help when investigating serious crimes involving blacks. Pamplin frequently visited Wood Street, where he often picked up his dinner at Strickland's Café. Pamplin didn't interfere with African-Americans unless they did something to anger him or the white community, but Frank said the mere sight of him could strike terror among blacks.

CELEBRATING FALLS COUNTY

Falls County marked its centennial in 1950, and the Marlin Chamber of Commerce formed a special Centennial Commission to organize a weeklong celebration. The festivities started on Sunday, October 8, when preachers held special church services, while organizers designated Monday Homecoming Day, with parades, marching bands, and floats. Ranchers brought their best animals to the Empty Saddle Club Arena for Livestock Day on Tuesday, while Youth Day was on Wednesday and Agriculture Day was on Thursday. The chamber hired a carnival enterprise to provide rides and games on the courthouse grounds and the United Daughters of the Confederacy built a memorial log cabin as a special exhibit. The chamber also commissioned the John B. Rogers Production Company to produce a four-night historical pageant on the football field, complete with elaborate costumes and props. The company recruited three hundred citizens to pantomime the county's history on the football field while narrators read from a script over the loudspeakers. The pageant scenes included nomadic Native Americans, Spanish settlers, the early white pioneers, and the establishment of the first church. Others portrayed Civil War soldiers lowering the Confederate battle flag to signal their defeat. The spectacle ended with the queen of the centennial and her court parading across the field.[9]

The celebration provided a brief diversion from Marlin's growing economic problems. Recognizing his hometown needed a little help, U.S. Senator Tom Connally arranged for the construction of a 222-bed Veterans Administration hospital in 1950. If the doctors saw their business at the hot springs drop because of antibiotics, he figured they could shift to government work. The hospital employed 13 physicians and 290 other employees and quickly became the largest employer in Marlin.[10]

On Tomlinson Hill, Vincent's youngest son, O.T., quit high school to work odd jobs, while O.T.'s older brother Charles moved to Corpus Christi with his wife, Zelma.[11] J.K. preferred to hang out on Wood Street and shoot dice.[12]

LIVE OAK STREET

Every Saturday, when county residents flooded into Marlin to shop, the town's racial divide was clear for anyone to see. Live Oak was the dividing line between black and white, and whites walked on the north sidewalk, while blacks walked on the south.[13] When blacks and whites shared the same sidewalk, whites expected blacks to step into the street to make way.[14] The Wyman family lived a block away from the white neighborhood and Frank said he learned as a six-year-old in the early 1950s how their home's location put him in danger:

> A friend of mine and I were sitting on the curb and this man, this white man, and these two little boys came running down the street and he was shouting to them to "shoot them niggers." I had no idea what they were doing. I had heard of BB guns, but I had never held one. I didn't know anything about it, so they were directly across the street from us, just pumping the BB gun and just shooting as fast as

they could. [The white man] would get behind and say, "No, to the left, to the left, shoot him." The little boy would shoot and he missed.

So finally, one of them hit my friend on the shoulder and he said, "They're shooting at us." When I look back at it, I say, "How stupid could we have been?" We could have been blinded. But we just sat there looking at them until he hit Junior Bonner on the shoulder. So we just peeled off and ran away and they walked on down the street.

The next day I told Junior Bonner to bring a hammer and I'd find the steam to kill both of them little boys. I took these bullets out of my mother's sewing machine drawer. My father had a .32 revolver; it was an officer's revolver during World War I.

My plan was that I would steal those bullets and a pair of pliers and he would bring the hammer and I would hold the bullet with the pliers and he would hit the bullet from the back, and when it went off, we would be shooting back at them. We were going to sit on the curb as bait to trick them into coming to shoot at us again. Just before we left I was taking the last inventory of the bullets, when my mother saw me with them and asked me why did I have them. I just nonchalantly told her the entire story and the plot to commit first-degree murder. It was the first time I saw her do almost what people do in church when they're shouting, where they just become possessed.[15]

Wyman remembered that African-American parents spent a great deal of time training their children, particularly boys, to avoid getting into situations where they might be falsely accused of doing something wrong. Blacks did not speak to a white stranger unless spoken to first, and they avoided looking a white person directly in the eye. Frank said he was taught never to speak to a white woman without a witness present, preferably a white man. The most important rule for a black man was never to be alone with a white woman. Daily life offered routine humiliations, as well. Frank remembered walking down Live Oak one evening with two friends when he was twelve years old. Two slightly older white boys drove by.

They started screaming out "Niggers!" This was a favorite sport for them, this type of harassment.

My friend's friend shouted an insult back to them. Okay, they went down a block and pulled into the parking lot on the corner of Gretchen and Live Oak. They made a U-turn and came back, and when we saw the car coming back, our hearts fell. They came back shouting, "You niggers want to fight, you niggers want to fight!"

We ran across the parking lot, through the partial construction of the funeral home, and we were just trying to figure out which way to go, because we didn't want to go to either one of our homes. This would tell them where we lived and they would surely come back with men in sheets on horseback or something.

I have spent time punishing myself for having run and swearing that if the same thing happened again, I would run as far as I could and pick up a two-by-four. If they want[ed] to kill me, they would have to do it right then and there. I was ashamed and angry at myself for having run. They would never make me afraid enough to run from them again.[16]

Segregation in the 1950s provided both whites and blacks a chance to hide. Whites didn't want to share their power and privilege, and blacks found protection within their own communities. But segregation denied African-Americans equal opportunities and guaranteed a lesser quality of life. Many Marlin businesses refused to serve African-Americans, but those that did set up elaborate ways to keep their white customers separate. When Vincent took his children for ice cream, the parlor downtown had a special entrance in the back and uncomfortable seating. At the movie theater, blacks sat in the balcony and public water fountains came in pairs, one for each race.[17] At Houston's Restaurant, next to the Marlin bus station, cooks served blacks from a window in the back.[18] No matter how much pride, self-esteem, or education African-Americans enjoyed, segregation ate away at them, and it often ate away at the whites who came to recognize the unearned benefits it granted them.

In the summer of 1955, Albert's heart began to fail and he checked into the Buie Clinic in Marlin. There he bumped into a woman he vaguely recognized, Julia Ann Taylor. She was the schoolteacher from the Tomlinson Negro School and the daughter of Hezekiah Taylor, the man whom Albert had blackballed in the 1930s. Frank is Julia Ann's son, and he told the story of what happened that day:

> She saw this black orderly pushing this elderly white man in a wheel-chair and he passed her and she didn't pay any attention. Then she heard him say, "Whoa, Bully," one of the nicknames they would give to the orderlies. Or a black male, they called him "bully." He said, "Back up, back up," until he got right in front of her and he asked her, "Are you Hezekiah Taylor's daughter?"
>
> She said, "Yes."
>
> And then she remembered it was one of the Tomlinsons, Albert Tomlinson. She said that he just started talking as though it was pent-up and he wanted to release that he remembered something, and that it was how happy he was to see her and that he had great respect for her father.
>
> When [my mother] was telling the story to me, she said Albert had been the one who had blacklisted my grandfather. She told me that with all those mouths to feed at that time, no one would hire Hezekiah. . . . He was at a point of desperation until they started working on what they called the Roosevelt roads.
>
> She thought it was bitter irony. She would say, "These people get holy when death starts knocking on their door."
>
> And then she would clarify and say, "Heaven belongs to God, and I'm certainly not standing at the door with a clipboard in my hand as to who's going to make it. I'm not the maître d' to the Pearly Gate, so who He lets in is His business. But I am not going to open the side door to heaven to one of these racist hypocrites that come up to me talking about how we loved you all, when I know better."[19]

Albert died from heart disease on November 1, 1955, at the age of eighty-two.[20]

TEXAS VERSUS THE NAACP

Texas Democrats, long hostile to the NAACP, launched a legal attack against the organization in 1956. Texas attorney general John Ben Shepperd sued the organization, claiming that it had "exceeded the bounds of propriety and law" and was no longer operating as a non-profit. He wanted the NAACP to pay taxes as a corporation and pub-lish its membership list, knowing it would be used to harass civil rights supporters.[21]

Rather than sue in Travis County, where his office was located, or Dallas County, where the state NAACP was headquartered, Shepperd took his case to Smith County, one of the most conservative districts in Texas. Not surprisingly, Shepperd found a sympathetic ear in Judge Otis T. Dunagan, who ordered the NAACP to cease operations. The national NAACP sent their top lawyer, future Supreme Court justice Thurgood Marshall, to answer what he said was the most important case in the nation at the time because it was designed to force the NAACP to aban-don several school integration lawsuits.[22] The *Dallas Morning News'* editorial board also took a dim view of the NAACP, calling it "the National Association for the Agitation of Colored People." "In a free country, every citizen is as entitled to his personal prejudices as to his so-called civil rights," one editorial read.[23] Shepperd and the NAACP eventually settled out of court, with the state agreeing to stop challeng-ing the group's nonprofit status, and the NAACP agreeing to pay state franchise taxes.[24]

African-American parents filed a new lawsuit against the Dallas school board in 1957 after it failed to make any effort to integrate. Else-where in Texas, school districts that were integrating allowed wealthy white students to transfer out of schools that included blacks and re-fused to provide transportation for blacks who wanted to attend white schools. Integrated schools allowed white students to turn extracurricu-lar clubs into private after-school functions so they could legally exclude blacks. Superintendents retaliated against activist black teachers by dis-missing them, rather than transferring them to integrated schools. The effect was continued segregation.[25]

Yet more than 300 white ministers and 115 black clergy in Dallas issued a joint statement in 1958, calling for "simple justice" for all citizens. Small school districts in North and West Texas with negligible African-American populations embraced school integration because it saved them money by consolidating facilities and staff. Not surprisingly, the districts with the largest number of black students took the longest to integrate.[26]

THE BOWLING LIFE

Bob Tomlinson graduated from Woodrow Wilson High School in 1958, and Tommy ordered him to attend Texas A&M, just as he had and his father had before that. Tommy didn't seem to care that Bob had no interest in engineering, farming, or the military, the three things at which A&M excelled. But Bob followed his father's wishes and underwent the Corps of Cadets' military-style training and hazing.[27]

Bob spent as much time as possible bowling, joining two leagues and competing with the official A&M team. The Memorial Student Center had lanes, and the Knights of Columbus hosted a league that bowled in an eight-lane alley built with cinder blocks and steel beams, probably the loudest alley Bob ever experienced. "Every chance I got I went to the bowling alley, which is one reason why my grades sucked," he told me.[28]

In October 1959, Bob scored 297 in one game and a week later rolled his first perfect 300 game at the Memorial Student Center, a rare accomplishment for any bowler, let alone a seventeen-year-old college freshman.[29] By December, the A&M team took a wide lead with a 32–4 record in the conference. Their next closest competitor, Arlington State, had a 25–11 record.[30]

Howard Rogers was Bob's roommate that semester, and he set Bob up on a blind date with a cousin for the Texas A&M vs. Texas Christian University football game in Fort Worth. Beth Ward was a junior in high school and lived in Arlington, a suburb between Dallas and Fort Worth. Bob and Beth hit it off and started dating.

After that first semester, Bob didn't go back to College Station. He had stopped attending some classes completely and wanted to enroll at Arlington State, a community college near where Beth lived. But Tommy insisted Bob go to the more prestigious Southern Methodist University, an expensive private school, long known for its wealthy student body and active fraternities and sororities. But Bob didn't like parties, and he liked SMU even less than A&M. Bob again spent most of his time in bowling alleys, much to the chagrin of his conservative father.[31]

By the mid-1950s, more and more Texas conservatives were joining Tommy in the Republican party. Tommy and other Dallas County white voters in 1954 elected their first-ever Republican to Congress, Bruce Alger, who took increasingly white supremacist positions over the next decade to defeat conservative Democrat challengers. In the late 1950s, the *Dallas Morning News* reported on the transformation of the Texas Republican party into a conservative states' rights group and how the Democrats were moving toward liberalism and civil rights. By 1960, the *Dallas Morning News* was endorsing Alger's positions.[32]

Dallas's conservatism extended to many African-American leaders as well, who politely cooperated with the all-white Dallas Citizens Council. Together, they formed the Committee of 14, with seven members from each race, and they convinced middle-class stores to desegregate their lunch counters to avoid protests like those seen in other states. But younger African-Americans, inspired by those sit-ins and marches, organized dramatic protests across the city in 1960 and attracted condemnation from both black and white leaders. At conservative SMU, fifty-eight white students and two black students staged a protest at the University Drug Store lunch counter. The owner hired an exterminator to pump the restaurant full of insecticidal gas to drive the students out, but they held their ground.[33]

Bob wasn't a part of the protest; in fact, he was barely on campus. In April 1960, he traveled to Toledo, Ohio, with the five-member Dallas Bowling Association team to compete for a spot in the American

Bowling Congress's open division. He led the team and helped it earn a spot in the amateur tournament with a 618 three-game series.[34] Bob stopped attending classes in his favorite subject, English, because the lecturer appeared to be gay. While he didn't mind the lesbians he'd met at Lakewood Lanes, he couldn't accept an effeminate man. Bob spent only one semester at SMU.[35]

Bob became the deskman at Zangs Bowl in Dallas's Oak Cliff neighborhood, collecting the fees, handing out shoes, and switching on the alleys. Tommy knew Bob couldn't make a decent living working the counter of a bowling alley, but he recognized bowling was growing in popularity. Tommy floated the idea of building a bowling alley for his son, but Bob thought that was a bad idea. Tommy came out of retirement in 1961 to open a bowling-supply distributorship and retail shop for his son, Bowling Supplies, Inc., at 2012 Greenville Avenue in Dallas. Tommy became the North Texas sales and service representative for Ace Bowling Balls and the Vulcan Corp.'s bowling-pin division.[36] Tommy managed the business while Bob hit the road for three weeks out of the month, selling supplies to bowling alleys across Texas and western Louisiana. The company offered everything from pin-setting equipment to the chemicals needed to treat the lanes.[37] Bob proposed to Beth, then a high school senior, and they wed in June 1961:

> She wore a gown of silk organza with scoop neckline and voluminous skirt with formal train. Her veil was a Chantilly lace mantilla, and she carried roses and valley lilies.
>
> Miss Joan Clare of Arlington was maid-of-honor and the bridegroom's sister, Miss Sally Tomlinson, was bridesmaid.
>
> Howard Rogers of San Antonio served as best man, and groomsman was Ken McKenzie. Guests were seated by Robert D. Ward of Ardmore, Okla. and Emil Fretz Jr.
>
> A reception was held at the Midway Savings Community Room.[38]

Bob traveled the state but still bowled in local and national amateur tournaments, with varying success. He was very skilled for someone in his early twenties, and many thought he had the potential to turn pro. On March 9, 1963, Bob bowled his first perfect 300 game in a sanctioned tournament, leading his Bowling Supplies, Inc., team in the Dallas Open Class league. He carried a 199 average, a professional-level score at the time.[39]

Bob found it difficult working for his father, though. The two engaged in screaming arguments at least once a week and Bob felt unappreciated.

> I wanted a little bit of stroking, right. Everyone likes to hear they did well. I'm the only one he could never tell that. He'd tell everyone else I'd done well, but he wouldn't let me know it. One time I came back from a trip to East Texas; I had, for those days, a ridiculous amount of orders, three or four thousand dollars.
>
> I came back with all of these orders. But he was so full of himself, he was so proud of himself, he had orders for six dozen bags. That was more important than the three thousand–dollars plus in orders I'd brought in.
>
> When Lakewood Lanes was still open, I'd go over sometimes and someone would say, "Man, your dad sure was bragging on what a good job you're doing on things." I never heard it.[40]

Bowling was a distinctly blue-collar sport, and Bob enjoyed how it put him in contact with a wide variety of Texans. But in the early 1960s, it was hard to make friends with people from other races. Dallas was geographically segregated, with thirty-six out of more than two hundred census tracts reporting no blacks, while six tracts were more than 90 percent African-American.[41] Bowling alleys were equally segregated for customers, but African-Americans provided most of the labor, working as porters, lane men, and mechanics. Bob came to respect and like the blacks he encountered, but he couldn't understand why he wasn't allowed to befriend them.[42] Genuine, if unequal, friendships could develop between blacks and whites, particularly with domestic workers who knew their employers most intimate secrets, but the inequality was always there. When an African-

American team won a citywide bowling award, whites refused to recognize them:

> The bowling industry was slow to change in a lot of ways and a good
> example is there used to be an awards banquet at the end of each
> bowling season. There would be the banquet and a dance, and they
> would give out [to] all the winners of the city tournament their awards.
> If somebody had won a 300 award, or something like that, within a
> couple of months of the banquet they would wait and give it to them
> then.
>
> A couple of guys, named Julius Lamar and Ray Williams, won the
> doubles one year. They canceled the banquet because they were black
> and didn't want to have the mixing.
>
> When Denver Ray and Julius were kind of shuffled off to the
> side—[organizers] didn't want to take a chance on having them win
> anything else in the city tournament—I thought, That's not right.
> They won it. They deserve their honors. That's an injustice. It's just
> minor, but it's there.[43]

When asked, Bob couldn't recall a single moment when he recognized the injustice of racial segregation and consciously decided to
support civil rights:

> It just seemed pretty apparent that some things were wrong and I
> don't know that there was any particular incident or moment that
> made the decision for me.
>
> The only thing that it could have been, I guess, was the people that
> I knew, the people that I had actually dealt with. Not in the sense of
> going out together socially, but you get to know people and you kind
> of have to figure out that these people are individuals.[44]

KENNEDY IN DALLAS

Bob was crossing class lines when he was twenty-one, something certainly not lost on his father, who understood Dallas's stratified society.

Dating back to the rise of the Klan in the 1920s, the Dallas elite constantly worried about what the unwashed masses might do. Builders and bankers like Tommy were at the top and controlled the city, and under them came, in order, working-class whites, poor whites, Mexican-Americans, and finally African-Americans. Tommy and Mary socialized at the Lakewood Country Club, but Bob spent his time in bowling alleys and enjoyed a camaraderie with working-class whites and upper-class blacks who shared his love for the game. This difference divided the two men.[45]

The starkest example of the division between Dallas's elite and the working class was the election of President John F. Kennedy in 1960. He carried 45 percent of the working-class vote in Dallas, versus only 23 percent of the upper-class vote. The addition of Texas Senator Lyndon B. Johnson to the ticket did little to assuage fears among conservative Democrats that Kennedy was a civil rights–promoting socialist. In fact, Kennedy hurt Johnson's reputation.[46] Tommy, who bore a distinct resemblance to Johnson, got angry every time someone brought it up.[47] In many ways, the 1960 presidential election marked the beginning of the end for Democrats in Texas.

The Dallas elite's disgust for Kennedy was expressed in a full-page advertisement that the American Fact-Finding Committee bought in the *Dallas Morning News* on November 22, 1963, which proclaimed, "Welcome, Mr. Kennedy," then went on to attack almost all of his policies as dangerous to the United States.[48] Members of the John Birch Society distributed leaflets along Kennedy's motorcade route that morning. Showing his face from the front and in profile, the leaflet declared him "Wanted for Treason." In contrast, more than 250,000 working-class Dallasites enthusiastically welcomed Kennedy on that clear, cool fall morning. When Kennedy's open-topped limousine passed through Dealey Plaza, Lee Harvey Oswald shot and killed Kennedy and wounded Governor John Connally.

Outsiders considered Dallas's leaders culpable in the assassination because they had so vociferously denounced Kennedy. Neiman-Marcus executive Warren Leslie blamed Dallas's right-wing extremism on nouveau-riche Republican women. Yet the real right-wing ideologues in

Dallas were oilmen H. J. Hunt and Clint Murchison, who were behind the American Fact-Finding Committee, and John Birch Society leader Gen. Edwin Walker.[49]

Moderate whites in Dallas recognized that change was inevitable and supported conservative African-Americans. The white business community backed Joe Lockridge for the Texas House of Representatives, and he became one of the first three African-Americans to serve in the legislature since Reconstruction, along with Houston's Curtis Graves and Barbara Jordan, who won election to the state senate. In 1969, white elites backed George Allen, a conservative African-American who had served on the Committee of 14, in his successful bid for city councilman.

Bob wasn't involved in politics, but if asked at the time, he would have considered himself conservative. Beth, on the other hand, was a liberal, and Bob says she slowly convinced him to take more progressive stances. But he was mostly concerned about bowling.

Harless Wade, the bowling reporter for the *Dallas Morning News,* began chronicling Bob's successes and failures in city tournaments and often referred to him as a "rapidly-rising young star."[50] Bob qualified for the biggest amateur tournaments, such as the 1965 National All-Star in Philadelphia,[51] but he maintained his amateur status to qualify for local tournaments that often paid winners very well.[52] In 1965, he was a finalist in the Master's and chosen for the *Morning News*'s All-Greater Dallas men's team.[53]

Bob was driving back in March 1965 from a bowling tournament in Miami when the interstate highway in Alabama was abruptly shut down on one side and all the traffic was shifted onto one side of the divided highway. He saw thousands of marchers on the closed side of the road.

I saw Dr. King's march from Selma to Montgomery in person. It was only driving along the highway, but . . . it was impressive seeing all those people.

You couldn't avoid knowing what was going on and you would look at those cops beating people and turning fire hoses on them and

the people [weren't] doing anything except just trying to go from
point A to point B. It just wasn't right.[54]

A few months later, I was born in Dallas's Baylor Hospital on July
18, 1965. Bob and Beth named me Christopher Lee, maintaining the
family tradition of the eldest son bearing the name of the Confederacy's greatest general.

Bob looks back on the mid-1960s as a golden age in Dallas's bowling
scene. Nationally ranked players lived and bowled regularly in Dallas
and the alleys made solid profits. When the *Morning News* hosted the
annual Dallas Bowling Awards Dinner on May 21, 1966, the newspaper named Bob to its six-member All-Star men's team for the second
year in a row.[55] Bob wrote a column for a free weekly newspaper called
the *Bowling News*. He wrote about tournaments, teams, and products,
but he couldn't write about what he really loved about bowling alleys—
the people from all walks of life.

Most bowling alleys operated on the same schedule. Corporate
leagues brought in the city's businesspeople at 6:30 P.M. for corporate
leagues, and at 8:30 P.M. the social leagues bowled. Late at night, the city's
seedier crowd arrived to gamble, if not on the lanes, then at the billiard
tables or the pinball machines. One of the toughest places was the Cotton Bowling Palace, where the Dixie Mafia guys hung out.[56]

DESEGREGATION

Dallas had grown from an important Texas town to a nationally recognized city with a county population of 951,527 people. The Dallas
Cowboys football team set up shop in 1960, and direct flights to Europe started from Love Field in 1962.

Yet Dallas remained a southern city. The mayor in 1960 was Robert
L. Thornton, a former cotton picker, self-made millionaire, and former
Klansman. Seven elementary schools in Dallas bore the names of Confederate heroes, and the Thomas Jefferson High School mascot was the
rebel, the Confederate battle flag its emblem.[57] Dallas talk radio was
full of people spouting theories blaming the Soviet Union and the

devil for stirring up African-Americans, and Bob remembered hearing a regular caller nicknamed "Granny Hate." She called herself "Dixie Leber," for the word *rebel* spelled backward, and she claimed to be the chief Ku Klux Klan recruiter in Dallas. Bob knew Granny Hate's daughter from bowling, but she was polite enough not to discuss her views on race in the bowling alley.[58]

After four years of inaction by the Dallas school district, a federal judge in 1960 ordered board members to begin integrating one grade a year.[59] Dallas school administrators and teachers proclaimed that integration would spark violence, particularly among underprivileged students of both races. The district hired a public-relations firm to produce a film warning Dallasites not to cause trouble, because school violence would harm their children and hurt Dallas's reputation. Dallas police chief Jesse Curry promised that his force would go after those who tried to stir up trouble, warning that he already knew the likely suspects.

In the fall of 1961, police and school officials escorted eighteen African-American elementary pupils to eight white schools. Protestors hanged a dummy from the flagpole of one school, while police intercepted a nineteen-year-old protestor preparing to burn a cross at another. Despite such acts, Dallas took its first step toward school desegregation relatively peacefully.[60]

District Superintendent Warren T. White was in no hurry to do any more. Over the next three years, out of a population of 9,400 African-American students, he transferred only 113 blacks to previously all-white schools. The passage of the Civil Rights Act of 1964 placed additional pressure on White by authorizing federal officials to cut off funds to segregated schools. In 1967, he reported that 67 out of 171 schools were integrated, but in most cases, only a handful of black students were attending predominately white schools. By May 1970, 113 out of 177 Dallas schools remained all-white institutions. As Dallas school officials stalled, white parents moved to the suburbs.[61]

Dallas was not the only district dragging its feet. In 1964, only 18,000 out of 325,000 African-American students statewide attended a formerly all-white school. This unimpressive achievement, though, put Texas at the top among former Confederate states. The white Texas State Teachers Association merged with the Colored Teachers State Association in 1965, and by 1967, nearly 47 percent of black students attended an integrated school.[62]

The U.S. Supreme Court ruled in 1967 that whites had to stop using cleverly drawn district boundaries and student choice to avoid meaningful integration. The Department of Health, Education, and Welfare filed suit against all of the major districts in Texas, including Dallas, because they maintained schools that were "visible vestiges of the dual school structure." Both sides engaged in a war of statistics. The Texas Education Agency in the spring of 1970 reported that 70 percent of black students attended an integrated school, while the HEW pointed out that only 35 percent of African-American students attended a predominately white school. In Dallas, 97 percent of African-American students still attended a predominately black school.[63]

Federal judges drafted desegregation plans and redrew school boundaries, pairing up black and white schools and closing others. In 1971, the Supreme Court declared busing a viable solution for ending unconstitutional segregation, and the NAACP and HEW filed a new suit against the Dallas school board, demanding a desegregation plan that used busing.[64] That year, I started the first grade.

John Tower, the first Republican senator from Texas since Reconstruction, had built his career by appealing to conservative Democrats who'd lost faith in their party. He immediately condemned the Court's decision and vociferously opposed busing. Whites complained that riding the bus not only placed their children in danger of traffic accidents but that long bus rides resulted in increased drug use and immoral behavior. Blacks complained that their children would go to school outside their neighborhoods and spend the most time on the bus. As part of his southern strategy for reelection, President Richard Nixon came out against forced busing, and white Texans flocked to his party.

A NEW TOMLINSON HILL

After Albert Tomlinson died in 1955 with no heirs, his cousin John Peoples Tomlinson moved from Marlin to Tomlinson Hill and took over what was left of the farm. Known as "Uncle John," he and his wife, Olga, were well liked by both the white and black communities. John liked Vincent Tomlinson and hired him as a farm manager and handyman.[65] Early most mornings, Vincent walked a hundred yards to John's house, where they shared breakfast and discussed what needed to be done that day. Neighbors often saw the two men riding together in a pickup before John went to Marlin for the day, where he managed a bank. He and Olga were first cousins and chose not to have children, so the Hill was the center of their lives.[66]

The black Tomlinsons continued to grow their own vegetables, raise hogs, and work on nearby farms. In the spring and fall, Vincent and his family traveled to plant and harvest cotton around the state, but he reserved one weekend every summer to use the Old Settler's reunion grounds for a family reunion. He remained active in the church and the Masons, but his youngest sons were different. O.T. and J.K. preferred to go to Wood Street, listen to music, shoot dice, play pool, and hang out with their friends.[67]

O.T. was short and slight like his father, and he carried a chip on his shoulder. He never hesitated to say what he thought, but he also worked hard and could be generous to a fault. O.T. played baseball in high school and fought in underground boxing matches around Falls County. He kept a .410-gauge shotgun in his truck to hunt rabbits and squirrels for meat and raccoons for their pelts. O.T. and his friends on the Hill started a hunting tradition on Thanksgiving mornings, but they always returned home in time for dinner.[68]

O.T. turned twenty in 1955 and started dating Jewell Butler McClain, the nineteen-year-old daughter of a farm laborer from nearby Reagan.[69] Jewell was married, but her husband was serving time in a California prison. She became pregnant with her first child by O.T., Linda, and moved into a house on the Hill with O.T. In 1957 they had their first son, Oliver Terry Tomlinson, Jr., whom they called Terry. They had another son in 1958, Ronald, and a third son, Charles, in 1960. The name on the children's birth certificates was McClain, because Jewell and O.T. were not married, but the children grew up calling themselves Tomlinson. Some of the kids used the name McClain when they got their driver's licenses, but Terry officially changed his name to his father's. O.T. took a job constructing mobile homes with Centurion Homes in Waco, which paid him a decent wage.[70]

O.T. and his family lived in a small white wooden house on a sandy road around the corner from his parents. He often said the Hill was his favorite place on the planet. It offered quiet country living and he knew all of his neighbors, many of whom were family. He also loved that it bore his name. He felt a special responsibility to everyone who lived there, just as Vincent did.[71]

In the early 1960s, more than one hundred people lived on the Hill, and most worked on other people's farms. The older families had built their wooden bungalows in the late 1940s, but after Uncle John sold individual lots in later years, newcomers built new brick houses well into the 1960s.[72] The middle-class African-American village soon became known as Tomlinson Hill, and O.T.'s children grew up believing the village was named for their family and didn't know about the slave plantation.

Jewell worked at Frank Smith's chicken-processing plant in Waco, and O.T.'s mother, Julie, would care for the children during the day. O.T. and Jewell were both strong-willed and a little stubborn, and they often fought, upsetting Terry. One day, when he was four years old, Terry packed his things in a sack and walked one hundred yards up the street to his grandparents' house and moved in. Terry lived there until he graduated from high school, but even though he slept at his grandma's house, O.T. and Jewell saw him every day. The Hill was like a family compound, and it protected the family from the societal and racial problems afflicting Texas. Everyone looked out for one another, and no one was ever truly alone.[73]

SMALL-TOWN CIVIL RIGHTS

The Civil Rights movement didn't reach Marlin until the late 1960s, when a few African-Americans staged a sit-in at the lunch counter in Houston's Restaurant. J. C. Williams was working as a cook and described how Sheriff Pamplin convinced them to leave, but only after identifying the protesters' parents, many of whom worked for the school district or the city.[74] Their white bosses informed the protesters' parents the next day that if their children mounted any more demonstrations, they'd lose their jobs. Pamplin took a harsh view of anyone who wanted to stir up trouble, white or black.[75] He made it clear that neither the Ku Klux Klan nor the NAACP were welcome to protest in Falls County.[76] The *Dallas Morning News* published a fawning profile of Pamplin and his thirty-two-year career as a lawman in 1966:

> Pamplin was one of the original, most caustic critics of the new legal emphasis on the rights of defendants and suspects.
>
> Says Pamplin, "It has completely broken down law enforcement. Any place you look you can see proof of that. Everybody's 'rights' are getting well taken care of now except the law-abiding citizens'. What kind of a system is that?"

> One of Pamplin's favorite helpers is a shaggy 5-year-old German shepherd dog named Chief, trained by the sheriff to be both an excellent tracker and a guard. Chief loves his law work. He can follow a scent as good as most bloodhounds. If Pamplin posts him to guard the jail door it's dangerous to get close by it, particularly from the inside.
>
> The sheriff can bring in the worst of prisoners in a car, with only Chief's aid. Pamplin puts the two in the back seat and cautions the prisoner, "Now you just sit real quiet until we get to the jail and you'll be okay. I sure wouldn't make any sudden moves if I were you." With Chief staring him intently in the eye, no prisoner needs a reminder."[77]

Elsewhere in Texas, African-Americans were more active. Students from all-black Wiley and Bishop colleges staged protests in Marshall in the spring of 1960. Prairie View students protested in Hempstead in 1963, while the NAACP and the Congress for Racial Equality petitioned and protested segregation in Austin, Houston, and San Antonio. Protests continued against discrimination in small towns into the 1970s.[78]

Many African-Americans, though, voted with their feet by moving into the city, or leaving the South completely. In the twenty years from 1940 to 1960, the rural black population in Texas dropped by half, while the number of African-American farmers dropped from 52,751 to 15,041. The number of white farmers didn't drop nearly as precipitously. During that period, white farmers added acreage, while African-American land ownership was a third of what it averaged in 1940. Only 3,138 black sharecroppers remained by 1960.[79]

EIGHTEEN

I wish I was in the land of cotton,
Old times they are not forgotten;
Look away! Look away! Look away! Dixie Land.

— **Songwriter Dan Emmett, an Ohio native who sang in
blackface about the virtues of slavery.**

B̲ob's best chance to join the Professional Bowling Association's
tour came in 1966. At his first PBA-sanctioned tournament, he
bowled well enough in the opening matches to qualify for the national
tournament, which was held in New Orleans. He and Beth agreed that
if he won one thousand dollars, he would turn professional.

My first match was against Nelson Burton, Jr., and I won it. I lost
every other game after that. I was just completely out of gas. And I
don't know whether it affected me or not—or whether it was a part of
it—but I got a chiropractic workout that made me feel really good in
between shifts. Whether this made me feel too relaxed or whether I
was just out of gas or whether I just choked, I don't know. I just didn't
have the courage to finish. I guess that's what it was. I could get close,
but I couldn't win.[1]

Bob made only $650 and didn't join the PBA. The popularity of
bowling was also flagging, and Bob had to expand his sales route to
keep enough orders coming in to stay in business, which kept him out

of town most of the week. He gave up his dream of becoming a professional bowler and concentrated on selling supplies and raising a family, though he continued to bowl as a serious amateur at the American Bowling Congress's national tournament for the next forty years.

The Vietnam War and the turmoil in the Democratic party in 1968 motivated Bob to get involved in the hottest thing in Texas politics, the Republican party. I can vaguely remember a Richard Nixon lawn sign in front of our house. Bob told me about attending the party's 1968 state convention. Rather than finding the party of Nixon and Nelson Rockefeller, he discovered Texas favored Barry Goldwater and Ronald Reagan. "I'm not going to fit in here at all," he concluded.[2]

The Vietnam War played a bigger role in shaping Bob's political views than did the civil rights movement. The ability of wealthy white men to avoid going to war bothered Bob, even though he was exempt from the draft because he was married and had young children. He also believed the war itself was immoral and unnecessary.[3]

Bob and Beth moved into the Lake Highlands neighborhood in northeast Dallas and found themselves in a liberal enclave. Beth convinced Bob to join her in liberal Democratic party politics. After the 1970 election, Beth started hosting neighborhood meetings of the League of Women Voters at our house on Aldwick Drive.[4] The couple joined the Amigos, an organization that met once a month and brought together white, black, and Hispanic Dallasites to promote racial understanding. There Bob met Peter Johnson, who represented the Southern Christian Leadership Council in Dallas, and Dr. Charles Hunter, an assistant minister at St. Luke's African Methodist Episcopal Church, located downtown.[5]

In 1972, Bob became the Democratic party precinct chair and volunteered to promote the George McGovern campaign for president. He told me he enjoyed politics:

> I think it's the second-best indoor sport and bowling is my first. . . .
> It's a pretty wild swing going from a Republican state convention one
> year and being an organizer for McGovern four years later. But I was

much more at home with McGovern. I thought he was a very good man, but a lousy candidate.

[Beth always] considered herself to be a Democrat and she couldn't be just a Democrat. She had to be the leading rabble-rouser Democrat. She didn't have a pragmatic bone in her body; she was all or nothing.

When I was working for McGovern, some of our strongest opposition was within the Democratic party—George Wallace people [who supported segregation].[6]

When Bob and Beth attended their district's convention, conservative Democrats outnumbered them two to one, and the conservatives rejected everything the liberals said, often without listening first. Bob described one such incident: "We were at the district convention and from the chair there was a mathematical error. Joe and I stood up to try and correct that, and we started getting all these yells: 'Sit down, you dirty Commies!'"[7]

Texas voters chose conservative Dolph Briscoe for governor by a huge margin, while voting for Nixon over McGovern. But Houston's Barbara Jordan became the first African-American woman from a southern state to win election to the U.S. House of Representatives. Bob served as precinct captain again in 1974, but he failed to be reelected and was replaced by an oil-and-gas attorney.[8]

Bob also volunteered with Big Brothers, an organization where adult men act as mentors for boys at risk of dropping out of school or getting involved in crime. Bob's little brother was Jimmy Miller, an African-American who came from a family of four brothers, all boxers.

We were going to work with a young guy who had some legal problems and try and show him a better life than stealing. He visited with us every couple of weeks, I guess, for a year and after that I think he was tired of it. And we would run out of things to do with him, so we kind of drifted away. Unfortunately, I know he wound up in some legal problems later on, because he was a champion in the Golden

Gloves in the Dallas division, but his probation officer wouldn't let him go to the next step, to the state tournament.[9]

Bob had troubles of his own as Bowling Supplies, Inc., began to collapse. The rapid construction of bowling alleys in the early 1960s had created a bubble that burst by 1970. Most of the operators leased their buildings from landlords, so when hard times hit, they cleaned out the buildings and left without paying their debts, including those to Bowling Supplies, Inc. One bowling center accepted a delivery of pins, only to declare bankruptcy the next day. Bob said he and an employee went down to Waxahachie and took the pins back. A series of suspicious fires destroyed several bowling centers, including one where the fire burned only the back of the alley and the storerooms, not the snack bar or the arcade at the front. Within months, the owner used the insurance money to reopen as a skating rink. Bob said his company had made a profit only once in ten years, and it burned through Tommy's savings as his debts racked up.[10] Tommy and Mary still held a large investment in Lakewood Bank and Trust, where Tommy was a director, but that money was for their old age.

In the summer of 1972, Tommy was at Lakewood Bank when he suffered a stroke. He returned home weeks later from the hospital, but was bedridden. I remember him lying in his bedroom with the curtains drawn because the light gave him headaches. I could tell he was suffering, and his condition worsened until Mary readmitted him to the hospital later that year. He held on for Christmas but died on New Year's Eve.[11]

I was seven years old and asked to attend the funeral. I surprised my parents and grandmother because I wasn't distraught by Tommy's death. I agreed with what many of the adults had told me, that he was in a better place and no longer suffering. After an elaborate Episcopal service, we rode in a black limousine, and Mary asked the motorcade to pass through Tommy's beloved Lakewood Country Club on the way to the cemetery. I remember the golfers on the links as we drove by.

Mary no longer needed the huge house on Twin Tree Lane and looked for a smaller one nearby. She began sorting through old boxes.

I found the Fretz family scrapbooks on a bookshelf in Bob's old room. The first was filled with clipping from the Dallas German-language newspaper published by Swiss settlers during the early 1900s. The other scrapbook was where I first read the obituaries for Gus, Eldridge, and R. E. L. Tomlinson. I was thrilled to learn they were cowboys, Texas Rangers, and southern gentry. Tommy had only ever said, "Our family used to own slaves and we treated them so well that they took our last name." To me, these were precious documents. My grandmother even told me that a Tomlinson had died in the Alamo and that my middle name was the result of the Tomlinsons' marrying into Robert E. Lee's family. Armed with this information, I told my friends at all-white Lake Highlands Elementary that I was descended from aristocracy and I was the offspring of the greatest general ever. Only years later would I learn that the family had no connection to the Alamo or to the Lees of Virginia.

I never considered that nonwhites might look at my family history with anything less than awe. I felt proud of my family's slaveholding and Confederate past, not because I believed in slavery or racism, but because white Texans honored and celebrated that heritage. I learned in elementary school that the South's cause was lawful and noble, and that the northerners who came to Texas were evil carpetbaggers set on looting my family's belongings. I learned the words to "The Battle Hymn of the Republic," but at school we sang "Dixie" more often. My parents forbade me from using racist language, but they didn't explain the injustices all around me. The only black people I encountered before I met Jimmy, the young boxer, were servants.

A popular cartoon character on Saturday-morning television commercials when I was in elementary school was Frito Bandito, created by the Dallas-based company Frito-Lay. A kid at school told me that if I wrote to the company, they would send me free Frito Bandito erasers, a hot commodity at my elementary school. But Frito Bandito was a caricature of a swarthy Mexican with a sombrero and bandoliers across his chest. He waved pistols in the air, yelled, "¡Arriba!" and twirled his mustache while trying to steal Frito snacks from children. He even fired his pistols to the tune of "Cielito Lindo," an iconic ballad from the Mexican Revolution. Civil rights groups protested this depiction of Mexican-Americans as early as 1969, but I remember collecting the rubber figures well into the early 1970s without objection from any adult in my life.

The mythology of a great family legacy took on greater psychological importance as I watched my family fall apart. Bob and Beth first experimented with marijuana in 1972, and he smoked it on a regular basis for years to come. They also started having sex with other couples. One night, I witnessed some heavy petting between them and the parents of a friend. A few weeks later, my parents and the other couple thought it was cute when I wrapped my arm around the other couple's daughter. We were nine years old.[12]

Bob and Beth frequently argued, and they never enjoyed spending time with their own parents. Holiday gatherings ended in wine-fueled arguments, but by the mid-1970s, the fights began as soon as we got in the car. The fighting grew worse after Tommy's death, when money became tight. I spent more and more time imagining ever more grand fantasies about my ancestors.

Bob carried on with Bowling Supplies, Inc., for a few months after Tommy died, but he could see the business had no future. He sold as much inventory as he could, put the money in the bank, and declared bankruptcy. The bank seized the cash, which paid off most of the debts, and the suppliers fought over what remained. The move protected Mary's nest egg, but Bob's credit was destroyed.[13] Beth applied for a job for the first time since she had married Bob and worked as a teller at a bank near our house.

A NEW DALLAS

Eddie Bernice Johnson became the first African-American woman to win a public office in Dallas County when she won an election to the Texas legislature in 1972.[14] The Dallas Cowboys won their first Super Bowl that year, and the Washington Senators baseball team moved to Arlington and became the Texas Rangers. Between 1960 and 1973, more than 100,000 Anglos moved out of Dallas to avoid desegregation and took with them much-needed revenues for the schools.[15]

Racial tensions reached a fever pitch in July 1973, when Dallas police arrested twelve-year-old Santos Rodriguez and his thirteen-year-old brother as robbery suspects. The officers placed Santos in the front passenger seat of their patrol car and Officer Darrell L. Cain tried to convince him to confess by placing a .357-caliber revolver against his head during a game of Russian roulette. Cain pulled the trigger and killed Santos in what the officer later claimed was a mistake because he thought he'd removed all of the bullets first. Minority leaders pointed out that Cain had shot a black suspect three years earlier, and police arrested him for murder. A judge then released Cain on five thousand dollars' bail, setting off anger in the Mexican-American community. The case united blacks and Mexican-Americans, who often disagreed on civil rights.[16]

More than a thousand demonstrators protested outside of City Hall a week later, damaging a police motorcycle, smashing windows, and looting luxury department stores. Police arrested twenty-three Mexican-Americans and thirteen blacks. A court found Cain guilty of murder, but he served only three years of a five-year sentence.[17]

After Bob closed down Bowling Supplies, Inc., he took a job selling fire alarms, then left that for the Guardian Life Insurance Company. My parents did not have a lot of money, but we lived in a nice house in a safe neighborhood. At first, I attended a suburban school because it was closest to our house, even though it was not part of the Dallas school district.[18]

In the third grade, my teachers started observing February as Black History Month and taught us about the civil rights movement and Dr. Martin Luther King, Jr. My teacher read King's "I Have a Dream Speech," and I felt an instant connection when she read, "'I have a dream that one day on the red hills of Georgia the sons of former slaves and the sons of former slave owners will be able to sit down together at the table of brotherhood.'" I was the son of a slaveholder and out there, somewhere, were the sons of slaves my family had held. But rather than feel a sense of shame, I wondered where those slave descendants lived and if I'd ever meet them. My teacher taught that slavery was wrong, but I don't remember her saying anything bad about those responsible for it. She talked about how prejudice was wrong, but she never said anything bad about prejudiced people. She walked a careful line in teaching about race, holding no one responsible for the sins of the past. That allowed me to hold on to the love of my ancestry while embracing equality for all. She was letting me and all of the other white children have our cake and eat it, too.

The first African-American children attended Lake Highlands when I was in the fourth grade. The teacher invited one black student to come to the front of the class and asked him if he'd ever touched a white person's hair. The terrified child shook his head no, and she invited him to touch her hair and feel her white skin. Then she invited a white girl to come touch the boy's hair and skin. The teacher explained how the skin color and hair texture of a black person were no more significant than the hair and skin color of a white person. By this time, I'd met Jimmy and Faye and several other black people whom my father knew, and I thought the whole exercise was a little strange, but then at recess I spoke to my white friends. They explained that they'd never spoken to a black person before. Even my slight experience with African-Americans was more than what my classmates had. While a handful of African-Americans attended Lake Highlands that year, my classroom was still all white.

The situation at home, meanwhile, grew more tense. Bob couldn't get the hang of selling insurance and was becoming increasingly unhappy. He wasn't very good at selling what he considered a concept, not an actual product, and it gave him nightmares.[19] These dreams were part of a larger emotional breakdown, and he started seeing a psychotherapist. Bob learned to follow what made him happy, and that meant returning to bowling alleys.

Bob became the night deskman at Expressway Lanes in 1975. Expressway had all of the qualities that had made him love Lakewood Lanes almost twenty years earlier. It was just north of downtown, on Central Expressway. Suburban bowlers in big corporate leagues came in on their way home. The place was also cheap and central enough to attract blue-collar bowlers and the gambling crowd that showed up after the businessmen were gone. Bob worked nights and Beth worked during the day, so my sister, Dana, and I became latchkey kids. We let ourselves inside the house after school and waited for Mom, knowing Dad wouldn't come home until after we had gone to bed. But he was back in his element and didn't want to leave bowling again.[20]

CONFRONTING RACE

One afternoon, when I was about nine years old, a neighbor named Roger offered to introduce me to a star football player with the Dallas Cowboys, Harvey Martin. Roger had gone to college with the Dallas native at East Texas State, and it was my first chance to meet a celebrity. Roger didn't want to take any chances on my behaving badly, so he told me not to use the word *nigger* around Martin. I was shocked to hear Roger use the *n* word and I didn't understand at first why he had brought it up. I wondered if there was something about me that made Roger worry that I would say such a thing. Using the *n* word was taboo, and I felt like he was telling me not to set his cat on fire.

I explained to Roger that I had never used that word, not to mention that "Too Mean" Martin was three times my size and capable of throwing me like a football across Texas Stadium. Roger's attempt to educate me about race made me realize how naïve I was and that my grandfathers weren't the only ones who didn't know any better.

While Bob was strict about racism, he was flexible in other areas. When a cook's son showed up with a semitrailer full of electronics, no one questioned his story about a shop that was going out of business, rather than thinking it was a hijacking. The Expressway regulars, including Bob, bought microwave ovens and portable radios for pennies on the dollar. One of Bob's favorite criminals was a shoplifter named Pat Parks, who once gave me a stolen portable typewriter when he learned that I liked to write. Bob also liked to gamble, though not for big money. He made bets on his skills at bowling and pinball, or played the spread in college football. He enjoyed the company of petty criminals and smoking dope when he got home from work, but he liked to say, "I was still a good boy. I was being good with my weed and only smoked it at home."

Dallas schools finally got serious about desegregation in 1975, and past courtesies, such as allowing white children like me to cross district lines, came to an end. Administrators required my parents to enroll me in the Dallas Independent School District[21] and I left Lake Highlands and started fifth grade at Hexter Elementary. The biggest change came in my grades. I went from earning mostly C's at the rich school to straight A's at the poor one, because the standards were so much lower.

Toward the end of my first year at Hexter, federal judge William Taylor still didn't think Dallas officials were moving fast enough, and in March 1976, he ordered them to begin busing. The school board approved a plan to bus 18,223 students in fourth through eighth grades and create "magnet" schools, which would offer special classes to attract white students to minority parts of town. That year, students in the fourth through eighth grades were 47.1 percent black, 38.65 percent white, and 14.4 percent Mexican-American.[22] The district decided that when I entered the sixth grade, I should take a bus to Reilly Elementary, formerly an all-white school.

School officials scheduled a meeting to explain to parents how the plan would work. Our school actually got the good end of the deal, since we would attend a nearby elementary and middle school. The big difference would be the black students bused from South Dallas. My father took me to the meeting, and I remember that the father of one of my classmates became irate, insisting that the teachers couldn't protect his daughter Kelly from the black students. He proclaimed that blacks behaved no better than animals and would rape his little girl. The man's rant set off my father's hair-trigger temper, and he responded with a stream of expletives. Within minutes, the two stared each other down, the racist, with his crew cut, dress shirt, and cowboy boots, facing off against my father, who wore his hair over his ears, sported a disco mustache, and had on a paisley shirt. Desperate school officials begged them to calm down, and the other man left. My friends began talking about Kelly's initials, KKK.

The stark contrast in my class pictures from the fourth grade to the sixth shows how quickly change came. At Lake Highlands, I had shared a classroom with twenty-two all-white pupils. In my first year at Hexter, the class size jumped to twenty-seven, with one Hispanic student and the rest of the class white. At Reilly Elementary, Miss Smith's Class 6I numbered twenty-six students, with sixteen whites and ten African-Americans. I made friends easily with the black kids, but I could tell they were having a hard time. They woke up early to catch the bus and arrived tired. Since my education at Lake Highlands had put me far ahead of the others, the teachers at Reilly enrolled me in a talented and gifted program. The all-black schools had not prepared the African-American kids for the regular classes at Reilly, so they had to play catch-up.

I became close to the class clown, an African-American boy named Talbert. Talbert was a skinny kid and couldn't stay seated. He quickly figured out which of the white kids feared him and took advantage by pretending to be tougher than he was. I remember that my father asked me about him because other parents had complained. I told him Talbert was harmless if you got to know him. Talbert failed that year, and I never saw him again.

Under the desegregation plan, the district bused in students from three previously all-black elementary schools and four nearby white elementary schools the year I started Robert T. Hill Middle School. The kids had remained largely calm during the first year of busing, but the students at Hill took the gloves off the second year, and just about everyone fought. School discipline deteriorated, and teachers stepped up corporal punishment. Principals and male teachers paced the hallways carrying paddles, some with holes drilled in them to make the swat sting more. During class, we could hear the principals "giving pops" that echoed down the hallways. If the student made no sound, we giggled. If we could hear the child in pain, we squirmed. On at least two occasions, a student pulled a knife, prompting the police to arrest the student. In one fight, an African-American girl cut another badly enough to warrant an ambulance.

The greatest tension took place on the basketball court, where the black kids played a tougher game than the whites. A sharp elbow, perfectly normal for a South Dallas street game, triggered a fight with the white kids. I was small for my age, so I refereed.

After I had spent two years in Dallas schools and reached the onset of puberty, my grades dropped, and I fell out of the talented and gifted program. I wanted to be like my father, capable of moving in any circle but not belonging to any single one.

Bob tried to make some extra money by exploring his lifelong interest in photography. He took a few commercial assignments, shot some portraits, and even tried a few weddings. Working at Expressway had increased his exposure to homosexuals, and in 1977 he volunteered to take photos of his friends competing in the Mr. Gay Fort Worth pageant. I remember having seen the contestants in street clothes and then seeing the photos of them in drag when he made prints. He'd never taught me to discriminate against homosexuals, so I thought nothing of it. For him, though, this meant losing an old prejudice:

> I met a few gays along the way that I kind of liked—not sexually, but just as friends or customers or whatever. I used to enjoy running around town with Mr. Gay Fort Worth. Her name was Nancy, and she and her girlfriend took me out clubbing a couple of times, and it was a trip. Nancy really looked good, didn't she? She looked like a really good-looking guy.[23]

Bob left Expressway and moved to Circle Bowl on Dallas's west side, where the manager welcomed the Lambda League, a group of gay men. They held an annual Halloween party at the bowling alley and my father told stories of men wearing tutus and sprinkling fairy dust on people.[24] Bob describes himself as deeply antisocial, but he loves people who can tell a good story, or provide him with one to tell.

One thing he could never stand was an uninformed opinion. I once ridiculed the sound track of *Urban Cowboy*, a hit movie in 1980.

Knowing that he held Texas's contemporary faux-cowboy culture in low regard, I thought this would win his approval. Instead, he sat me down and made me listen to Boz Skaggs, Bonnie Raitt, and Linda Ronstadt and admit that they were something special. I realized then that my father was never going to tolerate any stereotyping on my part. He expected me to be curious about the things I didn't understand and to learn about them before judging. That was the greatest lesson of my life, and for that I will always thank him.

NINETEEN

A lot of times, when we look around, we think that we've come so far, and we have. Then somebody would come along and steal that peace that you had, that things are changing and we're making a difference.

—Loreane Tomlinson

The Marlin Independent School District began desegregating twelve years after *Brown v. Board of Education* by allowing students from either all-white Marlin High or all-black Booker T. Washington to voluntarily transfer beginning in the 1965–1966 school year. Only four African-American students chose to switch schools, including a junior named Lonnie Garrett. Garrett's father and grandfather were sharecroppers and preachers in Marlin and well respected. The Garrett family enjoyed a reputation as a hardworking, God-fearing family where the children treated elders with respect. But when Lonnie chose to attend the all-white school, his clean-cut reputation did not protect him.

As in many rural communities, Marlin's phone system used party lines, which meant that half a dozen or more homes used the same circuit. If someone called the Garrett home when someone from another household was on the phone, the caller got a busy signal. Residents could identify when a call was for them because of a distinctive ring pattern. But if you picked up the phone while another person was using the party line, you could listen in on your neighbors. The trick was to lift the receiver carefully so the people on the phone couldn't hear that you were getting on the line. Lonnie's family shared a party line with several white families, and that's how they learned how whites felt about Lonnie going to Marlin High. They called Lonnie horrible names and told their children that mixing with African-Americans would cause the latter's blackness to rub off on them and bring down their character. Lonnie said he once took a white teen's hand and rubbed it to show that his blackness did not come off:

> There was one thing my mother told me before I went to school, because she knew I wanted to go to that school regardless of whatever consequences there were. So she said, "I want to give you some tips. I want you to see your birth certificate. On that birth certificate it says Lonnie D. Garrett."
>
> I said, "Yes."
>
> "Now, if you hear any other name, good or bad, and it isn't that, they're not talking to you. So when the *n* word comes up, and all those names come up, you keep walking, 'cause they're not talking to you. Until they call this name. That's the only time you're supposed to respond."
>
> So that was a great thing; it really helped me to get going. Certainly my first day there was really chaos. I had a little briefcase my dad had before he died; I carried it to school with me. I walked into the building and one of the teachers said "Are you an insurance salesman?"
>
> I said, "No, ma'am, I'm just a student."[1]

Lonnie soldiered through the first month of school, trying to maintain his dignity as the white students tested him. He played the guitar for a talent show and impressed the white students, but the other black students had a tougher time:

> There was another African-American boy, Sammy Woodson; he went with me. But he lasted a week. I had learned, as my mother said, if they don't call that name, don't respond. Well, his mother never

told him that. So he was really, you know, that anger—he had built a wall up before we got there. You know, he'd say, "I'm not going to take this and that."[2]

Three years later, the school board closed Booker T. Washington and sent all the students to Marlin High and turned the old black high school into a junior high. Anna Steele was an eighth-grade teacher in Marlin's white junior high when the schools were combined. She said the decision staggered the white community:

They didn't really want it to happen. And I really doubt it seriously that the blacks wanted it to happen any more than we did. But when it was forced on us by our government, then we got in there and did everything we could to make it as easy of a transition as possible.

When we integrated, everything changed. I really sort of felt sorry for the black children. They gave up their school. They became Marlin High School kids, and it was very difficult for them, I'm certain. It was very difficult for us, as teachers, to try to blend, because they weren't as far along as our children were. So it was a very hard time trying to get them pulled up, and you could see some of them were so smart. They needed to be pulled ahead so they wouldn't have to repeat eighth grade. Some of them did. It was just a really difficult time for them and for us.

When the junior high went to the Booker T. Washington school, those were hard times. I know when we went into our classrooms, we cleaned and scrubbed to make them nice and clean. The black kids had been able to get up and walk out of class anytime they wanted to eat or whatever, and we didn't allow it. That was one thing that was very difficult. And in eighth grade, we had some young men that were way too old to be in eighth grade, so it took a lot of hard work for all of us to pull them up. So the classes were different than what they were when we just had the white children, but I'm glad we did.[3]

Teachers questioned whether to uphold the former white school's standards, thereby failing the African-American students, or adapt the grading system to give black students a chance. Steele said she gave extra attention to black students but then expected them to catch up. She said the parents ultimately made the difference: "The parents of the white children were always involved in their children's lives. There were lots of black families that were very involved with their children, but there were a lot that [weren't]. It's that parenting that I think we need in both the black and white race."[4]

Integration exacerbated racial problems in Marlin, Garrett said, with students from both races resenting the upheaval and loss of school traditions, including separate football teams. The district also kept more white teachers than black teachers, angering the black community. Garrett said the races were too far apart when they were forced together:

> Our backgrounds were so different. We were the servants in the community, and most of our mothers and fathers, we worked for the white[s]. So we were more like a servant, not equal. Because I've been here when they had the white water fountains and the black water fountains in the grocery store. They had it in the courthouse here, the black water fountain and the white water fountain.
>
> What it had done, it had built up in some of the students that "I was just as good as anyone else," which they were right [about], but how they had gone about doing it . . . the wrong way.
>
> They wanted to fight their way into it. If the white mention anything negative about a black person, there was a fight.[5]

African-Americans across the state were more actively asserting their rights, working to better their communities. Only 40 percent of African-Americans held a high school diploma in 1970, while 7 percent had completed college. By comparison, 59 percent of whites completed high school and 13 percent had a college degree.

African-Americans made up 20 percent of the Texans who lived in a dwelling with more than one person per room, and they lived in 25 percent of the buildings without complete plumbing. That year, 24 percent of black families had a female head of household.[6]

The African-American voter-registration rate peaked in 1968, with

83 percent of black Texans signing up to vote at a time when they made up 12 percent of the state's population. They were capable of swinging a statewide election.[7]

LAST OF THE COTTON PICKERS

For more than a decade, cotton farmers had developed equipment and modified seed so they would no longer need farmworkers to walk the rows, and in 1966 automatic picking machines came to Falls County. Farmers also let more land go fallow for cattle or hay production.[8] The Marlin Cotton Compress, which for sixty-seven years had packed cotton into huge bundles, shut down for lack of enough business in 1966.[9]

That same year, O.T. and Jewell Tomlinson had their third child, a daughter they named Flesphia. Tomlinson Hill was in the Rosebud-Lott School District, the first of the Falls County districts to integrate. Maintaining separate schools was a financial strain on the small rural district. O.T.'s son Terry was in the fifth grade when he first attended classes with white children. "Some people didn't get along with [the whites], but they didn't get along all together. I had some good white friends. The best good friend of mine, his name was Bubba Renfro, played football with me, too," Terry said.[10]

O.T. spent much of his free time in Marlin on Wood Street, and he was hanging out at Strickland's Café one hot September day in 1970 when his friend Tommy invited an attractive eighteen-year-old named Loreane Lowe to join them. O.T.'s good looks, big smile, and charm instantly attracted Loreane, despite their seventeen-year age difference. He looked young and was playful. Tommy and O.T. invited Loreane to go wading with them at the Falls of the Brazos to cool off from the sweltering heat. Loreane felt an instant, intense attraction. O.T. told Loreane about his four children but didn't want to introduce them quite yet.[11]

Doctors diagnosed O.T.'s father, Vincent, with lymphatic cancer in March 1971. He was seventy-five years old, and he passed away three months later at Scott and White Memorial Hospital in Temple. His wife, Julie, arranged his burial in the small cemetery next to the China

Grove church.[12] Loreane comforted O.T. as he dealt with the loss, and
O.T. became more devoted to his mother and son Terry.[13]

Terry had his first bad experience with white students when he
started Rosebud High School. He told me he wasn't afraid of them;
after all, he was growing up to be a big man and played outside linebacker on the varsity football team. Yet the hatred some of the white
teens felt toward him bothered him:

> You could tell the difference in the way that people was raised, and
> the people's parents. Some of them, they didn't want their kids to
> hang around with blacks. And you could tell because some of them
> would use that word, that *n* word. Their parents was very prejudiced.
> They didn't want their kids to even be around blacks. So I guess you
> could say that's the first time I experienced that. And it went on for a
> while, up until I finished high school.[14]

Julie also worried about her grandson mixing with white children.
She and Vincent had spent years on Tomlinson Hill avoiding situations where they could fall victim to racists. When Terry brought
white friends to the house, Julie often knew their parents and warned
him that they wouldn't like their children spending time with blacks:

> I was feeling confused. I'm wondering why? Because I wasn't raised
> like that. I wasn't raised around prejudice or whatever. Didn't no-
> body never teach me about it. I experienced it myself. But she'd tell
> me a few things, what not to do.
>
> Don't mess with the white girls, don't steal nothing, and don't
> take nothing that ain't yours. And always ask for what you want. I
> was raised to ask for what you want.[15]

Terry listened but had mixed feelings as Julie warned him to be
careful in Marlin, where police often assumed that when a black
man and a white man were together, it was for a drug deal. Terry
said he could feel the tension when he walked into a white business
in Marlin.

A family portrait of LaDainian Tomlinson as an infant. LaDainian is the son of Oliver Terry Tomlinson and Loreane Tomlinson, born in Marlin in 1979. He was the couple's second child, though O. T. had five children from a previous relationship. During his early childhood, LaDainian lived in his father's home on Tomlinson Hill, where he grew up near his grandparents, Vincent and Julia. He had a pet pig and, despite moving to the city when he was older, he still considers himself a country boy at heart.

A school portrait of LaDainian in elementary school. About this time LaDainian's father, O. T., fell through a roof while working in Waco and seriously injured his back. Despite several operations, O. T. remained in pain and eventually became addicted to drugs. LaDainian's mother, Loreane, asked O. T. to leave the house and moved the family to Waco, where LaDainian spent most of his childhood. He gained statewide attention as a high school football player, earning a scholarship to play for Texas Christian University in Fort Worth. Football was always at the center of LaDainian's life.

Photo courtesy of Loreane Tomlinson.

LaDainian (kneeling) and Lavar
suit up for Pop Warner football in
the mid-1980s.

LaDainian Tomlinson holds up
the ball while acknowledging the
cheers from fans as he leaves the
field after gaining 243 yards in
the Chargers' 21-14 victory over
the Oakland Raiders on Sunday,
Dec. 28, 2003, in San Diego.
Tomlinson became the first player
in NFL history to catch 100 passes
and gain 1,000 yards rushing.

AP Photo/Lenny Ignelzi

Oliver Terry Tomlinson at his parents' home on Tomlinson Hill in February 2007. A *New York Times* reporter interviewed O. T. about his famous son after learning about the family's history in Falls County. The report highlighted O. T.'s poverty while his son was becoming one of the best players in the NFL. LaDainian was embarrassed by the story, which made him look like an ungrateful son. The reporter was not aware of O. T.'s drug addiction.

The tabernacle built for Confederate veteran reunions on Tomlinson Hill in 1920, now renamed the Old Settlers' and Veterans' Reunion Grounds. The tabernacle was built using trees harvested on the land and reclaimed lumber. Businesses that supported the maintenance of the tabernacle placed signs in the eaves to advertise their support. The annual reunions always honored the oldest settler or veteran present and included prayers for those who had passed. The association also hosted an annual fiddle contest.

Chris shows LaDainian pre-Civil War corn cribs, the only surviving structures on Tomlinson Hill from before emancipation. LaDainian's grandfather Vincent died before he was born and his father, O. T., told him very little about the family's history on Tomlinson Hill. LaDainian visited the old compound where the white Tomlinsons lived for the first time while making a documentary about his football career for the NFL network.

Chris visits a cotton field with Zelma and Charles Tomlinson. Chris tracked down Charles and Zelma in Kansas and asked them to return to Falls County to show him where they lived and share their stories living on Tomlinson Hill. Charles picked cotton for his dad, Vincent Tomlinson, who sharecropped for Albert Tomlinson. Charles and Zelma also agreed to show Chris the different techniques for picking cotton.

David Tinsley, who now owns the land where the Tomlinson's built their homestead in 1859, talks to LaDainian and Chris about Tomlinson Hill today. David leases the land to cattlemen for grazing, but otherwise is keeping the fields fallow. He has a small grass airstrip where he keeps an antique, two-seat airplane for his personal use. David didn't know the age of the corn cribs on his land and was surprised they dated back to the Civil War.

LaDainian and Chris talk in front of the home Vincent Tomlinson built in 1946 after Albert Tomlinson ended sharecropping on Tomlinson Hill. Albert offered free land to all of the sharecropping families working for him in 1945 when he decided to sell much of the plantation or to switch to cattle grazing. Albert also offered loans so the families could build new houses in the community that now calls itself Tomlinson Hill. O. T. was living in the house in 2007 when he died, and no one has lived there since, leaving it in disrepair.

LaDainian Tomlinson holds up his son, Daylen, two years old, during a news conference at the San Diego Chargers' facility, on Monday, June 18, 2012, in San Diego. He signed a one-day contract with the San Diego Chargers and announced his retirement after a brilliant eleven-year NFL career.

LaDainian stands in front of the Tomlinson Hill sign and the Old Settlers' and Veterans' Reunion Grounds. After World War II, the organization dropped Confederate from their name and now welcomes all Falls County veterans, though the group is no longer active. Most of the residents of Tomlinson Hill are African-Americans and many trace their heritage to the Tomlinson Hill Plantation. LaDainian's father, O. T., was the last Tomlinson living on the Hill when he died in a car accident in 2007.

Chris talks to Lizzie Mae and Charles Tomlinson while sitting on the steps that once led to the Tomlinson Negro School in Falls County. Lizzie Mae remembers playing in the 1920s with her grandfather Peter, who was born into slavery. Lizzie Mae married Winston White in 1937 and they moved to Corpus Christi, ending her family's reliance on sharecropping. Note: Lizzie Mae passed away in February 2014.

Lizzie Mae Tomlinson sits with her brother Charles on the steps of the home she moved to in 1947 on Tomlinson Hill after she was married.

AFRICAN AMERICAN TOMLINSONS

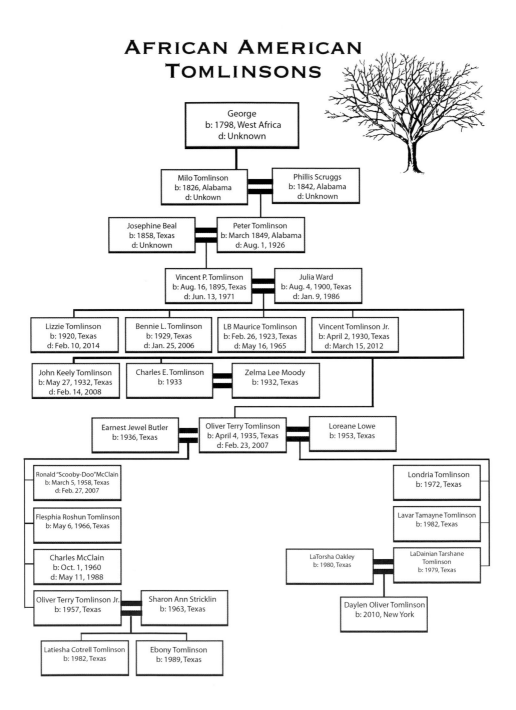

George
b: 1798, West Africa
d: Unknown

Milo Tomlinson
b: 1826, Alabama
d: Unkown

Phillis Scruggs
b: 1842, Alabama
d: Unknown

Josephine Beal
b: 1858, Texas
d: Unknown

Peter Tomlinson
b: March 1849, Alabama
d: Aug. 1, 1926

Vincent P. Tomlinson
b: Aug. 16, 1895, Texas
d: Jun. 13, 1971

Julia Ward
b: Aug. 4, 1900, Texas
d: Jan. 9, 1986

Lizzie Tomlinson
b: 1920, Texas
d: Feb. 10, 2014

Bennie L. Tomlinson
b: 1929, Texas
d: Jan. 25, 2006

LB Maurice Tomlinson
b: Feb. 26, 1923, Texas
d: May 16, 1965

Vincent Tomlinson Jr.
b: April 2, 1930, Texas
d: March 15, 2012

John Keely Tomlinson
b: May 27, 1932, Texas
d: Feb. 14, 2008

Charles E. Tomlinson
b: 1933

Zelma Lee Moody
b: 1932, Texas

Earnest Jewel Butler
b: 1936, Texas

Oliver Terry Tomlinson
b: April 4, 1935, Texas
d: Feb. 23, 2007

Loreane Lowe
b: 1953, Texas

Ronald "Scooby-Doo"McClain
b: March 5, 1958, Texas
d: Feb. 27, 2007

Londria Tomlinson
b: 1972, Texas

Flesphia Roshun Tomlinson
b: May 6, 1966, Texas

Lavar Tamayne Tomlinson
b: 1982, Texas

Charles McClain
b: Oct. 1, 1960
d: May 11, 1988

LaTorsha Oakley
b: 1980, Texas

LaDainian Tarshane Tomlinson
b: 1979, Texas

Oliver Terry Tomlinson Jr.
b: 1957, Texas

Sharon Ann Stricklin
b: 1963, Texas

Daylen Oliver Tomlinson
b: 2010, New York

Latiesha Cotrell Tomlinson
b: 1982, Texas

Ebony Tomlinson
b: 1989, Texas

Back on the Hill, though, life continued with little interference from the outside world. The Tomlinsons attended church every Sunday morning and on Wednesday nights, and Terry often found himself the only teen inside the chapel, where Julie expected him to serve as an example to others. When Terry had free time, he'd go fishing for channel cat or bass on Deer Creek, and if Julie saw Terry walking up the road with a stringer of fish, she'd have the grease hot in the pan by the time he reached the house. Terry was also old enough to join his dad on Thanksgiving hunting trips.[16]

Terry enjoyed a typical teen's life, playing football and basketball, but not concentrating too hard in class. He worked odd jobs painting houses or doing basic carpentry work during the summer months and saved enough money to buy a used Chevy Nova for $150. Terry and his friends, both boys and girls, would pile into the little car with some beer and a little marijuana and hang out together in the woods or next to a creek or pond.

O.T. and Terry may have loved rural life, but Falls County was not always a paradise, nor was it immune to big-city problems. Since the end of mineral-water tourism, and with the interstate highways bypassing Marlin, businesses and incomes suffered. World prices for cotton and beef hit all-time lows, and the city council resisted attracting outside businesses for fear of competition. In the early 1970s, Falls County ranked among the poorest counties in Texas, and one resident told a *Dallas Morning News* reporter that "if it weren't for the State Welfare Department, business would really suffer."[17] Marlin police and sheriff's deputies found themselves dealing with more drugs and social problems as poverty grew.

HOLLYWOOD COMES TO MARLIN

Paramount Pictures announced in 1974 they wanted to shoot part of a movie on Wood Street. Former *Life* magazine photographer Gordon Parks wanted to make a biopic about blues musician Lead Belly. Parks, perhaps the most famous black photojournalist of his generation, had turned to filmmaking and needed a place that looked like Shreveport,

Louisiana's Fannin Street in 1920. The real Fannin Street looked nothing like it had when Lead Belly played there, so location scouts chose Wood Street as a stand-in. No one had improved the low nineteenth-century buildings, and the Bloody Butcher had changed little over the previous fifty years. The only major change they needed to make before starting filming was to cover the potholed street with dirt.[18]

Parks hired black Marlinites as extras. Joyce Strickland walked down the street with a bundle of clothes balanced on her head. Elijah Polk's role involved walking a mule named Josephine laden with pots and pans. Lead Belly was played by Roger Mosley, a character actor who gained fame playing the helicopter pilot on the television show *Magnum, P.I.* Parks hired one of Texas's most famous authors, John Henry Faulk, to play Governor Pat Neff, the man who pardoned Lead Belly because his music was so beautiful. The film company spent $38,000 in Marlin.[19] As soon as the filming ended, Wood Street turned the jukeboxes back on, and the bars and restaurants resumed business.[20]

Jewell and O.T.'s relationship was faltering, and they spent more and more time apart. O.T. started taking Loreane to Terry's football games, but he always made sure to take another friend along to ride in the backseat with her. Terry saw through the ruse and knew there was something going on between his dad and Loreane, who was just four years older than he was. Jewell moved out of the house on the Hill in 1972 and took all of the children except Terry with her to Waco.[21]

O.T. stopped hiding his relationship, and Loreane met his four children and liked them. Loreane was enchanted by O.T.'s life on the Hill and discovered how important the community was to her boyfriend. O.T. would take Loreane fishing, cutting across Uncle John Tomlinson's land and waving at him as he sat on his porch. Loreane told me O.T. reminded her of her father, hardworking and generous. In early 1972, Loreane discovered she was pregnant with O.T.'s child, and O.T. asked her to marry him. On February 2, 1972, they drove to the justice of the peace in Lott. Loreane described those early years in her book, *LT & Me*:

It was difficult for O.T. to be away from his beloved Hill. If he could have, he would have spent all his time there. It was where he felt the most at ease and free to be himself. Every time we left that place after a visit, O.T.'s whole demeanor took on a slightly sad look.

O.T. and I had a good marriage. We were in love and laughed a lot. Even in my happiest moments, though, I knew O.T. had another love: Tomlinson Hill.[22]

That summer, Loreane gave birth to their first child, a daughter named Londria. Londria and her cousins called the Hill "our town" because it bore their name. She told me about Julie, now short, stout, and gray-haired, with a dimple on her cheek. Everyone called her "Big Mama Julie."

My earliest memories are [about] going over to Big Mama Julie's house and the tea cakes, and spending time with her in the kitchen and going up under—I think it was an oak tree—and playing around out there. And playing on the well with all my cousins and stuff. We knew once it got dark, we were supposed to be home. She'[d] have drawn our bath and everything and had our food like hot, you know, after we got out of the bath. And she would read to us.

The sand, it was just like sand I've never seen. . . . We would sit there for hours and play in that sand. Besides the cooking, and Big Mama Julie taking care of me while my parents were away at work, that was the most memorable thing . . . that sand.

And there just always [had] been a lot of food, a lot of family around. We were kids laughing and running up and down the street. And the houses, you could go to anybody's house. They didn't care. They [could] be sitting in there watching TV and we'[d] just walk in and go to the refrigerator. And we [were] like, "Hey, we're thirsty. We're on this part of the Hill."[23]

When both O.T. and Loreane worked, they dropped Londria with Julie to spend the day and Julie would fix her meals. Londria said her grandmother doted on her, encouraging her to be a good girl, get good grades, and stay away from "hardheaded boys."

O.T. raised hogs and cows, and Julie planted a half-acre vegetable garden, where anyone on the Hill could pick what they needed: corn, tomatoes, peas, sweet potatoes, and many other things. As the community began to shrink, Loreane said the preacher started coming only every other week, but the whole community would still come together in the little nineteenth-century Gravel Hill chapel. Relatives who had moved away would make a special trip to Tomlinson Hill on those Sundays.[24]

In the evenings, Julie would shell peas and watch one of her favorite television shows, *M*A*S*H*. She almost never left the Hill, and rarely left her house and yard, except to visit her relatives or walk to the neighborhood store. If she needed something from town, Julie usually asked someone to pick it up for her.[25]

Londria said she rarely saw whites in her neighborhood, but a white family did run a store down the road; it looked like an aluminum barn. Julie always wanted an older cousin to walk with Londria and the nine-year-old twins, because she felt it was too far to go alone, but that didn't keep them from sneaking down the gravel road:

> She was looking for us and I swear I heard her at that store calling my name. And I was like, "We're in trouble."
>
> So we go running down the road, and I'll never forget it. It was this white man in this pickup truck; it was a blue pickup. And he stopped and he said, "What y'all niggers doing down here?"
>
> The biggest [twin], she picked up this bottle and she threw it [and hit] his truck. And he went to get out and we stood there. She said some ugly words to that man.
>
> And I remember thinking, I'm gonna tell my daddy, my daddy going to shoot you.
>
> I was thinking that in my mind. But I said something kind of like "Let's go." And we took out running again. Big Mama knew that we were somewhere that we didn't have any business.

She was outside on the porch and we went in the house and stuff, and she said, "I told y'all not to go down there to that store."

Londria didn't tell her grandmother about the white man, but she told her dad. He was angry that Londria had disobeyed Julie, but he was also angry at the white man. He told her, "You know, racism is here. You know, everybody don't like black children." That was the first time that Londria remembered anyone saying that to her:

"I think I was embarrassed. I was embarrassed because I was some-where where I wasn't supposed to be, first of all. And then I heard something that made me feel dirty," she said.[26]

When Londria told me this story, her mother was sitting next to her and hearing it for the first time. Loreane looked down and shook her head. The story visibly saddened her:

That's something that I can attest to. It's kind of like an embarrass-ment, even though you're not the one that's acting like that. You're kind of embarrassed and you feel not only threatened, but you feel like you've done something wrong.

A lot of times, when we look around, we think that we've come so far, and we have. Then somebody would come along and steal that peace that you had, that things are changing, and we're making a dif-ference.[27]

Loreane took a job at the HEB grocery store in Marlin and asked O.T. to move to town to be closer to work, Londria's nursery school, and her family. O.T. agreed, but he missed the Hill. When the two ar-gued over money or he felt a need to get away, he drove out to his little house. He'd hunt for rabbit with the shotgun he carried in his car, skin the animal, and take it to his mother to cook.[28]

Family was the most important thing in O.T.'s life, and he wanted to protect the people he loved. He often visited his children, who were living in Waco with Jewell. But sometimes his parenting skills didn't measure up. O.T. found it difficult to discipline his children, leaving that responsibility to their mothers.[29] O.T. particularly doted on Londria, who was a daddy's girl. He took her fishing and hunting and taught her how to drive when she was twelve.[30]

O.T. warned all of his children against becoming attached to the animals he raised. Nevertheless, Londria wanted a pig of her own, so he tied a shoestring around its neck, and she fed the little piglet until it grew into a huge hog. One day, she noticed her pig was missing, and at dinner that night, as Londria put a piece of pork in her mouth, O.T. told her she was eating her pet pig. She said it took a while before she ate ham or bacon again.[31]

One day, Londria complained to her father about a boy at school shoving her. O.T. went straight to the principal's office to demand that the teachers stop the bully. But a few days later, Londria found O.T. playing dominoes with his friend Pookie and told him that the boy was still pushing her. They decided to teach her how to fight.

They got to talking about it and Uncle Pookie was like, "O.T., keep teaching her the upper cut." And "Hit him where it hurt[s]."

I was like, "Okay?" But my dad was really serious about teaching me how to fight.

He was teaching, "You keep them up, and you jab and you keep your arms straight." I might have been, what, seven, eight. But I would do it. And he would tell me, "Hit me harder. That's a sissy touching."

I was like, "I'm a girl!"

I went to school over the next few months and that bully boy, he pushed me down again. We were in the cafeteria. My lunch tray went one way and I went the other. I was on the cafeteria floor; everybody was laughing. And I just jumped up—and I remember it—I just popped him and popped him right in his mouth. His mouth was bleeding; he was crying.

I was like, "Oh my God, are you okay?" I started crying.

We went to the office and they called Mom. . . . She was not happy with me or Daddy.[32]

The shock didn't last long. Her father had taught her well. Londria told me she came to rely on her fists more than she should have, spending a lot of time in the principal's office.

O.T. had also taught Flesphia, whom everyone called "Fifi," how to fight, and she was getting in trouble in Waco. Sometimes she'd run away, and O.T. and Terry would go searching for her.[33] Waco was a much larger city than Marlin, with 100,000 people, some tough parts of town, and a no-nonsense police department.

A Marlin court fined Terry in February 1975 for possessing a small amount of marijuana.[34] Terry's brother Ron was convicted and fined for carrying a small amount of marijuana there in 1978.[35] Five years later, Waco police arrested Terry's brother Charles for larceny and fined him. But that wasn't the end of Charles's trouble. Waco Police arrested him in 1985 for burglary and the court sentenced him to five years in prison, though he was paroled after just one year.[36]

These kinds of arrests were not uncommon in African-American neighborhoods, where police aggressively charged blacks for minor offenses and prosecutors sought maximum sentences. President Richard Nixon had declared a "war on drugs" in 1971, and African-Americans found themselves the primary targets in an era when school integration spurred African-American dropout rates, and the loss of manufacturing jobs drove up black unemployment. Minor drug convictions also disqualified blacks from getting higher-paying jobs that could get them out of poverty.[37] For the first time in five generations of freedom, black Tomlinsons faced a standard of living lower than that of their parents.

LASTING CHANGE

Marlin's population reached 9,839 in 1976, and the city's budget was $1.2 million. Cattle provided most of the county's income, followed by the VA hospital, the regional hospital, and nursing homes. In a bid to diversify, the city recruited a carpet mill, a turkey-processing plant, and a business-forms printer for a new industrial park south of the city.[38] The older generation passed the baton to a younger generation, and no two people personified that better than Brady and Larry Pamplin.

Brady Pamplin was sixty-nine-years old and terminally ill during the 1976 sheriff's race. He urged his twenty-eight-year-old son, Larry, to run for the Democratic nomination, and once he won the primary, Brady stepped down. The county commissioners appointed Larry to serve out Brady's term. But both Pamplins had made enemies, particularly in the Marlin police force. Many of the officers had served under Brady Pamplin as deputies and didn't like him. Rumors circulated that Brady favored a particular wrecker service in return for kickbacks, and that he tried to intimidate supporters of the man who ran against his son in the primary.[39]

Nevertheless, Falls County voters elected Larry, and at first he appeared born for the job. In February 1977, he arrested two men for flying one thousand pounds of marijuana into a rural airstrip, a twenty-year-old Marlinite and a twenty-year-old from Austin.[40]

Federal regulators ruled in 1977 that the Marlin Independent School District was one of six districts in the United States that had failed to comply with the Civil Rights Act of 1964. Two of the other districts were in Texas, and the rest were in Arkansas. The secretary of the Department of Health, Education, and Welfare, Joseph Califano, Jr., threatened to cut off all federal funding, taking away $200,000 from the district's $2,647,000 budget. HEW said "racially identifiable and racially isolated classes" and "the exclusion of minority students from extracurricular activities," combined with the illegal "promotion, demotion, assignment and recruitment" of staff and faculty, were the reasons for the ruling.[41]

Harry Kenny, the president of Marlin's school board, insisted that the all-white school board had done all it could for the students, who were 51 percent black, 40 percent white, and 8 percent Hispanic. The faculty included 112 white teachers and 39 blacks, with only one out of seven administrators an African-American. The golf team was the only segregated extracurricular activity, but that was because the private Marlin Country Club, where the team practiced, did not allow African-Americans. Eventually, the district reached a deal with federal authorities.[42]

Most Texas schools had found meeting the federal integration standard not that difficult. After busing and court-ordered desegregation, 42 percent of Houston schools and 37 percent of Dallas schools in 1978 remained virtually single-race institutions, and federal officials considered those districts in compliance. However, many white parents considered that level of integration too much, and by the 1980s, blacks and Hispanics were the majority in the Dallas and Houston school districts.[43] In 1979, African-Americans served as superintendents at two of Texas's one thousand school districts.[44]

The federally mandated changes to Texas society angered white conservatives, who amplified their calls for greater states' rights. Civil rights activists, though, believed almost every institution needed to change, particularly with regard to criminal justice. In Dallas, a police force of 2,000 had only 106 blacks in 1980, prompting a federal judge to declare the department guilty of discrimination. The Houston police force was only 8 percent nonwhite when minorities made up 45 percent of the city. In the 1980s, when prospective jurors showed up for a murder trial in Texas, one in three whites made it onto the jury, while only one in twelve African-Americans were selected.[45]

Texas Democrats, who had controlled Texas since the end of Reconstruction, reached a tipping point in 1976. Jimmy Carter, whom many Texans considered a leftist, won the party's nomination for president and prompted conservative Texas Democrats to defect. In 1978, Texans elected the first Republican governor since Reconstruction, Bill Clements. In a move conservatives considered Washington meddling, Carter named Gabrielle McDonald the first African-American federal judge in Texas, based in Houston.[46]

The poverty rate for Texas blacks dropped from 55 percent to 28 percent between 1959 and 1980, but it was still more than double the white rate of 12 percent. The percentage of African-Americans who graduated from college reached 9 percent in 1980, an all-time high, compared to 18 percent for whites. But perhaps the most symbolic step came in 1979, when the Texas legislature declared Juneteenth a state holiday.[47]

TWENTY

There was so much I didn't see because I was white. My privilege allowed me a blindness to the realities that my African-American friends faced every waking minute.

—Chris Tomlinson

In the 1970s, the Dallas Independent School District wanted to use voluntary busing to desegregate high schools, so they built a huge new high school in the Pleasant Grove neighborhood called Skyline, advertising it as a "career development center." The school offered a number of "vocational clusters" that taught real skills so graduates could find jobs straight out of high school. I was obsessed with airplanes and wanted to be a pilot, so when I heard Skyline offered an aeronautics cluster that taught aircraft mechanics and private pilot's ground training, I begged my parents to let me go.

I got a little rush every time I walked into the aircraft hangar, where teens worked on helicopters that the instructors flew from a helipad next to the athletics field. I wanted to attend the Coast Guard Academy to fly helicopters, though no one mentioned to me that a vocational high school probably wasn't the best way to get there. Convinced that the closer to aviation I got, the more likely I would make a life of it, I never gave a second thought in 1979 to attending a school where African-Americans made up the majority.

Dallas businesses felt differently, among them the Dallas Cowboys, American Airlines, and Exxon, and moved to predominately white suburban school districts. When JCPenney relocated from New York, it chose mostly white Plano.[1]

Forty Klan members marched through downtown Dallas in 1979 for the first time since the 1920s. More than two thousand counter-protesters showed up to shout them down. The *Dallas Morning News* reported on the parade, billed as the "March of the Christian Soldiers." Police shut it down after only twenty minutes and put the Klan members on a bus:

> "Oh my God," said the unnerved bus driver, 38-year-old Jay Irizarry, as he looked around with bulging eyes and surveyed his passengers. "Nobody told me I'd have to do this. This bus doesn't even have bulletproof windows. Oh my God."
>
> Dallas County Sheriff Carl Thomas was standing nearby in civilian clothes, but wearing his badge and a revolver stuffed in his belt.
>
> He watched the bus leave and said, "Judge Porter never should have let the Klan march"—a reference to U.S. Dist. Judge Robert Porter, who ended two weeks of controversy Friday by ruling that the Klan had a constitutional right to march after the city issued its representatives a permit.
>
> "In my opinion it was a very bad ruling and created the potential for a lot of trouble—although, of course, I'm not the judge," Thomas said. "It's getting so federal judges think they can run the country."[2]

Among the marchers was Addie Barlow Frazier, the seventy-three-year-old Dixie Leber herself. "You bet I'm mad at the police," said the petite Mrs. Frazier, wearing a bright crimson robe and cross-shaped earrings, as she stomped her foot on the concrete floor. Then with a wide grin and twinkling eyes she said, "I guess they didn't want to have a riot."[3]

FITTING IN

Early in my freshman year at Skyline, an older boy recognized me from middle school and invited me to join the German Club and learn how to folk dance. Kevin Hunt was the only person I recognized in the school of four thousand students, so I agreed to attend a practice. The folk dancers reflected the diversity of the school, with whites, blacks, Hispanics, and foreign students represented. The troupe promised I would get to dance with girls and go on weekend trips to German festivals all over the state. The other kids seemed a lot like me, not too rich or popular, but not too geeky, either. I learned later that while they wore German costumes to dance, most of the kids liked to drink, have sex, and drive around in cars at night, and nothing in the world appealed to me more.

My parents fought when they were both at home, which was usually only on Saturday mornings or Sunday and Monday evenings. To finance my new lifestyle, two friends in the German Club convinced their manager at Kip's Big Boy restaurant to hire me as a dishwasher and busboy on the weekends. I spent as little time at home as possible.

Bob had left his hourly wage job for self-employment, leasing a pro shop inside the bowling alley, where he sold and drilled balls and also sold accessories. He was happy with our small house and simple life as long as he was his own boss.[4] Beth, on the other hand, was working at a company called Jet Fleet, which trained pilots and chartered executive jets and helicopters. She earned more money than Bob and had rubbed shoulders with rich people. Beth wanted more than a lower-middle-class existence, and after years of unhappiness, she asked for a divorce in early 1980.

I found out on a Saturday morning, when I happened to have a day off. I was watching cartoons while my parents yelled at each other. The fight ended when my father left for work. Then my sobbing younger sister, Dana, ran into the room, looked at me, and cried, "Now you know why Mom and Dad are getting a divorce."

Shortly after Dana slammed the door to her room, Beth stepped out of the kitchen and asked, "You did know we're getting a divorce, right?"

"No, but I can't say I'm surprised," I replied.

My mother finalized the divorce on June 19, 1980, their nineteenth wedding anniversary. My mother moved us into an apartment in a new neighborhood, but since Skyline was a magnet school, I had friends all over the city. I spent time in South Dallas with Jacky Donahue and Vernon Wesley, whose mother owned a beauty parlor in Exline. One afternoon, I sat in the salon, looking completely out of place as a blond, blue-eyed teen, and watched with fascination as the women used hot flatirons to straighten their hair. Wesley's mom laughed and said, "You've never seen anything like this before, have you?"

"No, ma'am, I haven't," I admitted.

"Well, let me tell you about a black woman's hair," she began, and I've never forgotten the lesson.

I dated both black and white girls, though at the time no couple in our group stuck together very long. We knew that interracial dating was taboo for many Texans, but no one made a big deal out of it at Skyline. Jacky's father was white, but they lived in an African-American neighborhood.

On one weekend trip, though, a German Club chaperone tried to convince us that dark skin was the mark of Cain and discouraged our interracial dating. We ignored her, but my father made me angry when I showed him a picture of a black girl named Vanessa, whom I had a crush on. He looked at the photo and said, "Oh, you like dark meat." Bob liked to say provocative things to get a rise out of people, but I considered this a betrayal. He'd threatened to spank me if I said anything racist, and here he was making a vulgar comment. I'd always admired him for supporting civil rights and teaching me about race and bigotry, but at that moment I realized that some liberal whites still retained the right to make an off-color joke.

In the parts of Dallas where we spent most of our time, no one gave our multiracial group a second look. But we did discuss race and how we could get into trouble on the road if we were not careful. The old German settlements in Central Texas held beer festivals from Septem-

ber through November, and we made four- to five-hour drives in bor-
rowed church vans almost every weekend. Our chaperones were
careful about where we stopped for bathroom breaks, because some
of the truck stops didn't like white teenagers with long hair, let alone
African-Americans. I remember escorting my black friends into a
couple of places and feeling the heat on the back of my neck from rednecks staring at us. This was probably the first time I'd felt how intimidating and frightening a nasty glare could feel. Those experiences,
along with dancing and drinking the weekends away, pulled us into a
tight clique.

On the long drives, we shared stories and I told my friends about
my family's supposedly glorious history. I impressed my white friends,
but if I offended my black ones, they never said anything. It never occurred to me that they would find it upsetting. We often joked how my
ancestors must have been rolling in their graves because their worst
nightmares had come to pass.

I thought of everyone in the group as equal. But I was acutely aware
that my family, which was just scraping by, was still better off than the
families of most of my African-American friends. When I worked
after school, I spent the money on going out. When they worked, most
of the money went to their families. I also learned that Wesley and
Jacky suffered from chronic health problems, which were exacerbated
by a lack of health insurance or regular doctor visits. And while my
parents fought and my sister cried, my friends dealt with family members who committed real violence and ended up in jail. We attended
the same classes at the same school, and we spent a lot of time doing
the same things, but that facade masked the differences that would
influence our futures.

None of us made very good grades—we were too caught up in the
melodrama of adolescence. I believed that our little group proved that
people from different backgrounds could love one another. Years later,
though, Jacky and I talked about the round-robin dating in high school,
and she told me that she and Vanessa figured that the white guys would
always end up with white girls and never consider a serious relationship
with them. When she told me that, my heart broke a little. I realized

that I'd seen our group through rose-colored glasses and that there was so much I didn't see because I was white. My privilege allowed me a blindness to the realities that my African-American friends faced every waking minute. I thought I was progressive; they thought I was dabbling.

LEAVING TEXAS

My mother was anxious for a clean slate after divorcing Bob and wanted to get out of Texas. In the fall of 1980, she accepted a job at Coors in Golden, Colorado. In the middle of my sophomore year at Skyline, she moved my sister and me to a middle-class suburb of Denver called Wheat Ridge. After my first day trudging through snow to high school, I wrote to my friends in Dallas, "Help! My Mom put me in a cracker school!"

The job in Denver made one of my mother's dreams come true, but I wasn't prepared for what I found in the suburbs. My mother had balanced proximity to her job with what we could afford and the best schools she could find. Wheat Ridge High School, one of the nation's best public schools, was twenty minutes from her office, and she could afford a duplex on the poor side of town.

About fifteen hundred students attended Wheat Ridge, and they called themselves "the Farmers." My freshman class at Skyline had had that many students, and Skyline High School's raider on horseback mascot could easily have kicked the ass of the happy farmer, clad in overalls, with a wheat stalk between his teeth. I remember only one African-American girl in the school and a handful of Asians and Hispanics, one of whom became my first friend. The football players called Daren Greening "Beaner," and I told him I understood that to be racist. He said he knew it was, but that's what they'd called him since elementary school.

Coloradoans didn't like Texans, either, and lots of the kids had NATIVE bumper stickers on their cars. They complained about rich Texans buying up the mountains and terrorizing the ski slopes. Many called me "Tex," though not with affection.

The vast majority of kids lived in upper-middle-class homes, and, as in most schools, they were obsessed with sports. I enrolled in photography and theater classes and even arranged independent study to spend more time as the school newspaper and yearbook photographer. I joined the lighting and sound crew for plays and gave up on my idea of attending the Coast Guard Academy, focusing instead on playwriting.

Furiously writing letters, I remained in touch with my Dallas friends. I spent most of my time with my friends Mike, Charles, and Jacky when I visited Dallas, and I made sure not to miss my older friends' graduations.

My mother told me after my junior year that I needed to decide what to do after graduation. She couldn't offer any financial help, and my father certainly didn't have any money to help me go to college, even if one admitted me. Wheat Ridge was much more demanding, and my grades had dropped. I decided to join the U.S. Army.

At the recruiter's office, I asked for a three-year contract to become a military policeman, where I could learn about law and maybe become an attorney. A sergeant measured my height and said that was impossible, since army regulations in 1982 required all MPs to be at least five feet ten inches in height. With a generous rounding off, I measured five eight. The army also trained legal assistants, who worked for military lawyers, and I had scored high enough on the military's IQ test to qualify me for any job, so I asked to do that. But they had already filled all of the legal assistant positions for the next two years.

The next time I went to his office, the recruiter said he'd found a job where they could take me immediately after graduation. The army would add a big bonus to my college fund. The military occupational specialty was 05K, which stood for Electronic Warfare/Signals Intelligence Non-Morse interceptor. He had no idea what the job entailed, but I had to pass a Morse code aptitude test to qualify. I was a little confused about why I needed to take a Morse code test to become a non-Morse interceptor, but he said it was military intelligence and sometimes they did things in a funny way. While I was at it, he suggested I take the foreign language aptitude test. I went back to the processing station, took the tests, and discovered that I could copy Morse code but was unlikely ever to learn a foreign language. The recruiter put together a contract where I would attend basic training at Fort Jackson, in Columbia, South Carolina, and signals intelligence training in Pensacola, Florida. After that, the army would most likely station me in Germany. He still couldn't explain exactly what the job entailed, but the contract promised twenty thousand dollars for college after only three years in the service.

A week after my seventeenth birthday, my mother signed the paperwork allowing me to enlist, and I went to the processing station for the last time. By the end of the day, I had a start date of June 19, 1983. My father was angry because he opposed everything the military stood for, but I didn't feel he'd given me much choice. My mother felt enlisting was probably the best of my limited options. I went back for my senior year at Wheat Ridge High, dropped every advanced course on my schedule, and took just enough courses to graduate. I enjoyed my senior year, drank a lot of beer, smoked pot, lettered in theater, and graduated in the bottom 40 percent of my class. I didn't win any of the official "Senior Superlatives," but an underground list named me "Most Likely to Date Outside My Species." I took that as a badge of honor, coming from Wheat Ridge kids.

ACTIVE DUTY

The morning my recruiter arrived in the lime green staff car to drive me to the airport, I was scared, but not sad about leaving Colorado. My platoon included people from many races and all walks of life, including rich kids. While some of the white kids from the country seemed uncomfortable with our multicultural unit, I felt more at home than I had at Wheat Ridge.

The army itself, however, scared me. I'd never dealt with such discipline, and the shock and awe of those early days set me back on my heels. My first reaction to the barking drill sergeants and exhausting exercise was to collapse and quit. I watched as a quarter of my fellow recruits dropped out and headed home. I was seriously considering asking my drill sergeant to let me drop out, when my girlfriend sent me a Dear John letter, explaining how she was dating a mutual friend.

Staff Sergeant Hicks ordered me to toughen up and showed compassion by giving me additional training time to pass the physical-fitness test. Some of the older men in my platoon recognized the mind games Hicks was playing on us, but I fell for them, and that helped me succeed. I let Hicks tear me down, instill me with discipline, and build me back up with new self-esteem. I decided I could make the army work for me and looked forward to going overseas.

At Pensacola, the navy taught me how to intercept foreign teletype signals. It turned out we needed to understand Morse code because that's how our targets made initial contact, agreed on a frequency, and initiated the Teletype machines. I felt pity for the Morse code operators. They listened to dots and dashes and typed out five-digit encoded messages all day. The worst part of my job was listening to the racket of four Teletype machines running at once. I watched the students ahead of me graduate and go to Germany, and I was excited about going abroad. But when my class graduated, the army said it had recruited too many 05Ks and all the overseas posts were full. The army sent me back to Texas to join a combat intelligence brigade at Fort Hood.

Missing out on Germany hurt, but returning to Texas was a consolation. The 163rd Military Intelligence Battalion was next to the airport at West Fort Hood, where the reconnaissance battalion kept their aircraft. Once I settled into the barracks, I learned that peacetime duty meant a lot of busywork for a combat unit assigned to keeping the base spotless. About once a month, we'd deploy to a training field, where we'd set up our equipment and pull guard duty. As an 05K, I drove a two-and-a-half-ton truck with a radio-intercept cabin at the back. We'd raise the antenna, but we had no signals to intercept in the middle of Texas. Our commander explained that our equipment was so old, we were driving a useless anachronism. We didn't belong on the battlefield at all, he said; our job required us to sit in air-conditioned buildings in far-off countries.

On the weekends, I drove to Dallas to see my friends, but they were moving on with their lives. Mike had moved to Austin to attend the University of Texas, Jacky had found a job as a bookkeeper, Wesley was a cook at Luby's cafeteria, and Charles was installing air-conditioning units. Charles's growing drug use made him more and more unreliable. Mike impregnated his sixteen-year-old girlfriend and was trying to care for her while a freshman in college. Jacky's family relied on her more, and her ulcers grew worse. Wesley had problems with his pancreas and needed medical attention he couldn't afford. Meanwhile, I was perpetually broke and had stopped my contributions to the army's college fund, which was a matching program. I stopped going to Dallas so often, not only because of the gas money but also because my friends had less time for me.

In November 1984, our first sergeant called all of the 05Ks together to discuss a special offer. A drug bust at Field Station Okinawa had forced the army to revoke the security clearances of half a dozen 05Ks and they needed replacements as quickly as possible. The station was scheduled to close in 1985, so we would barely get to spend a year there, but I really wanted to see the world. Within weeks I was on a plane headed for Japan.

Okinawa is a tropical island in the Ryukyu chain, about halfway between the Japanese mainland and Taiwan. The listening post was in the middle of the island, on Torii Station, which we shared with a Special Forces brigade. The only time I'd left the country before was to go to the Cadillac Bar in Mexico, and Okinawa challenged all of my senses. The smell of the food, the look of the concrete homes, the tropical climate, and the sound of a completely foreign language all washed over me. The field station operated on a twenty-four-hour basis, and I worked a lot of nights and slept during the day. Whenever I had free time and some extra cash, I left the base to explore the archipelago. I learned a little about Japanese culture, discovered Buddhism, and realized how big the world truly is. When we shuttered the field station, I didn't want to leave, but my orders sent me to Fort Meade, Maryland, home of the National Security Agency.

I arrived in January 1986, with only six months left on my enlistment. The 504th Military Intelligence Brigade's mission was to supply uniformed personnel to work at the NSA, just a few blocks from our headquarters. The NSA, though, had too many 05Ks, so I was assigned to the brigade commander's staff and, inexplicably, was placed in charge of training the unit's linguists and promoted to sergeant. I began to think about getting out, but I found myself in a quandary. I'd failed to put enough money in my college fund to get the full army match and I hadn't applied to any colleges. Several of my superiors warned me not to leave the army unless I had a solid plan, since several of them had left, only to reenlist a few months later. I had to admit I wasn't prepared for civilian life and decided to reenlist. On the morning I retook my oath, I privately promised myself that I would never do it again.

While in Maryland, I started dating a friend of a Colorado friend. Her name was Lisa Horenstein and she lived in Philadelphia, where she attended pharmacy school. In the summer of 1986, Lisa's father and stepmother, Birgit, decided to move to Copenhagen, and Lisa went with them.

Lisa and I wrote every day, and I negotiated a job in Germany as part of my reenlistment. My contract called for spending all four years in Bad Aibling, a small town halfway between Munich and Salzburg. I hoped to regularly visit Copenhagen to see Lisa. But Dick, Birgit, and Lisa had no sooner settled in Denmark than Birgit wanted to return to Philadelphia. Lisa was back within driving distance of Fort Meade, and we grew more in love, but her relocation threw a wrinkle in our plan. I was leaving for Germany, and the only way the army would let us live together is if we got married. Lisa wanted to live in Europe and accepted my marriage proposal. I was twenty-one years old and she was twenty.

AN AWAKENING

We settled into an idyllic Bavarian village called Bruckmühl in early 1987, a short drive from the mountains and a covert National Security

Agency base. Lisa got a job at the base library and I worked as a crypt-analyst, which involved studying Russian telecommunications. My unit worked a week of days, followed by a week of evenings, and then a week of overnight shifts. My commander gave me a squad of soldiers to supervise, and I led them in physical fitness and rifle training to keep their skills up. The University of Maryland offered college classes on base, and Lisa and I attended as many as we could manage. I started reading about race, and *The Autobiography of Malcolm X* left a lasting impression. For a hobby, I joined a community theater group on base, where I starred in, directed, and produced plays.

With our busy schedules, Lisa and I struggled to find time for each other. She made friends with the other civilians and spouses, and my world rotated around the people I worked with. Birgit visited often and never hid her feeling that her stepdaughter had made a mistake by marrying an army sergeant. I had no tolerance for her bullying and often upset Birgit when I used my sergeant's tone while speaking to her. Lisa could not tolerate any criticism toward the woman who had raised her. Lisa thought that my head was getting too big, and every time I received an award or directed a play, her attempts to keep me grounded felt like she was robbing me of the joy of success.

Neither Lisa nor I understood that to make a marriage work, it must be your highest priority. Lisa put her mother's happiness over mine, and I spent more time with my friends than I did with Lisa. Part of the problem, I'm sure, is that from the day I proposed, we both saw the marriage as a means of living together. We never considered having children and always focused on what we would do once I got out of the army. By the fall of 1989, when I applied to transfer my col-lege credits to the University of Texas at Austin, our marriage was in trouble. That December, Lisa wanted to go to Copenhagen for Christ-mas, while I had to remain in Bad Aibling for work. Before she left, she said, "I'm not sure I want to be married to you anymore." We agreed we needed to make a decision about our future before I left the service in June 1990. When Lisa returned from Copenhagen in January, I told her I felt certain we shouldn't be married anymore. She moved to Denmark.

My last performance at the Bad Aibling community theater was for Black History Month in February 1990. I wrote a one-act play about race, which would be followed by a famous play called *The Meeting*, about a fictional encounter between Martin Luther King, Jr., and Malcolm X. I put Lisa out of my mind, worked my shifts, and rehearsed the plays. During this tumultuous period, the University of Texas invited me to begin school in the fall of 1990. I counted down the days until my discharge.

RETURNING TO TEXAS

My best friend, Mike, was working at a bank in Austin, supporting his wife and daughter, and preparing for UT's law school. I rented an attic apartment not far from campus from a retired professor. I tried to reintegrate into civilian life, taking off my sergeant's stripes and becoming a college undergraduate at the age of twenty-five. I started UT with a ferocious hunger to take advantage of everything such a huge school offered. I attended my classes religiously and read everything my lecturers assigned. I joined the Student Union and volunteered with the Multi-Cultural Committee to promote greater understanding on a campus that ranked third in the nation in international students. I became close friends with people from all over the world and was exposed to a wide spectrum of cultural and political points of view. I joined the University Buddhist Association and eventually committed myself to Buddhism.

After my first year at UT, I joined the Humanities Department, electing to enroll in an honors program that allowed students to design their own degree plan from classes offered in the various departments of the university. Each student needed to complete a thesis, and I studied how nations share responsibility for global common areas and wrote my thesis on the Montreal Protocol, a treaty to protect the ozone layer. I still considered becoming an environmental lawyer, but my score on the law school admissions test put me only in the seventy-fifth percentile. I wanted to go back overseas.

Through my work with international students, and their causes, I met a student named Keith, who had gone to South Africa in the late 1980s, when the African National Congress stepped up the fight against apartheid. He'd taught computer classes in a township north of Johannesburg, and had helped the ANC's military wing communicate by using computer bulletin boards. When we approached graduation, he invited me to go to South Africa with him and "join the revolution."

TWENTY-ONE

We didn't really have to go to the 'hood area, because those kids, they didn't really do the things we did. They didn't have the opportunity to go to a Boys Club. Their moms didn't care for them like that.

—LaVar Tomlinson

L oreane and O.T. had their ups and downs in the late 1970s, but they both worked hard, O.T. building mobile homes and Loreane working at the Veterans Administration hospital in Marlin. They lived in an old bungalow on Park Street, on Marlin's black southeast side. Seven years after Londria's birth, Loreane became pregnant again, this time with a son. LaDainian Tarshane Tomlinson was born on June 23, 1979, at the Torbett Clinic in Marlin.[1] Their joy was short-lived, though, when a fire destroyed their house while they were away. O.T. moved his family into a rental on Commerce Street in Marlin, but they didn't have enough money to rebuild their home.[2]

O.T. visited his mother and family on the Hill once a day, stopping by on his way home from Waco. Julie would often give O.T. a pie or some other food for his family in Marlin.[3] O.T. remained part of his older children's lives, though Terry was the only one still living in Falls County. Terry's mother, Jewell, helped him get his first job at Waco's Plantation Foods, hanging sixty-pound live turkeys on the conveyor belt leading to the slaughterhouse.[4] After Terry made enough money to buy a used car, his dad found him a job with Centurion Homes.

The two men enjoyed working side by side and made a decent living. Terry married Sharon Strickland in 1980, and the following year he took a job as a machine operator with Southern Pacific Railroad. He spent the next fifteen years riding the rails, repairing track, bridges, and signals across Texas. Sometimes his crew worked in empty fields; other times they walked to a café for lunch, if the locals let them. In 1989, the company sent Terry's crew to Vidor, a southeast Texas town that was the state KKK headquarters and didn't have a single black resident. "We drove all the machines up on a side and we was getting out, fixing to go to work, and them people come out with shotguns and told us to get back on the track. Vidor was very racial. They wouldn't let us get nothing to eat in Vidor," Terry said.[5]

O.T.'s new family continued to grow in 1982 with the birth of their second son, LaVar Tramayne Tomlinson.[6] O.T. tried to make all of his children feel like part of the same family.[7] LaDainian's earliest memories are of the Hill and his extended family:

> What I remember was just having a lot of brothers and sisters. Having great family picnics and reunions and things like that on the Hill.
>
> There was no area off-limits for us. We could do whatever, whenever we wanted to do something. So pretty much what I remember is a lot of time I actually spent at Grandma Julie's house. But I also remember at times having to go to the well to get water, and pouring water in the bathtub and those type of things as a kid. It was a way of life.[8]

As idyllic as the Hill seemed, it offered few opportunities. Farmwork was hard to find and paid little. The public schools were acceptable, but there were no community colleges or universities nearby. The 1980s were tough on Marlin, and local businesses shuttered, turning Live Oak Street into a ghost town. Young people left in droves to find jobs or an education elsewhere. Those left behind often found themselves in worsening poverty. Loreane didn't like the way her hometown was changing. Unemployed men and teenagers loitered around the corner store, and drugs became more common. For the first time, she was afraid.[9]

Wanting a better life for her children, Loreane convinced O.T. to move the family to Waco in 1985, cutting his thirty-mile commute every day. Loreane became a clerk at a convenience store near the family's new house.[10] To LaDainian, Waco was a big, noisy city compared to the Hill:

> It was a culture shock. It was so different from what I was used to, and so I remember for a while I didn't want to go outside. I was kind of depressed because I felt like I had left what I had known, my comfort zone of running from Aunt Emma's house to Grandma Julie's house to my dad's house to the store up the street. I didn't embrace it at first.[11]

LaDainian was shy, and Londria had just turned thirteen. City life didn't suit her, and she chose to spend her school breaks in Marlin, staying with family and friends.[12] The family would always visit Julie's house for holidays, putting on barbecues for Juneteenth and traditional meals for Thanksgiving.[13]

O.T. was proud that his sons showed an aptitude for sports, teaching them football, basketball, and baseball. LaDainian joined his father on Sunday afternoons to watch the Chicago Bears, their favorite team, and Walter Payton, his favorite running back:

> Every Sunday was a family time, but football was on and my dad would always quiz me on what I was seeing. He would leave the room on purpose sometimes and come back and I would have to brief him on everything that [had] happened while he was gone. It was great times really, and I think it really shaped my love for the game early on, having to know the details.[14]

O.T.'s greatest love, though, was boxing. He was small but very muscular, and while LaDainian never saw his father fight, he heard stories about his father's legendary uppercut.[15] Loreane encouraged her children to participate in sports, but she drew the line at boxing.[16]

THE HILL'S LAST WHITE TOMLINSONS

John and Olga Tomlinson spent their retirement in the Victorian house their ancestors had built in the late 1890s. Uncle John leased the Hill to cattlemen, who brought cows to feed on the grass. Looking down to the river, John could still make out the patterns of the one-hundred-year-old cotton fields, but no one planted there anymore. On January 13, 1981, he passed away in his grandfather's house, with his wife by his side.

Olga lived on the Hill for two more years, but after she turned eighty-three, her family moved her out of the rickety old house and into a retirement home in Marlin. In 1985, her relatives sold the land to David Tinsley, a fried-chicken entrepreneur, ending 129 years of white Tomlinsons on the Hill. Both the first and last white Tomlinson residents were women.

The following year, O.T. suffered the biggest losses of his life. Julie died at the age of eighty-six, and, a few months later, the roof underneath him at work collapsed, dropping him twelve feet to the concrete floor. While the X-rays showed no broken bones, O.T. suffered extensive muscle and ligament damage to his back. The doctors put him on painkillers, but even after weeks of rest, the pain did not subside. He tried going back to work, but he never lasted more than a day. After six months, O.T. finally went to a specialist, who decided to operate.[17]

Doctors replaced two disks and put him in physical therapy, but O.T. never fully recovered. The constant pain, inability to work, and the need to use a cane left the fifty-one-year-old depressed. O.T.'s doctor decided he needed to replace another disk in O.T.'s neck, but O.T. refused to go through with another operation, even if he would experience pain for the rest of his life. He started collecting disability checks.[18]

To cheer himself up, O.T. invited his friends to the house during the day while Loreane worked at the convenience store and the children were at school. The number of friends grew, and Loreane became suspicious that something untoward was going on. O.T. became forgetful and jittery, and by 1987 Loreane suspected he and his friends were using illegal drugs. He denied it, but she couldn't explain his behavior any other way. After months of bickering, Loreane accepted that O.T. was addicted to his pain medication, at best, and, at worst, selling his pills and using crack cocaine. She said, "He tried drugs and just got hooked. And it was bigger than he was. That's where it started, I believe, because he was on heavy, heavy pain medication. Sometimes you don't realize what you've done, or how much you've taken. You're in pain, and you just want it to stop."[19]

Neither Loreane nor O.T. understood addiction, or how to overcome it. The two argued more and more, with Loreane demanding that O.T. get off the drugs, while he denied there was a problem. Often O.T. would go to his mother's empty house on the Hill for days at a time, escaping to the place he loved the most. He found comfort with his cousins and the simple farm life of his childhood. Worried that O.T.'s bad habits would harm their children, Loreane asked O.T. to move out.[20]

The night he left, O.T. sat down with his children and explained that while he still loved them, he was leaving. He told eight-year-old LaDainian that he needed to step up. LaDainian said later that he was too young to understand what was happening, or why:

> I just remember him saying "You're the man of the house now. You're the oldest son, and you're going to have to take care of your momma and your brother." I remember him talking about that, but I didn't understand why. That was a lot of responsibility for a kid that was eight years old at the time.
>
> My mom just said, "Well, your father and I just need a break from each other and we're going to break up for a little while." Of course, I [didn't] know what that means. I just took it as my dad is never coming back. For a while, I think all those things of moving away and being around a different environment, different kids—that was depressing. I love my dad, you know, and so there were times I didn't want to go outside. I really wanted to go back to Tomlinson Hill and Marlin and the area that I knew, where my family and I was comfortable running around from house to house and being a kid.[21]

Loreane moved her three children into an apartment complex on Waco's south side, where she struggled as a single mother relying on a meager income. A country girl herself, she didn't like the crowded conditions and people living on top of one another in apartment buildings. She could hear other couples fighting and babies crying through the thin walls. Her children no longer had their own yard to play in, and the complex's courtyard was full of children without adult supervision. The children made friends, but Loreane missed her family back in Marlin. She sent money to them each month, even though her own finances were tight. In time, she found a better job at the HEB grocery store in Waco. She also took a second job working in the cafeteria at a Veterans Administration hospital. Soon she was earning enough to move out of the apartment and into a house. Loreane even tried to reconcile with O.T. But he hadn't kicked the drugs, so she asked him to leave again. She, too, became depressed. Even with two jobs, she simply couldn't give her three children the life she felt they deserved.[22]

Loreane was not alone. The number of African-American households headed by a woman rose to 40 percent in 1990, the highest recorded up to that date. Of the two million blacks living in Texas in 1990—the third-largest population after California and New York—30 percent lived in poverty, up from 28 percent in 1980.[23] The African-American standard of living was slipping backward.

THE BOYS AND GIRLS CLUB

When Londria turned sixteen in 1988, she took a job at the Boys Club in Waco and suggested that her brothers enroll there. Loreane was reluctant because LaDainian and LaVar were both under ten years old, but when she found that the club provided tutoring and organized activities, she relented. Most important, it provided a safe place after school, and she knew that Londria was at the front desk.[24] LaDainian counted the Boys Club as one of his biggest influences:

The Boys and Girls Club became my crutch, where I needed to go to find myself and to become who I wanted to be. I think it was the greatest thing that my mom did for us, and particularly me.

I felt like there were people there that really cared, because there was a time when my mom was working two, three jobs and there was no way she could be around. If it wasn't for the Boys and Girls Club, who knows where I would have been, what crowd I would have got involved with.[25]

LaVar said the Boys Club kept him and LaDainian away from gangs and drugs:

Five bucks for the summer, man. We was there. It was fun. I loved it; we had something to do. We didn't really have to go to the 'hood area, because those kids, they didn't really do the things we did. They didn't have the opportunity to go to a Boys Club. Their moms didn't care for them like that.[26]

One day, LaDainian came home with a special request: He wanted to join the Pop Warner football league.[27] Pop Warner is a nonprofit organization that runs football leagues and cheerleading programs for young children and requires them to maintain their grades.[28] Loreane looked at the application, the schedule, and the costs, but she wasn't sure she should spend what little extra money the family had on something that was not a necessity. Nine-year-old LaDainian was crushed when his mother told him she'd have to think about it, but Loreane met with the coaches and asked what support the league could offer a single mom with two jobs. After reminding herself that the reason she had moved to Waco was to give her children more opportunities, she signed up both LaDainian and LaVar. LaDainian said he found his calling:

The first time I touched a ball, I ran a touchdown. I guess at that point it was destiny. I found my gift. My mother and my father, they nurtured that gift. They pushed me, never made me do anything, but they pushed me. Every year since, I have played football. I look forward to it, and I played with blacks, whites, and Hispanic kids.[29]

LaDainian ended every practice wanting more. Loreane said he listened to his coaches' every word, including their advice about always knowing where the ball is. LaDainian took that literally, carrying his ball with him everywhere and even sleeping with it.[30]

LaDainian and LaVar traveled around the region, but while LaVar enjoyed playing, he didn't feel the same way LaDainian did. LaVar enjoyed history and social studies and generally liked school, except for math.[31] That was one of many differences between LaDainian and LaVar. LaDainian said he loved math and could perform calculations quickly in his head. He was a decent student, but for him school was what he did to play football.[32]

O.T. was a good dad, when he was around. LaVar enjoyed visiting the Hill, where his father cooked him hamburgers and he could run around with his cousins without a care in the world. But LaDainian and LaVar said their father never talked about the Hill's history.

When LaVar was ten years old, he learned in Waco that when some people looked at him, they didn't see a big country boy who liked to fish and play football; they saw a suspect:

A cop pulled up right next to me, and he tells me to stop. He asked me where I'm going. I say I'm going home, and he starts talking about arresting me.

It's amazing that that kind of stuff still happens. Broad daylight. There's nothing going on. Quiet neighborhood. I still remember the crew cut on this guy. I remember the look on his face. He could have been about thirtysomething.

I never looked at another officer the same. Even black police officers, I question. "Are you really trying to do what our ancestors and our civil rights leaders fought for in equality, or are you trying to be one of these guys?" I'm in awe at a black man in a police uniform, to be honest with you, because I'm sure he's experienced that.[33]

O.T. lived on the Hill, but he also spent a lot of time on Wood Street, where he smoked marijuana and crack with his friends. He may have become an addict, but by all accounts he dressed well and functioned. Occasionally, he'd knock on Jewell's door, looking for a place to sleep, or go to Terry's house, asking for a ride back to the Hill, but he never became homeless or a street junkie.[34] He would, however, sell his possessions, including gifts from his children, to get money for drugs.[35]

O.T. told Londria, LaDainian, and LaVar that they were good kids who could rely on their mother. He said Ronald, Terry, and Fifi needed him more, a sentiment that hurt Londria, who said she needed her father.[36] LaDainian said he tried to become a role model for LaVar, coaching him at sports, teaching him how to fight, even how to cook pancakes.[37] But O.T.'s older kids were experiencing tough times.

Terry's wife was losing patience with his spending Monday through Friday working for the railroad while she raised their children alone.[38] Fifi was mixing with the wrong crowd, using drugs, and breaking into homes.[39] O.T.'s third son, Charles, then twenty-seven, was selling drugs in Waco,[40] and in May 1988 a woman stabbed him to death.[41]

The black Tomlinsons faced the same problems with unemployment, drugs, and crime that damaged many African-American families. Black unemployment was twice the rate of that of whites in Texas, creating widespread despair. Racism remained rampant. A 1995 study found that when African-Americans drove in white suburbs, they received double the number of traffic tickets that whites received. Between 1985 and 1991, the percentage of African-Americans in Texas prisons rose from 36 percent to 46 percent as lawmakers waged their war on drugs. Even though African-Americans constituted only 12 percent of the population, 29 percent of those executed were African-American.[42] Almost every academic study of criminal justice in the early 1990s concluded that police disproportionately pursued and arrested African-Americans, and the courts handed down tougher sentences when the defendant was black.

African-American Texans were dancing the Texas two-step, taking two steps forward and one step back. But while economic conditions were challenging, the political climate was improving. Major court decisions in the 1980s gave minority candidates better chances at winning elections. Single-member districts provided minorities greater influence, and schools and city officials began responding to their needs.[43]

When a 1992 survey showed that banks rejected African-American loan applications in Texas five times more often than they did white applications, the legislature passed stricter laws against "redlining" minority neighborhoods. In response to violent crimes where blacks were attacked, lawmakers passed hate-crime laws in 1993, and the Texas Commission on Human Rights sued Klan groups for harassment in 1994.[44]

POWER OF PERSISTENCE

Loreane held her family together largely through her faith, and even during the hardest periods, she made the drive every Wednesday night and Sunday morning to her church in Marlin, where Lonnie Garrett was a pastor. Her kids rarely saw O.T. as his addiction worsened.[45]

The Pop Warner coaches recognized LaDainian's speed and made him a running back. Loreane tried to encourage him, but money remained tight and she often couldn't give her children the things they wanted. She signed up for more shifts to pay for extras, such as when LaDainian wanted to attend a football camp put on by Jay Novacek, a tight end for the Dallas Cowboys. One day at the camp, LaDainian took a hand-off from one of his heroes, Emmitt Smith, a running back for the Cowboys. From that day on, LaDainian felt destined to play professional football.[46]

Loreane met another single parent, a construction worker named Herman Chappell, at Lonnie Garrett's church. The two began dating, and he steadily won the children's trust. After eighteen months, Loreane and Herman married, and the children had a new man in their lives.

TWENTY-TWO

I hear you're going to Rwanda for Alex. We need someone
there, too. We pay ten cents a word . . .

—Reid Miller

I arrived in Johannesburg in late October 1992 and soon discovered
that my friend Keith was not going to deliver on his promises to get
me into the African National Congress. He said his comrades had
gotten into trouble for corruption and that the ANC had kicked them
out. I'm still not sure what I believe. Keith may never have had any
high-level connections. But it was clear that South African revolution-
aries didn't need me, or any other white guys from Texas. Nelson
Mandela was leading the ANC campaign to win the first democratic
elections in the country's history, and thousands of ANC cadre needed
work. Giving up on becoming a revolutionary, I walked down to one
of South Africa's two Mexican restaurants and asked for a job.

Bandito's primary purpose was to qualify the pub upstairs for a
liquor license, but I knew how to cook Tex-Mex, and the Afrikaner
owners let me rewrite and tweak their recipes. Most of their customers
came from an Afrikaner university located down the street. Two blacks
who lived in the Soweto township worked in the kitchen, one a profes-
sionally trained chef and the other a helper. The chef did not like me
in his kitchen, but he accepted the fact that I could teach him about

dishes he'd never cooked before. I introduced the quesadilla to South Africa.

One of the first things I noticed about my black coworkers were their scars. An inordinate number of black working-class men in South Africa had scars on their faces or arms, and probably in places I couldn't see. They were part of a generation that had started the Soweto uprising in 1976 to protest apartheid.

Black students frequently staged strikes to express their displeasure with school policies, but on April 30, 1976, junior high students marched out of their classrooms to protest a new policy that required some classes be taught in Afrikaans, a languge that had first been used by Dutch settlers. On the morning of June 16, somewhere between three thousand and ten thousand black students left their Soweto classrooms and marched to the Orlando soccer stadium. Police set up barricades to block the students' routes, forcing them toward Orlando High School. Police said that the children threw stones, so the police responded by firing their weapons into the air and releasing attack dogs. When the teens used stones to fight off the dogs, the police opened fire. Twenty-three people died.

The news and images of white police opening fire on black high school students set off six months of protests and riots, and the security forces responded with ferocious violence. By the end of 1976, six hundred people had died and four thousand had suffered serious injuries. Students staged similar demonstrations in 1980, 1983, 1985, and 1986, clashing with police and ultimately South African soldiers. Many of the people I encountered wore their personal experiences fighting apartheid on their faces.

One evening, the kitchen helper at Bandito's made a mistake that led to some food spoiling. When one of the owners found out, he came into the kitchen and immediately began punching the kitchen helper in the face and body. The helper didn't attempt to fight back; he dropped to the floor and curled into a ball, while the much larger white man continued to punch him and yell in Afrikaans. I looked to the chef for some kind of reaction, but he stood still, coolly watching the beat down. Before I could say anything, the beating ended and the owner saw the stunned look on my face. I could tell the kitchen assistant was not seriously hurt, but he was humiliated. I mumbled something like "That's not acceptable," and the owner and I walked out of the kitchen. I told him that as far as I was concerned, I'd just witnessed a crime, but the passivity of the helper and the chef bothered me as much as the owner's violence. The owner said such beatings were routine, though he acknowledged that with apartheid ending, that would probably change. He promised it would never happen again.

I returned to the kitchen, confused about what to do, and the chef also took me aside. He said the helper had screwed up and that he had realized he would suffer a beating for his mistake. More important, he explained that the helper's family depended on this one job for their survival. If the helper lost it, and the Afrikaner's reference, he might not find another one. I decided that I'd made my feelings clear, and that it was up to the helper and the chef to take any further action. After I finished teaching the chef my recipes, the owner fired me.

Armed with my southern accent and knowledge of my culture's food, I applied for a job at Fat Frank's Cajun Restaurant in downtown Johannesburg. The high-end establishment was located next to a sister restaurant that served gourmet Afrikaner food, the Linger Longer. The neighborhood was going downhill fast, but rich whites from the suburbs still made the trek downtown for New Orleans cuisine lifted directly from Paul Prudhomme's cookbooks. The manager hired me to wait tables, knowing that customers would enjoy talking to a real-life Southerner. The other waiters came from diverse backgrounds, including black college students who attended the University of the Witwatersrand and working-class whites, both English and Afrikaner. The team reminded me of my friends at Skyline, and we all got along and hung out together outside of work. But the tips we earned varied, depending on our backgrounds. The black staff made the least and the Texan faking a Cajun accent made the most, on average about eighty dollars a day, good money in South Africa. I also witnessed another side of apartheid's perversity when I discovered that one of the old racist white men at the restaurant paid a black male parking attendant to give him blow jobs in the alley.

I moved into an apartment with some of the other waiters in Hillbrow, a mixed-race inner-city ghetto with Stalinist-type housing blocks and Art Deco apartments. Low-income folks of every race and creed mixed in Hillbrow, where dance clubs blared from dusk until dawn, vendors sold street food on every corner, and cheap restaurants set up tables on the sidewalks twenty-four hours a day. Cops, prostitutes, and drug dealers all walked the streets in groups of four or more for safety, and rarely did a night go by without the crackle of gunfire. The other waiters and I would go to neighborhood joints to unwind after work.

I'd always wanted to become a writer, so I decided I would begin working on a book about my time in South Africa. I asked my manager to give me time off to attend the big events that I could see scheduled in the newspaper, such as the Day of the Vow, when Afrikaners celebrated their heritage. One day in March 1994, I opened the newspaper to find that Lucas Mangope, the leader of a black homeland called Bophuthatswana, was refusing to step down as apartheid was ending. The people who lived there took to the streets to demand Mangope relinquish power. I had the next two days off, so I bought a bus ticket to the capital, Mmabatho.

The bus dropped me off in the middle of town, where rioters were looting anything of value. Mangope's police made a halfhearted attempt to stop them, but most appeared more concerned about surviving the revolt. I took photos and talked to the looters, who said they were attacking only the stores that belonged to Mangope and his family. As evening set in, I asked journalists on the streets where they were staying, and they told me to head for the four-star Mmabatho Sun Hotel. Luckily, I was carrying every penny to my name and could pay for one night at the hotel, but I had no transportation. I walked in the hotel's direction, sticking out my thumb at every car that passed me. Luckily, Japanese journalist Takeshi "Go" Kawasaki picked me up.

Go gave me a lift to the hotel and asked me for whom I worked. I said I was freelancing. He'd come straight from the airport and said he needed an assistant. He offered me one hundred dollars a day, on those days he needed me, and I quickly agreed. That's how I became a journalist.

Go hired me when he wanted to go someplace dangerous or difficult, particularly when we investigated violence in the townships between forces loyal to the ANC and the Zulus. He asked me to work every day during the three weeks leading up to the April 27 election and assigned me to dig up any dirt on Mandela. But after twenty-seven years in prison and four more years in varying levels of custody, Mandela had little opportunity to get into trouble. On occasion, Go asked me to go to the townships around Johannesburg when violence flared, handing me a flak jacket and a mobile phone to call in what I saw. I tried to convince him to run pictures I'd taken, but he said the paper preferred to rely on him or wire services like the Associated Press. He transmitted his photos to Japan from the AP office, so I came to know it well.

On the Sunday before the election was set to begin, I caught a taxi at my apartment and began the trip through downtown to the *Asahi* office. About halfway there, a car bomb exploded, blowing in the taxi's windshield. Through the dust and smoke, I could see the shell of a car flipped over and burning on the sidewalk. The blast had knocked out hundreds of windows in the tall buildings along the road, leaving a thick layer of shattered glass covering the street. I counted at least a dozen bodies and only eight frames of film left in my Nikon. A South African police truck pulled up just as I was taking my last frames and warned me that another car bomb was nearby. I walked toward the hotel and saw where police had set up a barricade, and behind it were dozens of photojournalists. That's when I realized the value of the photos I'd just taken and remembered how *Asahi* never wanted any of my photos. I grabbed a taxi and told the driver to take me to the AP office.

Mike Feldman, a top photo editor at the time, grabbed my film, stuck it in a processing machine, and peppered me with questions. He looked at my amateur camera and asked if I'd focused it properly and set the exposure. Looking down at the spots of blood where shards of windshield glass had pierced my shirt, I struggled to hear him through the ringing in my ears. The film processor would give him his answer. He pulled the negatives out of the machine, took out a loop to examine them, and smiled. He offered me two thousand dollars for all eight, and I had my first AP byline.

Feldman gave me a cup of coffee and sent me to talk to Tina Sussman, an AP reporter. My hands shook as I sipped my coffee and told her what I'd seen. I told her as a freelance journalist, I could write the story, but she politely told me no, that I was a witness and not an AP reporter.

Go was annoyed that I'd taken the photos to the AP, but he accepted my explanation and knew *Asahi* would still run my photos. Thousands of newspapers used them on their front pages, including all of the South African papers and the *New York Times*.

Go let me spend Election Day with South African troops in Katlehong, the most dangerous township in the Johannesburg area. If there was any violence, the troops would serve as a quick reaction force. But Election Day was one of the most peaceful in South Africa's history. Two weeks later, I watched Mandela take the oath of office along with 150,000 other people on the grounds of the capitol in Pretoria.

A week later, I returned to Texas with plans to write a book, but I found no publishers interested in my adventures. My friend Mike helped me get a job as a speechwriter for a state senator, but when Go called from Japan and asked if I'd be willing to work for him at his new assignment in Nairobi, where he would cover events in East Africa, I immediately agreed.

I arrived in Nairobi in January 1995, and Go provided housing, food, a car, and a salary of nine hundred dollars a month. Soon after I arrived, we flew to Rwanda to report on the country's recovery from the genocide and the refugee crisis in Zaire. But Go's budget was not large enough to take me everywhere, and he already had a Kenyan office manager.

My goal in taking the job with *Asahi* was to build a reputation to get a job with the AP, but I was worried that Go would lay me off before I had a chance. I asked the Voice of America bureau chief, Alex Belida, to have lunch and tell me about getting a master's degree from his alma mater, Columbia University. Alex told me it wasn't worth the student loans and suggested I move to Rwanda and work for him instead.

Alex explained that the VOA had recently won a grant to start a Kinyarwanda and Kirundi service to broadcast objective news in those languages to Rwanda and Burundi. He had tried to hire local journalists, but they couldn't seem to overcome sectarian politics enough to send in decent stories. For two thousand dollars a month, he needed someone to file every weekday, but first I needed to write radio news scripts, learn how to use the equipment, and pass a voice test. Alex also said his close friend, AP bureau chief Reid Miller, needed more copy from Rwanda and that I could probably cut a deal with him, too.

Reid scared me. He talked tough, looked tough, and always had a cup of coffee in one hand and a cigarette dangling from his lip. I'd heard his voice echo down the hallway in the press center when he lost his temper, and other reporters warned me that he did not suffer fools gladly. When I went into the AP office, I was prepared to explain why he should give me a chance, but I never got it out. He pointed me to a seat, finished editing a story, and then took a long drag off his cigarette and released a lungful of smoke. "I hear you're going to Rwanda for Alex," he said. "We need someone there, too. We pay ten cents a word, fifty dollars a photograph, and if you shoot video, we'll pay you for that, too, when there's a big story. I'll give you a two-hundred-dollar-a-month retainer and pay your expenses whenever we ask you to leave Kigali."

He asked if I had a laptop, and when I said yes, he told correspondent Terry Leonard to set me up with some software and teach me how to file stories. He then shook my hand and said good-bye. The conversation lasted fifteen minutes at most, and I wondered if he even knew my last name.

In September, I took a short trip to Kigali to look for a place to live, but during that logistics trip, an aid worker friend, Samantha Bolton, told me about a massacre and took me to the hospital where Médecins Sans Frontières was treating survivors. I dictated the story to Reid's wife, Pauline Jelinek, also an AP reporter, and she faxed me a copy after it hit the wire.

Sitting on the front step of the hotel where I was staying, I saw my name at the top of the fax: "Chris Tomlinson, Associated Press Writer." Tears welled up in my eyes as I read the story and saw how Pauline had taken my notes and quotes and created an AP dispatch. I'd never been happier, and I knew this was how I wanted to spend the rest of my life.

LIFE AFTER GENOCIDE

I returned to Kigali for good in October and eventually moved in with some people who worked at the UN Children's Fund. Terry and Pauline patiently took my horrible copy and transformed it into readable journalism. At first, none of my sentences survived editing. At Reid's urging, I always printed out my original and compared it line by line with what Terry and Pauline had put on the wire. Slowly, I improved, and during a visit to Nairobi, Terry showed me, sentence by sentence, how to write a feature story from my first muddled draft. He taught me more about writing in that single hour than I'd learned up to that point in my life. After the first six months, Reid and Alex asked me to report on Burundi and the refugee camps in Zaire, Uganda, and Tanzania.

A coup in Burundi took up much of my time late in 1996, followed by the insurgency in Zaire. My VOA stories prompted the leader of the Rwandan genocide, Colonel Théoneste Bagosora, to place a one-thousand-dollar bounty on my head, the same price he was offering for the assassination of the U.S. ambassador to Rwanda. Congolese rebels attacked the Rwandan refugee camps in late 1996, and my reports on the crisis hit hundreds of American front pages and appeared in the world's top newspapers. The AP was thrilled with my work and offered me a chance to become a staff reporter if I would agree to return to the United States and spend a year in a local bureau. The first bureau chief to offer me a job was in Minneapolis. Dave Pyle needed someone to fill in while another reporter went on maternity leave. Over two weeks in January 1997, I went from standing over the bodies of murdered Spanish aid workers in Rwanda to interviewing shoppers in the Mall of America.

After my year in Minneapolis, I moved to the AP's International Desk in New York, the last step before assuming an overseas post. The East Africa correspondent's job in Nairobi opened in the summer of 2000, and I returned to Africa. In the first year, the AP sent me to cover an Ebola outbreak in Uganda, President Bill Clinton's visit to Tanzania for Burundi peace talks, and, of course, trips to my old stomping grounds in Rwanda, Burundi, and Congo.

In August 2001, my college friend Shalini Ramanathan dropped me a note, asking if she could visit. She was living in Washington, D.C., and her work required her to make frequent trips to South Africa. I invited her along on a reporting trip to Tanzania's Serengeti National Park, where I planned to report on poaching by Arab royalty and write a second story about luxury travel in Africa. We spent a week driving around northern Tanzania in a 1976 Range Rover I'd bought from a *National Geographic* photographer. By the time I dropped her off at the airport in Nairobi, we were dating. Two weeks later, nineteen terrorists hijacked four airliners and flew them into the World Trade Center, the Pentagon, and into the ground in Pennsylvania.

THE WAR ON TERROR

All foreign correspondents in the world saw their careers take a dramatic turn on September 11. Within a week, I was in Lebanon, visiting Palestinian refugee camps and interviewing members of Hezbollah to see what they knew about al-Qaeda. A month later, I was in Bahrain, reporting on the buildup at the U.S. Navy base there, and a few weeks after that, the bombing began in Afghanistan. I spent a month on the USS *Theodore Roosevelt* aircraft carrier before AP sent me to Tajikistan, for insertion into Afghanistan.

The day after I arrived in Kabul, bureau chief Kathy Gannon sent me to Jalalabad, and after I survived an ambush on the road there, she ordered me to stay. Osama bin Laden was hiding in a cave complex called Tora Bora just to the south, so I moved to the front lines with the mujahideen until bin Laden fled to Pakistan and the mountain redoubt fell on December 17, 2001.

I went back to covering Africa and developed a terrorism beat. Bin Laden's first attacks on the United States were the 1998 embassy bombings in Nairobi and Dar-es-Salaam, Tanzania. The men responsible had fled to Somalia, where fighting between clan-based warlords kept the country from establishing a functioning government. Fearing that the anarchy in Somalia might attract a greater al-Qaeda presence, the Pentagon set up a command post on a former French Foreign Legion base in Djibouti. I wrote about Islamic extremists trying to undermine the moderate leaders in local mosques across East Africa and recruiting young men to fight in Afghanistan.

In the summer of 2002, I got a call from AP headquarters, asking me to make a trip through Bahrain, Qatar, and the United Arab Emirates to write about the military buildup for a war against Iraq. With the war in Afghanistan still raging, I couldn't believe the Pentagon would open up another front, yet by November, U.S. Central Command had relocated to Doha, Qatar. Gen. Tommy Franks's top public affairs adviser, a civilian on loan from the White House, showed me around a brand-new command center the Defense Department was building. By the adviser's tone and confidence, I knew then the United States was going to invade Iraq, and I settled into life in the Middle East.

The AP moved me to Kuwait in January, where I embedded with Company A, Third Battalion, Seventh Infantry Regiment. The embed put me at the biggest battles, including the capture of Baghdad and fighting in Fallujah. I accompanied the unit from Kuwait to their homes at Fort Stewart, Georgia, writing about every detail along the way.

Shalini and I continued to see each other when we could, between my long reporting trips and endless travel. She moved to Kenya in 2004, and we were married in a three-day Hindu ceremony in Bangalore, India, that year.

The situation in Somalia began to deteriorate in 2005, and by 2006 al-Qaeda-backed extremists were fighting Somali moderates backed by Ethiopia and the United States. The fighting continued in the spring of 2007, and after six years covering death, I was growing weary. In addition to war, I'd also covered earthquakes, volcanoes, and a tsunami. I could feel my nerves fraying, and my readiness to throw myself into horror evaporated. When I learned that a reporter who worked for me, Anthony Mitchell, had been killed in a plane crash while returning from covering a story I'd assigned him, I felt I couldn't take any more. He was the twelfth friend I'd lost to the job, and I'd hit my limit for sorrow.

Shalini worked in renewable energy and applied for a job with a company in Austin. They offered her a deal we couldn't refuse in a city we both adored. We moved to Texas in July 2007. I worked part-time for the AP on special assignments and decided to spend my free time writing a book I'd been thinking about since I was eight years old: a story of two families from a Texas slave plantation, one white and one black, with the same name.

TWENTY-THREE

I would score touchdowns and people would then yell out,
"Nigger! Nigger!"

—LaDainian Tomlinson

The Waco school district in the late 1980s had an unusual program where all of the city's sixth graders attended the same school before moving on to junior high. LaDainian said the Carver Center had the toughest kids in the city; there were fights almost every day, and thirteen-year-olds were dealing drugs. He managed to stay out of trouble, and for the seventh grade he went to University Junior High, where he had his first encounter with racism between blacks and Hispanics. But playing sports meant spending a lot of time with Mexican-Americans:

> You get to see people for who they are, and in times where they're tired, they're hurt. They may be going through something and you get to see them for who they are, rather than their skin color, especially when you're all trying to win a game, and after that game, when you all celebrate winning. It's a happy time that you all worked together for one goal, to accomplish one thing. To fight and try to break that apart, I always felt like it was silly, because there was no purpose in the fight.[1]

LaDainian also met an African-American history teacher named Mrs. Miles, who taught him the importance of learning and the opportunities that college offered. She helped him see that going to school was more than just an avenue to play sports.[2]

It was just as LaDainian was hitting his stride in junior high sports and LaVar was happy at his school in 1991 that Loreane learned that her mother's doctors planned to amputate her leg. Loreane's brothers and sisters in Marlin had cared for their declining mother, but the amputation meant she would need more help than ever, so Loreane packed up the family and went home.[3]

Loreane also hoped that living in Marlin would encourage O.T. to see more of her boys, but he rarely kept his promises anymore. Loreane explained O.T.'s problems to LaDainian, and he finally had to accept that his father was human and flawed. LaDainian started his freshman year at Marlin High School and made the varsity football, basketball, and baseball teams. But he didn't get along with the coaches or the kids anymore. He wanted to return to Waco, which he had come to consider his true home. After Loreane's mother learned to walk on her prosthesis, the family moved back to Waco.[4]

LaDainian made the varsity team at University High and became the class leader along with a white childhood friend, Wayne Rogers. LaDainian was a starting player, either as fullback or outside linebacker, but he really wanted to start as running back. Loreane counseled her son to listen to his coach, learn new skills, and work hard toward his goals. The *Waco Tribune Herald* frequently praised LaDainian's performance at Friday-night games.[5]

Texas high school football is notoriously competitive, and during a game in Lampasas, seventy miles southwest of Waco, people in the stands started heckling LaDainian:

I would score touchdowns and people would then yell out, "Nigger! Nigger!" And so that's when it kind of started to really sink in.

I felt bad for the one or two black guys that was on their team more than anything, because I knew I was going back to a place where people accepted me for who I was.

I looked at it as them trying to make me angry. The little things that I remembered growing up about my father telling me about working in the cotton fields, my slave ancestors, my grandfather working in cotton fields. I knew that I wasn't a part of that.

We were moving forward now and I didn't have to do those things. Yeah, my ancestors did, but I didn't have to, and there was no way we were going back.[6]

For the next sixteen years, through college and a professional career, football fans would continue to call LaDainian a nigger from the stands, and he said he never let it make him angry.[7]

Just as LaDainian found his stride at University High, his stepfather, Herman, got a job in Dallas. At first, Loreane intended to take LaDainian and LaVar to their new home, but LaDainian was panicking. He knew he needed to get into a great football college to make the pros, and after moving from Marlin High to University High, he knew a new coach wouldn't know him, recognize his talent, or make him a starter. The college recruiters also wouldn't know where to find him, since they'd been watching him play at University High for two years. He convinced Loreane to let him stay with friends in Waco for his senior year.[8]

Always LaDainian's biggest fan, Loreane made the two-hour drive from Garland, a Dallas suburb, to watch her son play, and he excelled. Smaller than most players, only five ten, LaDainian was fast, nimble, and capable of taking a hit and getting back up.[9]

Fans recognized LaDainian wherever he went in Waco, and he told me the attention and living away from his mother made his senior year difficult. He had to deal with the same temptations as any other teenager, and one evening an older cousin visited LaDainian and brought with him some alcohol. LaDainian said he didn't get drunk that night, but his mother found out and was furious. She'd seen alcohol ruin the lives of too many young black men. LaDainian said he also knew the dangers:

Even in my neighborhood there were certain drug dealers that would always try to get us younger kids to sell some drugs for them, and I always resisted drugs and partying and drinking and all those things. I mean, don't get me wrong; I did go to a party here and there, but it wasn't something that I hung at all the time on weekends.

Honestly, I had seen it from older cousins that had played in high school but didn't do the right thing, didn't continue on playing. I didn't want to be like that. I remember my dad telling me about my older brother, Terry Tomlinson, that he had potential to be a great running back but couldn't deal with the fame and being talked about. He kind of succumbed to alcohol and all those things.[10]

LaDainian wrote his mother to apologize:

Hello Mom, how are you doing, I guess you're wondering why I am writing you a letter when I can talk to you on the phone or face to face. The reason is I want this letter kept until I fulfill my goals, and when I am feeling low I want to look at this letter and remember what I said on this letter. Mom I love you so much that every time I say it or write it, it brings tears to my eyes. One day you will be the proudest Mom in the whole world, because I am going to college and graduate and, if God is willing, go on to play pro football. And be the best person I can because that's how you raised me. Mom, I thank you so much for everything you have and is [sic] still doing for me, because it is hard not having a father who I could talk to and get advice from. You did the very best.

(Sorry so sloppy. Kept crying.)[11]

LaDainian was Waco's star football player, college recruiters were calling him, and he was living with another family while his mother was two hours away in Garland. He had to grow up fast and learned from his temporary family:

They had a great family structure. His dad was there, his mom, the whole family. I think more than anything it allowed me to see what I wanted in life, the structure of the family that I wanted because I never had that.

I feel like God always does things and puts you in certain positions to help you down the road, to help you become the person that he wants you to become. So seeing that family structure allowed me to say, "This is what I want one day."[12]

His senior year, LaDainian set the University High record for yards gained—2,254—and the team made it to the state championship, no small feat in the nation's second-largest state, where football is a religion. The University High Trojans eventually lost to the Calallen High team from Corpus Christi, but LaDainian was the star. Coaches in his district named him the year's most valuable player.[13]

COLLEGE BALL

LaDainian knew he needed to play for a university with a high profile, a good record, and a shortage of running backs if he were to reach the National Football League. Unfortunately, many coaches thought LaDainian was too small for college ball, let alone the pros. He also suffered from a lack of statistics, since he had played running back only in his senior year. Only three schools offered him scholarships: Baylor University, in Waco; the University of North Texas, in Denton; and Texas Christian University, in Fort Worth. On National Signing Day in 1996, La Dainian sat before dozens of journalists in Waco to announce he'd chosen TCU. He was one of only two players at University High to get full scholarships.

TCU's team, the Horned Frogs, held several advantages for LaDainian. He wanted to play on natural turf, which he felt was easier on his body, and his mom and brother could easily make the forty-five-minute drive to attend home games. During that first year, LaDainian began to suffer migraines, made worse by direct sunlight or bright stadium lights. His doctor recommended wearing a shaded visor on his helmet, and this became LaDainian's trademark. LaDainian also continued a habit he'd started in high school, remaining silent on game day to prepare mentally for the field.[14]

LaDainian started TCU when African-Americans topped 9 percent of the students at Texas universities, but those who got into college sometimes found a hostile environment. White fraternities at many schools continued holding racially charged events celebrating ante-bellum southern culture and portraying negative images of blacks, of-ten attracting protests. The University of Texas at Austin employed only 52 African-Americans on its faculty of 2,300 in 1993, and officials complained they couldn't find enough blacks with Ph.Ds.[15]

LaDainian's first season with the Horned Frogs was an unmitigated disaster. As a freshman, he rarely took the field, so he bore none of the blame, but the ten-game losing streak in 1997 was one of the school's worst records. TCU fired Coach Pat Sullivan and brought in Dennis Franchione, who emphasized weight training, something LaDainian loved. Within a year, LaDainian weighed 210 pounds and could bench-press 450.[16]

Franchione made LaDainian the starting fullback, but the sopho-more really wanted to be a running back. He bitterly remembered how the Waco coach didn't make him a running back until his senior year, hurting his chances with college teams. He worried Franchione would hurt his chances to go pro, but LaDainian's coaches expected him to wait until the senior starting running back, Basil Mitchell, graduated.[17] Three games into his sophomore year, LaDainian confronted his coaches, and Franchione made LaDainian the backup. Even with less time on the field, LaDainian managed seven hundred yards of rushing that year. The Horned Frogs recorded seven wins and four losses, good enough to make the Sun Bowl in El Paso. They beat the University of Southern California 28–19, the first bowl game victory for TCU in forty-one years.[18]

His junior year, LaDainian was the starting running back, and TCU won five out of their first nine games before they traveled to the Univer-sity of Texas at El Paso. In that game, LaDainian rushed for 406 yards—an NCAA record that year—and scored six touchdowns, to lead the team to a 52–24 victory. They ended the season with a 7–4 record, which earned them a trip to face East Carolina in the Mobile Alabama Bowl. Loreane went to the game and listened to East Carolina fans com-plain that LaDainian was unstoppable, and TCU won 28–14. LaDainian's end-of-season stats set records, with 1,850 yards in rushing and eighteen touchdowns. LaDainian became a national football star.[19]

That same year, LaDainian began dating another TCU student, LaTorsha Oakley, a Bill Gates Millennium Scholar from Dallas with a 4.0 grade average. LaDainian hadn't dated much, so when he took Torsha to Loreane's house, she knew he was serious about her. Loreane held high expectations for the women in her boys' lives and was happy to learn LaTorsha was a committed Christian.

Loreane had earned her ordination as a preacher as well as a real estate license. She started selling houses and making decent money, and perhaps for the first time in her life, thanks to Herman, she felt financially secure. LaVar was still in high school, and she spent her Friday nights watching him play for South Garland High, and her Saturdays watching LaDainian.[20]

Moving to the Dallas suburb of Garland at age thirteen proved tough for LaVar. He went from a town of 150,000 to a metropolis of more than one million, and he went from a high school that was largely black and Hispanic to one that was mostly white. The strict dress code and preppy culture made LaVar feel horribly out of place. Race relations were also a much bigger problem, and he said blacks sought refuge in sports:

> Those [white kids] were raised differently than a lot of black kids. Those kids tend to be a little more rough, you know. They might not come with the *n* word, or the slander, but you know it's there. They look at you. They look at you in that way. The way they talk to you, there's no respect in their tone when they speak to you. That's what is overwhelming, to be able to stand that, to go through it and actually stand there and to be like, "Are you really the way that I'm feeling like you are, because I can be a jerk, too? You know?"
>
> I think it was important to be a bigger person and to go on with my sports, and let them be who they are, because I'm going to be who I am.[21]

One thing South Garland High was not ready to change was its school mascot, the "Southern Colonel," or the fight song, "Dixie." Even though the school had officially dropped it in 1991—the year Martin Luther King, Jr. Day became a state holiday—fans still used the school's old banner, the Confederate battle flag. The symbols offended LaVar:

> When you're taught about the Confederate flag in fourth-grade social studies, you learn in elementary what the Confederate flag meant. I knew and I think the parents knew; everybody knew. But sports kept me out of trouble.

> The apartments we stayed in, there were gangs over there. If I didn't play football or if I wasn't in sports, then I could have ended up with them. I don't know where a lot of those guys are today. I heard a few of them went to jail. It could have been me. So, you make a decision, a conscious decision: What's worse? Listening to a racist fight song or going and sitting in jail for the next fifteen years. I'll take the racist fight song.[22]

LaVar made it through his freshman year at South Garland, but he didn't want to return. He transferred to Lakeview, another Garland school, but one where African-Americans made up the majority. That fall, he played football against the South Garland Colonels and beat them.[23]

That wasn't the last move for LaVar, though. His parents moved again to Pleasant Grove, one of the toughest neighborhoods on the southeast side of Dallas, and he enrolled in W. W Samuell, a school known for gangs. LaVar felt whipsawed, but he concentrated on football:

> I [had] my friends; they were gang members. But they were my buddies. We ran around together and went to parties together. They had my back; I had theirs. They'd come to my house; I'd go to theirs. My mom loved them; their moms loved me. It was all love, man.

> They wanted me to do certain things with them, but at the same time, they knew what I had going and they actually cared enough to try to keep me away from certain stuff. So it truly wasn't that hard to stay focused.[24]

Herman and Loreane's struggle to move from manual labor to professional jobs reflected the experiences of many Texans. Between 1972 and 1987, the number of African-American businesses in the state increased from 15,001 to 35,725. Overall, though, blacks owned only 6 percent of Texas's businesses. The African-American high school dropout rate also fell from 41 percent in 1988 to 23 percent in 1993.[25]

In 1995, Dallas became the first major Texas city to elect a black mayor, Ron Kirk. Former Dallas Cowboy quarterback Roger Staubach and real estate developers had backed Kirk's campaign, and community leaders complained that he spent more time defending white developers' interests than those of poor African-Americans.[26]

Barriers, however, did remain. A *Dallas Morning News* study found that among the thousands of partners in major Texas law firms, only eleven were African-Americans. Only 37 percent of black Texans attended integrated schools, largely due to white flight to suburban districts, and between 1984 and 1990, minorities lodged more civil rights complaints against Texas law-enforcement officers than any other state in the nation. The statewide investigative agency, the Texas Rangers, did not appoint its first African-American until 1988. And only in 1990 did Morris Overstreet become the first African-American elected to statewide office, as a justice on the Texas Court of Criminal Appeals.[27]

TRAGEDY AND TRIUMPH

Loreane's life took a turn for the worse when Herman suffered a stroke. She nursed him back to health, but she discovered he had no intention of giving up the cigarettes, liquor, and fried foods that had put him in the hospital, refusing to believe that his health was in jeopardy. Loreane pressed him to change his ways, but he only started drinking more and began screaming at her and calling her names. He complained that she spent too much time at church, and he refused to go anymore. He left the house for days at a time and didn't tell her where he'd been. During one of their fights, he raised his hand to hit Loreane, and LaVar caught Herman from behind and slammed him into a wall.[28]

Loreane filed for divorce, but after Herman's illness, she was nearly broke. Her real estate business had turned sour, and all at once, Loreane again found herself wondering how she was going to buy groceries and pay the bills. Creditors called at all hours of the night, and at one point the city turned off the water until a Christian ministry stepped in and paid the bill. Eventually, Loreane began closing real estate deals again, and she started the slow climb back to financial security.[29]

LaVar's football performance as a defensive linebacker at Samuell High earned him a scholarship to Sam Houston State University, the small school in Huntsville where R. E. L. Tomlinson had earned his teaching certificate. The school's football team did not compete in a major league, but suiting up with the Bearkats gave LaVar a chance to prove himself worthy of transferring to a better football program, or at least the opportunity to earn a degree. LaVar's plans nearly got derailed when a man at a party in Denton hit his girlfriend and LaVar beat the man down. A few days later, police asked LaVar to turn himself in. He hired a lawyer and pleaded guilty to aggravated assault, a second-degree felony. The judge sentenced him to six years' probation.[30]

LaVar played well his freshman year and tried to get into the University of Arkansas, but his grades weren't good enough. Instead, he ended up studying at a community college in Independence, Kansas, trying to improve his academic standing. But the math classes he had taken in the Garland and Dallas schools had not prepared him for college, and LaVar grew tired of coaches comparing him to LaDainian. Football became too much like work. LaVar looks back now and sees a system that fails young African-Americans, particularly boys. He said too many think the only means for success is through sports or entertainment. The school systems also promote the kids based on their athletic ability, not academic standards. LaVar said he felt betrayed:

> When we get up to the college level, we're dumb as rocks and we're trying to figure out how we're going to make it through college, and we don't make it. Our dreams of playing football are dashed because did nobody teach us how to do the math or how to read this four-syllable word or even how to speak. We'll want to do interviews with

gold teeth in our mouth, and dreadlocks in our hair. You know, that's not smart. That's not intelligent at all, but we don't know.

Black people are known for [physical prowess]. We're known as that warrior race; that's why we were enslaved, because we had the build. We had the muscle mass. We had the longevity to endure these kind of hardships, the physical beatings. We can endure that. And to this day we're just in another form of slavery.[31]

LaDainian, though, never lost his love for and obsession with football. He entered his senior year at TCU in 2000 as the undisputed star of the Horned Frogs football team, and the excitement of his final season swirled around the twenty-year-old. Loreane discovered that her son had a new nickname, "LT." Fans chanted these initials at football games and bumper stickers proclaimed LT's greatness. Loreane took a moment to reflect on her son's years of hard work from Pop Warner to TCU, and she realized that not once had O.T. seen his son play college ball. Loreane invited O.T. to attend a game and offered to let him stay in her guest room. He agreed, and she drove down to the Hill to get him.[32] That day, LaDainian looked up into the stands and found his father's smiling face next to his mother's:

It's emotional, because it was his first time seeing me play. I remembered when I seen him. I would always spot my family in the stands before the game. I had to find them to see where they were, because if I scored, I would point to my family, or tap my heart, or whatever.

So I saw my dad and I remember trying so hard to impress him. I tried so hard that I probably didn't have the best game. I mean, I probably had one of the worst games that I possibly could have because I was trying to impress him.

After the game, he gave me a hug. He said, "Great job. I know you was trying real hard."

It was a moment that I never wanted to end because it was special. I finally felt like all those years of watching football with my dad had come full circle, where he was now able to watch me in real life. He could finally say, "Son, you did it. You know, you did it."[33]

LaDainian gained only seventy-five yards on twenty-one carries that game, and years of disappointment still overshadowed the relationship between the two men. O.T. stayed with Loreane the entire season and attended every home game. Slowly, father and son reconnected, and LaDainian overcame his resentment toward his absentee father. They started to talk again, and for LaDainian, those were the best years he spent with his father. LaDainian finally forgave him.[34]

O.T. appeared to keep his addiction under control while he stayed with Loreane. LaDainian even started driving to Waco to visit with O.T. and his older stepbrother Ronald. Sitting on Ronald's porch and talking to his father gave LaDainian a chance to feel more like a Tomlinson. But after Loreane bought O.T. an old truck to commute to and from the Hill, he began spending more and more time down there.[35] That allowed O.T. to fall back into his old habits, and while he never missed a TCU home game, Loreane and LaDainian noticed the change. O.T. resented them trying to control his life and tell him how to live it.[36]

The Horned Frogs and LT, however, had a great season, blowing out the competition in their first seven games. They ended the regular season with a 10–1 record, and LaDainian racked up 2,158 yards in running, 354 yards in receiving, and scored twenty-two touchdowns. TCU lost the Mobile Alabama Bowl to Southern Mississippi, but LaDainian won most valuable player for the game and ended his college career with the sixth-best record in Division I NCAA football history: 5,263 rushing yards. After the Mobile Alabama Bowl game, LaDainian signed with an agent, who pulled him out of school for a special training camp. He was going to the NFL Scouting Combines and needed to get in the best shape of his life.[37] His agent also handed him an envelope. La Dainian described it:

> I remember going back to the hotel with my mom, and it had to be like $75,000, all in a big envelope.
> I remember dumping it all on the bed, like, "Mom, I can't believe this. I cannot believe this. I've made it to the NFL. I'm going to the NFL."

That was one of the most exciting times in my life, knowing that not only did I just do something that nobody else in my family had done. I had just changed my family's life forever.[38]

Groups across the country named LaDainian an All-American and Senior Bowl most valuable player. He won the Doak Walker Award as the nation's best college running back and the Jim Brown Trophy for the NCAA's top running back. He also earned a nomination for the Heisman Trophy, the award for the best all-around college football player of the year.

In February 2001, LaDainian flew to Indianapolis for the NFL Scouting Combines, an invitation-only opportunity for scouts to evaluate three hundred potential players. I am not alone in drawing the obvious and uncomfortable comparison between the recruiters inspecting players and buyers at a nineteenth-century slave market inspecting a slave's teeth. The recruits undergo an extraordinarily thorough physical, and every major muscle group is measured and evaluated. Then the scouts put them through a series of workouts, including a forty-yard dash, a bench press, a vertical jump, broad jumps, a slalom run, and a shuttle run. Players undergo interviews and tests to see if they are psychologically prepared, and scouts use these measurements to determine whether to draft them and how much to pay them. LaDainian said the multimillion-dollar job offer makes it worthwhile.

The NFL uses a draft system, where teams each take turns choosing one player at a time from the pool of new recruits. The order is determined by a team's record the previous year, and coaches often trade their place in line to get a player they really want. The thirty-one teams can choose from 254 players. The NFL held the 2001 draft at Madison Square Garden, in New York.[39] LaDainian took his family and LaTorsha with him.

Despite the fact that LaDainian ran quick times at the combine, football pundits argued that he was too small for professional football, even at 221 pounds. But LaDainian was used to being underestimated.

The San Diego Chargers called his name when they made the fifth pick in the first round of the draft.[40] San Diego was LaDainian's first pick, too, since he knew they needed a starting running back. The nine-year-old's dream of playing professional football had, twelve years later, become a reality. The little boy who had worried about his mother making ends meet in Waco would now earn enough money to make sure she never made another mortgage payment. Loreane saw the reward for all the sacrifices she'd made so that LaDainian could take advantage of every opportunity.

LaDainian's agent sat down with the Chargers and began hammering out an agreement. As the negotiations dragged on, LaDainian moved to San Diego, and Torsha transferred her credits from TCU to the University of California-San Diego.[41] The two sides only reached agreement in time for LaDainian to play in the last preseason game against the Arizona Cardinals in Phoenix. The six-year, $38 million contract instantly transformed LaDainian's life.[42] Loreane, LaVar, and Londria watched him play in his first professional game.

Playing against the Washington Redskins, LaDainian proved that he was capable of delivering at the professional level, running for 113 yards, catching one pass, and scoring two touchdowns. The Chargers had ended the previous season 1–15, so LaDainian was already making a difference.[43]

LaDainian started in all sixteen games, ran for 1,236 yards, and scored ten touchdowns. His performance belied a seriousness not often found in rookies. He never celebrated touchdowns with an end-zone routine; he merely tossed the ball to a referee. Sportswriters started describing him as the quiet rookie, who rarely spoke up, but when he did, his teammates knew to listen because it was something important. The Chargers ended the 2001 season with five wins and eleven losses, but the team had made remarkable progress.

LaDainian hired a financial adviser and told him to prioritize saving money. Running backs are fragile, and small ones like LaDainian could see their careers end in a single tackle if hit the wrong way. In those early years, when the checks came only after he'd played the game, he chose to live frugally until he could build up a nest egg. He married LaTorsha on March 21, 2003.[44]

During his first three years in the NFL, LaDainian racked up statistics seldom seen before. He became the fifth player in NFL history to run more than two hundred yards in four games in a single season. He became the first to rush one thousand yards and catch one hundred passes in a single season. In 2004, LaDainian negotiated an extension on his contract, agreeing to play for San Diego until 2010 for as much as $60 million, with $24 million guaranteed. Chargers fans felt relieved to see their star player stay in San Diego.

Throughout those years, LaDainian reached out to his father, asking, cajoling, and even begging O.T. to get help. LaDainian understood that if O.T. was ever going to get control of his drug use, he needed to get off the Hill and into a stable, supportive, and drug-free environment. O.T., however, refused all attempts to help him.[45] Terry said his dad was stubborn: "I know he probably wasn't going. You wasn't going to tell him to do something what you wanted him to do, not if he didn't want to do it. And he'd talk plenty of trash, too. 'Leave me the f——— alone or you'll have a problem.' Yeah, he didn't play."[46]

O.T. lived in his mother's house, which was now falling into severe disrepair. He didn't want to leave the place and people he'd known his entire life. Every tree, every well-trod path, every nook and cranny of Tomlinson Hill reminded O.T. of the happiest days of his life. No amount of money or luxury could lure him away.[47] He also knew he could rely on Terry and Terry's mother, Jewell, who often gave him a meal or a place to sleep.[48] He watched his son play football on television but otherwise refused to change his lifestyle.

In the 2006 season, LaDainian set a league record by scoring nineteen touchdowns in a span of only six games and was the first player ever to score three touchdowns in each of four consecutive games. He started in all sixteen regular-season games and ran for 1,815 yards. He caught fifty-six passes for 508 yards and scored a total of thirty-one touchdowns. He also passed the ball for two touchdowns. He protected the ball, just as he had as a child, only fumbling once to the opposing team. The Chargers had their best season ever, with a 14–2 record. The Chargers lost to the New England Patriots in the play-offs, but national sportswriters named LaDainian the league's most valuable player for the season.[49]

LaDainian had achieved superstar status and made the pro bowl for the fourth year. The Associated Press named him Offensive Player of the Year and the NFL named him Man of the Year for his charity work, which included football camps for kids in San Diego and Waco. ESPN gave him awards for Male Athlete of the Year, Best Record-Breaking Performance, and Best NFL Athlete.[50] Those awards led to endorsement deals with Nike, AT&T, and the Campbell Soup Co., and the latter asked Loreane to be in a commercial with her son.

During the 2007 play-offs, a reporter from the *New York Times* wrote a feature story about an old slave plantation that bore LaDainian's name. The reporter tracked down O.T. at Vincent and Julie's old house:

> Standing in his front yard, next to a rusty pickup truck and a car that needs new spark plugs, Oliver Tomlinson sorted through his mail. "I'm looking for Super Bowl tickets," he said. "I know they're coming."
>
> Oliver explains to anyone passing by that his son plays football for the San Diego Chargers and that they are going to the Super Bowl. When it is suggested that they first need to win two playoff games, he waves his hand dismissively.
>
> Oliver lives in a one-story white house on a corner. He watches his son's games on a television set with a rabbit-ears antenna. He surrounds himself with space heaters. Rain clatters off his tin roof. He has no phone. Among the few decorations on the walls is an unframed photograph of the Rev. Dr. Martin Luther King Jr.
>
> "LaDainian has asked me to move to San Diego," Oliver said, spitting a stream of tobacco juice into a peanut can. "But I can't leave this hill. It's been too good to me. This hill has given me everything I need. The Lord blessed me with that boy on this hill."[51]

The story angered and embarrassed LaDainian, because it made him look like he didn't care about his father:

> It upset me because it portrayed it in a way that I wasn't helping my father. I didn't appreciate that because they didn't know the relationship we had and what I had tried to do for him.

Europeans' sense of superiority. European culture also considered the color white a symbol of purity, while equating black with evil. The fact that many Africans were Muslims also contributed to Christian bigotry against them.

A German physician named Franz Joseph Gall pioneered the study of the brain and believed that by measuring the size and shape of the skull, and mapping the bumps, scientists could accurately predict a person's intellect, personality, and character.[5] Phrenology developed alongside physiognomy, the study of the face, which claimed to explain an individual's behavior and personality.[6] These pseudoscientists believed that the less European a person appeared, the more inferior he or she was. Early anthropologists placed whites at the top of the hierarchy and decided blacks should go on the opposite end of the scale, just above apes, which Europeans had also first seen in Africa.[7] When Susan Tomlinson Jones first stepped on Tomlinson Hill, these ideas were widely accepted.

POWER AND PRIVILEGE

Until I got to Africa, I really didn't understand the power of my white skin to give me privileges denied to nonwhites. Shopkeepers and bureaucrats always sat up when a white person walked into the room and would order the African they were helping to get lost and empty the chair so I could sit down. When Kenyan police set up roadblocks to shake drivers down for bribes, I could confidently refuse to pay and know they'd wave me through. Even when I was broke and loitering, security guards at fine hotels always let me through, but they chased equally impoverished Africans away. My skin indicated that I was wealthy and potentially important, and I was always treated that way.

Upon returning to the United States, where whites are the majority, I came to see how easy it is for white Americans to dismiss their privileges. After all, if a person is one among many, he tends to compare himself to others like him. What such people don't see, and often willfully refuse to accept, is that white society has preserved privileges for itself while subtly denying them to nonwhites.

To overcome these prejudices, prosperous blacks rely on conspicu-
ous displays of wealth to signal to whites that they belong in expensive
restaurants or in the finest hotels. I can show up to a top restaurant
wearing a three-hundred-dollar suit and expect service, but a black
man knows that to get equal treatment he needs to arrive in a sports
car and a one-thousand-dollar suit. That's the power of whiteness.

Many white Americans ridicule African-Americans for being paranoid and accuse them of playing the race card to cover up their inad-
equacies. As an American who has worked in countries where people
hate the United States, I've felt the heat on the back of my neck from
people staring at me. While a soldier in Europe, I could sense hostility
from Germans who showed me perfect courtesy but still somehow
made their distaste for me clear with slow-motion service, the roll of
an eye, or the click of a tongue. These observations are not paranoia,
scientists call them microaggressions.

Scientists watched how people of different groups interacted to see
what was happening to make minorities detect hostility where none
was obvious. They documented tiny verbal and nonverbal snubs that
members of dominant groups displayed toward people in the minority
group. Classic examples are the white woman who clutches her purse
tighter when she sees a black person, or the hostess who seats a black
couple next to the kitchen when there are better tables available. People
who are part of the dominant culture will show microaggression
against anyone they perceive as "the other," whether from a different
race, country, culture, or gender.[8] The person who perpetrates them
usually doesn't notice what he's done and denies acting out of prejudice. Oftentimes, the victim will not realize what happened, either,
but that person will still feel vaguely humiliated. The person who rec-
ognizes the microaggression feels even more like an outsider and a
second-class citizen.[9]

Microaggressions are not limited only to social niceties, and if
unchecked, they can ruin the lives of minorities. That woman who unconsciously clutches her purse when she sees an African-American
might work as a personnel manager for a major corporation. When she
looks at a job applicant, she may react unconsciously when she sees a

black-sounding name on a résumé or interviews someone with a black-sounding voice. She doesn't think of herself as racist, doesn't intentionally make racially motivated decisions, but she also doesn't recognize her racist behavior. She will insist that she doesn't care if someone is black, not realizing that denying the role race plays in our society is itself a microaggression that negates some individuals' real experiences of discrimination.[10]

Some leaders routinely call for an end to affirmative action, an end to political correctness, and an end to talking about race. A white woman in Marlin told me that since I wasn't alive during slave times, there was no reason to confront that history. In my research, I found that people love to embrace their heritage until they're asked to talk about America's racist history. Few people are ready to publicly acknowledge that their ancestors murdered, raped, and maimed others to maintain a racist regime that guaranteed their and their offspring's prosperity.

Writing this book profoundly changed how I feel about my homeland and led me to question the factors behind my successes. Did my elementary school teachers give me more attention because I was blond and blue-eyed? Did the army promotion boards relate to me more than to black soldiers because I used proper diction and mirrored my white superiors? Did I get my first journalism job because I was a white man in Africa, someone fellow foreign correspondents could better relate to? Was my success largely because as a white man I could more easily gain access to the big stories in Africa and the Middle East? The answer can only be yes to all of these, and it's because of my ancestors. Whites born into middle-class or wealthy homes must acknowledge that they started out in pole position.

When examining the history of American race relations, one can focus on the progress made by the brave and talented few or focus instead on the thousands of racial injustices that take place every day. What one should never do, however, is assume that progress is constant and inevitable. The history of the Ku Klux Klan and the pushback of African-American economic power shows that setbacks are possible. The embers of our racist past are far from cold, but they are easily extinguished.

A CURE FOR RACISM

Many bigots say the hatred and disgust they feel is powerful, and the strength of that hatred gives them certainty in their feelings. The impulse to hate feels instinctive, which again raises the question, Is bigotry part of our nature, or the product of nurture? The answer, neuroscientists are discovering, is both.

Humans can recognize a person's skin color, gender, age, body shape, clothing, cleanliness, and an enormous amount of other information in just a few milliseconds. Depending on our analysis, other parts of our brain will react. When average people are shown a photograph of a homeless person or a drug addict while in a functional magnetic resonance imaging scanner, or fMRI, the insula of the brain lights up. That is the part of the brain associated with disgust; the normal parts of the brain that react to people shut down. The test subjects' brains don't conceive of those people as fellow humans. When researchers showed white American men images of unfamiliar black men, the amygdala activated. That's the limbic part of the brain, which is associated with the processing of emotions, such as fear and vigilance. White men looking at images of blacks also didn't use the parts of their brains normally activated when looking at white faces. Whites also had a more difficult time remembering the faces of black strangers than those of other whites. The more people look like us, the more our brain reacts positively, while the less familiar the face, the greater the hostility.[11]

Yet researchers discovered that what our brains are really determining is whether a stranger is one of "us." Physical traits are only one part of the story. If someone is wearing clothes similar to ours, our brains react differently than if someone is wearing an item that identifies them as an enemy. Clothing and community emblems were important for humans when they lived in tribes that competed for limited resources. In those early millennia, neighboring tribes shared a common skin color, making that factor irrelevant in determining whether a stranger was a friend or foe.[12] We use clothing and adornments to identify one another and rely on generations of experiences.

The power of culture and tradition is clear because people are more likely to act on their bigotry when they feel under pressure or are commanded by an authority figure, or if they think they will win societal approval.[13] Oftentimes, this tradition of bigotry is passed on subconsciously.

In the study of white men looking at images of black men, Ohio State researcher William Cunningham found that the amount of activity in the amygdala was directly related to how high the subjects had scored previously on a test for racism, but the reaction was easily mitigated. When shown an image of a black man they recognized, they showed no amygdala reaction. Cunningham also found that the fear and vigilance reaction was most consistently activated when the image of an unfamiliar black man was flashed for only thirty milliseconds, just long enough for the subconscious to register it. When he left the image up long enough for the brain to process it, about 525 milliseconds, the amygdala did not activate and the parts of the brain associated with inhibition and self-control took over.[14] The neocortex, home of more advanced thinking, was overriding the instinctive impulses of the amygdala.[15] Biological instincts exist, but what activates them is learned and easily overcome.

The brain rewires itself as we learn. For instance, a white American may at first perceive a black man as a threat, until he notices a police uniform. The more a white person sees a black person as a source of security, the less the brain will consider people of that race a threat. As time passes, the amygdala will spark less and the neocortex will require less energy to override it. David Amodio, an assistant professor of psychology at New York University, found that less prejudiced people used their neocortex to regulate their behavior more than racists.[16]

Social psychologists have found the best way to stop prejudice is to place members of different races on the same team with a common goal, a dynamic LaDainian recognized when playing high school football. In dozens of studies, researchers documented that once people form bonds through team work, they overcome the prejudices they learned as children. This is called the "ingroup identity model." The more you make people feel part of the same group, or tribe, the less prejudice they feel based on racial, ethnic, or religious differences.[17] This theory has special application when it comes to school desegregation.

American children in the twenty-first century are by any measure the least racially bigoted of any generation ever tested, thanks largely to integration. However, 25 percent still report experiencing ethnic or racial bias, 10 percent report being called a bigoted name, and 40 percent have seen bigoted graffiti on campus, according to 2007 federal data. While those statistics indicate a lot remains to be done, only two generations ago southern lawmakers forbade black and white children from attending the same schools. The key to the progress has been genuine, face-to-face cooperation in the classroom. Where children of different races took part in programs that made them feel part of a single group, 94 percent showed no outward signs of bigotry based on race or ethnicity.[18] I can attest that my experience in desegregated schools made a difference in my life, and LaDainian has said similar interactions affected him and those around him the same way.

THE HILL

I made my first trip to Tomlinson Hill a few years after LaDainian's father died. I'll never forget reaching the tabernacle and seeing for the first time the red tin letters that spell out the name Tomlinson Hill. Exploring the Hill created a tangle of conflicting emotions. I was thrilled to visit my ancestral home but aware of the bad things that had happened there. I was enthralled by the fields, the wildflowers, and the quietness, but ashamed of its original sin. The Hill was where I took the first step on a journey that led me to fascinating people who were generous with their stories.

Currently, no black or white Tomlinson lives on the Hill, though Terry owns what is left of Vincent and Julie's old home, now uninhabitable. LaDainian told me he is looking to buy a ranch in Falls County but is quick to add that his wife doesn't share his enthusiasm for country living. I have no desire to live there, and my curiosity about our families' history is quenched. LaDainian and I both feel more complete knowing our heritage.

Many people have asked whether I felt bad about revealing my ancestors' dirty laundry. I emphatically tell them no. In South Africa and

Rwanda, I learned that the only way a civilization can heal after one community commits a heinous crime against another is to confess and make amends. That was done by the Truth and Reconciliation Commission in South Africa, and at the Gacaca courts in Rwanda. In that spirit, I offer this unflinching account of the past and its impact on the present. Perhaps if we all were to do the same, we could start the painful but essential conversation about America's original sin and create a more perfect nation.

ENDNOTES

CHAPTER 1

1. Marjorie Rogers, "Beloved Pioneer and Leader Expires Tuesday," *Marlin Democrat,* January 23, 1943.
2. Ibid.
3. Marjorie Rogers, "Obituary for Col. William G. Etheridge," *Dallas Morning News,* September 17, 1922.

CHAPTER 2

1. Randolph B. Campbell, *An Empire for Slavery: The Peculiar Institution in Texas 1821–1865* (Baton Rouge: Louisiana State University Press, 1989), 55.
2. U.S. Bureau of the Census, 1850 Census for Conecuh County, Alabama.
3. Frank Calvert Oltorf, *The Marlin Compound: Letters of a Singular Family* (Austin: University of Texas Press, 1968), 64.
4. U.S. Bureau of the Census, 1850 Census for Conecuh County, Alabama.
5. Oltorf, *The Marlin Compound,* 42.
6. Ibid., 43.
7. Campbell, *An Empire for Slavery,* 61.
8. Oltorf, *The Marlin Compound,* 46.
9. Campbell, *An Empire for Slavery,* 68.
10. Oltorf, *The Marlin Compound,* 47.
11. Ibid.

12. Ibid.

13. Ibid.

14. Ibid.

15. Falls County Commissioner's Court, "Minutes Book 1A," in *County Court Minutes* (Falls County, TX, January 1852).

16. Ibid.

17. Oltorf, *The Marlin Compound*, 47.

18. Ibid., 48.

19. Alwyn Barr, *Black Texans: A History of African Americans in Texas, 1528–1995* (Norman: University of Oklahoma Press, 1996), 18.

20. Ibid.

21. Campbell, *An Empire for Slavery*, 134.

22. Barr, *Black Texans*, 20.

23. Campbell, *An Empire for Slavery*, 193.

24. Barr, *Black Texans*, 18.

25. Ibid., 20.

26. Oltorf, *The Marlin Compound*, 62.

27. Ibid., 53.

28. Ibid.

29. Ibid., 65.

30. Lillian Schiller St. Romain, *Western Falls County, Texas* (Austin: Texas State Historical Association, 1951), 96.

31. Oltorf, *The Marlin Compound*, 58.

32. Barr, *Black Texans*, 19.

33. Oltorf, *The Marlin Compound*, 58.

34. Ibid., 62.

35. Ibid., 58.

36. Ibid., 64.

37. Ibid., 66.

38. Ibid., 65.

39. Ibid., 66.

40. Paul Sniderman and Edward Carmines. "Tangled Politics," In *Racism*, ed. Martin Bulmer and John Solomos (Oxford: Oxford University Press, 1999), 401.

41. Oltorf, *The Marlin Compound*, 70.

CHAPTER 3

1. Lillian Schiller St. Romain, *Western Falls County, Texas* (Austin: Texas State Historical Association, 1951), 45.

2. Ibid., 48.

3. Frank Calvert Oltorf, *The Marlin Compound: Letters of a Singular Family* (Austin: University of Texas Press, 1968), 71.

4. Ibid., 75.

5. Randolph B. Campbell, *Gone to Texas: A History of the Lone Star State* (New York: Oxford University Press, 2012), 216.

6. Oltorf, *The Marlin Compound*, 74.

7. Ibid., 100.

8. Ibid., 105.

9. Ibid., 79.

10. Alwyn Barr, *Black Texans: A History of African Americans in Texas, 1528–1994* (Norman: University of Oklahoma Press, 1996), 20.

11. Randolph B. Campbell, *An Empire for Slavery: The Peculiar Institution in Texas 1821–1865* (Baton Rouge: Louisiana State University Press, 1989), 133.

12. Abigail Curlee Holbrook, "A Glimpse of Life on Antebellum Slave Plantations in Texas," *The Southwestern Historical Quarterly* 76, (1973): 361–83.

13. Ibid.

14. *A Memorial and Biographical History of McLennan, Falls, Bell and Coryell Counties, Texas* (Chicago: Lewis Publishing Company, 1893) 483–485.

15. Ibid.

16. Oltorf, *The Marlin Compound*, 79.

17. Barr, *Black Texans*, 17.

18. Ron Tyler and Lawrence Murphy, eds., *The Slave Narratives of Texas* (Austin: State House Press, 1997), vii.

19. Federal Writers' Project, Work Projects Administration, *Slave Narratives: A Folk History of Slavery in the United States from Interviews with Former Slaves,* Vol. 2: *Texas Narratives* (Washington, D.C.: Library of Congress, 1936–1938), 534.

20. Ibid., 8.

21. Ibid., 11.

22. Ibid., 8.

23. Campbell, *An Empire for Slavery*, 138.

24. Tyler, Murphy, eds., *The Slave Narratives of Texas*, 38.

25. Federal Writers' Project, Work Projects Administration, *Slave Narratives: A Folk History of Slavery in the United States from Interviews with Former Slaves,* Vol. 16: *Texas Narratives* (Washington, D.C.: Library of Congress, 1936–1938). These interviews are available online.

26. Ibid.

27. Barr, *Black Texans*, 15.

28. Holbrook, "A Glimpse of Life on Antebellum Slave Plantations in Texas."

29. Barr, *Black Texans*, 17.

30. Campbell, *An Empire for Slavery*, 138.

31. Tyler and Murphy, eds., *The Slave Narratives of Texas*, 50.

32. Ibid., 37.

33. *A Memorial and Biographical History of McLennan, Falls, Bell and Coryell Counties, Texas*, 882.

34. Ibid.

35. Oltorf, *The Marlin Compound*, 75.

36. Ibid., 79.
37. Falls County Probate Court, "Estate of J. K. Tomlinson," in *Minutes*, vol. 1 (Falls County, TX, Probate Court, 1865–1867), 149.
38. Marjorie Rogers, "Obituary for Col. William G. Etheridge," *Dallas Morning News*, September 17, 1922.
39. *A Memorial and Biographical History of McLennan, Falls, Bell and Coryell Counties, Texas*, 882.
40. "Arrival of the Steamship Matagorda, the Coldest Week on Record," *Galveston Weekly News*, December 27, 1859.
41. *A Memorial and Biographical History of McLennan, Falls, Bell and Coryell Counties, Texas*, 882.
42. Rogers, "Obituary for Col. William G. Etheridge."
43. Effie Cowan, "Interview with Robert E. L. Tomlinson, White Pioneer of Marlin, Texas," oral history, Federal Writers' Project (Washington, D.C.: Library of Congress, 1936).
44. U.S. Bureau of the Census, Census for Falls County, Texas, film 653–1293, p. 146, Family History Library, Salt Lake City, UT.
45. Barr, *Black Texans*, 22.
46. Federal Writers' Project, Work Projects Administration, *Slave Narratives*.
47. Author's interview with Robert Stem, state district court judge for Falls County, May 2010.
48. Author's interview with David Tinsley, owner of the Tomlinson Hill homestead in 2010, May 15, 2010.
49. Manford Eugene Jones, "A History of Cotton Culture Along the Brazos" (master's thesis, University of New Mexico, 1939), 36.
50. Ibid., 37.
51. Ibid.
52. Barr, *Black Texans*, 25.
53. Jones, "A History of Cotton Culture Along the Brazos."
54. Ibid.

CHAPTER 4

1. U.S. Bureau of the Census, 1860 Census for Falls County, Texas, film M653_1293, p. 8, Family History Library, Salt Lake City, UT.
2. Randolph B. Campbell, *An Empire for Slavery: The Peculiar Institution in Texas 1821–1865* (Baton Rouge: Louisiana State University Press, 1989), 274.
3. Effie Cowan, "Interview with Robert E. L. Tomlinson, White Pioneer of Marlin, Texas," oral history, Federal Writers' Project (Washington, D.C.: Library of Congress, 1936).
4. Lillian Schiller St. Romain, *Western Falls County, Texas* (Austin: Texas State Historical Association, 1951), 51.
5. Ibid., 94.
6. Campbell, *An Empire for Slavery*, 224.

7. Frank Calvert Oltorf, *The Marlin Compound: Letters of a Singular Family* (Austin: University of Texas Press, 1968), 105.

8. Campbell, *An Empire for Slavery,* 227–30.

9. Ibid.

10. Ibid., 224.

11. Ibid., 225.

12. Ibid., 226.

13. Ibid., 225.

14. Oltorf, *The Marlin Compound,* 106.

15. Campbell, *An Empire for Slavery,* 227.

16. Ibid., 224.

17. Sam Houston, "Address at the Union Mass Meeting, Austin, Texas, September 22, 1860," in *The Writings of Sam Houston, 1813–1863,* Vol. 8, ed. Amelia W. Williams and Eugene C. Barker (Austin: University of Texas Press, 1943), 154–55.

18. Campbell, *An Empire for Slavery,* 228.

19. Oltorf, *The Marlin Compound,* 74.

20. *A Memorial and Biographical History of McLennan, Falls, Bell and Coryell Counties, Texas* (Chicago: Lewis Publishing Company, 1893), 194.

21. Frank Calvert Oltorf, "Under the Confederacy," in *History of Falls County,* ed. Roy Eddins (Marlin: Old Settlers and Veterans Associations of Falls County, Texas, 1947), 126.

22. Ibid.

23. "Declaration of Causes," February 2, 1861, at http://www.tsl.state.tx.us/ref /abouttx/secession/2feb1861.html (accessed December 11, 2012).

24. Campbell, *An Empire for Slavery,* 230.

25. Marjorie Rogers, "Obituary for Col. William G. Etheridge," *Dallas Morning News,* September 17, 1922.

26. Oltorf, *The Marlin Compound,* 106.

CHAPTER 5

1. Clayton E. Jewett, *Texas in the Confederacy: An Experiment in Nation Building* (Columbia: University of Missouri Press, 2002), 65.

2. James M. McPherson, *Battle Cry of Freedom: The Civil War Era* (New York: Oxford University Press, 1988), 333.

3. Ralph A. Wooster, *Texas and Texans in the Civil War* (Austin, TX: Eakin Press, 1995), 19.

4. Randolph B. Campbell, *Gone to Texas: The Lone Star State* (New York: Oxford University Press, 2012), 244–245.

5. Ralph A. Wooster, *Texas and Texans in the Civil War,* 25.

6. Randolph B. Campbell, *An Empire for Slavery: The Peculiar Institution in Texas 1821–1865* (Baton Rouge: Louisiana State University Press, 1989), 71.

7. Lillian Schiller St. Romain, *Western Falls County, Texas* (Austin: Texas State Historical Association, 1951), 51.

8. Marjorie Rogers, "More Than the Passing of a Good Man." *Marlin Democrat,* January 23, 1943.

9. "Bills of Sale," Evergreen, Alabama, 1861–1862, Confederate Army Records ("Rebel Archives"), Natural Archives, Washington, D.C.

10. Churchill Jones, "Letter Requesting Assistance in Gaining a Pardon," Falls on the Brazos, September 21, 1865. "Rebel Archives," National Archives, Washington, D.C.

11. "Bills of Sale," Evergreen, Alabama, 1861–1862.

12. David J. Eicher, *The Longest Night: A Military History of the Civil War* (New York: Simon & Schuster, 2001), p. 99.

13. Carl H. Moneyhon, *Texas After the Civil War: The Struggle of Reconstruction* (College Station: Texas A&M University Press, 2004), 8.

14. "Estate of Mary Travis," Falls County, TX, Probate Court, February 1865.

15. Oltorf, Frank Calvert. *The Marlin Compound: Letters of a Singular Family* (Austin: University of Texas Press, 1968), 155.

16. "Enlistment Records," Waco, Texas, 1861–1862, Confederate Army Records ("Rebel Archives"), National Archives, Washington, D.C.

17. Ibid.

18. Campbell, *Gone to Texas,* 216.

19. Barr, "Texas Coastal Defense, 1861–1865," 4.

20. "Enlistment Records," Waco, Texas, 1861–1862.

21. Oltorf, *The Marlin Compound,* 107.

22. Ibid., 109.

23. William Scurry, letter, *Tri-Weekly Telegraph* (Houston, TX), April 24, 1863.

24. *War of the Rebellion: Official Records of the Union and Confederate Armies,* series 1, vol. 15 (Washington, D.C.: Government Printing Office, 1896), 1064.

25. Barr, "Texas Coastal Defense, 1861–1865," 10.

26. Wooster, *Texas and Texans in the Civil War,* 65.

27. Ibid., 63.

28. "Unit Records," Company K, First Texas Heavy Artillery, Galveston, Texas, 1861–1862, Confederate Army Records ("Rebel Archives"), National Archives, Washington, D.C.

29. Wooster, *Texas and Texans in the Civil War,* 63.

30. Ibid.

31. Ibid., 64.

32. Frank Moore, ed., *The Rebellion Record: A Diary of American Events,* vol. 9. (New York: Van Nostrand, 1865), 726.

33. "Unit Records," Company K, First Texas Heavy Artillery, Galveston, Texas, 1861–1862.

34. Moore, ed., *The Rebellion Record,* 343.

35. Author's interview with Alwyn Barr, September 17, 2010.

36. Moore, ed., *The Rebellion Record,* 343.

37. Barr, "Texas Coastal Defense, 1861–1865," 2–13, 11–13.

38. Moore, ed., *The Rebellion Record,* 339.

39. Barr, "Texas Coastal Defense, 1861–1865," 14–15.

40. Ibid., 16.

41. "Unit Records," Company K, First Texas Heavy Artillery, Galveston, Texas, 1861–1862.

42. Moore, ed., *The Rebellion Record,* 338.

43. Barr, "Texas Coastal Defense, 1861–1865," 16.

44. Ibid.

45. Ibid., 18.

46. Wooster, *Texas and Texans in the Civil War,* 67.

CHAPTER 6

1. Ralph A. Wooster, *Texas and Texans in the Civil War* (Austin, TX: Eakin Press, 1995), 69.

2. Alwyn Barr, "Texas Coastal Defense, 1861–1865," *Southwestern Historical Quarterly,* 65 (July 1961): 23.

3. Frank Calvert Oltorf, *The Marlin Compound: Letters of a Singular Family* (Austin: University of Texas Press, 1968), 116.

4. Ibid., 115.

5. Ibid., 118.

6. Wooster, *Texas and Texans in the Civil War,* 76.

7. Oltorf, *The Marlin Compound,* 121.

8. Ibid., 126.

9. Wooster, *Texas and Texans in the Civil War,* 77.

10. Frank, Moore, ed., *The Rebellion Record: A Diary of American Events,* vol. 9 (New York: Van Nostrand, 1865), 734.

11. Barr, "Texas Coastal Defense, 1861–1865," 28–29.

12. Moore, ed., *The Rebellion Record,* 245.

13. "Unit Records," Company K, First Texas Heavy Artillery. Galveston, Texas, 1861–1862, Confederate Army Records ("Rebel Archives"), National Archives, Washington, D.C.

14. Wooster, *Texas and Texans in the Civil War,* 92.

15. Moore, ed. *The Rebellion Record,* 736.

16. Ibid.

17. Wooster, *Texas and Texans in the Civil War,* 138.

18. Ibid., 140.

19. Oltorf, *The Marlin Compound,* 137–139.

20. Moore, ed., *The Rebellion Record,* 740.

21. Oltorf, *The Marlin Compound,* 139.

22. Ibid., 140.

23. Moore, ed. *The Rebellion Record,* 733.

24. *War of the Rebellion: Official Records of the Union and Confederate Armies,* Series I, vol. 34, Part II (Washington, D.C.: Government Printing Office, 1896), 320; Wooster, *Texas and Texan in Texans in the Civil War,* 148.

25. Oltorf, *The Marlin Compound,* 142.

26. Henry Cheaver, "Certificate of Disablity for Discharge," Army of the Confederate States, Galveston, Texas, May 13, 1864.

27. "Unit Records," Fourth Texas Cavalry, Galveston, Texas, 1861–1862, Confederate Army Records ("Rebel Archives"), National Archives, Washington, D.C.

28. Wooster, *Texas and Texans in the Civil War,* 171.

29. *A Memorial and Biographical History of McLennan, Falls, Bell and Coryell Counties, Texas* (Chicago: Lewis Publishing Company, 1893), 882.

30. Wooster, *Texas and Texans in the Civil War,* 185.

31. Author's interview with Robert Stem, state district court judge for Falls County, TX, May 2010.

32. Federal Writers' Project, Works Progress Administration, *Slave Narratives: A Folk History of Slavery in the United States from Interviews with Former Slaves,* vol. 16: *Texas Narratives* (Washington, D.C.: Library of Congress, 1936–1938). These interviews are available online.

CHAPTER 7

1. *A Memorial and Biographical History of McLennan, Falls, Bell and Coryell Counties, Texas* (Chicago: Lewis Publishing Company, 1893) 882.

2. "Estate of J. K. Tomlinson," in *Minutes,* vol 1 (Falls County, TX, Probate Court, 1865–1867), 391.

3. Carl H. Moneyhon, *Texas After the Civil War: The Struggle of Reconstruction* (College Station: Texas A&M University Press, 2004), 29.

4. Ibid., 16.

5. Ibid.

6. Ibid., 21.

7. Ibid.

8. Ibid., 15.

9. Ibid., 22.

10. Ibid., 24.

11. Ibid., 27–28.

12. William L. Richter, *Overreached on All Sides: The Freedmen's Bureau Administrators in Texas, 1865–1868* (College Station: Texas A&M University Press, 1991), 23.

13. Ibid., 19.

14. Ibid., 20.

15. Ibid., 25.

16. Moneyhon, *Texas After the Civil War,* p. 33.

17. Richter, *Overreached on All Sides,* 30–32.

18. Moneyhon, *Texas After the Civil War*, 66.

19. Richter, *Overreached on All Sides*, 37.

20. Ibid.

21. Ibid., 49.

22. Ibid., 54.

23. Christopher B. Bean, "A Stranger Amongst Strangers: An Analysis of the Freedmen's Bureau's Sub-Assistant Commissioners in Texas." (Ph.D. diss. University of North Texas, 2008), 253–245.

24. Richter, *Overreached on All Sides*, 253.

25. Churchill Jones, "Application for Amnesty," September 21, 1865, National Archives, Washington, D.C.

26. Bureau of Refugees, Freedmen, and Abandoned Lands. Records of the Assistant Commissioner for the State of Texas, 1865–1869, National Archives, Washington, D.C.

27. Ibid.

28. Barry A. Crouch, *The Freedmen's Bureau and Black Texans*, Austin: University of Texas Press, 1992, 20.

29. Richter, *Overreached on All Sides*, 88.

30. Ibid., 105.

31. Moneyhon, *Texas After the Civil War*, 27.

32. Ibid., 48.

33. Ibid., 50.

34. Ibid., 52–53.

35. Richter, *Overreached on All Sides*, 99.

36. Ibid., 86.

37. Moneyhon, *Texas After the Civil War*, 55–56.

38. Ibid., 60.

39. Ibid., 45.

40. Ibid., 60.

41. Ibid.

42. Ibid.

43. Ibid.

44. Ibid., 62.

45. Richter, *Overreached on All Sides*, 432.

46. Ibid., 90.

47. Ibid., 99.

48. Ibid.

49. Ibid., 202.

50. "Estate of J. K. Tomlinson," *Minutes*, vol. 1 (Falls County, TX, Probate Court, 1865–1867), 152.

51. Moneyhon, *Texas After the Civil War*, 65.

52. "Estate of J. K. Tomlinson." *Minutes*, vol. 1, 152.

53. Ibid.

54. Ibid.

55. Richter, *Overreached on All Sides,* 481.
56. "Letters Sent and Received," Officials Records of the Bureau of Freedmen, Marlin, TX, 1867, National Archives, Washington, D.C.
57. Ibid.
58. Ibid.
59. Ibid.
60. F. B. Sturgis, "Field Office Records of the Bureau of Freedmen for Marlin, Texas," May 23, 1867, National Archives, Washington, D.C.
61. Richter, *Overreached on All Sides,* 250.
62. Sturgis, "Field Office Records of the Bureau of Freedmen for Marlin, Texas," May 23, 1867.
63. Moneyhon, *Texas After the Civil War,* 67.
64. Sturgis, "Field Office Records of the Bureau of Freedmen for Marlin, Texas," May 23, 1867.
65. "Letters Sent and Received."
66. Moneyhon, *Texas After the Civil War,* 87.

CHAPTER 8

1. Carl H. Moneyhon, *Texas After the Civil War: The Struggle of Reconstruction* (College Station: Texas A&M University Press, 2004), 69.
2. Ibid.
3. Ibid., 70.
4. Ibid., 71.
5. Ibid.
6. F. B. Sturgis, "Field Office Records of the Bureau of Freedmen for Marlin, Texas," May 23, 1867, National Archives, Washington, D.C.
7. Moneyhon, *Texas After the Civil War,* 73.
8. Ibid., 75.
9. Ibid., 77.
10. Ibid.
11. Ibid., 79.
12. Ibid., 82.
13. Ibid.
14. Ibid., 85.
15. Ibid., 85, 100.
16. Ibid., 94–95.
17. Ibid.
18. United States Congress, House of Representatives, Committee on Elections, *Papers in the Contested Election Case of Grafton vs. Conner in the Second District of Texas* (Washington, D.C.: Government Printing Office, 1870), 8.
19. Ibid.
20. Moneyhon, *Texas After the Civil War,* 95.
21. William L. Richter, *Overreached on All Sides: The Freedmen's Bureau Admin-*

istrators in Texas, 1865–1868 (College Station: Texas A&M University Press, 1991), 273.

22. Old Settlers and Veterans Association of Falls County, Texas, *History of Falls County, Texas*, ed. Roy Eddins (Marlin, TX: Old Settlers and Veterans Association of Falls County, Texas, 1947), 62.

23. United States Congress, House of Representatives, Committee on Elections. *Papers in the Contested Election of Grafton vs. Conner in the Second District of Texas.*

24. Moneyhon, *Texas After the Civil War*, 98.

25. "Estate of J. K. Tomlinson," in *Minutes*, vol. 1 (Falls County, TX, Probate Court, 1865–1867), 452.

26. Ibid.

27. Ibid.

28. Ibid.

29. Falls County Historical Commission, *Families of Falls County* (Austin, TX: Eakin Press, 1987), 454–455.

30. U.S. Bureau of the Census, 1870 Census fr Falls, Texas, film 553083, page 116A, Family History Library, Salt Lake City, UT.

31. Frank Calvert Oltorf. *The Marlin Compound: Letters of a Singular Family* (Austin: University of Texas Press, 1968), 158.

32. Ibid.

33. Moneyhon, *Texas After the Civil War*, 100.

34. Ibid., 100–101.

35. Ibid.

36. Ibid., 110.

37. Ibid.

38. Ibid., 115.

39. Ibid., 116.

40. Ibid.

41. Ibid.

42. Ibid., 118.

43. Ibid.

CHAPTER 9

1. Carl H. Moneyhon, *Texas After the Civil War: The Struggle of Reconstruction* (College Station: Texas A&M University Press, 2004), 119.

2. Ibid., 121.

3. Ibid., 122–123.

4. Ibid., 124.

5. Ibid., 127–128.

6. Ibid., 135.

7. Lillian Schiller St. Romain, *Western Falls County, Texas* (Austin: Texas State Historical Association, 1951) 62.

8. Moneyhon, *Texas After the Civil War*, 158.

9. Ibid. 160.

10. Edward King, *The Great South* (Hartford Conn.: American Publishing Company, 1875), 65.

11. Randolph B. Campbell, *Grass-roots Reconstruction in Texas, 1865–1880* (Baton Rouge: Louisiana State University Press, 1997), 186–187.

12. Moneyhon, *Texas After the Civil War,* 171–172.

13. Ibid., 172–173.

14. Ibid., 174.

15. Ibid., 176–177.

16. Ibid., 178.

17. Ibid., 182.

18. Ibid., 183.

19. Ibid., 185.

20. Ibid., 184.

21. Old Settlers and Veterans Association of Falls County, Texas, *History of Falls County, Texas,* ed. Roy Eddins (Marlin, TX: Old Settlers and Veterans Association of Falls County, Texas, 1947), 165.

22. Ibid., 167–168.

23. Effie Cowan, "Interview with Robert E. L. Tomlinson, White Pioneer of Marlin, Texas," oral history, Federal Writers' Project (Washington, D.C.: Library of Congress, 1936).

24. Moneyhon, *Texas After the Civil War,* 186.

25. Ibid., 188.

CHAPTER 10

1. U.S. Bureau of the Census, 1870 Census for Falls County, Texas, film 553083, page 116A, Family History Library, Salt Lake City, UT.

2. Ibid.

3. Old Settlers and Veterans Association of Falls County, Texas, *History of Falls County, Texas,* ed. Roy Eddins (Marlin, TX: Old Settlers and Veterans Association of Falls County, Texas, 1947), 171.

4. Marlin Bicentennial Heritage Committee, *Marlin 1851–1976* (Marlin, TX: Marlin Chamber of Commerce, 1976), 11.

5. Carl H. Moneyhon, *Texas After the Civil War: The Struggle of Reconstruction* (College Station: Texas A&M University Press, 2004), 189.

6. Ibid.

7. Ibid.

8. Ibid., 190.

9. Ibid., 191.

10. Ibid.

11. Ibid., 194.

12. Ibid., 197.

13. Ibid.

14. Ibid.
15. Marlin Bicentennial Heritage Committee, *Marlin 1851–1976* (Marlin, TX: Marlin Chamber of Commerce, 1976), 12.
16. Ibid., 15.
17. Ibid., 25.
18. Ibid., 17.
19. Ibid.
20. Roy Eddins, *Marlin's Public Schools from the 1840s to 1960* (Marlin, TX: Marlin Ex-Students Association, 1960), 33.
21. Randolph B. Campbell, *Grass-Roots Reconstruction in Texas, 1865–1880* (Baton Rouge: Louisiana State University Press, 1997).
22. Eddins, *Marlin's Public Schools from the 1840s to 1960,* 32.
23. Ibid., 34.
24. Lillian Schiller St. Romain, *Western Falls County, Texas* (Austin: Texas State Historical Association, 1951), 62.
25. Alwyn Barr, *Black Texans: A History of African Americans in Texas, 1528-1995* (Norman: University of Oklahoma Press, 1996), 100.
26. St. Romain, *Western Falls County, Texas,* 62.
27. Ibid., 65.
28. Falls County Historial Commission, *Families of Falls County* (Austin, TX: Eakin Press, 1987), 454.
29. Ibid., 456.
30. Moneyhon, *Texas After the Civil War,* 203.
31. Ibid., 204.
32. Ibid., 205.
33. Thad Sitton and James H. Conrad, *Freedom Colonies: Independent Black Texans in the Time of Jim Crow* (Austin: University of Texas Press, 2005), 2.
34. St. Romain, *Western Falls County, Texas,* 112.
35. Sitton and Conrad, *Freedom Colonies,* 18.
36. Ibid., 16.
37. Ibid., 17.
38. Ibid.
39. Federal Writers' Project, Works Progress Administration, "*Slave Narratives: A Folk History of Slavery in the United States from Interviews with Former Slaves,* Vol. 16: *Texas Narratives* (Washington, D.C.: Library of Congress, 1936–1938). These interviews are available online.
40. Sitton and Conrad, *Freedom Colonies,* 18.
41. Ibid., 23.
42. Ibid., 44.
43. Ibid., 23.
44. Ibid., 43.
45. Ibid., 110.
46. Old Settlers and Veterans Association of Falls County, Texas, *History of Falls County, Texas,* ed. Roy Eddins, 185.

47. Sitton and Conrad, *Freedom Colonies,* 58.

48. Ibid., 59.

49. Ibid., 70.

50. U.S. Bureau of the Census, 1870 Census for Falls County, Texas, film 553083, p. 117B.

51. Wedding license for "Tomlinson, Milo and Phillis," issued by the Falls County clerk, Marlin, Texas, April 16, 1869.

52. U.S. Bureau of the Census, 1870 Census for Falls County, Texas, film 553083, p. 117B.

53. Ibid.

54. St. Romain, *Western Falls County, Texas,* 112.

55. Barr, *Black Texans,* 107.

56. Sitton and Conrad, *Freedom Colonies,* 90.

57. Barr, *Black Texans,* 109.

58. Ibid.

59. This quote and the subsequent one are from an interview by Lisa Kaselak with Pinkie Taylor Price, April 17, 2011.

60. Barr, *Black Texans,* 89.

61. Ibid., 90.

62. Ibid., 96.

63. Ibid.

64. Ibid., 101.

65. Ibid., 73.

66. U.S. Bureau of the Census, 1880 Census for Falls County, Texas, film 1255302, p. 252C, Family History Library, Salt Lake City, UT.

CHAPTER 11

1. Marlin Bicentennial Heritage Committee, *Marlin 1851–1976* (Marlin, TX: Marlin Chamber of Commerce, 1976), 17.

2. Alwyn Barr, *Black Texans: A History of African Americans in Texas, 1528–1994* (Norman: University of Oklahoma Press, 1996), 83.

3. Lillian Schiller St. Romain, *Western Falls County, Texas* (Austin: Texas State Historical Association, 1951), 51.

4. Barr, *Black Texans,* 58.

5. Obituary of Eldridge Alexander Tomlinson, *Marlin Democrat,* August 1936.

6. Homer K. Davidson, *Black Jack Davidson: A Cavalry Commander on the Western Frontier* (Glendale, CA: Arthur Clark, 1974), 33.

7. H. Allen Anderson, entry on George Washington Arrington, at http://www .tshaonline.org/handbook/online/articles/far20 (accessed May 26, 2012).

8. Davidson, *Black Jack Davidson,* 227.

9. Anderson, entry on George Washington Arrington, at http://www.tshaonline .org/handbook/online/articles/far20.

10. Obituary of Eldridge Alexander Tomlinson, *Marlin Democrat,* August 1936.

11. Marjorie Rogers, "Beloved Pioneer and Leader Expires Tuesday," *Marlin Democrat*, January 23, 1943.

12. St. Romain, *Western Falls County, Texas*, 69.

13. Barr, *Black Texans*, 83.

14. Ibid.

15. Ibid.

16. U.S. Bureau of the Census, 1880 Census for Falls County, Texas, film 1255302, p. 252C, Family History Library, Salt Lake City, UT.

17. St. Romain, *Western Falls County, Texas*, 62.

18. U.S. Bureau of the Census, 1880 Census for Falls County, Texas, film 1255302, p. 252C.

19. Barr, *Black Texans*, 99.

20. St. Romain, *Western Falls County, Texas*, 111.

21. Old Settlers and Veterans Association of Falls County, Texas, *History of Falls County, Texas*, ed. Roy Eddins (Marlin: Old Settlers and Veterans Association of Falls County, Texas, 1947), 186.

22. Falls County Historial Commission, *Families of Falls County* (Austin, TX: Eakin Press, 1987), 454.

23. Barr, *Black Texans*, 100.

24. Old Settlers and Veterans Association of Falls County, Texas, *History of Falls County, Texas*, ed. Roy Eddins, 172.

25. Alwyn Barr, *Reconstruction to Reform: Texas Politics, 1876–1906* (Dallas: Southern Methodist University Press, 1971), 82.

26. Barr, *Black Texans*, 73.

27. Ibid., 75.

28. Ibid., 77.

29. Booker T. Washington, "Booker T. Washington Delivers the 1895 Atlanta Compromise Speech," available at http://historymatters.gmu.edu/d/39/ (accessed October 6, 2012).

30. *Plessy v. Ferguson*, 163 U.S. 537; U.S. Supreme Court decision rendered May 18, 1896.

31. Barr, *Black Texans*, 102.

32. J. M. Kennedy, editorial, *Marlin Democrat*, May 20, 1897.

33. "Violence at Leonard," *Dallas Morning News*, August 16–22, 1897.

34. Ibid.

35. J. M. Kennedy, editorial, *Marlin Democrat*, August 25, 1897.

36. Falls County Historial Commission, *Families of Falls County*, 454.

37. St. Romain, *Western Falls County, Texas*, 110.

38. Rogers, "Beloved Pioneer and Leader Expires Tuesday."

39. Roy Eddins, *Marlin's Public Schools from the 1840s to 1960* (Marlin, TX: Marlin Ex-Students Association, 1960), 39.

40. Falls County Historial Commission, *Families of Falls County*, 455.

41. Ibid., 456.

42. "School Reports," *Marlin Democrat*, January 12, 1897.

43. Rogers, "Beloved Pioneer and Leader Expires Tuesday."

44. Ibid.

45. Marlin Bicentennial Heritage Committee, *Marlin 1851–1976*, 33.

46. Ibid., 34.

47. Ibid., 35.

48. Ibid.

49. Ibid.

50. Ibid., 37.

51. Ibid.

52. Various articles, *Marlin Democrat*, March–June 1897.

53. Ibid.

54. "UCV Meets," *Marlin Democrat*, September 4, 1897.

55. J. M. Kennedy, "Emancipation Day Observed in Marlin," *Marlin Democrat*, June 24, 1897.

56. Walter L. Fleming, *Ex-Slave Pension Frauds* (Baton Rouge, LA: Ortlieb's Printing House, 1910), 3, 13.

CHAPTER 12

1. Wiliam D. Carrigan, *The Making of a Lynching Culture: Violence and Vigilantism in Central Texas 1836–1916* (Urbana: University of Illinois Press, 2004), 63.

2. Ibid., Appendix A.

3. Marlin Bicentennial Heritage Committee, *Marlin 1851–1976* (Marlin, TX: Marlin Chamber of Commerce, 1976), 25.

4. "New Year Lynching," *Dallas Morning News,* January 2, 1891.

5. Ibid.

6. "Awaiting the Lynchers," *Dallas Morning News,* January 5, 1891.

7. U. S. Bureau of the Census, 1880 Census for Falls County, Texas, film 1255302, p. 252C, Family History Library, Salt Lake City, UT.

8. "More Blood Near Lang," *Dallas Morning News,* January 6, 1891.

9. Ibid.

10. Alwyn Barr, *Black Texans: A History of African Americans in Texas, 1528–1995* (Norman: University of Oklahoma Press, 1996), 84.

11. Carrigan, *The Making of a Lynching Culture,* Appendix A.

12. "A Word as to Lynching," *Dallas Morning News,* March 1, 1893.

13. Carrigan, *The Making of a Lynching Culture,* 113.

14. "That Terrible Explosion," *Dallas Morning News,* August 5, 1895.

15. "Negro Shot and Killed," *Dallas Morning News,* April 18, 1895.

16. "That Terrible Explosion," *Dallas Morning News.*

17. Ibid.

18. Ibid.

19. Carrigan, *The Making of a Lynching Culture,* 160.

20. "That Terrible Explosion," *Dallas Morning News.*

21. J. M. Kennedy, "Columbus Fendrick, Colored Man, Convicted of Murdering R. H. Boyd," *Marlin Democrat*, August 26, 1897.
22. Ibid.
23. Ibid.
24. Ibid.
25. J. M. Kennedy, "Rumor of a Mob," *Marlin Democrat*, May 6, 1897.
26. Kennedy, "Columbus Fendrick, Colored Man, Convicted of Murdering R. H. Boyd."
27. "Three Negro Men Were Lynched," *Dallas Morning News*, May 15, 1897.
28. "Three Lynched," *Marlin Democrat*, May 20, 1897.
29. J. M. Kennedy, editorial, *Marlin Democrat*, May 20, 1897.
30. Carrigan, *The Making of a Lynching Culture*, 164.

CHAPTER 13

1. "Brazos Valley Flood," *Dallas Morning News*, July 16, 1899.
2. "Situation at Waco," *Dallas Morning News*, July 5, 1899.
3. Ibid.
4. "Brazos River Planters," *Dallas Morning News*, January 21, 1900.
5. "Flood in Falls County," *Dallas Morning News*, May 4, 1900.
6. Author's interview with Robert Lee Tomlinson, May 28, 2008.
7. Marlin Bicentennial Heritage Committee, *Marlin 1851–1976* (Marlin, TX: Marlin Chamber of Commerce, 1976), 92.
8. Ibid., 68.
9. Roy Eddins, *Marlin's Public Schools from the 1840s to 1960.* (Marlin, TX: Marlin Ex-Students Association, 1960), 38.
10. Alwyn Barr, *Black Texans: A History of African Americans in Texas, 1528–1995.* (Norman: University of Oklahoma Press, 1996), 101.
11. Eddins, *Marlin's Public Schools from the 1840s to 1960,* 46.
12. "School Reports," *Marlin Democrat*, December 10, 1903.
13. Marlin Bicentennial Heritage Committee, *Marlin 1851–1976,* 61.
14. Ibid., 167.
15. Ibid., 63.
16. Ibid., 77.
17. Barr, *Black Texans,* 147.
18. Marlin Bicentennial Heritage Committee, *Marlin 1851–1976,* 68.
19. Ibid., 55.
20. Barr, *Black Texans,* 79.
21. Ibid.
22. Ibid., 176.
23. Ibid., 80.
24. Ibid., 84.
25. Ibid., 82.

26. Marlin Bicentennial Heritage Committee, *Marlin 1851–1976*, 134.

27. Eddins, *Marlin's Public Schools from the 1840s to 1960*, 64.

28. Barr, *Black Texans*, 165.

29. Ibid., 153.

30. Ibid., 112–13, 144.

31. "Texas Judge Whips John R. Shillady," *New York Times*, August 23, 1919.

32. Ibid.

33. Barr, *Black Texans*, 91, 97.

34. Web site for the film *Unforgivable Blackness: The Rise and Fall of Jack Johnson* at http://www.pbs.org/unforgivableblackness/index.html (accessed October 13, 2012).

35. "Whites and Blacks Riot," *New York Tribune*, July 5, 1901.

36. Barr, *Black Texans*, 137.

37. See http://www.pbs.org/unforgivableblackness/index.html.

38. Ibid.

39. Randolph B. Campbell, *Gone to Texas: A History of the Lone Star State* (New York: Oxford University Press, 2012), 338.

40. Falls County Historial Commission, *Families of Falls County* (Austin, TX: Eakin Press, 1987), 456.

41. Author's interview with Charles Tomlinson, September 21–22, 2012.

42. Old Settlers and Veterans Association of Falls County, Texas, *History of Falls County, Texas*, ed. Roy Eddins (Marlin, TX: Old Settlers and Veterans Association of Falls County, Texas, 1947), 294.

43. Ibid., 295.

44. Ibid.

45. Ibid., 298.

46. Ibid., 302.

47. Marjorie Rogers, "Beloved Pioneer and Leader Expires Tuesday," *Marlin Democrat*, January 23, 1943.

48. Marlin Bicentennial Heritage Committee, *Marlin 1851–1976*, 72.

49. Ibid., 134.

50. "Sophs Lose to Juniors," *Marlin Democrat*, April 18, 1918.

51. Author's interview with Robert Lee Tomlinson, May 28, 2008.

52. Old Settlers and Veterans Association of Falls County, Texas, *History of Falls County, Texas*, ed. Roy Eddins, 205–09.

53. Barr, *Black Texans*, 114–115.

54. Old Settlers and Veterans Association of Falls County, Texas, *History of Falls County, Texas*, ed. Roy Eddins, 208.

55. Marlin Bicentennial Heritage Committee, *Marlin 1851–1976*, 73.

56. "Award Athletic Letters," *Marlin Democrat*, May 9, 1919.

57. Classified ad in the *Dallas Morning News*, October 17–18, 1918.

58. Falls County Historial Commission, *Families of Falls County*, 280.

59. "Ten Votes Decide Race," *Marlin Democrat*, March 2, 1921.

60. "Census Counters Names," *Marlin Democrat*, February 9, 1922.

61. "Three River Victims Still Missing," *Marlin Democrat,* May 17, 1922.

62. Ibid.

63. Ibid.

64. "Pontoon Bridge Ready, Will be Shipped at Once" *Marlin Democrat,* May 19, 1922.

65. U.S. Bureau of the Census, 1900 Census for Falls County, Texas, Justice Precinct 4, District 21. (Washington, D.C.: U.S. Government Printing Office, June 16, 1900).

66. "Marriage Certificate for Peter Tomlinson and Josephine Beal," August 23, 1875, Falls County Records, Marlin, TX.

67. U.S. Bureau of the Census, 1900 Census for Falls County, Texas, Justice Precinct 4, District 21.

68. Barr, *Black Texans,* 158.

69. Author's interview with Frank Wyman, June 10, 2012.

70. Author's interview with Lizzie Mae Tomlinson Scott, June 10, 2012.

71. Barr, *Black Texans,* 167.

72. Old Settlers and Veterans Association of Falls County, Texas, *History of Falls County, Texas,* ed. Roy Eddins, 199.

CHAPTER 14

1. "Reunion is Great Event," *Marlin Democrat,* July 14, 1922.

2. "Old Settler Passes Away," *Marlin Democrat,* September 16, 1922.

3. Alwyn Barr, *Black Texans: A History of African Americans in Texas, 1528–1995* (Norman: University of Oklahoma Press, 1996), 165.

4. Michael Gillespie and Randal L. Hall, *Thomas Dixon, Jr. and the Birth of Modern America* (Baton Rouge: Louisiana State University Press, 2006).

5. Richard Shickel, *D. W. Griffith: His Life and Work* (New York: Simon & Schuster, 1984).

6. Southern Poverty Law Center, *The Ku Klux Klan: A History of Racism and Violence,* at http://www.splcenter.org.

7. Ibid.

8. Annie Burton Cooper, *The Ku Klux Klan* (Los Angeles: W. T. Potter, 1916), 9–10.

9. "Give Woman a Tar Coat," *Marlin Democrat,* July 18, 1918.

10. Michael Phillips, *White Metropolis: Race, Ethnicity and Religion in Dallas, 1841–2001* (Austin: University of Texas Press, 2006), 67.

11. Barr, *Black Texans,* 140.

12. Mark E. Lender and James K. Martin, *Drinking in America* (New York: Free Press, 1982), 11.

13. Southern Poverty Law Center, *The Ku Klux Klan.*

14. Silliman Evans, "Texas Congressional Democrats Oppose National Anti-Lynching Bill," Associated Press, December 20, 1921.

15. Phillips, *White Metropolis,* 83.

16. Bryan Woolley, "At Its Peak, KKK Gripped Dallas," *Dallas Morning News,* October 15, 2010.

17. "Thousand Knights of the Ku Klux Klan Parade in Dallas," *Dallas Times Herald,* May 22, 1921.

18. Alonzo Wasson, "Dallas Slandered," *Dallas Morning News*, May 24, 1921.

19. Woolley, "At Its Peak, KKK Gripped Dallas."

20. "Ku Klux Treasury Swells with Fees Paid by Members," *Marlin Democrat,* September 6, 1921.

21. Phillips, *White Metropolis,* 100.

22. Barr, *Black Texans,* 116, 139.

23. David Ritz, "Inside the Jewish Establishment," *D: The Magazine of Dallas,* November 1, 1975 (accessed digitally: www.dmagazine.com/publications /-magazine/1975/November/inside-the-jewish-establishment/).

24. Phillips, *White Metropolis,* 98.

25. Author's interview with Mary Jane Ward, April 10, 2012.

26. Author's interview with Robert Lee Tomlinson, March 17, 2010.

27. Ibid.

28. Woolley, "At Its Peak, KKK Gripped Dallas."

29. Phillips, *White Metropolis,* 89.

30. Ibid.

31. "Evans Arrives for Klan Day at the Fair," *Dallas Morning News,* October 24, 1923.

32. Phillips, *White Metropolis,* 86.

33. Ibid., 87.

34. "Hope Cottage is Dedicated by Klan," *Dallas Morning News,* October 24, 1923.

35. Phillips, *White Metropolis,* 89.

36. Ibid., 91.

37. Woolley, "At Its Peak, KKK Gripped Dallas."

38. "Klan Party Held," *Dallas Morning News,* December 26, 1924.

39. Michael Newton and Judy Ann Newton, *The Ku Klux Klan: An Encyclopedia* (New York: Garland Publishing, 1991), 70.

40. Ibid.

41. Marlin Bicentennial Heritage Committee, *Marlin 1851–1976* (Marlin, TX: Marlin Chamber of Commerce, 1976), 77.

42. "Parade Is Staged by Klan," *Marlin Democrat,* September 14, 1921.

43. Ibid.

44. "Klan Clashes with Law," *Marlin Democrat,* October 3, 1921.

45. Ibid.

46. "Citizens Endorse Parade," *Marlin Democrat,* October 3, 1921.

47. "Ku Klux Klan in Texas Unlawful Organization Attorney General Rules," *Fort Worth Star-Telegram,* October 16, 1921.

48. Ibid.

49. "Minstrels Make Big Hit," *Marlin Democrat,* March 4, 1922.

12. Author's interview with Robert L. Tomlinson, May 28, 2008.
13. Margaret Milam, "Dallas Journey's End for Many Out-of-Towners," *Dallas Morning News,* July 21, 1938.
14. Flippen-Prather advertisement, *Dallas Morning News,* September 1, 1940.
15. Author's interview with Robert L. Tomlinson, May 28, 2008.
16. Old Settlers and Veterans Association of Falls County, Texas, *History of Falls County, Texas,* ed. Roy Eddins (Marlin, TX: Old Settlers and Veterans Association of Falls County, Texas, 1947), 239.
17. "J. M. Kennedy, Publisher of Marlin, Dies," *Dallas Morning News,* April 20, 1942.
18. "Quiet Reunion Marks Fiftieth Anniversary," *Dallas Morning News,* January 23, 1942.
19. Death certificate for R. E. L. Tomlinson, January 27, 1943, Falls County Clerk's Office, Marlin, TX.
20. Author's interview with Robert L. Tomlinson, May 28, 2008.
21. Alwyn Barr, *Black Texans: A History of African Americans in Texas, 1528–1995* (Norman: University of Oklahoma Press, 1996), 197.
22. "Texas, Deaths, 1890–1976," at https://familysearch.org/pal:/MM9.1.1/KSBB-2HH (accessed August 21, 2012. Certificate 32086).
23. Author's interview with Robert L. Tomlinson, March 2010.
24. Ibid.
25. Ibid.
26. Author's interview with Sarah Lee Tomlinson, March 18, 2010.
27. Author's interview with Robert L. Tomlinson, March 17, 2010.
28. Author's interview with Sarah Lee Tomlinson.
29. Author's interview with Robert L. Tomlinson.
30. Author's interview with Sarah Lee Tomlinson.
31. Author's interview with Robert L. Tomlinson.
32. "Mrs. R. E. L. Tomlinson Dies Here Saturday, Funeral Monday A.M.," *Marlin Democrat,* August 13, 1951.
33. Author's interview with Robert L. Tomlinson, May 28, 2008.
34. Ken Hand, "Miss Jacobs to Head Bank," *Dallas Morning News,* May 6, 1955.
35. Author's interview with Robert L. Tomlinson, March 17, 2010.
36. Author's interview with Robert L. Tomlinson, May 28, 2008.
37. Author's, interview with Robert L. Tomlinson, September 10, 2012.
38. Author's, interview with Robert L. Tomlinson, March 17, 2010.
39. Ibid.
40. Michael Phillips, *White Metropolis: Race, Ethnicity and Religion in Dallas, 1841–2001* (Austin: University of Texas Press, 2006), 102.
41. Ibid., 104.
42. Barr, *Black Texans,* 147.
43. "Negroes Stage Big Juneteenth at Centennial," *Dallas Morning News,* June 20, 1936.
44. Barr, *Black Texans,* 171.

50. "Attention Is Called to the Kriss Kross Karnival," *Marlin Democrat,* July 27, 1922.
51. "Poll Tax Records Broken," *Marlin Democrat,* February 8, 1922.
52. Rosebud Klan No. 110, "Letter to Nick Potts," *Marlin Democrat,* February 21, 1922.
53. "Klan Takes Convention," *Marlin Democrat,* July 22, 1922.
54. Ibid.
55. Ibid.
56. "Marlin Klan Entertains," *Marlin Democrat,* August 17, 1923.
57. Ibid.
58. Ibid.
59. Old Settlers and Veterans Association of Falls County, Texas, *History of Falls County, Texas,* ed. Roy Eddins (Marlin: Old Settlers and Veterans Association of Falls County, Texas, 1947), 220.
60. Marlin Bicentennial Heritage Committee, *Marlin 1851–1976* (Marlin, TX: Marlin Chamber of Commerce, 1976), 77.
61. J. M. Kennedy, "Anonymity," *Marlin Democrat,* August 8, 1924.
62. J. M. Kennedy, "The Klan Bolts," *Marlin Democrat,* August 4, 1924.
63. Ibid.
64. "Invisibles Hold Meet," *Marlin Democrat,* August 6, 1924.
65. "Klansmen Turned Down," *Marlin Democrat,* September 3, 1924.
66. "Says K.K.K. Out of Politics," *Marlin Democrat,* September 8, 1924.
67. Marlin Bicentennial Heritage Committee, *Marlin 1851–1976,* 85.
68. Southern Poverty Law Center, *The Ku Klux Klan.*
69. Phillips, *White Metropolis,* 101.
70. Ibid., 102.

CHAPTER 15

1. Alwyn Barr, *Black Texans: A History of African Americans in Texas, 1528–1995.* (Norman: University of Oklahoma Press, 1996), 169.
2. Robert Uzzel, *Blind Lemon Jefferson: His Life, His Death and His Legacy* (Austin, TX: Eakin Press, 2002), 4.
3. Barr, *Black Texans,* 165, 168.
4. Marlin Bicentennial Heritage Committee, *Marlin 1851–1976* (Marlin, TX: Marlin Chamber of Commerce, 1976), 81.
5. Greg Johnson, "Henry 'Ragtime Texas' Thomas," at http://www.cascadeblues.org/History/HenryThomas.htm (accessed Aug. 12, 2012).
6. Barr, *Black Texans,* 169.
7. Christine Hamm, "Ledbetter, Huddie [Lead Belly]," at http://www.tshaonline.org/handbook/online/articles/fle10 (accessed Aug. 12, 2012).
8. Ibid.
9. Alan Lee Haworth, "Hopkins, Sam [Lightnin']," at http://www.tshaonline.org/handbook/online/articles/fhoab (accessed Aug. 12, 2012).

10. Barr, *Black Texans,* 169.

11. Uzzel, *Blind Lemon Jefferson,* 29.

12. Ibid., 46.

13. Michael Hall, "The Soul of a Man," *Texas Monthly,* December 2010 (accessed www.texasmonthly.com/story/soul-man).

14. Ibid.

15. "Men Arrested by Rangers No Billed by Grand Jury," *Dallas Morning News,* November 7, 1924.

16. Author's interview with Lizzie Mae Tomlinson Scott, June 10, 2012.

17. Author's interview with Frank Wyman, June 10, 2012.

18. Ibid.

19. Ibid.

20. Thomas Turner, "Marlin Policeman Acquitted of Murder," *Dallas Morning News,* May 12, 1961.

21. Author's interview with Robert Lee Tomlinson, May 28, 2008.

22. "Make Awards in Yard Contest at Marlin," *Dallas Morning News,* June 11, 1928.

23. Marlin Bicentennial Heritage Committee, *Marlin 1851–1976,* 74.

24. Ibid., 152.

25. Ibid., 172.

26. Ibid., 83.

27. Ibid., 219.

28. Barr, *Black Texans,* 153.

29. Old Settlers and Veterans Association of Falls County, Texas, *History of Falls County, Texas,* ed. Roy Eddins (Marlin, TX: Old Settlers and Veterans Association of Falls County, Texas, 1947), 223.

30. Ibid., 224.

31. Marlin Bicentennial Heritage Committee, *Marlin 1851–1976,* 84.

32. Marjorie Rogers, "Old Settlers' and Confederates' Reunion," *Lockhard Post Register,* August 26, 1937.

33. Old Settlers and Veterans Association of Falls County, Texas. *History of Falls County, Texas,* ed. Roy Eddins, 224.

34. Barr, *Black Texans,* 154.

35. Author's interview with Charles Tomlinson, Sept. 21–22, 2012.

36. Author's interview with Lizzie Mae Tomlinson Scott.

37. Peter Tomlinson's Death Certificate, August 1, 1926, Falls County Clerk's Office, Lott, TX.

38. Author's interview with Lizzie Mae Tomlinson Scott.

39. Ibid.

40. Author's interview with Charles Tomlinson.

41. Author's interview with Lizzie Mae Tomlinson Scott.

42. Author's interview with Charles Tomlinson.

43. Author's interview with Lizzie Mae Tomlinson Scott.

44. Interview by Lisa Kaselak with Pinkie Taylor Price, April 17, 2011.

45. Barr, *Black Texans,* 157–59.

46. Author's interview with Charles Tomlinson.

47. Author's interview with Lizzie Mae Tomlinson Scott.

48. Author's interview with Charles Tomlinson.

49. Author's interview with Lizzie Mae Tomlinson Scott.

50. Loreane Tomlinson, with Patti M. Britton and Ginger Kolbaba, *LT & Me: What Raising a Champion Taught Me about Life, Faith, and Listening to Your Dream* (Carol Stream, IL: Tyndale House, 2009), 35.

51. Author's interview with Charles Tomlinson.

52. Ibid.

53. Ibid.

54. Ibid.

55. Author's interview with Lizzie Mae Tomlinson Scott.

56. Ibid.

57. Ibid.

58. Ibid.

59. Author's interview with Charles Tomlinson.

60. Interview by Lisa Kaselak with Pinkie Taylor Price.

61. Ibid.

62. Ibid.

63. Author's interview with Frank Wyman.

64. Author's interview with Lizzie Mae Tomlinson Scott.

65. Ibid.

CHAPTER 16

1. Flippen-Prather advertisement, *Dallas Morning News,* September 1, 1940.

2. Highland Park Shopping Village, designated a National Historic Landmark, February 16, 2000, at http://tps.cr.nps.gov/nhl/detail.cfm?ResourceId=1048910856 &ResourceType=Building (accessed August 17, 2012).

3. Ibid.

4. See www.nps.gov/nhl/designation/samples/tx/highland.pdf (accessed August 17, 2012).

5. W. S. Adair, "Emil Fretz Tells of Early Dallas," *Dallas Morning News,* November 13, 1924.

6. Author's interview with Robert L. Tomlinson, March 17, 2010.

7. "Emil Fretz Funeral to Be Held Thursday," *Dallas Morning News,* October 18, 1928.

8. "Carl Wiesemann Club Is Organized," *Dallas Morning News,* January 17, 1931.

9. "To Wed in June," *Dallas Morning News,* April 23, 1933.

10. "A. E. Tomlinson Weds Miss Fretz In Chapel Rites," *Dallas Morning News,* June 9, 1933.

11. Marlin Bicentennial Heritage Committee, *Marlin 1851–1976* (Marlin, TX: Marlin Chamber of Commerce, 1976), 177.

45. Phillips, *White Metropolis,* 116.
46. Ibid.
47. "Colored Gentry to Celebrate June 19 with Cab Calloway," *Dallas Morning News,* June 16, 1936.
48. Barr, *Black Texans,* 172.
49. "Negroes Stage Big Juneteenth at Centennial," *Dallas Morning News.*
50. Phillips, *White Metropolis,* 116.
51. Ibid., 107.
52. Ibid., 110.
53. Marlin Bicentennial Heritage Committee, *Marlin 1851–1976,* 92.
54. Barr, *Black Texans,* 142–43.
55. Phillips, *White Metropolis,* 116.
56. Ibid., 117.
57. Ibid., 120.
58. Barr, *Black Texans,* 173–74.
59. Phillips, *White Metropolis,* 116.
60. Barr, *Black Texans,* 175.
61. Ibid., 199.
62. Phillips, *White Metropolis,* 106.
63. Ibid., 120.
64. Barr, *Black Texans,* 177.
65. Ibid., 207.
66. Ibid., 207–08.
67. Phillips, *White Metropolis,* 122.

CHAPTER 17

1. Author's interview with Charles Tomlinson, September 21–22, 2012.
2. Author's interview with Robert Stem, state district court judge for Falls County, Texas, May 9, 2010.
3. Author's interview with Charles Tomlinson.
4. Ibid.
5. Author's interview with Robert Stem.
6. Lillian Schiller St. Romain, *Western Falls County, Texas* (Austin: Texas State Historical Association, 1951), 112.
7. Thomas E. Turner, "Sheriff and Dog: Friendly, Tough," *Dallas Morning News,* September 24, 1966.
8. Author's interview with Frank Wyman, June 10, 2012.
9. Marlin Bicentennial Heritage Committee, *Marlin 1851–1976* (Marlin, TX: Marlin Chamber of Commerce, 1976), 89.
10. Ibid., 201.
11. Author's interview with Charles Tomlinson.
12. Author's interview with Lizzie Mae Tomlinson Scott, June 10, 2012.

13. Interview by Lisa Kaselak with Anna Steele, February 26, 2012.

14. Author's interview with Charles Tomlinson.

15. Interview by Tamela Jackson with Frank Wyman.

16. Ibid.

17. Author's interview with Lizzie Mae Tomlinson Scott.

18. Author's interview with Lonnie Garrett, June 15, 2009.

19. Author's interview with Frank Wyman.

20. "Texas, Deaths, 1890–1976," at https://familysearch.org/pal:/MM9.1.1/LC26 -40M (accessed August 22, 2012. Certificate 54603).

21. Michael Phillips, *White Metropolis: Race, Ethnicity and Religion in Dallas, 1841–2001.* (Austin: University of Texas Press, 2006), 153.

22. Harvey Bogen and Mike Quinn, "Court Order Closes Dallas NAACP Office," *Dallas Morning News,* September 23, 1956.

23. "Texas Suit Uncovers NAACP," *Dallas Morning News*, October 10, 1956.

24. Phillips, *White Metropolis,* 153.

25. Alwyn Barr, *Black Texans: A History of African Americans in Texas, 1528– 1995* (Norman: University of Oklahoma Press, 1996), 206–09.

26. Phillips, *White Metropolis,* 152.

27. Author's interview with Robert L. Tomlinson, September 10, 2012.

28. Ibid.

29. "Dallas Aggie Rolls a '300,'" *Dallas Morning News,* October 11, 1959.

30. The Associated Press, "Texas A&M Pin Team Sets Pace," *Dallas Morning News*, December 14, 1959.

31. Author's interview with Robert L. Tomlinson.

32. Phillips, *White Metropolis,* 155.

33. Ibid., 156.

34. "Conkling's 629 Paces Dallasites," *Dallas Morning News,* April 9, 1960.

35. Author's interview with Robert L. Tomlinson.

36. "New Titles," *Dallas Morning News,* April 7, 1961.

37. Author's interview with Robert L. Tomlinson.

38. "Edna Ward Marries in Arlington," *Dallas Morning News,* June 18, 1961.

39. "Tomlinson Rolls 300 at Jupiter," *Dallas Morning News,* March 10, 1963.

40. Author's interview with Robert L. Tomlinson.

41. Barr, *Black Texans,* 220.

42. Author's interview with Robert L. Tomlinson, March 17, 2010.

43. Ibid.

44. Ibid.

45. Author's interview with Robert L. Tomlinson, May 28, 2008.

46. Phillips, *White Metropolis,* 158.

47. Author's interview with Robert L. Tomlinson.

48. "Welcome, Mr. Kennedy," *Dallas Morning News,* November 22, 1963.

49. Phillips, *White Metropolis,* 158.

50. Harless Wade, "State Match Games Near," *Dallas Morning News,* December 3, 1964.

51. Harless Wade, "Once They 'Struck' for Goodness," *Dallas Morning News*, November 4, 1964.
52. Harless Wade, "Young Keglers Top Teams," *Dallas Morning News*, May 16, 1965.
53. "Two Share Spotlight as Match Games Roll," *Dallas Morning News*, July 26, 1965.
54. Author's interview with Robert L. Tomlinson, March 17, 2010.
55. Harless Wade, "Local Bowling Stars Honored," *Dallas Morning News*, May 22, 1966.
56. Author's interview with Robert L. Tomlinson, September 10, 2012.
57. Phillips, *White Metropolis*, 156.
58. Author's interview with Robert L. Tomlinson.
59. Barr, *Black Texans*, 208.
60. Phillips, *White Metropolis*, 157.
61. Ibid., 158.
62. Barr, *Black Texans*, 209–10.
63. Ibid., 210.
64. Ibid., 212.
65. Author's interview with Oliver Terry Tomlinson, Jr., September 25, 2012.
66. Author's interview with Robert Stem.
67. Author's interview with Oliver Terry Tomlinson, Jr.
68. Author's interview with Loreane Tomlinson, June 24, 2012.
69. U.S. Bureau of the Census, 1948 Census for Falls County, Texas, film T627_4030j, p. 7A, Family History Library, Salt Lake City, UT.
70. Author's interview with Oliver Terry Tomlinson, Jr.
71. Loreane Tomlinson, with Patti M. Britton and Ginger Kolbaba, *LT & Me: What Raising a Champion Taught Me about Life, Faith, and Listening to Your Dream* (Carol Stream, IL: Tyndale House, 2009), 29.
72. Author's interview with Robert Stem.
73. Author's interview with Oliver Terry Tomlinson, Jr.
74. Author's interview with J. C. Williams, July 27, 2010.
75. Author's interview with Frank Wyman, June 10, 2012.
76. Author's interview with J. C. Williams.
77. Turner, "Sheriff and Dog: Friendly, Tough."
78. Barr, *Black Texans*, 187.
79. Ibid., 196–97.

CHAPTER 18

1. Author's interview with Robert L. Tomlinson, September 10, 2012.
2. Author's interview with Robert L. Tomlinson, March 17, 2010.
3. Ibid.
4. "Urban Design Process Women Voters' Topic," *Dallas Morning News*, February 8, 1971.

5. Author's interview with Robert L. Tomlinson, September 10, 2012.

6. Author's interview with Robert L. Tomlinson, March 17, 2010.

7. Author's interview with Robert L. Tomlinson, September 10, 2012.

8. Ibid.

9. Ibid.

10. Ibid.

11. Ibid.

12. Ibid.

13. Ibid.

14. Ruthe Winegarten, *Black Texas Women: 150 Years of Trial and Triumph* (Austin: Universty of Texas Press, 1995), 276.

15. Michael Phillips, *White Metropolis: Race, Ethnicity and Religion in Dallas, 1841–2001* (Austin: University of Texas Press, 2006), 167.

16. Ibid., 164.

17. Ibid.

18. Author's interview with Robert L. Tomlinson.

19. Ibid.

20. Ibid.

21. Ibid.

22. Mark Seibel, "Board Approves Student Assignment Plan," *Dallas Morning News,* March 23, 1976.

23. Author's interview with Robert L. Tomlinson.

24. Ibid.

CHAPTER 19

1. Author's interview with Lonnie Garrett, June 15, 2009.

2. Ibid.

3. Interview by Lisa Kaselak with Anna Steele, February 26, 2012.

4. Ibid.

5. Author's interview with Lonnie Garrett.

6. Alwyn Barr, *Black Texans: A History of African Americans in Texas, 1528–1995* (Norman: University of Oklahoma Press, 1996), 243.

7. Ibid., 230.

8. Author's interview with Frank Wyman, June 10, 2012.

9. Marlin Bicentennial Heritage Committee, *Marlin 1851–1976* (Marlin, TX: Marlin Chamber of Commerce, 1976), 74.

10. Author's interview with Oliver Terry Tomlinson, Jr., September 25, 2012.

11. Loreane Tomlinson, with Patti M. Britton and Ginger Kolbaba, *LT & Me: What Raising a Champion Taught Me about Life, Faith, and Listening to Your Dreams* (Carol Stream, IL. Tyndale House, 2009), 27.

12. Death Certificate for Vincent Tomlinson, June 13, 1971, Temple, Texas.

13. Tomlinson, *LT & Me*, 30.

14. Author's interview with Oliver Terry Tomlinson, Jr.
15. Ibid.
16. Ibid.
17. Jim Lewis, "Anthrax Weakens Pocket, Spirit in Central Texas," *Dallas Morning News*, July 21, 1974.
18. Frank X. Tolbert, "'Lead Belly' Walks a Street in Marlin," *Dallas Morning News*, November 16, 1974.
19. Ibid.
20. Marlin Bicentennial Heritage Committee, *Marlin 1851–1976*, 82.
21. Author's interview with Oliver Terry Tomlinson, Jr.
22. Tomlinson, *LT & Me*, 29.
23. Author's interview with Londria Tomlinson, June 24, 2012.
24. Author's interview with Loreane Tomlinson, June 24, 2012.
25. Author's interview with Londria Tomlinson.
26. Ibid.
27. Author's interview with Loreane Tomlinson.
28. Tomlinson, *LT & Me*, 45.
29. Ibid., 47.
30. Author's interview with Londria Tomlinson.
31. Ibid.
32. Ibid.
33. Author's interview with Oliver Terry Tomlinson, Jr.
34. Texas Department of Public Safety, "Tomlinson, Oliver Terry, Jr.," SID: 02073002, criminal history search, Austin, TX, 2012.
35. Texas Department of Public Safety, "McClain, Ronald Carl," SID: 02442756, criminal history search, Austin, TX, 2012.
36. Texas Department of Public Safety, "McClain, Charles Allen," SID: 03263867, criminal history search, Austin, TX, 2012.
37. Michelle Alexander, *The New Jim Crow: Mass Incarceration in the Age of Colorblindness* (New York: New Press, 2010), 59–87.
38. Marlin Bicentennial Heritage Committee, *Marlin 1851–1976*, 201.
39. Kent Biffle, "Tempers in Falls Rise Over Sheriff's Controversy," *Dallas Morning News*, December 12, 1976.
40. United Press International, "Marijuana Seizure Announced," *Dallas Morning News*, February 11, 1977.
41. Carlton Stowers, "HEW's Review Perplexes Marlin," *Dallas Morning News*, February 16, 1977.
42. Ibid.
43. Barr, *Black Texans*, 239.
44. Ibid., 240.
45. Ibid., 234–35.
46. Ibid., 235.
47. Ibid., 245.

CHAPTER 20

1. Michael Phillips, *White Metropolis: Race, Ethnicity and Religion in Dallas, 1841–2001* (Austin: University of Texas Press, 2006), 167.
2. Lloyd Grove, Doug Domeier, and Dan Watson. "40 Klansmen March in Dallas," *Dallas Morning News*, November 4, 1979.
3. Ibid.
4. Author's interview with Robert L. Tomlinson, September 10, 2012.

CHAPTER 21

1. Author's interview with Loreane Tomlinson, June 24, 2012.
2. Author's interview with Oliver Terry Tomlinson, Jr., September 25, 2012.
3. Author's interview with Loreane Tomlinson.
4. Author's interview with Oliver Terry Tomlinson, Jr.
5. Ibid.
6. Author's interview with Loreane Tomlinson.
7. Author's interview with LaDainian Tomlinson, January 15, 2013.
8. Ibid.
9. Loreane Tomlinson, with Patti M. Britton and Ginger Kolbaba, *LT & Me: What Raising a Champion Taught Me about Life, Faith, and Listening to Your Dreams* (Carol Stream, IL: Tyndale House, 2009), 43.
10. Ibid., 52.
11. Author's interview with LaDainian Tomlinson.
12. Author's interview with Londria Tomlinson, June 24, 2012.
13. Author's interview with Loreane Tomlinson.
14. Author's interview with LaDainian Tomlinson.
15. Ibid.
16. Author's interview with Loreane Tomlinson.
17. Tomlinson, *LT & Me*, 44.
18. Ibid., 45.
19. Author's interview with Loreane Tomlinson.
20. Tomlinson, *LT & Me*, 48.
21. Author's interview with LaDainian Tomlinson.
22. Tomlinson, *LT & Me*, 52.
23. Alwyn Barr, *Black Texans: A History of African Americans in Texas, 1528–1995.* (Norman: University of Oklahoma Press, 1996), 236–37, 244.
24. Tomlinson, *LT & Me*, 54.
25. Author's interview with LaDainian Tomlinson.
26. Author's interview with LaVar Tomlinson, November 7, 2012.
27. Tomlinson, *LT & Me*, 55.
28. See http://www.popwarner.com/About_Us.htm (accessed September 27, 2012).
29. Author's interview with LaDainian Tomlinson.
30. Tomlinson, *LT & Me*, 56.
31. Author's interview with LaVar Tomlinson.

32. Author's interview with LaDainian Tomlinson.
33. Author's interview with LaVar Tomlinson.
34. Author's interview with Oliver Terry Tomlinson, Jr.
35. Author's interview with Loreane Tomlinson.
36. Author's interview with Londria Tomlinson.
37. Author's interview with LaDainian Tomlinson.
38. Author's interview with Oliver Terry Tomlinson, Jr.
39. Author's interview with Loreane Tomlinson.
40. Author's interview with Oliver Terry Tomlinson, Jr.
41. Tomlinson, *LT & Me*, 73.
42. Barr, *Black Texans*, 235–36.
43. Ibid., 232.
44. Ibid., 233–34.
45. Tomlinson, *LT & Me*, 60.
46. Ibid., 63.

CHAPTER 23

1. Author's interview with LaDainian Tomlinson, January 15, 2013.
2. Ibid.
3. Loreane Tomlinson, with Patti M. Britton and Ginger Kolbaba, *LT & Me: What Raising a Champion Taught Me about Life, Faith, and Listening to Your Dreams* (Carol Stream, IL: Tyndale House, 2009), 89.
4. Tomlinson, *LT & Me*, 90.
5. Tomlinson, *LT & Me*, 103.
6. Author's interview with LaDainian Tomlinson.
7. Ibid.
8. Ibid.
9. Ibid.
10. Ibid.
11. Tomlinson, *LT & Me*, 106.
12. Author's interview with LaDainian Tomlinson.
13. Tomlinson, *LT & Me*, 103.
14. Ibid., 118.
15. Alwyn Barr, *Black Texans: A History of African Americans in Texas, 1528–1995* (Norman: University of Oklahoma Press, 1996), 241–42.
16. Tomlinson, *LT & Me*, 125.
17. Author's interview with LaDainian Tomlinson.
18. Tomlinson, *LT & Me*, 131.
19. Ibid., 134.
20. Ibid., 132.
21. Author's interview with LaVar Tomlinson, November 7, 2012.
22. Ibid.
23. Ibid.

24. Ibid.
25. Barr, *Black Texans*, 237–38, 240, 245.
26. Michael Phillips, *White Metropolis: Race, Ethnicity and Religion in Dallas, 1841–2001* (Austin: University of Texas Press, 2006), 168.
27. Barr, *Black Texans*, 234–35, 237, 239.
28. Tomlinson, *LT & Me*, 139.
29. Ibid., 142.
30. Texas Department of Public Safety, "Tomlinson, LaVar Tramayne," SID: 06761774, criminal history search, Austin, TX, 2012.
31. Author's interview with LaVar Tomlinson.
32. Tomlinson, *LT & Me*, 145.
33. Author's interview with LaDainian Tomlinson.
34. Ibid.
35. Tomlinson, *LT & Me*, 145.
36. Author's interview with Zelma Tomlinson, January 22, 2013.
37. Tomlinson, *LT & Me*, 148.
38. Author's interview with LaDainian Tomlinson.
39. National Football League's 2001 draft, April 2001, at http://www.nfl.com/draft/history/fulldraft?season=2001 (accessed September 29, 2012).
40. Ibid.
41. Tomlinson, *LT & Me*, 163.
42. "N.F.L.: Roundup," *New York Times*, August 23, 2001.
43. Washington versus San Diego box score, September 9, 2001, at http://www.nfl.com/gamecenter/2001090912/2001/REG1/redskins@chargers#tab=analyze (accessed September 29, 2012).
44. Tomlinson, *LT & Me*, 176.
45. Author's interview with Londria Tomlinson, June 24, 2012.
46. Author's interview with Oliver Terry Tomlinson, Jr., September 25, 2012.
47. Tomlinson, *LT & Me*, 196.
48. Author's interview with Oliver Terry Tomlinson, Jr.
49. LaDainian Tomlinson profile, 2012, at http://www.nfl.com/player/ladainian-tomlinson/2504778/profile (accessed September 29, 2012).
50. Beth Harris, "Tomlinson Named Male Athlete of the Year," Associated Press, July 27, 2007.
51. Lee Jenkins, "Links to Slavery and N.F.L. Star on a Hill in Texas," *New York Times*, January 7, 2007.
52. Author's interview with LaDainian Tomlinson.
53. Author's interview with Londria Tomlinson.
54. Author's interview with LaDainian Tomlinson.
55. Tomlinson, *LT & Me*, 192.
56. Author's interview with LaDainian Tomlinson.
57. Tomlinson, *LT & Me*, 194.
58. Ibid., 195.
59. Ibid.

EPILOGUE

1. Natalie Angier, "Do Races Differ? Not Really, DNA Shows," *New York Times*, August 22, 2000.
2. Frank Snowden, "Images and Attitudes," in *Racism*, ed. Martin Bulmer and John Solomos (New York: Oxford University Press, 1999), 27–28.
3. Reginald Horsman, "Superior and Inferior Races," in *Racism*, ed. Martin Bulmer and John Solomos (New York: Oxford University Press, 1999), 45.
4. George Mosse, "Eighteenth-Century Foundations," in *Racism*, ed. Bulmer and Solomos, 40–41.
5. Ibid., 42.
6. Ibid., 47.
7. Ibid.
8. Derald Wing Sue, "Microaggressions, Marginality, and Oppression: An Introduction," in *Microaggressions and Marginality: Manifestation, Dynamics, and Impact*, ed. Derald Wing Sue (Hoboken, NJ: John Wiley & Sons, 2010), 3.
9. Ibid., 3–4.
10. Ibid., 5–6.
11. Susan T. Fiske, "Are We Born Racist?" in *Are We Born Racist? New Insights from Neuroscience and Positive Pyschology*, ed. Jason Marsh, Rodolfo Mendoza-Denton, and Jeremy Adam Smith (Boston: Beacon Press, 2010), 10.
12. Ibid., 11.
13. Ibid.
14. Ibid., 12.
15. David Amodio, "The Egalitarian Brain," in *Are We Born Racist?*, ed. Marsh, Mendoza-Denton, and Smith, 48.
16. Ibid.
17. Ibid., 51.
18. Jennifer Holladay, "Promoting Tolerance and Equity in Public Schools," in *Are We Born Racist?* ed. Marsh, Mendoza-Denton, and Smith, 64, 67.

ACKNOWLEDGMENTS

Special thanks goes to John Silbersack at Trident Media Group and Marcia Markland at Thomas Dunne Books for believing in this project, supporting it, and providing peerless advice.

I would like to thank Loreane Tomlinson for accepting me into her heart and family and opening the door for me to meet the African-American Tomlinsons, including her children LaDainian, Londria, and LaVar. They graciously accepted me and generously shared their stories. I owe special thanks to Sandra Tyron for introducing me to her mother, Lizzie Mae Scott, and her uncle Charles and his wife Zelma. They taught me more about the Hill than anyone else. Sandra also introduced me to Sherry and Gladys Scott, who graciously shared the story of their lives. I could not have written this book without their cooperation.

My expert advisers, Dr. Alwyn Barr and Dr. Fred McGhee, fact-checked my work and helped me keep it in context. Tami Jackson spent hours searching through archival material in Austin and Waco, gathering many of the newspaper excerpts and original documents included in this book. Former Marlin residents Sharon Styles, Steve Swinnea, and Bettie Beard shared their love of Marlin history and provided invaluable assistance.

The residents of Marlin spent hours telling me their stories and providing me with incredible insight. District Judge Robert Stem, Mayor Elizabeth Nelson, Mayor Norm Erskine, Bishop Lonnie Garrett, Dr. James Bryan, Frank Wyman, Pinkie Taylor Price, David Tinsley, Pam Kelly, and Anna Steele all provided important accounts for this book.

A special thanks goes to one of my oldest friends, Lisa Kaselak, who participated in many of the interviews as part of the production of the book's companion documentary film, *Tomlinson Hill*. Her insights and hard work provided major contributions.

Most of all, though, I thank my wife, Shalini Ramanathan, whose unflagging support for the project and belief in me as a writer buoyed me through the toughest periods of my life, and she shared in my joy during the most triumphant. *More!*

INDEX

abolitionist movement, 34–35, 42, 50–52, 55

Adair, Garland, 217

Adolphus Hotel, Dallas, 201, 207

Afghanistan, 349–50

African Americans, 336. *See also* farming; racism; slaves

abuse of, 83–86, 94, 96–99, 101, 103, 115, 118, 125, 133, 142, 144, 151–53

Black Codes and, 264, 268, 305, 307

education of, 83, 89, 110, 116, 128–29, 134, 138, 145, 150, 179, 182, 192, 234–35, 264–65, 315, 361

entertainment/arts and, 183–84, 221–27

labor/market shifts and, 193, 229, 232, 240–41, 248, 286

land ownership by, 131, 133–34, 137, 177–78, 180, 239, 286

living conditions, post-emancipation, of, 131–39, 221–41

lynching of, 161–76, 181, 184, 247

miscegenation and, 144, 184, 196–97

organizations formed by, 138, 146, 182–83, 192–93, 204, 255–59

political participation by, 89–90, 97, 102–6, 111–13, 125–26, 141, 144, 146–51, 181, 213, 254–59, 279, 288, 289, 292, 304–5, 315, 339–40, 361

in prison, 141–42, 154, 339

sharecropping by, 91, 97–98, 132–34, 137–39, 143, 145, 177–78, 180, 232–41, 264, 286

wage contract farm work by, 83–91, 97, 132–34, 137, 177–78, 180

African Methodist Episcopal normal school, Denison, 138

African National Congress (ANC), 330, 341, 345

Alabama, 14, 20–22, 26–35, 41–43, 57–59, 123, 142, 148, 220

civil rights marches in, 279–80

Albright, J. H., 151

Alger, Bruce, 274

Allen, George, 279

Allen, Walter, 190

al-Qaeda, 2, 7–8, 349–50

American Colonization Society, 138

American Fact-Finding Committee, 278–79

American Legion, 217
the Amigos organization, 288
Amodio, David, 377
Anderson, L. C., 146
Anthology of American Folk Music, 225
Anti-Defamation League, 220
Anti-Lynching bill of 1937, 258
anti-Semitism, 208, 216, 261
A. P. Tomlinson Development, 263
Army Corps of Engineers, Texas, 191
Arnold, Ed, 167–70
Arnold, Phil, 167–70
Arrington, George Washington, 142–43
Aryan Nations, 261
Asahi, 345–46
Asberry, Alexander, 151
Associated Press, 162, 345–51, 368, 371
Atlanta Compromise, 148–50
The Autobiography of Malcolm X, 328

Bad Aibling, Germany, 327–29
Bagosora, Théoneste, 348
Ballinger, William P., 113
Bandito, Johannesburg, 341–43
Banks, Nathaniel, 71–75
Bartlett and Watkins, Marlin, 31–32, 69,
     120, 127
Bartlett, Churchill Jones, 179
Bartlett, Sarah Jones Green, 30–32
Bartlett, Tom, Sr., 227
Bartlett, Zenas, 31–32, 55, 95, 110, 127, 179
Barton, Harry, 228
Bates, L. J., 223
Bayou City (Confederate boat), 65–67
Beall, Charles, 162–65
Beall, Squire, 163–65
Beaty, John Owen, 261
Belida, Alex, 346–47
Bell, J. H., 59, 87
Belton Reporter, 176
Berry, Robert, 244
Beulah Church/School for blacks,
     Falls County, 116, 145
Beulah Church/School for whites,
     Falls County, 129, 155, 171
Big Brothers organization, 289
Bill Gates Millennium Scholarships, 359
Billingsley, J. C., 47–48

bin Laden, Osama, 7, 349
The Birth of a Nation (film), 197
Blackburn, W. R., 151
Black Codes, 91–94, 99
Black History Month, 293
Blaylock, Louis, 195, 198, 208
Bluitt, Benjamin, 146
Bolton, Samantha, 347
Bomar, Buddy, 253
Bonner, Junior, 268–69
Booker T. Washington High School,
     Marlin, 182, 241, 301–4
Boston Tea Party, 217
Bowdon, Bill, 218
Bowling News (Dallas), 280
Bowling Supplies, Inc., Dallas, 275–76
Boyd, Robert J., 170–72
Boyd, Ruth, 170
Boys and Girls Club organization, 336–37
Brady, Wes, 31, 39–40
Bragg, Wesley, 167–70
Brazos River, Texas, 21–22, 44, 57,
     116–17, 133, 155, 186
     flooding along, 15, 139, 177–78, 190–91
Breckinridge, John C., 51
Briggs, B. J., 190
Briscoe, Dolph, 289
Broadus, Henry, 38, 43, 383n25
Broadus, Ned, 78–79, 388n32
Broadus, Tom, 191
Brooks, George, 106
Brown, Henry Billings, 150
Browning, John, 152
Brown, John, 42, 50
Brown v. Board of Education, 261, 301
Buchanan, Bob, 211–12
Buddhism, 326, 329
buffalo soldiers, 143
Bureau of Refugees, Freedmen and
     Abandoned Lands. *See* Freedmen's
     Bureau
Burrell, Wesley, 36
Burton, Nelson, Jr., 287
Burundi, 347–48
Byrd, Dave, 123, 132, 393n39

Cain, Darrell L., 293
Calhoun, John C., 34

Califano, Joseph, Jr., 314
Calloway, Cab, 255–57
Calvert, Robert, 96
Cameron, Lucille, 184
Canby, E. R. S., 111, 113
carpetbaggers, 115, 124–25, 291
Carter, Amon, 228
Carter, George, 213
Carter, Jimmy, 315
Carter, Robert, 227
cattle industry, 116–17, 130, 133, 142–43,
    145, 178, 185, 210, 229, 264, 305, 313,
    334
Cedar Valley, Texas, 131, 135–37, 144,
    154, 234, 241
Centurion Homes, Waco, 284, 331
Chapin, Dennis C., 244
Chapin, Margaret, 244
Chapman, Lloyd, 252
Chappell, Herman, 340, 355, 361
Cheek, James B., 244
Chicago White Sox, 181
China Grove, Texas, 131, 135–36, 145,
    164–65, 239–40, 305–6
Cincinnati Reds, 181
Civil Rights Act of 1964, 281, 314
civil rights movement, 2, 253, 257,
    279–80, 281, 285–86, 314. See also
    African Americans; racism;
    segregation
  school curriculum and, 293
  Texas Exposition and, 255–57
Civil War, U.S., 13, 60, 142, 146
  Battle at Yellow Bayou in, 75–76
  Battle of Bull Run in, 59
  Battle of Galveston in, 60–68
  Battle of Gettysburg in, 71
  Battle of Pleasant Hill in, 74
  economic blockades in, 57–58, 82
  emancipation of slaves post-, 77–99
  end of, 77–79
  origins of, 42–43, 56, 57
  Red River Campaign in, 72–76
  remembrance of, 53, 157–59, 166, 186,
    195–96
The Clansmen (Dixon), 197, 199
Clare, Joan, 275
Clark, Amos, 37

Clark, Edward, 58
Clarke, Edward, 204
Clements, Bill, 315
Cline, Walter D., 255
Clinton, Bill, 348
Coates, Lillie, 172
Coke, Richard, 126–27
Colored Farmers Association, 138
Colored State Grange, Texas, 138
Colored Teachers State Association,
    282
Comiskey, Charlie, 181
Comité des Citovens (Citizens
    Committee), 150
Company A, Third Battalion, Seventh
    Infantry Regiment, 350
Compromise of 1850 (U.S.), 50
Confederate States of America
    (Confederacy), 83, 89, 157–58.
    See also Civil War, U.S.
  conscription enacted by, 63
  economic blockades against, 57–58
  slaves' assistance to, 61–63
  Texas's membership in, 54
Congo, 17, 348
Congress for Racial Equality, 286
Connally, John, 278
Connally, Tom, 179, 188, 195, 228–29,
    247, 258, 268
Convention of Colored Men, 138, 144
Cooper, Annie Burton, 198–99
Cotton, Dave, 172–75
cotton industry, 1. See also farming
  decline in, 116–17, 145, 264, 305, 307
Cotton States and International
    Exhibition, Atlanta, 148–49
Craft, Juanita, 259
Crane, Martin McNulty, 204
Crow, Louis, 212
Cumbria (Union boat), 66
Cuney, N. W., 147–48
Cunningham, William, 377
Cureton, Calvin, 212
Curry, Irby, 188
Curry, Jesse, 281

Daffan, George, 22–29
Dallas Bowling Association, 274, 280

Dallas County Citizens League, 204–5, 220, 274
the Dallas Cowboys, 280, 292, 318, 340
Dallas Express, 204, 258
Dallas Herald, 51
Dallas Morning News, 11, 151–52, 162, 166–69, 189, 229, 243, 245–46, 255–57, 272, 274, 278–79, 285, 307, 361
    on KKK, 203–4, 207, 209, 213, 318
Dallas Negro Chamber of Commerce, 255
Dallas, Texas, 11, 245–47
    Chamber of Commerce, 245
    Kennedy assassination in, 277–79
    KKK in, 201–9, 214, 318
    racism in, 201–9, 214, 276–78, 280–81
    segregation in, 199–205, 258–61, 272–73, 276–77, 280–82, 294, 296–98, 315, 317–18
    shopping mall's birth in, 243–44
    World's Fair in, 255–57
Dallas Times Herald, 201–2, 207
"Dark Was the Night, Cold Was the Ground," 225
Davidson, Lynch, 212
Davis, Edmund J., 54, 112, 115–19, 123, 124, 126–27
Davis, Jefferson, 59, 195–96
Davis, L. J., 214
Davis, Miles, 243, 254
Dealey, George, 203, 209
Dean, Aylett, 22
Dean, John, 108
Deer Creek Oil and Gas Company, Falls County, 189
Delano, Asa P., 85–96
Democratic Party, Texas
    as conservative party, 82–83, 87–89, 102–8, 111–13, 115–21, 123–27, 130, 147–48, 181, 204–5, 213–15, 219, 253, 259–61, 272, 274, 278, 288–89, 314–15
    constitution of 1876 by, 130
    KKK and, 213–15, 219
    liberal shift by, 274, 278–79, 282, 289, 315
    "New Departure" campaign by, 117–18
Democratic Statesman (Austin), 117
Denson, Nelson, 147
Dixon, Thomas, Jr., 197, 199

Donahue, Jacky, 320–22, 323, 326
Donaldsonville, Fort, Louisiana, 71
Dred Scott decision, 49
DuBois, W. E. B., 148
Dunagan, Otis T., 272

Eddins, Roy, 107, 119–20, 128, 141, 231
Eisenhower, Dwight D., 260
Emancipation Proclamation, U.S., 77–79
Emerson, D. R., 170–71
Emmett, Dan, 287
ESPN, 368
Etheridge, William G., 13, 48, 53, 55–56, 85, 102, 129, 154–55
    death of, 196
Evans, Hiram Wesley, 207–9

Falls Bridge, Falls County, 190–91
Falls County, Texas, 13, 44, 53, 129.
    See also Marlin, Texas
    centennial celebration by, 267–68
    Courthouse, 20, 59, 108, 135, 229
    economic troubles in, 49, 82, 116, 264, 268, 305, 307
    floods in, 177–78, 191
    lynching/vigilante justice in, 162–76, 209–19, 247
    wars and, 60–62, 82, 188, 191
Falls Hotel, Marlin, 228, 246, 250
Farmers Improvement Society of Texas, 146
farming. *See also* cattle industry
    as contracted laborer, 83–91, 97, 132–34, 137, 177–78, 180
    cooperatives, 138
    labor/demographic shifts in, 193, 286
    as land owner, 131, 133–34, 137, 177–78, 180, 239, 286
    living conditions, post-emancipation, 131–39, 221–41
    as sharecropper, 91, 97–98, 132–34, 137–39, 143, 145, 177–78, 180, 191, 232–41, 264, 286
    technology's impact on, 305
Fat Frank's, Johannesburg, 343
Faust, 157
Federal Writers' Project, 35–40, 120–21, 383*n*25

Feldman, Mike, 345
Fendrick, Columbus, 170–72
Fendrick, Hattie, 170–72
Ferguson, Jim, 219
Ferguson, Miriam "Ma," 219
Fifteenth Amendment, U.S. Constitution, 113
Fifth Texas Cavalry Regiment (Confederacy), 63–67, 69–71, 73–76, 180
First Baptist Church, Dallas, 206, 244
First Baptist Church, Marlin, 155, 187, 188, 210, 228
First Texas Heavy Artillery (Confederacy), 60–61, 64–67, 69
Fisher, James/Joseph, 162–65
Fisher, Mrs. James, 162–65
504th Military Intelligence Brigade, 327
Flake's Daily Galveston Bulletin, 86
Flippen, Edgar, 243
Flippen-Prather firm, 205, 243–44, 246
Floyd, Troy, 223
Fooshee, Marion Fresenius, 244
Ford, Dan, 164
Ford Metal Moulding Company, 252
Fort Jackson (Union steamer), 77
Fort Worth Star Telegram, 228
Forward Dallas Association, 258
Fourteenth Amendment, U.S. Constitution, 91–93, 101, 113, 150
Fox, Phillip, 207
Franchione, Dennis, 358
Franks, Tommy, 350
Frazier, Addie Barlow "Dixie Leber," 281, 318
Freedmen's Bureau, 83–99, 104, 110, 111, 124–25
"freedom colonies," 131
Fretz, Emil, Jr., 245, 275
Fretz, Emil, Sr., 5, 11, 244–45, 248
Fretz, Jacob, 244
Fretz, Minnie, 251

Gall, Franz Joseph, 373
Galveston Daily News, 78
Galveston News, 105, 209
Galveston, Texas, battle for, 58–68
Galveston Weekly News, 42

Gannon, Kathy, 349
Garcia, Pete, 260
Garrett, Finis J., 201
Garrett, Lonnie, 301–2, 304, 340
Gassaway, George, 186
Gassaway, Henrietta, 116, 129
Goldwater, Barry, 288
Gordon, John B., 180
Granger, Gordon, 77, 83
Grant, Ulysses S., 70–72, 111
Gravel Hill, Texas, 131, 135–36, 191–92, 238, 241, 310
Graves, Curtis, 279
Great Depression, 36, 120, 228–29, 232–41
Greeks, 372
Green and Bartlett, Marlin, 31–32
Green, George, 30–32
Greening, Daren, 322
Green, Sue, 30
Green, Tom, 63–67, 70–74
Gregory, Edgar, 81, 83–89
Griffin, Charles, 101–3
Griffith, D. W., 197
Grimes, Jesse, 109
Guardian Life Insurance Company, 293

Hamby, Charles, 183
Hamilton, A. J., 83, 87
Harlan, John Marshall, 150
Harriet Lane (gunboat), 64–65, 67–68
Harris, Benjamin, 88
Harrison, Ben (sharecropper), 168–70
Harrison, Benjamin (president), 147
Harrison, J. E., 60
Harris, Willie B., 225
Harston, Don, 201
Harvey, Wash, 249
Haughn, Charles, 106
Hay, L. O., 226
Hayward, Willie S., 239
Hébert, Paul Octave, 64–65
Hedrick, Justice, 163
Hereford, John, 105
Hill, Henry, 168–70
Hilton, Conrad, 228
Hispanic Americans, 251–52, 288, 291–92, 293, 296, 315, 353

History of Falls County (Old Settlers and
    Veterans), 107, 119–20
Hobby, William P., 183
Hodges, A. M., 96
Hodges, Annie, 154
Hodges, W. E., 189, 214
Hogg, James, 148
Holman, Eliza, 36
Honduras (Union boat), 66
Hopkins, Sam, 223
Horenstein, Birgit, 327–28
Horenstein, Dick, 327
Horenstein, Lisa, 327–29
"A House Divided" speech (Lincoln), 49
House & Garden, 246
Houston Informer, 204
Houston, Sam, 42, 49–54
Houston & Texas Central Railroad, 127
Hunter, Charles, 288
Hunt, H. J., 279
Hunt, Kevin, 319

"I Have a Dream" (King, Jr.), 293
integration. *See* segregation
Irizarry, Jay, 318
The Iron Curtain Over America (Beaty),
    261

Jacobs, Maurine, 252
Japan, WWII and, 247
Jefferson, Blind Lemon, 223–25
Jeffries, James, 184
*Jeffries-Johnson World's Championship
    Boxing Contest,* 184
Jelinek, Pauline, 347–48
Jim Crow laws, 254
John Birch Society, 278–79
John F. Carr (Confederate boat),
    66–67
Johnson, Andrew, 78, 82, 88–89, 94–95,
    101
Johnson, Blind Willie, 224
Johnson, Budd, 223
Johnson, Eddie Bernice, 292
Johnson, Jack "the Galveston Giant,"
    183–84
Johnson, Lyndon B., 6, 278
Johnson, Monk, 163–65

Johnson, Peter, 288
Jones, Churchill, 31–32, 40–43, 81, 95,
    97–98, 108–9, 110, 189, 214
    citizenship of, 82, 87, 110
    Civil War and, 59–61
    secession and, 53, 55–56, 59
    slave management by, 19, 23–25, 27–29,
        33–35, 38, 48, 78, 144
    Texas migration by, 20–29
Jones, James Sanford, 22–29, 57, 60–61,
    67, 69
Jones, Son, 180
Jones, Susan Tomlinson, 20, 25, 30–31,
    33, 38, 40, 60, 373
Joplin, Scott, 183
Jordan, Barbara, 279, 289
Julius Rosenwald Fund, 192
Juneteenth, 134, 158–59, 236, 239, 255,
    315, 333

Kabila, Laurent, 9
Kawasaki, Takeshi "Go," 344–46
Kennedy, J. M., 151–53, 156, 157, 161–62,
    172–75
    KKK and, 200, 204, 215, 218–19, 247
    political service by, 179, 219, 247–48
Kennedy, John F., 277–79
Kenny, Harry, 314
Kiddoo, Joseph B., 89–95
Kigali, Rwanda, 346–48
King, Martin Luther, Jr., 2, 279–80, 293,
    329
King, Silvia, 40
Kirk, Ben, 370
Kirk, Ron, 361
Knights of Pythias, 166, 193, 198
Ku Klux Klan (KKK), 7, 16, 115, 150, 152,
    195, 247, 254, 281–82, 285, 318, 332,
    340
    decline of, 212, 219–20, 375
    founding of, 204, 216
    intimidation campaigns by, 105–8,
        111–12, 118
    membership statistics for, 205, 206
    spread of, 196–220, 278
    at Texas State Fair, 207–9
The Ku Klux Klan (Cooper), 198–99
Kuwait, 350

Kyser, E. E. "Bud," 218
Kyser, William Daniel, 210
Kyser, William Earnest, 210, 215–16

Lakewood Country Club, Dallas, 246,
    251, 252–53, 278, 290
Lamar, Julius, 277
Landlord and Tenant Act, 1876, Texas, 130
Landrum, Benjamin, 123, 145
Landrum, Pete, 186
Landrum, Samuel, 48
Lea, Alfred, 68
Lea, Edward, 68
League of Women Voters, 288
Ledbetter, Huddie "Lead Belly," 222–23,
    307–8
Lee, Robert E., 42, 54, 71, 195, 255, 291
Leonard, Terry, 347–48
Leslie, Warren, 278
Levy, Albert, 180
Levy, Marx, 189
Levy, Moses, 189
Levy, Skeeter, 218
Lewis, William, 106
Lincoln, Abraham, 49, 52, 54, 58, 82.
    See also Civil War, U.S.
    assassination of, 78
    Emancipation Proclamation by, 77–78
Llewellyn, N. J., 214
Lockridge, Joe, 279
Lomax, John, 223
Lone Star State Medical Association, 146
Longstreet, James, 180
Lott Clarion, 174
LT & Me (Tomlinson), 308–9
Lubbock, Francis, 59
Lucy Gwinn (Confederate boat), 66
lynching, 161–76, 181, 184, 247

Magee, Billy, 129
Magee, Calvin, 135
Magruder, John Bankhead, 65–68,
    71–73, 77
Malcolm X, 328–29
Mandela, Nelson, 9, 17, 341, 345–46
Mangope, Lucas, 344
Mann Act, U.S., 184
Marlin Cotton Compress, 179, 305

Marlin Cotton Oil Company Mill, 210
Marlin Democrat, 148, 151–54, 157–59,
    177, 179–80, 187, 189–90, 195, 229,
    248, 252
    on KKK, 200, 204, 211, 213–15, 217–19,
    247
    on lynching, 162, 172–75, 247
Marlin High School, 301–4, 354, 355
Marlin [Moving] Ball, 127, 155, 162
Marlin Sanitorium Company, 156
Marlin, Texas, 20, 30–31, 60, 141–42, 285.
    See also Falls County, Texas
    Bluebonnet Festival in, 246
    centennial celebration by, 267–68
    Chamber of Commerce, 124–25, 189,
    217–18, 228–29, 267
    economic struggles in/near, 228–29,
    232–41, 264, 268, 305, 307, 332–33
    floods in, 177–78, 191
    Freedmen's Bureau in, 85–99, 110,
    124–25
    growth of, 127–29, 155–57, 178–91,
    222–28, 313
    lynching/vigilante justice in, 162–76,
    209–19, 247
    major league baseball in, 181
    mineral springs of, 15, 155–57, 178,
    180–81, 189, 228, 250, 264, 268, 307
    Reconstruction and, 81–99, 102–13,
    124–25
    red light district of, 222–27, 307–8
    segregation in, 270, 301–4, 313, 314
    voting in, 120–21, 147
Marsalis Dallas Zoo, 11, 245
Marshall, Thurgood, 272
Martin, Harvey, 295
Martin Luther King, Jr. Day, 360
Masonic Society, African American, 182,
    192–93, 238, 283
Masonic Society, white, 129, 155, 166,
    198, 205, 207, 209–10
Matagorda (steamship), 42
Maverick, Maury, 258
Maxwell, Granny, 230
Mayfield, Earle B., 205
McCarroll, William, 76
McClain, Charles, 284, 313, 339
McClain, Flesphia "Fifi," 305, 313, 339

McClain, Jewell Butler, 283–84, 305, 308,
     312, 331, 339, 367, 370
McClain, Linda, 283
McClain, Ronald, 284, 313, 339, 364, 369
McClure, Sam, 219
McCullogh, Tom, 119
McDonald, Gabrielle, 315
McGovern, George, 288–89
McKenzie, Ken, 275
Meadows, Earl, 151
Médecins Sans Frontières, 347
The Meeting (play), 329
*Memories of the Hills of Home and
     Countryside* (McCullogh), 119
Mexia Daily News, 217
Mexia Democrat, 162
Mexican-American War, 20–21, 58, 63
Miller, B. J., 214
Miller, Jimmy, 289, 291
Miller, Reid, 347–48
Mitchell, Anthony, 8–9, 350
Mitchell, Basil, 358
Mitchell, Catherine, 9
Montreal Protocol, 329
Moore, Oscar, 223
Mosby, John "Gray Ghost," 142
Mower, Joseph, 76
Mukagasana, Cecile, 3
Murchison, Clint, 279
Murmer, J. S., 145

NAACP, 183, 220, 255, 259, 261, 272–73,
     282, 285
Nairobi, Kenya, 346–48, 349, 371
NASA, 225
Nathan, I. J., 179–80
National Bank of Commerce, 248, 252
National Football League (NFL), 7, 357
National Guard, 188, 259
National Negro Bankers Association, 182
National Negro Business League, 182
National Negro Protective Association,
     146
National Security Agency, 326–29
NCAA, 7–8, 358, 364–65
Neff, Pat, 212
Negro Protection Congress of Texas, 182
Neiman-Marcus, 244, 278

Nemeye, Xavier, 3
Neptune (Confederate gunboat), 65–67
New York Giants, 181
New York Times, 346, 368
New York Tribune, 67
New York World News, 203–4
NFL, xi, 8, 364–68
Nixon, Richard, 282, 288–89, 313
Norton, A. B., 51
Norwood, John, 76
Novacek, Jay, 340

Obama, Barack, 16–17, 159
Okinawa, Japan, 326–27
Old Settlers and Confederate Veterans
     Association, 198
   fairground reunions, 185–87, 229–32,
     239, 283
   historical book by, 107, 119–20
   KKK and, 214, 217
Oliver, John W., 117–21, 123, 124, 127
Oltorf, Frank, 214
Oltorf, James D., 108–9, 120, 127,
     141–42
Oltorf, Thomas, 155, 162
O'Neal, Arthur, 170–72
101 Ranch Wild West Show, 183
163rd Military Intelligence Battalion,
     325–26
Orrick, John C., Jr., 142
Oswald, Lee Harvey, 278
Overstreet, Morris, 361
Owasco (Union warship), 64
Owens, Roe, 172

Pamplin, Brady, 265–67, 285, 313–14
Pamplin, Larry, 313–14
Paramount, 223–24, 307–8
Parks, Gordon, 307–8
Parks, Pat, 295
Paul Quinn College, Austin, 138, 159
Paul, William, 163–65
Payton, Walter, 333
Peabody Foundation, 129
Pearl Harbor, attack on, 247
Pease, Elisha, 90, 103, 108
Peterson, Robert, 227
Philadelphia Phillies, 181

Phillips, Abe, 167–70
Phillips, Fannie, 168–70
phrenology, 373
physiognomy, 373
Pickett, Bill, 183
Pickle, Dave, 183
Pierce, Ben, 183
Pinson, Jerry, 76
Plessy, Homer, 150
Plessy v. Ferguson, 150
Polk, James K., 34
Pop Warner organization, 337–38, 340
Porter, Robert, 318
Prairie View College, Hempstead, 138, 159, 286
Prather, Hugh, 243
Price, Pinkie Taylor, 136–37, 239–41
Progressive Voters League, 258
Prohibition, 181, 187, 200, 219, 225–27
Pryor, Charles R., 51
Pyle, Dave, 348

racism, x–xi, 13–14, 16–17, 212–13, 315, 320–22, 338, 354–55, 359–63, 374–75. *See also* African Americans; Ku Klux Klan; segregation; slaves
    in Africa, 342–43, 371, 373, 378–79
    via Black Codes, 91–94, 99
    causes of, 207, 371–73
    cure for, 376–78
    via Jim Crow laws, 254
    between minorities, 353
    statistics on, 339–40, 361
Ramanathan, Shalini, 9–10, 349–51
Read, Thomas, 127
Reagan, Ronald, 288
Reconstruction Acts, U.S., 101, 103
Red River Ordnance Depot, 247
Reed, W. M., 109
Renfro, Bubba, 305
Renshaw, William B., 64–67
Republican National Committee, 1883, 147–48
Republican Party, Texas
    blacks holding office in, 116, 147–48
    civil rights position by, 111, 118, 138, 253, 260–61

conservative shift by, 274, 278–79, 282, 288, 315
    as progressive party, 92–95, 101–8, 111–13, 115–21, 123, 126–27, 147–48, 201
Reynolds, Joseph J., 101, 103–4, 107
Robertson, Felix, 207, 219
Rodriguez, Santos, 293
Rogers, Howard, 273, 275
Rogers, Marjorie, 229–30
Rogers, Wayne, 354
Roosevelt, Franklin, 35–36, 229, 255, 258
Rosebud High School, 306
Rosebud News, 174
Ross, Lawrence Sullivan, 165
Rural Electrification Administration, 229
Rwanda genocide, 2–3, 17, 379

St. Louis Browns, 181
Sam Houston (schooner), 63
Sam Houston State University, Huntsville, 15, 146, 153, 362
Sanders, Abe, 170–71
San Diego Chargers, 8, 365–69
Sanger, Alex, 205
Sanger-Harris Department Store, Dallas, 205, 244
scalawags, 85, 124, 126
Schreiber, Belle, 184
Scott, Samuel R., 175
Scott, Winfield, 58
Scurry, W. R., 62
segregation, 6, 13, 361
    benefits of, 258, 259, 270, 313
    in Dallas, 199–205, 258–61, 272–73, 276–77, 280–82, 294, 296–98, 315, 317–18
    in Marlin, 301–4, 313, 314
    spread of, 147–50, 181–82, 200–205
Selectman, C. C., 207
Separate Car Act, Louisiana, 150
September 11th attacks, 7, 349
Shannon, Denman, 71
Shelton, William, 129
Shepperd, John Ben, 272
Sheridan, Philip, 101
Shields, Benjamin G., 34, 48–49, 53, 55, 85, 102, 129, 145

Shields, Ed, 96
Shillady, John R., 183
Shivers, Allan, 260–61
Simmons, William J., 198, 204, 207
Simpson, Ben, 36–37
Skyline School, Dallas, 317, 319–22, 343
Slaughter, T. J., 216
slaves, x–xii, 1–4, 22, 372. *See also*
    African Americans
  abolition movement and, 34–35,
    42–43, 50, 52, 55
  Census count of, 48
  Confederacy's use of, 61–63
  living conditions of, 24–25, 36–40,
    44–45
  management of, 19, 23–25, 27–29,
    33–35
  oral accounts by, 35–40, 383n25
  plantation hierarchy and, 33–35, 40
  school curriculum on, 293–94
  sexual exploitation of, 40
Slave Trade Act, 1802 (Britain), 50
Smith, Antonio Maceo, 255, 258
Smith, Ed, 230
Smith, Emmitt, 340
Smith, Frank, 284
Smith, Henry "Buster," 223
Smith, Kirby, 77
Smith, Leon, 68
Smith, R. L., 146, 182
Somalia, 2, 8
South Africa, 378–79
  apartheid in, 2–3, 330, 342–43
  elections in, 17, 341, 345–46
  Soweto uprising in, 342
South Carolina, 52, 56, 57
Southern Christian Leadership Council,
  288
Southern Intelligencer (Austin), 51
Southern Methodist University, 261,
  274–75
Southern Pacific Railroad, 332
Soweto uprising, South Africa, 342
Speight, J. W., 60
Spivey, J. W., 214
Stallworth, Billah Etheridge, 12, 154–55,
  185, 196
Stallworth, Calloway, 26–28

Stallworth, Dosh, 157
Stallworth, Francis Marion "Frank," 35,
  40–41, 48, 56, 145, 157–58
  death of, 190
  marriage of, 12, 154–55, 185
  political service by, 179, 189–90
Stallworth, Harry, 186
Stallworth, Lucinda Jones, 35, 41, 56
Stallworth, Martha, 35, 56
Stallworth, Nicholas, 26–28, 35
Stallworth, Sanford J., 189, 214
Stamps, P. A., 182
Staubach, Roger, 361
Steele, Anna, 303–4
Steen, Fannie, 179
Stephenson, David, 219–20
Sterns, Christopher, 22
Stevenson, Adlai, 260–61
Stockdale, Fletcher, 113
Strickland, Sharon, 332
Stuart, Sabe, 172–75
Sturgis, F. B., 95–99
Sulakowski, Valery, 62–63
Sullivan, Pat, 358
Summers, Alice, 195
Sumter, Fort, South Carolina, 56, 57
Sussman, Tina, 346

Taylor, George, 165
Taylor, Hezekiah, 239–41, 271
Taylor, Julia Ann, 234–35, 263, 271
Taylor, Kid, 168–70
Taylor, Richard, 73–76
Taylor, Roberta, 239–41
Taylor, William, 296
Taylor, Zachary, 73
Texas. *See also* Democratic Party, Texas;
  Republican Party, Texas
  Black Codes in, 264, 268, 305, 307
  centennial exposition by, 255–57
  Civil War and, 42–43, 56, 57–79
  constitution of 1876, 130
  emancipation resistance in, 82–99
  Juneteenth in, 134, 158–59, 236, 239,
    255, 315, 333
  lynching in, 161–76, 181, 184, 247
  migration to, 20–29, 32–33, 40–45
  oil industry in, 185, 189

Reconstruction of, 82–99, 101–13, 124–25, 128, 131, 146, 196–97, 259, 279, 315
secession by, 47–56, 89
segregation/desegregation in, 6, 13, 147–50, 181–82, 199–205, 258–61, 270, 272–73, 276–77, 280–82, 294, 296–98, 301–4, 313–15, 317–18, 361
State Fair of 1952 in, 260
whitecapping in, 175–76
Texas A&M, 15, 138, 143, 145, 189, 244, 273–74
KKK and, 199
Texas Christian University, 8, 357–59, 363–64
Texas Colored Teachers' Association, 146
Texas Commission on Human Rights, 340
Texas Employment Commission, 259
Texas Negro Chamber of Commerce, 255
Texas Rangers, 6, 12, 142–43, 212, 261, 265, 361
Texas Rangers (baseball team), 292
Texas Republican (Marshall), 50
Texas State Fair, 1923, 207–9
Texas State Teachers Association, 282
Thirteenth Amendment, U.S. Constitution, 89, 91, 113
Thirty-sixth Infantry Division, WWI, 188
Thomas, Carl, 318
Thomas, Henry "Ragtime Texas," 222–23
Thomas, J. A., 152
Thornton, Robert L., 207, 280
Throckmorton, James, 90, 94, 103–4
Tinsley, David, 334
Titche, Edward, 205
Tomlinson, Albert Edward Lee "Tommy," 5, 6, 11, 14–16, 19, 187–89, 273–74, 278
birth of, 185
death of, 7, 290–91
KKK and, 206, 209
marriage of, 244–46
professions of, 205–6, 243, 246, 275–76, 290
racism and, 16, 206, 209, 249–50

Tomlinson, Albert Perry, 109–10, 123, 186–87
death of, 270–71, 283
farm management by, 185, 191–92, 234, 237, 239–41, 263–64
Tomlinson, Amanda, 48, 81
Tomlinson, Annie, 144
Tomlinson, Augustus "Gus," 48, 81, 109–10, 129–30, 291
cattle ranching by, 117, 143, 145
marriage of, 123, 153
Old Settlers founding by, 185–86
Tomlinson, Bennie Etheridge, 185
Tomlinson, Beth Ward, 279, 288–89, 291–92, 295, 319–20
Tomlinson, Bettie Etheridge, 12, 15, 154–55, 179, 185, 227–28, 245
death of, 252
Tomlinson, Bob, 7, 8, 11, 14–16, 206, 243, 248–52, 254
birth/adoption of, 247
bowling and, 10, 253–54, 273–77, 279–80, 287–88, 292, 294–95
marriage of, 275
political views of, 276–77, 279, 288–89
professions of, 6, 275–76, 287–88, 293–95, 298, 319
Tomlinson, Britton, 92
Tomlinson, Charles (son of Milo), 92, 135
Tomlinson, Charles (son of Vincent), 1–2, 232–38, 268
Tomlinson, Chris, 341–44
AP reporting by, 345–50
Army service by, 323–29
birth of, 280
desegregation and, 296–98, 317
education of, 317, 319–24, 328–30
marriages of, 327–29, 350
Tomlinson, Christian McPherson, 130
Tomlinson, Dana, 295, 319
Tomlinson, Daylen Oliver, xii
Tomlinson, Eldridge Alexander, 12, 48, 123, 142, 153, 291
Tomlinson, Elizabeth Jane Landrum, 123, 129–30, 145, 153
Tomlinson, Ella Louise Landrum, 153
Tomlinson, Ellie, 192

Tomlinson, Emma Diantha Perry,
    109–10, 154
Tomlinson, George (grandfather), 79, 92
Tomlinson, George (grandson), 92
Tomlinson, Harriet People, 154
Tomlinson Hill, Texas, x, 30, 284, 370,
    378. *See also* Falls County, Texas;
    Marlin, Texas; Tomlinson, James
    Kendrick "Jim"
    emancipation of slaves on, 78–79
    floods of 1899–1900 and, 177–78, 191
    oil and gas speculation on, 189
    reunion celebrations, 185–87, 229–32,
        239, 283
    sales of, 263
Tomlinson, James, 192
Tomlinson, James Eldridge, Jr., 109
Tomlinson, James Eldridge, Sr., 48, 96,
    109–10, 117, 123, 143, 154
    school opened by, 116, 145, 154
    war service by, 60–61, 64–67, 69, 76–77
Tomlinson, James Kendrick "Jim," 13, 14,
    26, 28, 33, 35, 59–60, 81
    Civil War and, 53–60, 63, 72, 77–79
    slave statistics for, 47–48
    Texas migration by, 40–45
Tomlinson, Jede, 144
Tomlinson, Jessie, 92
Tomlinson, John K. "J.K.", 233, 236, 268,
    283, 308
Tomlinson, John Nicholas, 48, 81, 123,
    130
Tomlinson, John Peoples, 283, 334
Tomlinson, Josephine Beall, 92, 139, 144,
    154, 164, 191
Tomlinson, Julie Ward, ix–xi, 191–92,
    232–41, 264, 284, 305–7, 309–11,
    331–33, 378
    death of, 334
Tomlinson, LaDainian, 7–8, 332–33, 335,
    339, 356
    birth of, 331
    college football and, 357–59, 363–64
    father's death and, 369–70
    honors received by, 365, 368
    marriage of, 366
    NFL football and, 365–69
    racism against, xi, 353–55, 377–78

youth program participation by,
    336–37, 337–38, 340
Tomlinson, LaTorsha Oakley, 19, 359,
    365–66, 369, 378
Tomlinson, LaVar Tramayne, 331, 332,
    336–39, 354, 359, 369
    sports and, 359–60, 362–63
Tomlinson, Londria, 309–13, 331, 333,
    336, 339, 369
Tomlinson, Loreane Lowe, 301, 305–6,
    310–12, 331–32, 356–59, 361–64,
    369–70
    marriages by, 308–9, 340
    relocation by, 333–40, 354–55
Tomlinson, Martha, 79, 92, 135
Tomlinson, Mary (daughter of John), 130
Tomlinson, Mary (daughter of Milo), 92
Tomlinson, Mary Eliza, 110
Tomlinson, Mary Frances Fretz, 5, 6,
    11–12, 248, 278, 290–91
    marriage of, 244–46
    racism and, 249–50
Tomlinson, Milo, 92, 97, 142
    marriage of, 135
    sharecropping by, 135, 138–39, 154
    as slave, 43, 63
Tomlinson, Minnie Augustus, 123
Tomlinson Negro School, Falls County, 116,
    129, 145, 154, 179, 191, 234, 265, 271
Tomlinson, Olga, 283, 334
Tomlinson, Oliver Terry, Jr. "Terry,"
    305–8, 313, 331, 356, 367, 378
    birth of, 283–84
    marriage of, 332, 339
Tomlinson, Oliver Terry "O.T.", x, xii,
    236, 268, 283–84, 305–7, 309–13,
    331, 333, 338, 363–64, 368
    birth of, 233
    death of, 369–70, 371
    drug addiction by, 334–36, 339–40,
        354, 367, 369
    marriage of, 308
Tomlinson, Peter, 92, 97, 154, 164
    death of, x, xii, 233
    sharecropping by, 135, 139, 144, 178, 191
    as slave, 43–44, 63, 236–37
Tomlinson, Phyllis Scruggs, 43–44, 79,
    92, 135, 138–39

Tomlinson, Robert Edward Lee (R. E. L.), 5, 19, 81, 115, 120–21, 123, 161–75, 179, 181, 185–86, 188, 213, 227–28, 245, 252, 291
  birth of, 58, 177
  death of, 13, 14, 176, 248
  education of, 143, 145–46, 153, 362
  KKK and, 205, 210, 214
  marriage of, 12, 154–55
  professions of, 12, 153–54, 178, 187, 189
Tomlinson, Ruth, 245, 248
Tomlinson, Sarah Elizabeth, 42, 48, 81
Tomlinson, Sarah Jemima Stallworth, 13, 20, 28, 35, 47, 58, 59, 123
  plantation management by, 81, 95–97, 108–10, 117
  Texas migration by, 40–44
Tomlinson, Sarah Lee "Sally," 248–53, 275
Tomlinson, Sarah "Sally," 130
Tomlinson, Vincent, Jr., 233
Tomlinson, Vincent, Sr., 191, 193, 225, 283, 378
  birth of, 154
  death of, x, xii, 305–6
  land purchase by, 263–64
  marriage of, 191–92
  sharecropping by, 192–93, 232–41, 264
Tomlinson, William, 48, 60–61, 63–64, 69, 76, 81
Tomlinson, William Augustus, 109, 154, 185–86
Tomlinson, Zelma, 1–2, 233, 268
Torbett, John W., Jr., 195
Torbett, John W., Sr., 180
Torbett Sanatorium/Clinic, Marlin, 180–81, 248, 331
Touchstone, J. R. M., 12, 145, 155
Tower, John, 282
Travis, Caroline, 48, 60
Travis, John, 48, 60
Travis, Martha, 136–37, 239
Travis, Mary (daughter), 48, 60
Travis, Mary Stallworth (mother), 28, 41–43, 48, 59–60
Travis, Milo, 136–37, 239
Travis, Nicholas, 48
Treaty of Guadalupe Hidalgo, 20
Trent, Alphonso, 223

Tri-Weekly Telegraph (Houston), 62
Truett, George, 256
Truth and Reconciliation Commission (South Africa), 3, 379
Tryon, Sandra, 232–33
Tucker, Dick, 163–64
Turley, Louis, 207
Tuskegee Institute, Alabama, 148
Tutu, Desmond, 3
Twain, Mark, 2
Twiggs, D. E., 58
Tyler, John, 34
Tyler, Mabel, 234
typhoid fever, 26–29, 35, 238

Union Army, U.S., 59–68, 159
Unionist Party, 13, 50, 52–54, 59, 66, 111, 154, 197
  Reconstruction by, 85, 89–95, 102–8
United Confederate Veterans, Marlin, 157–58, 186, 198
United Daughters of the Confederacy, 186, 195, 198–99, 231, 267
University of California–San Diego, 366
University of Texas, Austin, 328–30, 358
Urban Cowboy (movie), 298–99
U.S. Census, 47–48
U.S. Department of Agriculture, 116
U.S. Department of Health, Education, and Welfare, 282, 314
USS Theodore Roosevelt, 349
U.S. Supreme Court, 150, 259, 282

Veterans Administration, U.S., 263, 331, 336
Voice of America, 346, 348
voting
  intimidation/obstruction, 103–8, 111–12, 118–20, 125–26, 181
  in primary elections, 181, 213, 258–59
  taxes charged for, 181, 213, 258–59
Voyager (spacecraft), 225

Waco Daily News, 162
Waco, Texas, 60, 190, 312, 331–35, 353–54
  Boys and Girls Clubs of, 336–37
  KKK in, 107, 211, 214
  Pop Warner in, 337–38, 340

Waco Tribune Herald, 354
Wade, Harless, 279
Wainwright, Jonathan M., 68
Walker, Edwin, 279
Wallace, George, 289
Ward, Emma Sorillas, 192
Ward, John, 163–64
Ward, Nathan, 192
Ward, Robert D., 275
Washington, Booker T., 148–49, 182, 254
Wasson, Alonzo, 203
Watkins, John W., 69–71, 73–76
Webb, Tom, 227
Weber, Reverend, 266–67
Welle, Gus, 157
Wesley, Vernon, 320–21, 326
West, Decca Lamar, 195
Westfield (Union boat), 67
Wheat Ridge, Colorado, 322–24
Whig Party, 20, 34, 49, 102
whitecapping, 175–76
White, John, 238, 241
White, Lizzie Mae Tomlinson, 192,
    225–26, 232–41
White, Warren T., 281
White, Winston, 238, 241
Wigfall, Louis, 42
Wiley College, Marshall, 138, 286
Willard, Jess, 184
Williams, Berry, 172–75

Williams, Hannah, 169–70
Williams, J. C., 285
Williams, L. K., 256
Williams, Nelson, 173
Williams, Ray, 277
Wilson, Teddy, 223
Wilson, Woodrow, 188, 201
Women of the Ku Klux Klan, 200
Women's Christian Temperance Union,
    200
Wood, George Rodgers, 245
Woodrow Wilson High School, Dallas,
    252, 273
Woodson, Sammy, 303
Work Progress Administration (WPA),
    35–36, 229, 240
World War I (WWI), 187–88, 191, 249
World War II (WWII), 227, 247, 248, 263,
    265
Wyman, Charles, 267
Wyman, Frank, 221, 226–27, 265–67,
    268–71

Yeager, Mike, 151–52
Yellow Bayou, Louisiana, 75–76, 81
yellow fever, 26–29, 42, 60, 64, 77, 103
The Yokohama Maid, 188
Young, Horace, 76

Zaire, 346, 348